LEFT BEHIND: THE PUBLIC EDUCATION CRISIS IN THE UNITED STATES

This book addresses the harmful influences that the cultural, social, economic, political and ideological dimensions, in current 'American' society, have upon the delivery of elementary, secondary and university education. It examines the effects of poverty, funding at the local, state and federal levels and racial and ethnic discrimination. Arguing against the continuation of standardized testing – an ill-conceived methodology to 'measure' the performance of children – the author advocates more one-on-one teaching and evaluation. He charges that students' rights to education are not respected and, in elementary and high school, receive little in the way of instruction that translates into life skills and proposes what some of those skills should be. A critique of the extreme ethnocentric approach to education in the United States, *Left Behind* advocates strong instruction in the humanities and foreign languages and the establishment of education abroad as a permanent program in high school and university. The author identifies capitalism as the basic influence that, in the form of employing 'business model' constructs, has slowly transformed our children into obedient consumers. Physical education has waned and become a major contributor to adolescent obesity. Seeking to replace children's complacency with critical thinking instruction, the author demonstrates how the corporate mass media occupy their minds. He also fears the erosion of the profession of teaching by an 'online' instruction frenzy. The book explores the possibilities for a viable nationwide education institution, in which decision-making is in the hands of teachers, parents and education experts, instead of politicians and business people. The remedies that could be taken up by ordinary people are accessible at the common-sense level; what prevents change are the lack of political will and economic greed, bolstered by the ideological power of the mass media.

Paul L. Jalbert is Associate Professor *Emeritus* of Communication at the University of Connecticut, Stamford, Connecticut, USA, and Editor of *Media Studies: Ethnomethodological Approaches*. He has also published papers in the areas of political communication, qualitative sociology and the analysis of ideologies.

"A powerful book, and it comes at a moment when the privatizing buccaneers and the corporate 'colonizers of our children's minds,' as Jalbert puts it, are riding high and threatening the very essence of democratic schooling. I hope it's widely read, not just by academics but by all who care about our children's lives."

Jonathan Kozol, author of *Death at an Early Age*, *Rachel and Her Children*, *Savage Inequalities*, *Amazing Grace*, *The Shame of the Nation*, and *Fire in the Ashes*.

"Paul Jalbert views schooling from a rich perspective, and illuminates not only some of the most primary problems in schooling today, and, unlike most other critiques, he offers many feasible and basic suggestions for improving our educational systems. We see in his writing a view that has been powerfully influenced by theoreticians such as Paulo Friere and Henry Giroux, a view that highlights how schools are especially dismal for those at the lower socioeconomic levels. Jalbert properly perceives schooling to lack an emphasis on critical thinking and self- development, while it victimizes the intellects of students, prepares them for the military, and treats them as prisoners in unjust pathological systems from the beginning of the schooling process. But again, unlike many school critiques, Jalbert correctly does not blame teachers; in fact he defends them, focusing instead on the problems caused by the rampant capitalism and politics running our school systems, and ruining our children's minds. Jalbert understands that today's schools systematically and routinely violate the right of our students to develop their minds in ways unique to them as unique persons, and he calls for major reforms to deal with these and other deeply embedded problems in schooling today. He is to be especially applauded for his strong emphasis on the need for critical thinking in our schools, and for offering suggestions for bringing critical thinking into instruction. We need many more intelligent and elucidating critiques of our schools such as the one Jalbert offers. I highly recommend this book to all education administrators, teachers and faculty at any level who want to help solve the public education crisis we now face in this country."

Dr. Linda Elder, Educational Psychologist, Senior Fellow and President of the Foundation for Critical Thinking, USA. Co-author of *Critical Thinking: Tools for Taking Charge of Your Professional and Personal Life* and *30 Days to Better Thinking and Better Living Through Critical Thinking*.

LEFT BEHIND: THE PUBLIC EDUCATION CRISIS IN THE UNITED STATES

Paul L. Jalbert

LONDON AND NEW YORK

First published 2018
by Routledge
2 Park Square, Milton Park, Abingdon, Oxon OX14 4RN

and by Routledge
711 Third Avenue, New York, NY 10017

Routledge is an imprint of the Taylor & Francis Group, an informa business

© 2018 Paul L. Jalbert

The right of Paul L. Jalbert to be identified as author of this work has been asserted by him in accordance with sections 77 and 78 of the Copyright, Designs and Patents Act 1988.

All rights reserved. No part of this book may be reprinted or reproduced or utilised in any form or by any electronic, mechanical, or other means, now known or hereafter invented, including photocopying and recording, or in any information storage or retrieval system, without permission in writing from the publishers.

Trademark notice: Product or corporate names may be trademarks or registered trademarks, and are used only for identification and explanation without intent to infringe.

British Library Cataloguing-in-Publication Data

A catalogue record for this book is available from the British Library

Library of Congress Cataloging-in-Publication Data

A catalog record for this book has been requested

ISBN: 978-1-138-09181-8 (hbk)
ISBN: 978-1-138-09182-5 (pbk)
ISBN: 978-1-315-10781-3 (ebk)

Typeset in Bembo
by Servis Filmsetting Ltd, Stockport, Cheshire

 Printed in the United Kingdom by Henry Ling Limited

For
Mary Anne
Nicole
and
Anna

CONTENTS

Acknowledgements	ix
Foreword	xii
Preface: a challenging philosophy of education	xiv
Introduction: the crisis in public education	**1**
1. The *Right* to Education	17
2. 'The Free Press' – on a corporate leash!	34
3. The Business Model	57
4. A Political Economy of Education	72
5. Poverty: the perennial problem	96
6. Discrimination: some structural suspects	109
7. The Teaching Profession	134
8. The Mismeasure of Students	164
9. What our Children do not Learn in High School, But Should	180
10. "What? I Need to Learn a Second Language?"	223

viii Contents

11. Cultural Arrogance   **239**

**12. Orwell's Nightmare Achieved: the 'Colonization of the
Mind' vs. Critical Thinking**   **255**

Postscript: What to do?   267
Appendix: Plyometrics Movement Program   293
Index   300

ACKNOWLEDGMENTS

By appreciation, we make excellence in others our own...
— Voltaire [Francois-Marie Arouet (1694–1778)]

No one who achieves success does so without acknowledging the help of others. The wise and confident acknowledge this help with gratitude.
— Alfred North Whitehead (1861–1947)

Having worked on this book for ten years, naturally, there are many people to recognize and thank for their guidance, their insights, their emotional support and their patience.

Jeff Coulter is the most important teacher I have ever had. As my mentor, he has monitored my professional life for more than 40 years. His detailed comments throughout this undertaking were indispensable. We are brothers. I also thank him for agreeing to write the Foreword.

I thank the following selfless and insightful colleagues, friends and acquaintances for their kind assistance and conversations, which, on countless occasions, led me to rethink, reorganize or rewrite the many discussions contained in this book; all the remaining errors are mine: Reza Kefayati, my classmate, friend and brother, who insisted I not forget the troublesome reality of untenured and part-time teachers/professors; Evelyn Harris, a long-standing colleague and friend, whose own research in education inspired me; Lou Gesualdi, my colleague, friend and benefactor; Tim Berard, whose expert scholarship in discrimination and racism has clarified my understandings of these social problems; Jerry Sehulster and Joel Blatt, my two favorite faculty colleagues, who both encouraged me along in this journey and from whom I learned much over the years; Dave Schulz, my mentor while I

x Acknowledgments

coached girl's high school ice hockey, taught me about the struggles to maintain good physical education programs and the many parameters of athletic performance at the secondary level; Rick Sirois, whose 'plyometrics' system of physical education I advocate be adopted in elementary, middle and high schools and who I thank for permission to publish his program and its results; Ed Marth, former Executive Director of the AAUP, UCONN, a long-standing colleague and friend, whose experience enlightened me on issues political-economic in post-secondary education; Stacy Holmes, a former high school teacher in Bridgeport, CT, who afforded me insights about how standardized testing affects children and teachers; Andrew Greif and Lydia Phillips of the Community Bicycle Center program in Biddeford, ME (whose current Executive Director is Bronwyn Barnett), where children are taught many skills through a 'project-based' methodology of education; Elizabeth Caron-St. Cyr, former Superintendent of Schools, Sanford, ME, whose disclosures helped me understand the mission of superintendents at the elementary and secondary levels; Nancy Conroy, career special education teacher in Trumbull, CT, from whom I gained some understanding of the complicated problems such teachers endure in order to deliver instruction in this singularly difficult learning environment; the University of Connecticut for granting me a sabbatical in 2009 to launch this work; Lynn Gentry for granting me permission to publish his succinct and poignant poem *On Racism*; Denis Hayes for granting me permission to publish his wonderful oration on Earth Day 2017, in Washington, DC; the several undergraduate students who helped me with searches on the internet: Allison Schilling, Ashley Flynn, Amanda Harris, Amanda Boyd, Carly Sheahan, Seung Chu, Victor Poon and Nicholas Matthews; to Jaime Mastrorio for our discussions about the Teach For America program, its strengths and flaws; and to my long-time pals, who have encouraged me to press on with this project, expressing their confidence in me and the value of this work: Jay & Pat Meehan, Wes Sharrock, Peter Eglin, Rod Watson, Michael Lynch, Dusan Bjelic, Joel & Kathy Jacaruso, Milt (my coaching brother) & Sharon Peckham, Michael & Alison Mastrorio, Terry Reilly, Bobby & Lisa Martire, Sally Keelan, Doug Scott (my coaching brother), Helen Lucke, Mike & Linda Kosko, Rita Koenig, Doug Hallengren, Cathy & Ed Bozzi, Bud Campanelli, Tony & Cathy Aquila, Jon Halls, Mark & Dave Altieri, Joe Gargiulo, Dave Brenton and the late Clif Palmer and his wife, Kay. I also include my two brothers and their wives, Marc & Claire and Roland & Patricia, in this caring group of people. I also want to give a 'shout out' to my mates at The Fitness Nut House in Kennebunk, ME.

Special thanks to Neil Jordan, Editor, Alice Salt, Editorial Assistant: and Kevin Selmes, Senior Production Editor, all of Taylor & Francis Group, Routledge Books and Cinqué Hicks, Director of Bookbright Media; their assistance took me 'by the hand' throughout the process of typescript preparation and the procedural, ethical and legal ramifications of publication.

My family has embraced this project from the beginning. The support that I have received from my partner and spouse of 40 years, Mary Anne DeVeau, is monumental. She has always been my first and last critic on anything, providing me with the leveling I needed, when I needed it, the compassion for the crafting of this book, the love and patience on the many occasions when I felt like this project would never be completed, the many readings she did of the different drafts of the manuscript, catching the many inconsistencies and ramblings I often committed. She is my *wonderful woman* always. My two daughters, Nicole and Anna DeVeau-Jalbert, were always ready to discuss the many topics addressed in the book, offering suggestions on how to develop the trajectory of the points I wanted to make. Nicole proofed some of the manuscript and Anna helped me find my way on the internet. Throughout, their support was always imbued with compassion and love. They are so smart and clever and funny; I thank them both for their wonder.

FOREWORD

Education, its content and methods of delivery, is intertwined with the character of the citizenry it serves, and, in so many respects, creates. In this engaging, well-documented and original work, Professor Jalbert explores many facets of contemporary education in the United States (curricula, administration, funding and related components), focusing upon what he astutely identifies as the various contributors to the *crises* afflicting this most significant institution of all of our lives.

Describing in considerable detail how the contours of education are profoundly enmeshed in our political and economic reality, he provides a range of proposals for solving the problems he identifies. One theme which distinguishes Jalbert's treatment of the issues is his insistence that a sound education must involve the inculcation of a capacity for *critical thinking*. The philosophy and sociology of education, as academic specializations, have too often neglected this topic, tending to leave it by the wayside. This segregation of concerns has been debilitating, when what is required is a truly *comprehensive* approach. Just to select one pertinent instance of a relevant but very rarely discussed factor: the impact of proper nutrition on a student's ability to concentrate and engage in serious study. Adequate diets are surely a prerequisite for maintaining an adequate level of attention; further, a program of physical education, well-integrated into the curriculum, is surely of great benefit in this regard.

With critical aplomb, Jalbert calls out a disturbing array of suspects which contribute to the crisis in education. Among them are: curricular decisions must be made by teachers, and not by bureaucrats, politicians or members of the business community; standardized testing, which is often narrowly crafted to serve these latter interests, should be abolished and replaced by one-on-one teacher and student assessments; school days must be shortened and 'project-based' programs implemented; learning at least one foreign language from an early age, along with an exposure to major elements of other cultures. Such approaches best prepare our youngsters for a mature participation in our global relationships. Finally, education must be treated as a universal *right*, not a (mere) benefit for the few whose position in life affords them the privileges they enjoy.

It has been a long time since I have read a study so poignant in this area. This study is refreshingly clear in its prose style and in the choice of pointed examples of the problems it identifies. A fundamental strength of this book is that the many problems plaguing education, some of which are addressed elsewhere, are investigated in one volume, allowing the reader to appreciate the interrelationships among them. It is a lucid contribution which will, I am confident, be welcomed by anyone who is concerned about education, including academics, parents and prospective (as well as current) students alike: it is a call to action in the service of our children.

Jeff Coulter, Ph.D.
Professor *Emeritus*
Boston University
May, 2018

PREFACE

This approach involves a conversation in which a student is asked to question their assumptions. It is a forum for open-ended inquiry, one in which both student and teacher can use probing questions to develop a deeper understanding of the topic.[1]

– The Socratic conversation method

A challenging philosophy of education

An essential part of being a teacher or coach or professor must include the subscription to a philosophy of education. After decades of asking teachers the question, "What is your philosophy of education?", whether off-the-cuff in a conversation or at academic conferences or to prospective candidates for teaching positions in university, the most common response I have received has been of virtual consternation; that is, a response of reflection and wonder about the question. While these findings are anecdotal, I find that my experience with this query informs me quite well about how overwhelmingly most teachers whom I have encountered are not guided by a philosophy of education. Stunning![2] The few who avowed that they possessed any ideas that directed their practice as teachers expressed something like, "I want to pass on knowledge that can inform students and help them succeed in school" or "I want to prepare students to deal with the real world" or "I want to

---

1 Philosophy 101, "What is the Socratic Method? Definition & Examples", Chapter 1, Lesson 9; Instructor: Christine Serva http://study.com/academy/lesson/what-is-the-socratic-method-definition-examples.html.
2 No doubt many teachers practice education with very solid theoretical and philosophical guidance. My point here is to highlight that education, as an institution, pays inconsistent attention to the possession of a philosophy of education.

teach students what will be necessary for them to get a good job". While these kinds of expressions are appropriate, they do not express any set of guiding principles; they are teleological in nature, not expressions of theoretical principles, informing their daily work of teaching. They do not actually address 'the practice of education', of teaching, of coaching, of professing. I wonder just how many teachers own no philosophy, no accompanying set of principles – of whatever kind and apart from my own principles – to inform and position their educational practice.

In the mid-1970s, I was introduced to a philosophy of education that has remained my compass for almost 40 years. I was taking a philosophy class which introduced me to the work of Paulo Freire, the most lucid and compelling of which was his essay entitled *Pedagogy of the Oppressed*[3] (Freire, 1970). Since then, I have witnessed the difference having such a philosophy of education can make in the classroom, in conference with students and, over the long term, in how students recall much more of what they have learned and appreciate how their education has been useful to them in their everyday lives. This is in sharp contrast to the students' avowals that have been shared with me over the years about how little they remember about so many topics they had 'studied' in high school and college. The key, as was explained by Freire, is that true education takes place in a context, a "dialogical encounter", instead of in a relative "vacuum", devoid of a proper *milieu* for learning.

I share much of what Freire contributed to a viable and critical theory of education. However, the concept of 'pedagogy' can elicit somewhat mixed ideas. Its origin is in the Latin word *paedagogus* and the Greek word *paidagogos*, meaning the act, art, science and practice of teaching. That's its denotative sense, the one with which we are most familiar. However, its usage is not so straightforward. When we delve a little into how it has sometimes been used, we find that its meaning often lent itself to the understanding that teaching categorized as *pedagogy* was largely, if not exclusively, of a kind that required unwavering replication of what the teacher proclaimed.[4] In other words, the kind of scenario that Freire describes, in *Pedagogy of the Oppressed*, as the "banking" method of teaching, one through which students *absorb* what the teacher says and *regurgitate* what they have been told. To the extent that the use of the concept 'pedagogy' means this kind of 'transfer' of knowledge, to that extent I am not in agreement with its use. I argue that education can never be a 'transfer' of information; it must be a result of a discussion, a 'dialogical encounter' of some kind. Moreover, this encounter must be conducted in a context of interactional competence so as to elicit only the best knowledge and understanding possible, emerging from that intimate encounter.

---

3 Paulo Freire's (1970), originally published in 1968) *Pedagogy of the Oppressed*, New York: The Seabury Press.

4 I thank John Taylor Gatto for this point; see his *Underground History of American Education* (2006) p. 13 ff.

xvi Preface

Henry Giroux, arguably the foremost scholar of Paulo Freire's work, talks about 'philosophy of education' as 'theory'. He asserts that

> Teachers really don't understand two things: they don't understand the relevance of theory for what they do and … they often find themselves in a place where time is such a deprivation that it becomes difficult to really think about what role theory might have in their lives; or … where theory has been expunged from the possibility of what they do as teachers because they have been utterly deskilled and technicised. I think the second issue is: you should never engage in a practice for which you are not reflective about that practice … You can talk about a practice without theory, but to do that is to deny the fact that it is already informed by theoretical presuppositions, many of which you are just simply not aware of … What I don't think theory does … and should not do, is provide a prescription for what to do that bypasses the need to understand that you have to think about what to do in the context in which you find yourself.
>
> *(Giroux, in Welsch & Yousman, 2006)*[5]

All theories must be able to 'explain' something, whether in the natural sciences like physics, chemistry, biology, *etc.* or in the social sciences like sociology, anthropology, political science, *etc. and in education.* Also, all theories are populated by sets of concepts or analytical constructs which do the work of 'explaining'. We can express them in terms of principles that guide teachers and that can be called upon to help them assess the present set of circumstances at hand. For example, in geometry, the concepts of 'angles' and 'sides' help us understand the Pythagorean theorem: $a^2+b^2=c^2$. In sociology, the concepts of 'class' and 'mode of production' help us understand the disparity of wealth in society; as in more recent references to the 1% versus the 99% in the United States economy. This is very different from a system or attitude in which a pre-packaged set of elements in a *curriculum* prescribe what should happen in the classroom. The teacher who is theoretically informed, or subscribes to a guiding philosophy, and knows how to manage learning 'in the making' must be the situated arbiter of what is needed to conduct learning in that moment. This is the essence of 'academic freedom', that freedom to implement *curricula* in the ways that are most efficacious in that setting and in that moment. That does not mean that the teacher becomes a *dictator* in the classroom. It only means that the teacher is the best person to direct the discussions at hand, allowing for full participation of students.

Any practice and preservation of academic freedom also requires that school

---

5 Dr. Janice Welsch and Bill Yousman, 2006, *Culture, Politics & Pedagogy: A Conversation with Henry Giroux*, DVD documentary. For a more comprehensive discussion of these insights, see Henry Giroux (2011) *On Critical Pedagogy*, especially Chapter 8, "Rethinking Education as a Practice of Freedom: Paulo Freire and the Promise of Critical Pedagogy".

administrators be consonant with those theories and methodologies and those who respect the fact that education can never be dictated to, out of context, and that true, critical learning can only be a result of a hands-on approach in the classroom. Administrators must have been teachers themselves so that they can support teachers in the classroom, instead of being at odds with them. This is a common problem in elementary and high schools. Teachers I have talked to, who want to challenge their students in a more organic manner, are regularly prevented from embarking upon a truly effective mode of student engagement, the substance of which could be deploying perhaps some critical thinking concepts, or by offering students the opportunity to discuss issues that affect them in everyday life. The constraints are real against this kind of learning; the proverbial 'blinkers' are on, thereby shunting out real-life contexts because of the mechanistic manner of *curriculum* construction, and because of the very training of our teachers.

Consequently, we do not see much critical education in the United States. My own experience has demonstrated to me that the training programs in graduate schools are partly responsible for this. I have talked to graduate students in education about these matters and they complain that their readings are treated as 'gospel', constituting ends in themselves, rather than a point of departure. They have also shared with me the kinds of discussions which dominate their classes about these sages in the absence of criticality; the discourse is around who wrote what and how those ideas developed and how important they were/are to our profession. In other words, they continue to engage in the creation of 'sacred cows', rather than the critical assessment of what those sages wrote in relationship to what we, as teachers/coaches/professors, must do to achieve the stated goals of enlightening cohorts of new students, what we do in classrooms as informed by theories.

In spite of all the well-intentioned efforts to prepare teachers for the classroom, what is missing in the training plan is serious inquiry into how to conduct education itself, what the daily project looks like outside of the *curricula's* rubric (having a *curriculum* is important, but the delivery should be left to the professional in the learning context). Internships are largely cheap labor for those institutions – not the real, hands-on training that they should be – and often they are a nightmare for the graduate students who are required to do them, because the oversight is lacking. The claim here is not that no undergraduate or graduate program in the U.S. addresses these matters at all, only that there seems to be a noticeable paucity of discussion, *in situ*, about what is probably the most important element of good teaching practice: a clear philosophy or theory of education. Even where some efforts are made to include "critical pedagogy", (Giroux's addition of the category "critical" in his construct does mitigate my earlier comments about the practice of pedagogy.) it is usually because of the efforts of a single teacher and not something which is part of the whole program. The 'training' of teachers is no less flawed than the rest of education in the United States.

There are prescribed methodologies of education in place, creating a regimented environment, in which students are trained to accept what the teacher says and question very little, so that, in the long run, they are *protected from* variations in

xviii Preface

thinking, thereby creating a false sense that what they understand must be correct because they encounter few, if any, challenging points of view. This approach is rampant in the United States. Moreover, teachers are often coerced to subscribe to a method of learning that focuses upon the *minutiae* of processes and outcomes that students must memorize and retain because our society is a reservoir of sound bites and trivial preoccupations. Or, as advocated in this book, educators could adopt a view that learning is a context of collective activity directed toward a discovery process which can yield a multiplicity of outcomes, not prepackaged and predetermined at the outset, and arrived at through the deployment of a set of critical thinking constructs, through which not only education can ensue, but liberation and freedom and enlightenment can prevail. Not much of this is going on. I advocate such a philosophy here.

I am reminded of the Reverend Doctor Martin Luther King, Jr.'s comment about the relationship between *freedom* and *education*: "As long as the mind is enslaved, the body can never be free"[6] (MLK, 1967). Education well-delivered can lay the foundation for freedom and liberation; liberate us from the constraints of arcane thinking and free us to pursue the enlightenment that awaits us.

This kind of teaching requires the inclusion of *critical thinking*, that is

> self-directed, self-disciplined, self-monitored and self-corrective thinking. It requires rigorous standards of excellence and mindful command of their use. It entails effective communication and problem solving abilities and the commitment to overcoming our native egocentrism and socio-centrism.
> *(Paul & Elder, 2009)*[7]

Peter McLaren is a scholar who is concerned with these issues of criticality and collaborative education between teachers and students. His take on what should be done is also akin to Freire's insights. He asserts that "education does not only *literate* people [italics added]", it is the opportunity to engage a critical practice to reestablish students as "agents" in their education to investigate the roles of mediation and oppression and social justice, because "human beings are unfinished" and are an ongoing project (McLaren, 2007).[8] This approach emphasizes the 'organic' nature of education I have been describing, instead of the regimented character of traditional schooling, in which, for example, the very seating arrangements can be

---

6 From the speech of the Rev. Dr. Martin Luther King, Jr., entitled "Where Do We Go From Here?", delivered to the Southern Christian Leadership Conference in Atlanta, GA, August 16, 1967.

7 Richard Paul & Linda Elder, *The Miniature Guide to Critical Thinking: Concepts and Tools* (2009) announcing the 31st Annual International Conference on Critical Thinking, Tomales: Critical Thinking Press, p. 2. See Chapter 12 for details.

8 Peter McLaren, March 10, 2007, interview by Joe Kincheloe at McGill University, Montreal for The Freire Project: The Paulo and Nita Freire International Project for Critical Pedagogy.

changed from being in rows to forming circles or semi-circles so that all students can see each other and are able to interact with one another.

From the standpoint of students, the educational experience today is very similar to some 60 years ago.[9] Children go to school, listen, participate in all sorts of activities, have recess, suffer detention. They have textbooks to read and homework to do; exams to take and grades to worry about. Back then, as now, there were *criteria* we had to satisfy in order to move along through the grades. It was not always clear to us just what we had to do, according to the *curriculum*, but we were taken through it by our teachers and somehow we did move ahead, some of us in style and others of us 'by the seat of our pants'. However, did we understand what had happened in that last year of school? Did we really know what we were 'supposed to know'? I am still at a loss to answer those questions in today's context.

Having expressed that, the experience that children have today is different for several reasons: more testing, fewer 'shop' classes, diminished physical education classes, poor food at lunch time, *etc.* Probably the most impactful difference is that, while some children in the '50s and '60s were exposed to television, today, virtually all children are influenced by the daily 'bombardment' by television, radio, internet messages and 'social media', most of which is commercial in character.[10] This becomes the main mechanism for the 'colonization of the mind'[11], which interferes with the ability of students to set their minds to learning and robs them of their critical faculties to realize that they are (or should be) in command of their ways of understanding their immediate circumstances and their views of the world around them. Without a focused and competent curriculum and faculty, these dazzling pressures from the outside and some from the inside, our children can become bewildered.

From the standpoint of teachers, whose professional charge has always been a difficult one for many reasons – low pay, long hours, tough students, *etc.* – the challenges they face today are much more complicated and demanding. For the teachers who want to do critical education, this hyper-mediated scenario maximizes the distractions that students experience and prevents the learning day from spilling into the lives of the students. If there is anything that we should be doing, it is precisely to make the real connections between what we address in classes and what public life constitutes. Instead, teachers are preoccupied with redirecting students' attention to the work at hand.

---

9 There are widespread conditions that existed in the past which do not exist today, most notably, school racial segregation *a la* 1950s. While most of those laws are no longer on the books today, we continue to have a significant level of segregation in schools. See Nikole Hannah-Jones (September 6, 2017) "The Resegregation of Jefferson County", *The New York Times Magazine*, The Education Issue.

10 I am not arguing here that education 60 years ago was just fine; rather, that the experience today is far more distorted than back then, because of the overwhelming presence of mass mediated communication, especially broadcast and internet.

11 This construct arises out of the work of Franz Fanon (1968) *The Wretched of the Earth*, and John Henrick Clark, "In Our Image" (1989) and *Christopher Columbus and the Afrikan Holocaust: Slavery and the Rise of European Capitalism* (1992), and Ivan van Sertima (1976) *They Came Before Columbus*. See Chapters 2 and 12 on the media and Orwell, respectively.

xx Preface

Further, they are reduced to technocrats who spend their time running practice sessions for test-taking, so that students 'score sufficiently well' to be promoted to the next grade and so that the school can retain funding from the state or federal governments; teacher salaries are also tied to the results of test scores. Instead, teachers are dictated to via *curricula* that are decided upon by functionaries in educational settings – non-teachers – whose agendas have little to do with education *per se*, but rather with occupying the minds of our children with questions and answers according to a myopic set of preoccupations.

Consequently, our children know little more than the narrow-minded versions of instruction that pass for history, science and social science, geared to distract them from a critical appraisal of what they are learning and guide them to a cursory and sound-bite character of knowledge. They are taught that life is a series of knee-jerk reactions, instead of something 'to be examined'– as Socrates instructed us – constantly requiring a depth of understanding that might increase the probability of an enlightened experience.

What if this were not what we observed in our schools? What if there were another way or ways to practice education which taught students that learning is a collective effort on the part of teachers and students; that learning is not predicated on test-taking, but on discussion; that learning is a matter of connecting those discussions with the real practicality of 'doing life'? I offer a closer look at what Freire proposed. He offered his criticism of establishment/orthodox education, demonstrating that 'true' education cannot be a matter of involving certain 'intelligent' individuals, presumably teachers, imparting their 'knowledge' to others, presumably students, thereby "banking" that knowledge through some kind of transfer process 'into' the student. Hence, education, in this mechanistic scheme, is seen as operating from the premise that the teacher's 'knowledge', if successful, will transfer to the student. Freire asserts:

> The banking concept … distinguishes two [steps] in the action of the educator. During the first, he cognizes a cognizable object while he prepares his lessons …; during the second, he expounds to his students about that object.
>
> *(Freire, 1968)*[12]

Students are not invited to *participate* in their education; they are expected simply to accept what the teacher says. He continues:

> Nor do the students practice any act of cognition, since the object towards which that act should be directed is the property rather than a medium evoking the critical reflection of both teacher and students. Hence … we have a system which achieves neither true knowledge nor true culture.
>
> *(Freire, 1968)*[13]

---

12 Freire, *Op. cit.*, pp. 67–68.
13 *Ibid.*

Freire's criticism of this system not only challenges the misunderstanding of the concept of 'education' itself, but also challenges the actual *doing* of education. While Freire does not use this category, the process he describes is tantamount to *cloning*. He offers another path, not only for understanding education *per se*, but also for *doing* it, which involves the practice of the "dialogical encounter", that process of education that recognizes that common sense discussion is the key to real education.

> The teacher's thinking is authenticated only by the authenticity of the students' thinking. The teacher cannot think for his students, nor can he impose his thoughts on them. Authentic thinking ... does not take place in ivory tower isolation, but only in communication.
>
> *(Freire, 1968)*[14]

Much like standardized test-based education, the banking system relies on memorizing and parroting what the teacher says, but the dialogical encounter stresses the importance of the interactional component, the very engagement of the interlocutors, teachers and students together, through which learners bring much to the table (among many other components, their common sense 'stock of knowledge' at hand). The argument is that the resulting understandings are a synthesis of meaning-options made available in the discussions themselves and not preordained exercises in transference. Instead of counting on their 'memory' in learning, students 'remember' what they learn because of the encounter itself, the interactional experience, not because of the ephemeral 'memorized object', which, overwhelmingly and eventually, save the odd occasion, evaporates. The result of the 'conversation' is instead a 'social product', emerging out of the actual social interaction. Hence, this approach allows for the critical element to enter into the considerations of the participants in any discussion, whose purpose is to learn about or to investigate anything. This is at the theoretical heart of the experience of learning.

I have been practicing this philosophy for 38 years (as best I could), implementing the simple and incisive insights that Freire introduced. They work. There is nothing more inviting for students than to realize that, in any given course, there will be no examinations (testing) of any kind and that the evaluation of their work will be based upon their performance in the form of writing assignments and their participation in the discussions conducted in class. To virtually all students, this methodology liberates them from the fears and pressures of testing. That is what testing generates in students: a sense of fear and anxiety that gets in the way of education. It doesn't do anything else; particularly, it does not 'measure' anything. Tests are, at best, dubious evaluations of what students remember at the time of the test; at worst, tests are deleterious to students, representing only the fear and anxiety of the hours they spent in submission to them.

---

14 Freire, *Op. cit.*, p. 64.

xxii Preface

However, the problems that plague education today do not begin and end with testing. Eliminating testing is only part of what needs to be done. Students must be able to relax and focus on the matters at hand in whatever subject matter they are investigating. They must be shown how to be open to what all members of the class say and do, not only the teacher. They must realize that as they converse, discuss and debate the issues at hand, they are able to be critical of themselves as well as others, with confidence and without anxiety. This method encourages a creative evolution of the practice of learning, thereby allowing for the development of broad and deep understandings of the subject. Students learn that *education is not a matter of agreeing with the teacher; it is a matter of understanding what is being discussed* for good reasons, and that, if students take up what is being offered, it is because it has merit independent of whomever said or wrote it, and not because 'the teacher said so'. Education should never be the transfer of what someone said; it has to be based upon sound thinking and argumentation. Mere *opinions* have no place in education. Education is about acquiring the capacity to form *sound judgments*, which must be argued for and for which evidence must be brought to bear on the claims made. This kind of approach allows students to discover what is at hand, instead of through 'directives' by the teacher. Teachers should be rewarded for providing such contexts to students for their collective enlightenment, not for the scores their students achieve on tests.

Benefits of this approach go well beyond the actual classroom. Students are challenged to connect what they learn in school with their everyday lives. Education cannot be separate from the realities of doing life; it should not be intangible.

> Education as the practice of freedom – as opposed to education as the practice of domination – denies that man is abstract, isolated, independent and unattached to the world; it also denies that the world exists as a reality apart from men.
>
> *(Freire, 1968)*[15]

In other words, good education cannot take place in a vacuum; it must be connected to what students encounter every day. They can learn about the complex interrelationships among the institutions in society by understanding, at the conceptual level, what they involve, including what makes them work, what problems can arise, what solutions could be applied and how to improve the conditions of those relationships. They also must learn to evaluate how they could help change those relationships when they are shown to be discrepant or unjust. According to Freire, one tactic of oppression is to serve up a menu of myths in order to subdue people and maintain passivity. For example,

---

15 Freire, *Op. cit.*, p. 69.

Preface **xxiii**

> the myth that anyone who is industrious can become an entrepreneur ...; the myth of the universal right of education ...; the myth that rebellion is a sin against God; the myth of private property as fundamental to personal human development ...; the myth of the industriousness of the oppressors and the laziness and dishonesty of the oppressed, as well as the myth of the natural inferiority of the latter and the superiority of the former.
>
> *(Freire, 1968)[16]*

Indeed, part of critical education must be about identifying the myths in society, myths that resound in the echo chamber of the corporate media, myths as tools in the hands of those who rule to distort reality in order to confuse and dominate people (all societies have some version of such mythologies). This kind of practice has virtually guaranteed that those myths be reconstructed to fit any changes in the society. As a result, students do not understand how and why they are prevalent, how to demystify them and how to change their reality. The current practice of education in the United States does all of this very well.

Part of criticality must also be to awaken and develop a sense of 'activism' in students. This means that young people must involve themselves in the democracy they hope to create in their lives. Like education, democracy is a messy practice, constantly needing to be recreated. Students must understand that a viable democracy requires consistent participation; it is not a phenomenon *sui generis*. Students must realize that people actually must make it happen and that a lifelong commitment is necessary, because there are many people who do not want democracy and who instead support the plutocracy that has developed over the last two hundred years. They must realize that the fullest life includes involvement in work of a kind that goes beyond their immediate circumstances. They should work to improve the lives of people in their community, or city/town, or state or country – and the world. They must learn to participate in life in the context of something bigger than themselves and work to exit the planet, when they expire, in better shape than it was when they arrived. *What a sad moment indeed to realize, at age 80, that all we have done in life was to satisfy only our own needs and desires and never to have engaged in something that was outside of our purview, but still within our reach, something that could have left things better than we found them!* Ultimately, Freire was interested in freedom and justice made possible via an achieved "conscientization" *(conscientizacao)* won through the kind of education that lives in the interactional practice present in the classroom.

I subscribe to this philosophy and advocate that this critical form of teaching practice be adopted by all schools at all levels finally to inform our children and allow their critical faculties to be unlocked and grow. If properly coached, they can affect the change that is needed, not only in their own lives, but also in the larger society to ensure the freedom and justice that all deserve and to understand and

---

16 Freire, *Op. cit.*, pp. 135–136.

xxiv Preface

struggle against oppression wherever it arises. *In the absence of theoretical and philosophical insight, we cannot do this.*

Bibliography

Clarke, J.H. (1989) "In Our Image". *Essence*, volume *20*, issue *5*, p. 159.

Clarke, J.H. (1992) *Christopher Columbus and the Afrikan Holocaust: Slavery and the Rise of European Capitalism*. Brooklyn, NY: A and B Books.

Fanon, F. (1968) *The Wretched of the Earth*. New York: Random House, Inc.

Freire, P. (1970) *Pedagogy of the Oppressed*. New York: The Seabury Press.

Gatto, J.T. (2006) *Underground History of American Education*. New York: Oxford Village Press.

Giroux, H. (2011) *On Critical Pedagogy*. New York: Continuum Publishing.

Hannah-Jones, N. (September 6, 2017) "The Resegregation of Jefferson County". *The New York Times Magazine*. Retrieved from www.nytimes.com/2017/09/06/magazine/the-resegregation-of-jefferson-county.html

King, M. L., Jr. (1967) "Where Do We Go from Here?". Speech delivered at the 11th Annual SCLC Convention in Atlanta, GA, August 16, 1967.

McLaren, P. (March 10, 2007) Interview by Joe Kincheloe at McGill University, Montreal for The Freire Project: The Paulo and Nita Freire International Project for Critical Pedagogy.

Paul, R. & Elder, L. (2009) *The Miniature Guide to Critical Thinking: Concepts and Tools*. Tomales, CA: Critical Thinking Press.

Paul, R. (n.d.) Foundation for Critical Thinking. www.criticalthinking.org/

van Sertima, I. (1976) *They Came Before Columbus*. New York: Random House.

Serva, C. (n.d.) "What is the Socratic Method? Definition & Examples", Philosophy 101. Chapter 1, Lesson 9. Retrieved from http://study.com/academy/lesson/what-is-the-socratic-method-definition-examples.html

Welsch, J. & Yousman, B. (Producers), & Traverso, M. (Director). (2006) *Culture, Politics & Pedagogy: A Conversation with Henry Giroux*. [Motion Picture].

INTRODUCTION

It is not light that is needed, but fire. It is not the gentle shower, but thunder. We need the storm, the whirlwind, the earthquake. The feeling of the nation must be quickened; the conscience of the nation must be roused; the propriety of the nation must be startled; the hypocrisy of the nation must be exposed; and the crimes against God and man must be proclaimed and denounced.

– Frederick Douglass (1818–1895)[1]

The crisis in education

Allow me to take a few minutes of your reading time to let you know what is in store for you in this book. I am a sociologist. The members of our profession study society; we investigate the many parts which comprise it. Some sociologists study data about populations of people in terms of age, education, income, *etc.* – called 'demographics'; some study the distribution of social rewards in a social hierarchy – called 'social stratification'; yet others study how people engage with one another – called 'social interaction'. All of these scholars are interested in understanding the complexities of societies and the people in them and offer insights into the phenomena they investigate. They study pretty much anything that has to do with how the society is organized in all of its major dimensions: cultural, social, economic, political and ideological.

I have primarily studied social phenomena in terms of their ideological characteristics. One of the major questions I have posed from the beginning of my

---

1 From Frederick Douglass' speech "The Meaning of July 4th for the Negro", July 5, 1852, addressing the Rochester Ladies Anti-Slavery Society, Rochester, NY. See Howard Zinn's (2014) *Voices of a People's History of the United States* (performed by James Earl Jones), 10th edition, New York: Seven Stories Press.

2 Left Behind

studies is "How do people come to have the ideas they have?" (*e.g.*, the perspectives they hold on different conditions of life, phenomena that affect their lives, the consequences of their and other's actions, *etc.*). This kind of question led me to concentrate on the 'sociology of knowledge'; that is 'specialized knowledge' (*e.g.*, what we learn in school) and 'common sense knowledge' (*e.g.*, what we learn just by being members of a society). Later, I directed my energies to the investigation of the mass media of communication (and subsequently taught communication in university), inquiring into the 'information' that they offer up for our consideration, because I realized that much of what we take to be 'knowledge' is provided to us by them.

The kind of knowledge I am considering here, of course, is knowledge that we receive from going to public schools: elementary, middle, high school and college. I am questioning the depth and breadth of the knowledge our children actually receive and, as the title suggests, I do not think that our children are delivered a fair shake for many reasons, some of which I address in the different chapters ahead of you.

My interest in writing this book is to share with you the experience I have had as a teacher for 38 years and indicate several signposts of concern I have identified with regard to the proper delivery of that education to our children. What I call for is a 'paradigm shift'[2] in the way in which we think about education as an institution and in the ways we go about 'doing education'. My claim is that we have been failing for quite some time now; others claim that we never got it right, but that is for you to decide. This book treats several of those failures and suggests some ways to address them. Solutions to them must always come from people 'on the ground' in their respective communities.

"Paradigm shift"

When Thomas Kuhn wrote his seminal essay about scientific revolutions,[3] I wonder if he thought that his insights would themselves be 'revolutionary'. He challenged established notions in the philosophy of science which proposed how the natural sciences are actually produced. He asserted that science should be understood in terms of an historical understanding of periods of scientific discovery, as well as periods of disorder, doubt and confusion, paying close attention to the context of those who had made contributions to how the physical world works. Kuhn argued that scientific development advances in a series of 'phases': 'normal science', the science of 'business as usual', characterized by Ian Hacking as a science that "does not aim at novelty but at clearing up the status quo. It tends to discover what it

---

2 A 'paradigm' is a way of thinking or a way of seeing; it includes the adoption of a particular theory or a *modus operandi*, a methodology or a way of doing.

3 Thomas Kuhn (1962) *The Structure of Scientific Revolutions*, Chicago: University of Chicago Press.

Introduction **3**

expects to discover".[4] The revolutionary route arises out of a *bona fide* 'crisis' or in conditions of questioning and doubts about the 'paradigm' or *modus operandi* of existing scientific practice, thereby suggesting the need for shifts in those theories or methodologies.

I am old enough to remember Mario Savio's speech at UC Berkeley in 1964, talking about 'free speech':

> There's a time when the operation of the machine becomes so odious, makes you so sick at heart, that you can't take part! You can't even passively take part! And you've got to put your bodies upon the gears and upon the wheels … upon the levers, upon all the apparatus, and you've got to make it stop! And you've got to indicate to the people who run it, to the people who own it, that unless you're free, the machine will be prevented from working at all!
>
> *(Savio, 1964)*[5]

His sentiment is appropriate with regard to the educational status quo we witness today, because it is "sick" and we must "make it stop" and reestablish a freedom to deliver only the best public education possible to our children or our educational institution "will be prevented from working at all".

We have witnessed many 'paradigm shifts' in the history of human experience: the transition from predominantly nomadic life to sedentary life due to agriculture and the 'domestication' of animals some 10,000 years ago; the invention of the steam engine, which revolutionized the manufacturing industry in the 19th century; the development of nuclear energy, including, fatefully, that of the atomic and hydrogen bombs; and the development of the internet, which has rendered the world into an even smaller 'global village' than the radio and television did. These inventions/discoveries and others represent moments in history that changed life in fundamental ways, such that there has been no significant return to our previous ways of thinking and acting in the world.

One major example, which Kuhn described, was the growing ideological conflict between the Church and scientific discovery. Investigations in astronomy raised many questions about the claims by the Church that the earth was at the center of the universe. The Church had adopted this way of thinking after Aristotle (350 BCE).[6] According to Christian dogma, God created the universe and 'man' within it "in his image"; therefore, man was at the center of that creation on

---

4 See "Preface" by Ian Hacking (2012) to new edition of *The Structure of Scientific Revolutions: 50th Anniversary Edition*, Chicago: University of Chicago Press.

5 From Mario Savio's famous speech "Bodies Upon the Gears", December 2, 1964, on the steps of Sproul Hall at the University of California, Berkeley. Savio was a central figure of the Free Speech Movement; protests had erupted that fall because the university had prohibited 'political activity' on campus.

6 Aristotle (384–322 BCE), *On the Heavens*, 350 BCE.

4 Left Behind

earth. Hence, if man is the central focus of God's creation in the universe, then it follows that the center of the universe must be 'the earth', the geocentric concept. Investigations in astronomy challenged this long-standing belief. This had to do with the transformation of thought from the Ptolemaic vision of the universe to the Copernican and, later, to the Galilean insight. Ptolemy (150 AD)[7] had argued, heavily influenced by the Church, that the universe was of a 'geocentric' configuration; he was able to *demonstrate* this mathematically because he interpreted the paths of the planets to be in concentric circles around the earth. Copernicus (1514)[8] argued that the planets did not orbit the earth, but the sun, the heliocentric configuration; however, he could not *prove* this mathematically, having retained Ptolemy's concentric circle format. It was not until Galileo (1610)[9] demonstrated that the planetary paths are elliptical that the heliocentric model could be mathematically *proven*; hence, establishing the unanimously accepted configuration of the universe.[10]

This controversy established the preeminence of the 'scientific' over the 'religious' points of view in the understanding of the universe, a real challenge to the status quo and constituted a 'paradigm shift'. While this change was not an abrupt one, as the dating indicates, it was still a major transformation in our grasp of how the universe works, the original thinking of which cannot be restored.

Strictly speaking, Kuhn was not writing about 'social' transformations *per se* (although he did briefly discuss some of the social ramifications of such scientific changes). However, I am taking a bit of license here in claiming that what is needed in our system of education is analogous to what Kuhn was presenting: what we must do about the current state of public education in the United States is arguably on the order of Kuhn's scientific strictures. We must transform our educational system which has become degraded to such an extent as to be virtually inoperable in the delivery of equal, high-quality public education for all our children. What we must work for immediately is a major disruption and reorganization of the educational status quo.

I chose this analogy because I want to impress upon the reader that the changes that are required in our educational scheme are not minor or reforming or cursory; rather they are major and fundamental and must go to the core of what we must abandon and what we must adopt. They represent an example of Kuhn's 'paradigm shift', in the social sense. In short, what I propose here is revolutionary.

Consider another perspective on this theme: when human beings evolved some 200,000 years ago, slowly, but surely, the balance of nature changed. Human beings, for mostly good reasons, and many not so good, adapted to nature around

---

7   Claudius Ptolemy (100–170 AD), *Almagest*, 150 AD.
8   Nicolaus Copernicus (1473–1543), *Commentariolus*, 1514.
9   Galileo Galilei (1564–1642), *Siderius Nuncius*, 1610.
10 Turns out that these great intellects, limited by their technology, were myopic. What they were observing was our galaxy, the *Milky Way*, not the *universe*. Recent reports from the Hubble spacecraft estimate that there are some 2 trillion galaxies in the universe.

Introduction **5**

them; at first becoming a part of nature to satisfy their *needs* and, later progressively, harnessing the powers of nature to benefit their constantly growing *wants*. The result has been a transformation of nature unprecedented in history, most notably since the beginning of the Industrial Revolution in the early 19th century. The natural paradigm of life, that eco-biological balance among the flora and fauna, was interrupted by an artificial paradigm, one which has disrupted nature itself. In other words, in the last 200,000 years, human intervention has changed life on this planet since its emergence 3.5 billion years ago. Stunning! Janine Benyus (Schmid, 2015) argues from a biomimicry perspective that

> Our work as a species is to create designs and strategies that move us toward being better adapted to life on earth over the long haul; and, when you ask how to be better adapted to this planet, there are no better models than the species that have preceded us for billions of years.

And, using the context of chemistry,

> *We need to replace our old industrial chemistry book with nature's recipe book.* Our synthetic chemistry is completely different [from] nature's chemistry. We use every element in the Periodic Table, even the toxic ones; and then we use brute force reactions to get elements to bond or break apart. Life uses a small subset of the Periodic Table, the safe elements, and then very, very elegant recipes: low temperature, low pressures, low toxicity. That's nature's chemistry. So, *a very different paradigm.* [italics added]

And

> In the natural world, the definition of success is the continuity of life. You keep yourself alive and you keep your offspring alive. That's success; but it's not the offspring in this generation. Success is keeping your offspring alive 10,000 generations and more. And that presents a conundrum because you cannot, you're not going to be there to take care of your offspring 10,000 generations from now. So *what organisms have learned to do is to take care of the place that is going to take care of their offspring. Life has learned to create conditions conducive to life.*[11] [italics added]

Benyus argues that human intervention, in the interest of adaptation initially and for the purposes of increasing exploitation of nature, for some 200 years now, has altered the balance which has taken 3.5 billion years to create and maintain on our planet. That has been made abundantly clear for decades, particularly since Rachel

---

11 From documentary film *Biomimicry* (Schmid, 2015).

6 Left Behind

Carson's poignant book *Silent Spring*,[12] in which she blows the whistle on industrial waste, pesticides/herbicides, DDT, *etc.*, the "elixirs of death" in Carson's words, and sounds the alarm on the pollution of our land, air and water. This has been violent *intervention*, not *adaptation*. The Indigenous peoples of the North American continent (Turtle Island) have been making these arguments for hundreds of years (the first LAW [Land, Air and Water] society). The rise of capitalism in the late 18th century and the ensuing hyper-industrialization of production have transformed our planet into, on the one hand, a place that is drained of its resources and, on the other, a receptacle for the waste generated from overproduction at the cost of negatively impacting ecosystems everywhere. Hence, the climate change reality we suffer today.

I want to make an analogy here: for quite specific reasons, our educational experience has taken a major hit. Just as our planet has deteriorated, posing a major threat to the viability or life for our species and countless others, so too have our educational traditions been in decline, often treating our children like receptacles of mediocre learning. I, and many others, argue that there is a difference between 'education' and 'schooling'. The impact of capitalism is central here. Our children are understood within the context of that hyper-production, the 'toxic' part of the 'table of options'. Their instruction is geared to satisfy the vagaries of commodity production (schooling) which means that our children need not learn about many subjects that do not directly facilitate their smooth transition from school to the sweatshops or other work contexts of low pay, dangerous working conditions and industrial health problems. You see, people do not need 'education' to serve in those capacities; all they need is 'schooling'. All they need are the isolated 'skills' to be able to perform repetitive tasks. However, if students are not taught a full and quality *curriculum* of subjects (education), they are much more easily exploited economically. This is an imposition upon an otherwise quite benign experience of learning; these parameters are 'forced' upon or into the system of education such that it becomes distorted in the direction of production interests. In order to assert our right to a viable life, one free of exploitation, we must be literate and informed way beyond what is expedient for production purposes. This imposition of external and deleterious pressures on an originally organic process[13] is the truly violent and interventionist reality our children suffer today in school.

Just as nature has been, and continues to be, altered and devastated by this frenetic abuse of everything for 'progress' (which means, from the abusers' perspective, the maximization of profit, especially in the short run), so too have the fundamental and essential precepts of education been eroded by the intervention

---

12 Rachel Carson (1962) *Silent Spring*, London: Hamish Hamilton.

13 I refer here to the originally culturally animated practices that existed in communal societies, where all members were taught everything they needed to know to survive and thrive. This included the comprehensive cultural, social, economic, political and ideological knowledge of the society, not only that very practical knowledge that could literally keep them alive. See Chapter 1 on the right to education.

of powerful special interests. Whether under the Greek or Roman empires or in early stratified societies or later ones, feudalism being the most egregious form, or under the 'American empire' today, those original educational precepts have been compromised beyond recognition, to the point at which they are inoperative and not even part of the calculus of education. The principles driving the mission of the New School and others should be preserved and practiced:

> Frustrated by the intellectual timidity of traditional colleges [all schools PLJ], they envisioned a new kind of academic institution where faculty and students would be free to address honestly and directly the problems facing societies ... to bring creative scholars together with citizens interested in improving their understanding of the key issues of the day through active questioning, debate, and discussion.
>
> *(The New School, 1919)*[14]

To 'cash the check' on my analogy here, I argue that what we need is to reestablish or to introduce those critical and central components of educational practice, including cultural literacy, social intercourse, economic democracy, political participation and ideological awareness; to turn education for the rich and powerful on its head and relaunch educational *schemata* for all our children.

In other words, we must change the paradigm from doing education for the purposes of perpetuating the status quo. Witness the unprecedented disparity in income distribution (the 1% versus the 99%, a predictable result of capitalism), the ignorance our population exhibits in the political process (the 2016 election cycle in the United States demonstrates this most starkly), the decline of our cultural forms (emulating symbols dominated by corporate interests), the reduction of social interaction to 'little boxes' (those electronic devices that mediate how we communicate with one another) and the deleterious effects of how the corporate mass media feed us a diet of convoluted half-truths, 'sound bites' and lies.

'Causes' of the crisis

There is no controversy about how our educational practices are falling short of the mark. Depending upon who you ask, respondents are in agreement that something serious has to be done about education. People respond by identifying flaws in terms of funding, poverty, the *curriculum*, the teaching, overcrowded classrooms, the lack of teaching materials, standardized testing, crumbling physical plants, the political content of textbooks, *etc.* This list can easily be expanded to encompass

---

14 Part of the text of the early 'mission' articulated by the founders of The New School in 1919, "among them Charles Beard, John Dewey, Jams Harvey Robinson, and Thorstein Veblen". Luminaries as W.E.B. DuBois, Margaret Mead, Erich Fromm, Harold Lasky, Franz Boas, John Maynard Keynes and Frank Lloyd Wright taught there. See www.newschool.edu.

8 Left Behind

several categories of problems; the truth is that all of these problems have something to do with the crisis.

This book will not address all of the problems plaguing the education of our children, only those which seem to be most fundamental or foundational. What is presupposed in the question, "What is wrong with our education?" is that there actually is a *crisis in education*; the question is not whether there *is* one, but of what does it consist? For most people, this observation is a common sense one. From whatever perspective one takes on the matter, there is almost an instant recognition that there are serious problems in education these days, and for some time now. However, when we look into the ways in which this crisis is talked about, we discover that most of the categories suggested above are ignored. The talk seems to be focused upon test scores.

One after another, political candidates, economists, or media purveyors and pundits complain about the 'crisis in education' in terms of where high school students in the United States are positioned on the 'test-score ladder'. Whether in a meeting of a town council, or a symposium at some university, or a report by the Department of Education itself, the focus has been on our students' test scores. That is, they all work on the assumption that standardized testing[15] is correct; the problem is how to get students to score well on them. Ours is the only country in the world where such tests are administered to such an extent and on such a regular basis. All countries have educational problems, but not with this testing frenzy. Many countries of quite remarkable success in their results in student performance have deployed other means to evaluate their students and very sparingly administer such tests.

In the United States, if we do not quantify our students (reify them as scores on tests), we do not seem to know how to evaluate them. We have fallen into a quantitative abyss, without which we cannot know how our students are doing. What happened to the face-to-face, *tête-a-tête* encounter I remember having in elementary and high school with my teachers about how I was doing in this or that subject? What is curious is that these standardized tests are a poor mechanism for determining how our students are doing. Study after study has found that such tests are flawed in the most fundamental ways. They pressure students at the very time they have to 'perform' with formal test rules, the running clock, the onerous reality that the test they are taking right then may determine their future. Whether students are good test-takers or bad ones, we should be mindful of the awesome weight that they carry with regard to students' futures and the consequences of the actions that are taken as a result of the scores they achieve. Some students have actually been told that test scores can 'make or break' their chances in life.

The reliance on standardized testing has been exacerbated in the last decade by the passing of the legislation referred to as No Child Left Behind (NCLB),[16] in

---

15 See Chapter 8 on the mismeasure of our students.
16 The title of this book is an *ironic* reference to this law.

Introduction **9**

which it is clear that *all* evaluations of our students are conducted by implementing standardized, mostly multiple-choice, tests. After some criticism, the NCLB was replaced by the Common Core, no less problematic, maintaining the old assumption that test-taking is the correct evaluation tool for our students *and teachers*.[17]

Among the top contributors to poor education delivery is the growing poverty in the U.S; this, in spite of official reports that, for a family of four, with a threshold of $22,314 in 2010, 15.1% of the U.S. population lived in poverty and that, with a threshold of $24,563 in 2016, 12.7% of the U.S. population lived in poverty, poverty has decreased.[18] What is not included in this comparison is that the threshold is much too low. Depending upon where it lives, a family of four requires at least twice the official threshold in order not to be poor.[19] Poverty is not an accident; it is a fundamental component of capitalism, the money-based economic behemoth, organized to guarantee a workforce that is eager to work for minimum wages, without access to the 'good life' promised to us as the 'American Dream'. The extraordinary wealth that has been created by this capitalist mode of production has been squandered by the capitalist class on fraudulent foreign military campaigns to 'spread democracy' all over the world. What that global propaganda has maintained is a false equivalence between capitalism and democracy; nothing could be further apart than these two concepts, indeed they are *in contradiction*. Capitalism is a dictatorship of the wealthy over the poor, in spite of a 'legal contract' (the slogan for which was "A Fair Day's Wages for a Fair Day's Work"[20]), between capitalist and worker. The fact is that any wealth created in this system is expropriated by the capitalist and used to support this economic inequality which manifests in all domains of life.

For the last 60 years, that wealth has supported the military industrial complex President Eisenhower warned us about and has been absorbed by the dictates of the U.S. global empire. Inextricably bound to the causes of poverty is the poor funding for education, relying heavily on the tax base of communities; more funding in wealthy ones, less in poor ones. The same system which creates poverty through the uneven distribution of social rewards also prevents proper funding for education.

In the context of ongoing and protracted foreign engagement in invasions and occupations, most recently Iraq and Afghanistan (with ample sabre-rattling toward Syria and Iran), the national budget is being drained by these illegal and criminal actions. This fact exacerbates the national debt circumstances post-'Bush 43'. The current (2018) national debt is calculated to be more than $21 trillion and

---

17 See Chapter 8 on the mismeasure of our students.
18 Readily viewed at "Poverty Thresholds", https://www.census.gov/data/tables/time-series/demo/income-poverty/historical-poverty-thresholds.html
19 See Aimee Picchi (August 26, 2015) "How Much Money Do U.S. Families Need to Get By?" CBS News Money Watch, and Chapter 5 on poverty
20 Friedrick Engels (May 1–2, 1881), "A Fair Day's Wages for a Fair Day's Work", *The Labour Standard*, London; this motto was adopted by the British working class in the late 19th century.

10 Left Behind

counting.[21] (The cost of the invasion and subsequent occupation of Iraq alone has been put at $3 trillion.).[22] With that kind of debt and no real program to pay it down, instead we have continued spending for wars and occupations, and there is no adequate funding for domestic needs, including education.

There are other elements which contribute to the lack of educational funding at the federal level, *e.g.*, wrangling over budget items in Congress, trimming this and that program, placing more and more responsibility in the hands of state and local governments to provide funds for educational needs. Those local property taxes, part of which are marked for education, increase accordingly and, while the funds raised in such ways increase, the actual delivery of educational services does not seem to increase, rather it decreases. If we agree that education is a right and that it should be provided for through tax dollars, *i.e.*, public funds (all indicators demonstrate this commitment), then something has to be done to correct the path we are on and take responsibility to 'make good' on this most critical promise to provide education for our children.

I propose that, in order properly to 'fund' education, and any other institution for that matter, we must, in the short run, reposition the responsibilities among local, state and federal governments with regard to the real dollars that are allotted to education so that all schools are funded in ways that provide for the same opportunities across the board, regardless of where the schools are located, whether in the poorer or richer communities. In the long run, the economic system in place now, a money-based economy, must be replaced by a resource-based economy, something that is virtually never discussed.[23] This means that the sustainable use of resources that are available to us in any particular location, with a connection to other locations, can be shared nationally, and globally, for the benefit of all people. But … I digress!

Another reason we have a crisis in education is the state of our teaching profession. Our teachers are taught to maintain the status quo of 'educational' methodologies. Teachers are still trained (and this is primarily, but not exclusively, in the elementary and secondary school environment) to conduct class using memorization and repetition. The separation between teacher and student is maintained, rather than closing that gap and teaching *with* the students. The "banking" method is promoted throughout. Teacher programs must cease the perpetuation of the idea

---

21 The Office of Management and Budget estimates that the national debt, in 2021, will be more than $23 trillion. See www.usdebtclock.org. The estimate registers $13 trillion plus as of the end of August 2010, on its way to $14 trillion at a rate of more than $4 billion per day. This estimate is commensurate with estimates by multiple economists and others who monitor this figure. There is little, if any, controversy about this estimate.

22 See the convincing 2008 analysis by Linda J. Bilmes and Joseph E. Stiglitz, *The Three Trillion Dollar War: The True Cost of the Iraq Conflict*, London: W.W. Norton and Company, LTD.

23 Increasingly, people's jobs are being taken away from them by robots. There are estimates that claim that, over the next 20 years, unemployment will soar. One solution proposed, advocated by Jaques Fresco, is actually to increase robotics and free up human energy to do more important things like engineering how to use the natural resources that are available. See The Venus Project (n.d.).

Introduction **11**

that education is about 'knowledge transfer' and replace that with the idea that teaching is an organic and participatory practice.[24]

Another issue about teachers is their salaries. We know that salary equity is not practiced in the United States. While one might expect that the practitioners of the most essential professions in a society (*e.g.*, farmers, health professionals, social services professionals, fire and police protection, teachers) would have the highest pay of all; not so in the United States. People in professions like the media, insurance, sports, the stock exchange, sales, *etc.*, collect salaries far greater. While their services are also important, their import does not rise to the level of those provided by our teachers, *et al.* (At least, their pay should be on par.) Part-time and non-tenure-track teaching is worse. Low teacher pay is a disincentive for young people to choose education as a profession. In addition, the conditions of so many schools are so dire (physical plants, staff shortages, tools of the trade, *etc.*) as to discourage potential teachers. These concerns have become chronic across the country.[25] Yet another problem involves the transformation of a public institution of learning into an institution of profit-making, rendering the practice of education a matter of "business" rather than the nurturing experience that it should be.[26]

The crisis in education is manifest at least in these ways. To talk about the crisis in education without talking about these fundamental issues *together* is to misrepresent where the problems lie and how they interact, indeed to 'miss the boat'. As already mentioned, I believe that the most fundamental problem is a misunderstanding of what education should entail; that is, the character of the enterprise, from a sound philosophical position. Once anchored in sound theory, several other problems come into view and are able to be addressed in a deliberate manner.

How this book addresses the crisis

While the discussions in this book are organized into separate and distinct sections within chapters, they are also meant to elicit from the reader a sensitivity to the many other components of the five major dimensions which influence education: the cultural, the social, the economic, the political and the ideological. All of the separate issues are so closely related to the others that, consequently, the discussions overlap with other issues discussed in other sections.

In terms of the cultural dimension, our current practices fall way short of providing adequate attention to the humanities, languages and the arts. In fact, whenever there is a threat of funding cuts for education (this should never happen in a scheme properly thought through, the type proposed here), these are the areas which are first on the chopping block. This is unnecessary in a proper scheme and only undermines our ability to deliver what everybody needs and wants in any

24 See Preface.
25 See Chapter 7 on the teaching profession.
26 See Chapter 3 on the business model.

12 Left Behind

society: the availability of the most creative and beautiful and entertaining of artful presentations possible, in music, dance, all the humanities. This would be possible if domestic and foreign policies at the national level were in line with the needs of the people and not in concert with the whims and greed of corporations and power-hungry cabals, either in government or in the corporate sector. We are taught extreme ethnocentrism and American exceptionalism[27] rather than an appreciation for the contributions of people from other countries in a world of diverse cultures and expressions. We are so limited as not to be able to communicate with anyone else unless they also speak English.[28] Part of maintaining cultural forms and 'ways of doing' is to teach our children some of those basic 'practical' skills that too few of them possess today. They do not know how a house works, what to do if something breaks down or how to use basic tools. That kind of technology is eluding our youngsters.[29]

With regard to the social dimension, we are remiss in our attempts to develop in our students the principles they need to function in society. While kindergarteners are taught to share and cooperate, when these youngsters observe how little their parents, corporate spokespeople and government officials (most egregiously, the Trump Administration) practice these values, they too allow those principles to fall by the wayside and adopt that kind of conduct. Those more dominant values are ones which overshadow those kindergarten values and are replaced by ideals of climbing the corporate ladder and achieving the 'American Dream', often to the detriment of their childhood neighbors and friends. Some of the resulting fallout from this means that, in order to 'succeed', students must compete in ways that eliminate the competitor rather cooperating with classmates in this or that contest. Greed and exclusivity enter into the formula for success, not sharing rewards, but building toward a 'winner take all' attitude. This is often manifest in sports, in which 'winning' is more important than 'competing'.

Elements of racism and sexism become incidental signposts along the way because they are so ingrained into the 'consciousness' of people and affect our social experiences. While individuals may not overtly subscribe to these discriminatory practices, they come to see them as "the way things are" and move on toward their millionaire aspirations, while facilitating the continued exploitation of "those other people".[30] Face-to-face communication becomes very difficult to achieve because the tendency is to observe the world through the television, the internet, the "game boy" and the "smart" phone more and more youngsters carry around with them. Virtually everything experienced any more is mediated through these hand-held electronic windows to the fantasy worlds they constantly visit. Social interaction becomes estranged and stultified; being able to beat this or that game before their

27 See Chapter 11 on extreme ethnocentrism and American exceptionalism.
28 See Chapter 10 on second language instruction.
29 See Chapter 9 on high school.
30 See Chapter 6 on discrimination.

Introduction **13**

friends becomes paramount, not what they could learn in school or from their mates or, for that matter, at home from their parents. We are raising kids who are enticed into prioritizing relationships which are technologically mediated.

In the political dimension, the right to education is being challenged by right-wing ideologues. While not overtly expressed, except by the most rabid of reactionary individuals, education is understood by them as being a *privilege*, not a *right*.[31] They would have it that only certain people, those who can afford it due to the privatization of schools, could attend schools and that the *curricula* of those schools would be commensurate with their narrow, jingoistic understandings of the world. Hence, I address the matters of discrimination in terms of student access to education and that of teachers' ability to bring a fulsome *curriculum* to their students. Much of their *curricula* are dictated by politicians and businesspeople, not by teachers. The overwhelming developments in the technology entering the realm of teaching and education have transformed how the school experience is organized. In the name of 'making things easier and more transparent', computational exigencies have contaminated the students' and teachers' domains to the extent that they/we are constantly paying homage to the technology rather than concentrating on the tasks of education. As a result, students become estranged from their own histories, those histories that give them pause about who they are and where they come from.

The economic dimension hosts the foremost problem in education: poverty. There is no category more embedded in the deficient delivery of education than poverty. As long as poor communities are not properly supported in the scheme to fund equal, high-quality public education to all our children, those students will never realize their full potential.[32] We are faced with continued fiscal problems because we insist on understanding education to occupy a place in the 'profit' column on the ledger. Public education, and that is what we are talking about throughout this book, is tax-based and should not be understood as part of a scheme, whose benefits should include some kind of profit margin. No, education is a socio-economic expenditure, period. Most congressional members do not understand this and corporate interests are working to privatize *all* education, including our new Secretary of Education, Betsy DeVos. The cost of education is a perennial problem only because greed and political power dictate those decisions. Ample funding is available, but not delivered. Squabbles at all levels of government foreclose on the efficient realization of educational resources for our children. Meanwhile, the student loan industry is making a fortune on our students, who finish school without jobs, but with tens of thousands of dollars in loan debt. If we have public education – education paid for with tax dollars – then why should students have to pay anything to go to school? They, through their parents' taxes,

---

31 Whether or not a country proclaims that education is a right, the United Nations proclaimed that education is a human right in 1948; see Chapter 1 on the right to education.
32 See Chapter 5 on poverty.

14 Left Behind

already pay for that education. Why should they have to pay again? And why should students have to plan cookie sales to raise funds for this or that school program, when public monies are almost immediately available to corporations which build bombs and weapons of mass destruction?[33] This is not what people expect from a country which preaches 'democracy' and a government 'of the people, by the people and for the people'. Much of education is geared to develop individuals who will enter the workforce to serve, not their communities, but their corporate masters. The 'business' of education emphasizes fitting into a corporate landscape and undermines the broader considerations that education should engender.

In the arena of the ideological dimension, I discuss the problems with the kinds of ideas we inculcate in our children. The *monopolized mass media* are a focal point in this regard. We no longer have a healthy *fourth estate*. We have corporate media which have become the *lap dogs* of the powerful, not the *watch dogs* they were intended to be by the 'founding fathers'. Our children must become familiar with the *independent media*, those that work in the people's interests. Students are referred to as 'consumers' rather than 'students'. This is worrisome because our children are categorized in ways that shunt out the true character of who they are in school and suggest to them that all they are constitutes being *automata* who buy things. All they are is reducible to the transaction of money for objects or services? The mass media[34] reinforce these notions and dominate the everyday experiences of our students. They are fed a host of untruths, whether historical or political or economic, *etc.*, which count as the truth. Attempts on the part of reactionary ideologues to alter school *curricula* have already succeeded in part to reflect a version of the world which is sectarian and overwhelmingly understood as ridiculous, *e.g.*, the textbook controversy in Texas about not teaching evolution and advancing creationism and eliminating discussion of the separation of church and state.[35] In the final analysis, we cannot continue the way we have been going. Just as church must be separate from politics, it must also be separate from education. Education must also be separate from corporations, which continue to dominate the landscape of life and threaten to overtake everything of value for the species. These kinds of developments are chilling and remind us of the conditions suffered by people in Orwell's *1984*.[36]

Throughout this book, suggestions are made to ameliorate or eliminate some of these problems and offer up ways to replace practices with others that may address, head-on, what ails us. There are no 'magic bullets' here, only mechanisms which could halt the direction we are in and lay bare possibilities for advancement

---

33 I am reminded of the slogan that reads: "It will be a great day when our schools get all the money they need and the air force has to hold a bake sale to buy a bomber"; thought to have originated with the Women's International League for Peace and Freedom, 1979. See Library of Congress at http://www.loc.gov/pictures/item/2015649445/

34 See Chapter 2 on the mass media.

35 See Chapter 4 on a political economy of education.

36 See Chapter 12 on Orwell and critical thinking.

Introduction **15**

toward a viable methodology for education, based upon several considerations which address issues in our major dimensions. As always, hard work is required of all people who want to see changes to our current conditions that will address the problems discussed herein.[37]

A hope is that the reader will recognize the kinds of pitfalls identified in these pages and consider the alternatives proposed fundamentally to change them. No claim is made that the 'remedies' advanced in this work will solve *all* of the deep and overarching problems we have in our system of education. However, action in those directions will be a beginning. Life is a struggle. Some days, the struggle goes well; other days, not so well. Only through a sustained local vigilance can we hope to achieve the kinds of educational practices we claim to espouse, which have consistently eluded us over the past decades.

This is an ideological battle, nothing less. I am reminded of the controversy that the NCLB law of January 2002, sparked between those who espoused a rigorous curriculum monitored by professionals using four major parameters (content, expectations, time and teaching) as suggested in the findings of the report *A Nation at Risk*[38] and those whose narrow-mindedness directed them to advocate "making standardized test scores the primary measure of school quality".[39] This and the false mantra of 'choice', meaning that better education must include choices other than public: charter, magnet, religious, private or home. In fact, led by Betsy DeVos, these are masquerading as 'choices', hell bent on expropriating public funds for private enterprises and destroying public education.

Ours is a battle indeed, one which involves limiting, if not eliminating, the quantification of school children through test-taking. Ours is a battle to reignite the critical edge in our young minds so that they can evaluate the world around them, not accept and acquiesce to it. Ours is a battle to re-invigorate a collective concept of education that benefits not only the individual students, but the whole of the community and beyond. Part of that battle requires that students know how to take charge of their thinking, not how to say "sir, yes sir", like marine trainees or corporate underlings.

The thoughtful concerns and righteous appeals of Mario Savio in 1964 ring true again in this struggle for equal, high quality, public education for our children. The system is broken and corrupt and causing rampant damage to our youngsters. We need pervasive change now; so, let us begin *now*!

---

37 See Postscript.

38 *A Nation at Risk: The Imperative for Educational Reform*, a National Commission on Excellence in Education Report, chaired by David P. Gardner and including Nobel prize-winning chemist Glenn T. Seaborg, April, 1983.

39 Diane Ravitch (2010) *The Death and Life of the Great American School System: How Testing and Choice are Undermining Education*, New York: Basic Books, p. 15.

16 Left Behind

Bibliography

Aristotle (350 BCE) *On the Heavens*.

Bilmes, L.J. & Stiglitz, J.E. (2008) *The Three Trillion Dollar War: The True Cost of the Iraq Conflict*. London: W.W. Norton and Company.

Carson, R. (1962) *Silent Spring*. London: Hamish Hamilton.

Copernicus, N. (1514) *Commentariolus*.

Douglass, F. (July 5, 1852) "The Meaning of July 4th for the Negro". Speech given at Rochester, NY.

Engels, F. (May 1–2, 1881) "A Fair Day's Wages for a Fair Day's Work". *The Labour Standard*. London.

Galilei, G. (1610) *Sidereus Nuncius*.

Gardner, D.P. (April, 1983) *A Nation at Risk: The Imperative for Educational Reform*. National Commission on Excellence in Education Report.

Hacking, I. (2012) "Preface", in T. Kuhn, *The Structure of Scientific Revolutions: 50th Anniversary Edition*. Chicago, IL: University of Chicago Press.

Herman, J.L. & Golan, S. (1990) "Effects of Standardized Testing on Teachers and Learning – Another Look". Los Angeles, CA: Center for Research on Evaluation, Standards, and Student Testing.

Kuhn, T. (1962) *The Structure of Scientific Revolutions*. Chicago, IL: University of Chicago Press.

The New School (1919) Mission Statement. Retrieved from www.newschool.edu/about/mission-vision/

Picchi, A. (August 26, 2015) "How Much Money Do U.S. Families Need to Get By?" CBS News Moneywatch. Retrieved from www.cbsnews.com/news/how-much-money-do-us-families-need-to-get-by/

Ptolemy, C. (150AD) *Almagest*.

Ravitch, D. (2010) *The Death and Life of the Great American School System: How Testing and Choice are Undermining Education*. New York: Basic Books.

Savio, M. (December 2, 1964) "Bodies Upon the Gears". Speech delivered at University of California, Berkeley. Retrieved from www.americanrhetoric.com/speeches/mariosavi-osproulhallsitin.htm

Schmid, M. & Schwan, B. (Producers), & Conners, L. (Director). (2015). *Biomimicry* [A Tree Media Motion Picture].

United States Census Bureau (n.d.) "Poverty Thresholds". Retrieved from www.census.gov/data/tables/time-series/demo/income-poverty/historical-poverty-thresholds.html

U.S. Debt Clock.org (n.d.) "U.S. Debt Clock". Retrieved from www.usdebtclock.org/

The Venus Project (n.d.) "The Venus Project: Beyond Politics Poverty and War". Retrieved from www.thevenusproject.com/

Women's International League for Peace and Freedom (1979) "It will be a great day when our schools get all the money they need and the air force has to hold a bake sale to buy a bomber." Library of Congress. Retrieved from www.loc.gov/pictures/item/2015649445/

Zinn, H. (2014) *Voices of a People's History of the United States*, 10th edition. New York: Seven Stories Press.

1

THE *RIGHT* TO EDUCATION

Everyone has the right to education. Education shall be free, at least in the elementary and fundamental stages.

– United Nations Universal Declaration of Human Rights, Article 26

In early societies, passing on the practical knowledge of the culture was considered essential and necessary from the standpoint of daily survival. If one ignored the lessons from parents and extended family about the harsh environment which surrounded them all, one perished. Many hard lessons were learned through others' mistakes and inattention. There was little room for error. That accumulation of skills from the time children were old enough to walk and talk made it possible to live another day. Everyone had to pay attention to the most minute of details in order to be secure and carry on with daily activities that would provide the necessities of life. Mostly nomadic, these societies learned how to pay attention to the seasonal cycle and to use what their environs provided to be able to eat and drink, to preserve those sources for another day, to build shelter for protection from the weather and other animals at night when they slept. Education in those days was instituted in the family itself, the extended family, because more complex institutions outside the extended family had not yet been established.[1] The family and its ability to pass on knowledge to its offspring and their

---

1 We know that kinship relations were complex and very well developed. However, institutionalization of rules and traditions beyond the extended family were not developed in the ways we know today until literacy emerged. That is the only distinction being made here; no disrespect or disregard for the complexities of early/communal societies.

18 Left Behind

lineage encompassed all that was needed for the perpetuation of the group/clan/community.[2]

Because of its essential character, education was provided to all members of the tribe, not for a select few, unlike in the stratified societies that developed later on, *e.g.*, in Plato's *Republic*.[3] Everyone needed to know all of these skills, precautions, ways of doing things, procedures, *etc.*, because having access to the knowledge of the society, while it did not 'guarantee' survival, certainly went a long way to place one in a position to understand the environment such that the hazards of the day could be anticipated and managed.

Beyond these 'practical' skills, all members of the society also needed to be privy to the norms, the mores, the values, the beliefs, indeed, the 'stock of knowledge' made available by the society, however small or large. *I assert here the 'universality' of education; not only in the sense that all societies have the obligation to provide education to all their members, but also that all members of any society have a right to access that education if they are to thrive in that society and the world.*

An outline of legal history

Even though the concept of 'rights', as such, had not been established in these early societies, certainly the practices of those adults demonstrated their sensitivity to the 'need' for such a level of commitment to pass on knowledge to their new members. That 'need' today is the recognition that education is a right and that, as such, that right has become part of the legal rubric of most countries, worldwide. However, because education has become recognized as a human right does not mean that all societies provide universal public education to all their members. Indeed, much of the population of the planet does not have (yes, present tense) ready access to it;[4] hence, the need for this discussion. This claim is not meant to refer only to the many societies around the world that do not provide comprehensive education to its members, *e.g.*, Somalia, Eritrea, Ethiopia, Haiti, *etc.* For many of those countries, the reasons involve extreme poverty; but others involve sexism, *e.g.*, Saudi Arabia[5] and others or racism, *e.g.*, Israel[6] and others. Furthermore, the character of the education that is provided is often questionable in terms of its quantity and quality.

---

2 One of the most fundamental social-scientific discoveries about human beings is that *dialogue* is ontological to our species. *Thinking* and *talking* are necessary and essential to us. Moreover, it is most critical to successful education.

3 Education was different for each of the three major castes: the guardians were the philosophers, those who would be kings; the *auxiliaries* were those who defended the city/state; the artisans were the 'working' caste who performed the will of the guardians and produced the material conditions of life.

4 See Jessica Shepherd (2010) "70 Million Children Get No Education, Says Report", *The Guardian*.

5 The Saudi Kingdom does not accord equal rights to women. See Sandra Mackey (1990) *Saudi: Inside the Desert Kingdom*, New York: Signet, Penguin Books.

6 The "Apartheid" system presently operating in Israel forecloses access to education for many Palestinians. See Jimmy Carter (2007) *Palestine: Peace Not Apartheid*, New York: Simon & Shuster.

The *right* to education **19**

We know by now that the history of the United States is replete with examples of exclusion, discrimination and segregation, realities most people do not want to revisit. However, education is one area in which our historical practices have been particularly egregious. Following the examples of the British Empire, in which the indigenous populations in its colonies were not afforded education, whether in Asia or Africa or the continents which later became called the Americas. Attitudes established during those colonial experiences continue today. Many people still think that education is a 'privilege', that it is for the 'privileged' like it actually was in the early 1600s in many European countries and, by colonial association, here in the Americas as well. Perhaps a little known fact is that the documents of the Constitutional Convention of 1787[7] in our bourgeoning America (and later ratified) did not even include the words "education" or "school", demonstrating how little priority was accorded to education in those days. Considering this lack of attention to education by our early politicians and government agencies, it is no wonder that education rights have been won by struggle and not by *fiat* by the powers that be.

Education is not a privilege. It is one of the most essential of rights, along with safety, health and speech – and, depending upon how those rights are provided/practiced, it can influence the character and success of any society in terms of quality of life, prosperity and longevity. I remind the reader that education is among the 'human' rights declared by the United Nations.

> 1. Everyone has the right to education. Education shall be free, at least in the elementary and fundamental stages. Elementary education shall be compulsory. Technical and professional education shall be made generally available and higher education shall be equally accessible to all *on the basis of merit*. [Emphasis added; note that it is not "on the basis of" *wealth!*]
> 2. Education shall be directed to the full development of the human personality and to the strengthening of respect for human rights and fundamental freedoms. It shall promote understanding, tolerance and friendship among all nations, racial or religious groups, and shall further the activities of the United Nations for the maintenance of peace.
> 3. Parents have a prior right to choose the kind of education that shall be given to their children.[8]

These precepts are ensconced in the rubric of, not only, the United Nations, as an organization, but also of the member-countries of the U.N. The problems of educating people around the world are epic: deficiencies in facilities, funding, and

---

7 Most notably the *Federalist Papers*, the full text of which can be found at http://teachingamerican history.org.

8 Only three years after it was formed (July 28, 1945), the United Nations proclaimed the *Universal Declaration of Human Rights* (December 10, 1948); this is Article 26.

20 Left Behind

basic tools like books, paper and pencils continue today.[9] The United States has not escaped these basic problems; indeed, they have been maintained throughout our history. Even today, we hear stories about how teachers spend their own hard-earned money on classroom necessities because requisitioning them is routinely turned down, because of the poor funding they have. These and other perennial conditions must be addressed and remedied.

The United States has a long history of educational malfeasance and denial and suppression arising from chattel slavery, to the so-called 'Jim Crow' Laws, to discrimination against women, to language barriers in the 'melting pot'. It reflects what the overall struggle has been to establish more democratic forms. That history is replete with the 'back and forth' of gaining ground in favor of civil rights and losing that ground because of the sustained racist holdovers. Jim Crow Laws were particularly effective in the South in segregating the population along color lines. They began to be enacted in many southern states, during the period of Reconstruction, reaching northern states as well, thereby maintaining an overall segregated character to American society.[10] Please note that this is 100 years after the Declaration of Independence, in which there was a promise of equality ("All men are created equal."); this with the claim that the status of black Americans was "separate but equal". Brought to us by the faulty Supreme Court decision in *Plessy v. Ferguson*,[11] 163 US 537 (1896), it upheld state racial segregation laws for public facilities, including for education. In reality, these laws created *de jure* racial segregation in all aspects of public life. This segregation extended to all public facilities, transportation, rest rooms, drinking fountains and education, infrastructures often referred to as "the commons".[12]

One landmark decision by the United States Supreme Court was Brown v. Board of Education of Topeka, handed down on May 17, 1954. This unusual unanimous decision (9–0) declared that "separate educational facilities are inherently unequal" and violated the Equal Protection Clause of the Fourteenth

---

9 The reader may be aware of the many programs of UNICEF; one, in particular, the K.I.N.D. (Kids in Need of Desks) program, with its 'front man' Lawrence O'Donald of MSNBC News, provides classroom desks to students in Malawi; see www.unicefusa.org/mission/protect/education/kids-need-desks-kind. Unfortunately, these efforts, while laudable, are woefully inadequate. Education funding is far below what is needed all over the world. These funding efforts should only be supplementary to every country's full support of educational programs; any country should not rely solely on these altruistic grants.

10 Once President Lincoln's *Emancipation Proclamation* took effect (January 1, 1863), the Jim Crow Laws (1877–1954) brought back the harsh rules that had been in place under slavery, such that one could hardly tell the difference between them. Ida B. Wells (1862–1931) was an African American journalist and a most effective leader in the struggle against the Jim Crow Laws. Wells refused to give up her seat in a car of the Chesapeake and Ohio Railroad Company, May 4, 1884, 71 years before Rosa Parks in Montgomery, AL, December 1, 1955, the courageous act that sparked the civil rights movement. See Howard Zinn's (1980) *A People's History of the United States: 1492 – Present*, New York: Harper & Row.

11 *Plessy v. Ferguson*, 163 US 537 (1896).

12 See Chapter 4 on a political economy of education.

The *right* to education **21**

Amendment, which declares that "no state shall ... deny to any person within its jurisdiction the equal protection of the laws".[13] The Fourteenth Amendment was one of the Reconstruction Amendments which set the stage for later strides toward equality, in part by correcting the Dred Scott decision, March 1857, which had ruled that people of African descent were not protected under the Constitution and could never become citizens. This first sentence of the Fourteenth Amendment, known as the *Citizenship Clause* or the *Naturalization Clause*, reversed Dred Scott and laid the foundation for the *Brown v. Board of Education* decision almost a century later. Of paramount import in *Brown v. Board of Education* was that the category of 'education' became part of the rubric of the law, something that the Fourteenth Amendment had still not been explicit about.

Also, a decade after *Brown v. Board of Education*, the Civil Rights Act of 1964 (July 2) gave some teeth to the U.N. Declaration that all people have the right to education. Isn't it interesting that, once again, it required legal intervention to assert that education should be made available to all, something that came naturally to our ancestors in early societies? It stipulated that

> It is the policy of the United States that guidelines and criteria established pursuant to title VI of the Civil Rights Act or 1964 [42 U.C.C. 2000d *et seq.*] and section 182 of the Elementary and Secondary Education Amendment of 1966 [42 U.S.C. 2000d-5] dealing with conditions of segregation by race, whether *de jure* or *de facto*, in the schools of the local educational agencies of any State shall be applied uniformly in all regions of the United States whatever the origins or cause of such segregation.

And

> Such uniformity refers to one policy applied uniformly to *de jure* segregation wherever found and such other policy as may be provided pursuant to law applied uniformly to *de facto* segregation wherever found.[14]

One might have thought that the Civil Rights Act of 1875 (March 1) would have taken care of that, but not so. The assumption of the Act was that "it is essential to just government [that] we recognize the equality of all men before the law". Therefore,

> All persons within the jurisdiction of the United States shall be entitled to the full and equal enjoyment of the accommodations, advantages, facilities and

---

13 The Fourteenth Amendment, adopted July 9, 1868.
14 Civil Rights Act of 1964, 42 U.S.C., Sec. 2000d-6, a.

22 Left Behind

> privileges ... applicable alike to citizens of every race and color, regardless of any previous condition of servitude.[15]

Again, there was no explicit reference to 'education' or 'schools'. Because these categories were not unambiguously included in the phrase "accommodations, advantages, facilities and privileges", one would have to infer their inclusion because they are logically included under the categories of "facility" or "accommodation". *Brown v. Board of Education* clarified that once and for all.

Why was it necessary to struggle for the Civil Rights Act of 1964, 89 years later? Why did we need to do this again? Because, in 1883, consolidating five cases (*United States v. Stanley, United States v. Ryan, United States v. Nichols, United States v. Singleton,* and *Robinson and wife v. Memphis & Charleston R.R. Co.*), the Supreme Court declared the Civil Rights Act (1875) "unconstitutional". The Court argued that the Thirteenth Amendment was about 'slavery' and not 'race' and the Fourteenth Amendment (1868) was about the actions of the state (public) and not of individuals (private), thereby endorsing a tacit avenue for racial segregation.[16] Civil rights struggles were again thwarted and further complicated by the *Plessy v. Ferguson*[17] Supreme Court decision, which codified the "equal but separate" status for former slaves and their children. The majority white population in the United States, through its consolidation of power in government and public institutions and with the help of Jim Crow Laws and the criminal activities of the Ku Klux Klan, so-called 'colored' people (including Africans, South Americans, Asians, Indigenous peoples, Eastern Europeans, Irish, *etc.*) were denied their rights in general and to education in particular.

Encouraged by the spirit of the Civil Rights Act of 1964, the next attempt to establish equal rights for African Americans in the area of education did not come until 1974, when District Court Judge Garrity ruled, in *Morgan v. Hennigan,* that the Boston School Committee had "knowingly carried out a systematic program of segregation affecting all of the city's students, teachers and school facilities and have intentionally brought about and maintained a dual school system".[18] The decision was affirmed by the U.S. Court of Appeals. Garrity's ruling ordered the school committee to desegregate schools by implementing the busing of students in both directions, to and from, 'white' and 'black' schools. This citywide plan ordered adjusting student and teacher school assignments and creating school facilities to accommodate these changes. Essentially, schools with more than 50% 'white' or

---

15 Civil Rights Act of 1875, *US Statutes at Large, Vol. XVIII, p. 335 ff, sec. 1.*
16 See www.infoplease.com under the heading "Civil Rights Cases of 1883".
17 *Op. cit.* note 11 above.
18 From Judge W. Arthur Garrity's decision regarding Morgan v. Hennigan, 375 F, Supp. 410 – District Court, D. Massachusetts. See Kerri Anne-Marie Hutchinson (2009) Master Thesis, *Boston Divided: Representations and Perceptions of Judge Garrity and Morgan v. Hennigan,* Ontario, Canada: University of Waterloo for historical contexts and discussion regarding the decision and opposition.

'black' students had to 'equalize' their racial demographics by busing students from other schools or districts. The implementation was ordered to begin that fall. The opposition to this process was perhaps most represented by the organization *Return Our Alienated Rights (R.O.A.R.)*. One of the most prominent voices in opposition to busing was former Massachusetts Democratic Representative (1971–1973, a member of the House Committee on Education and Labor) Louise Day Hicks, a native of South Boston, 'ground zero' of the opposition. Her efforts were not effective partly because her real efforts were focused upon her bid for mayor of Boston.[19]

The controversy surrounding the 'busing decision' continued for the next two decades, and, in 1996, when two white students were denied entry to the Boston Latin School, there was yet again more court action. In 1998, the U.S. District Court of Massachusetts ruled supporting Garrity's 1974 desegregation decision; but the U.S. Court of Appeals reversed the ruling and held that the policy was unconstitutional.[20] This demonstrates how legal decisions themselves can be altered or overturned to satisfy the political current of the time. One would think, however, that such rudimentary matters could stand on solid bastions, unshakable by whim and folly. Since then, the proportion of 'black' students in 'white schools', as Jonathan Kozol aptly writes, is at "a level lower than in any year since 1969".[21]

Clearly, the legal history of education equality has not been exhausted here. Only one trajectory was followed to illustrate to the extent to which legal action was necessary to address the simple proposition that all children should have equal access to high-quality, public education. I chose this set of court decisions because I lived in Boston at the time these events were developing and the lively discussions we had were important to me for my understanding of the continued struggle that it has been to establish even the most fundamental of human rights.

One of the most controversial legal moves of the past decade, in my view, has been the legislation referred to as No Child Left Behind (NCLB).[22] The fundamental idea behind this law was not all that bad; it was supposed to guarantee, on some real level, proper education for our children. However, it fell short in many ways. This law was extensive and addressed multiple issues; in particular, skills in mathematics, reading and language arts in public elementary and secondary schools. Perhaps the most significant of these issues is the methodology for establishing and maintaining "academic standards, academic assessments, and accountability" (sec. 1111. State Plans). This section has come to be seen as the crux of the act: the use

---

19 More cogent opposition came from J. Michael Ross and William M. Berg (1981) in their tome, *I Respectfully Disagree with the Judge's Order*, Washington, DC: University Press of America.

20 See the Massachusetts Historical Society under the category of Education and the aftermath of the *Morgan v. Hennigan* case.

21 Jonathan Kozol (2005), "Overcoming Apartheid", *The Nation*, p. 26.

22 Public Law PL 107–110, the No Child Left Behind Act of 2001, introduced by Ted Kennedy in January and signed into law by G.W. Bush in May.

24 Left Behind

of standardized testing to "measure" the "adequate yearly progress" (1111, b, 2, B) of students.

This discussion is important here because one of the current issues before us is that some teachers are rebelling against this kind of *reification* of educational practices, *i.e.*, reducing what children learn to scores on a standardized test, rather than evaluating students individually according to principles of understanding, comprehension and performance. The right to education should not be 'fetishized' into mathematical *formulae*, which then serve as a rubric for decision-making that will affect students favorably or adversely in the short run, on the one hand, and, in many cases, for the rest of their lives, on the other.[23] That is not what we should be delivering as education. This impersonal methodology only serves those who need to answer to their superiors as to the condition of their student body: teachers to principals; principals to their boards of education; those boards to the department of education in their state; those departments to the U.S. DOE. Students are issued test scores to identify them along the testing continuum. Many well-intentioned parents encourage their children to 'measure up to' those upper percentiles on those scales. Education cannot proceed in this manner and succeed. This sterile approach is anathema to real education.

The curricula

Education is disheveled and messy. It is in constant flux; hence, it requires vigilant attention and adjustment. Teaching to the test stands outside of the changes witnessed in the classroom and does not lend itself to the many needs students have. One does not have to be a *teacher* to run students through a series of multiple-choice quizzes. To deliver on the right that our children have to education, we must tap into the competence that our teachers possess. They are, with few exceptions, caring and ethical problem-solvers.

The current system is wrought with practical problems that prevent such an experience. For example, the teacher-to-student ratios are not fair: teachers I have talked to over the years (some have better situations than others) have consistently complained that they have too many students to engage in learning. They almost universally argue, depending upon the subject matter, that 30 students in a classroom is too many for proper discussion to take place. In my own experience at the university level, years ago we had class caps at 25 students, then 30, then 35. The number of students always increased, never decreased, but the salary stayed the same and the quality of education suffered; not because we were less committed to our profession, but because, as in many other professions, there is a threshold at which quality decreases as quantity increases. We need more teachers across the board. There are several other examples of practical problems, deficiencies that prevent teachers from delivering proper learning: facilities, project-based programs,

---

23 See Chapter 8 on the mismeasure of our students' performance.

curricula that are viable and commensurate with the needs of students, *etc.* All of these require more funds for education.

While those − in whose hands lie the responsibilities to educate our children − conduct education in this manner, our children themselves can become virtual *automata*, forced to acquiesce to a system of measurement that does not really do justice to their promised education. They only go through the motions, while the process becomes akin to a 'cookie cutting' machine, delivering to the country a population of 'test-takers' instead of critically minded individuals. Our children have a right to much more. They deserve a one-on-one teacher/student evaluation that arises out of ongoing observation, assessment and critical judgement. This requires an increase in teacher populations across the board because, to achieve such a level of monitoring, we must decrease the current teacher-student ratio in elementary and secondary from 1:20 or 1:30 to 1:20 or less; and, in university settings, from (not always with graduate student assistants) 1:50, 1:70, 1:100, 1:300 to 1:20 or less. That is what could move us to the determination of real performance on the part of our students. However, the current trend is to hire part-time teachers/professors to replace career faculty and further increase the number of students in a class.

The manipulation of evaluation criteria and methodologies is only one area that jeopardizes the education rights of our children; another is the *curriculum* itself. Not only is the promise of a comprehensive education reified in test scores, it is also influenced and degraded by ideological shenanigans which either delete or emphasize particular historical moments or actors. Again, every country practices this kind of self-preservation in the light of their historical experience: hiding its crimes and highlighting its accomplishments.

More recently, there have been efforts to change history to the point that it becomes unrecognizable to many of us who take the routine embellishments and elisions into consideration as a matter of course. We are aware that there are different versions of history. We understand that these different versions are a product of a particular author or commentator, who has preserved the facts. Here, we are talking about the selection of particular historical epochs or events or actors in history and creating, through an ideologically motivated compilation, a history never before imagined. I would like to offer an example to illustrate the kind of mythology that has entered current parlance in regards to what we teach our children. The reader may have heard about Texas changing its *curricula* in public schools to reflect a somewhat narrower vision of the world.

On May 11, 2010, the State Board of Education (SBOE) in Texas, which has the legislative authority[24] to adopt the Texas Essential Knowledge and Skills (TEKS)

---

24 "Legislative authority" means that it has the "legal right" to decide what is appropriate to teach in public schools. This is critical because what we are talking about here is our children's "legal right" to a comprehensive education, not one which is deemed "appropriate" and altered beyond recognition by a "legislative" body, like the SBOE, that wants to regulate the content of history to suite

26 Left Behind

standards (every ten years), decided on a course of action unprecedented in U.S. history. It adopted a series of changes that belie the very foundations of our claims to guarantee education to our children and that erode the assertion that the content of that educational right be commensurate with a fair representation of human experience. The story flooded the media output for days and reflected some of the controversial character of these decisions. Here are some examples of the changes:

- The Board removed Thomas Jefferson from the Texas curriculum, "replacing him with religious right icon John Calvin."
- The Board refused to require that "students learn that the Constitution prevents the U.S. government from promoting one religion over all others."
- Teachers in Texas will be required to cover the Judeo-Christian influences of the nation's Founding Fathers, but not highlight the philosophical rationale for the separation of church and state.
- In addition to learning the Bill of Rights, the board specified a reference to the Second Amendment right to bear arms in a section about citizenship in a U.S. government class.
- Another amendment deleted a requirement that sociology students "explain how institutional racism is evident in American society."
- Conservatives beat back multiple attempts to include hip-hop as an example of a significant cultural movement.[25]

The Christian Right has landed, again – not only in the general sense for some time now – but in the very heartland of our public schools. People can have whatever religious beliefs they want; but, when those specific beliefs inform educational policy, education itself becomes the casualty of a reactionary political *coup* and students become set up for indoctrination. This should not be what we want for our children. Religious 'training' must always be separate from public education.

Some of the fallout from this kind of 'indoctrination' has to do with changing the significance of historical figures, such as the Reverend Dr. Martin Luther King, Jr. or Cesar Chavez or Charles Darwin, *etc.*, thereby enthroning or dethroning heroes of overwhelmingly accepted historical note or actually creating false heroes.

False heroes

What we have come to witness in education is akin to what is practiced in the media: the whole truth about something is not presented. Enter 'ideology'. The fundamental conceptual logic of *ideological expressions* is that they are partly true and

---

its ideological *penchant*, in this case a revisionist version that does not square with established and verifiable facts.

25 April Castro (2010) "Texas Education Board Approves Conservative Curriculum Changes by Far-Right", *The Huffington Post*, May 12.

The *right* to education **27**

partly false, at the same time. That is, the 'whole' truth is not expressed, only part of it – the part which news purveyors, or their advertisers, or politically motivated boards of education want to advance. If the whole truth were withheld, that would be *a lie*. Only when the whole truth is expressed is it *the truth*. For example, years ago, the American Dairy Association produced an advertisement campaign whose slogan was "Milk does a body good!" This is an ideological expression because it is partly true and partly false, at the same time. The true part is that milk can be 'good for you' in the sense that it can provide some nutrition to whomever drinks it. However, research has demonstrated that drinking milk over a lifetime can be deleterious to one's health and, in some cases, contribute to the development of cancer and other chronic conditions, *e.g.*, heart disease and stroke, osteoporosis because of the concentrated content of animal protein in milk. Now, because the media are routinely expressing only partial truths (hence, their expressions are ideological), they are not 'lying', but they are not providing the whole truth either. Many people have developed some sense for this, even if it is not in the terms I present here, *e.g.*, they do not necessarily believe everything they see/hear on television. However, many more believe that 'if it's on TV, it has to be true'; the media advertisers rely on this latter belief. Still, the success the media monopoly has had in the United States in transferring ideas and attitudes to us is mostly predicated upon commonly held misconceptions about how the mass media operate.

When it comes to education, people are often not even as critical as they may be about the media; apart from that vigilant parent or social scientist, by and large, people do not extend the same criticality to education. This does not mean that people do not have a visceral sense that something is wrong with education; they do. They just may not have the vocabulary to express what is wrong, because they may not understand how those problems are generated.[26]

Typically, people pay only marginal attention to the forms of ideological narratives in the *curricula*. One of the most glaring examples is the story of 'heroic' Christopher Columbus 'discovering' the 'New World'. With significant *caveats*, that claim is *partly true*. On the other hand, the part about the brutal and homicidal character of his, along with his *conquistadores*, actual conduct during that 'discovery' is also *partly true*. When one side or the other is expressed, the other side not expressed takes on a sense that it is *false*, hence the ideological character of either expression. Depending upon who the speaker is and which category is applied to this story, we could hear interchanges like: "Columbus was a 'hero'." "No he was not; he was a 'mass murderer'." To the supporter of Columbus' adventures, the category 'hero' is correct; to the detractor of Columbus' conquests, the categorial phrase 'mass murderer' is correct. According to Jeff Coulter, this category disconnection gives rise to a logical construct he calls the 'disjunctive category-pair'. He explains:

---

26 My hope is that this book will provide some of that understanding and vocabulary.

28 Left Behind

> At the level of the social organization of their use, we can speak of the categories 'belief' and 'knowledge' as forming a disjunctive category-pair … Other such pairs would include vision/hallucination, telepathy/trickery and ideology/science. Where one part of these pairs is invoked to characterize some phenomenon seriously, the speaker's belief commitment may be inferred, and the structure of subsequent discourse may be managed in terms provided for by the programmatic relevance of the disjunctive category-pair relationship. Thus, to the nonbeliever, Joan of Arc suffered hallucinations; to the believer, divine visions. To the nonbeliever, Uri Geller was a sophisticated conjurer; to the believer, a telepath and telekineticist, and so on.

> *(Coulter, 1979)*[27]

To the supporter, the category 'hero' is *true* and the categorial phrase 'mass murderer' is *false*; to the detractor, the categorial phrase 'mass murderer' is *true* and the category 'hero' is *false*. That is how ideological expressions work; the *partly true* version is always asserted by the speaker of the expression.

There are many examples of this kind of ideological mischief, in which only one side of an event/issue, is presented. One case which struck me was the announcement of the death of Richard Holbrooke.[28] The mainstream media filled the airwaves with praise and accolades of his long-standing service to our country from Vietnam, where he 'cut his teeth', to Indonesia, to Kosovo, to Afghanistan and Iraq. He was praised as a 'peace-maker' in an effusive array of corporate media reports. For example, among many others:

> Mr. Holbrooke's signal accomplishment in a distinguished career … was his role as chief architect of the 1995 Dayton peace accords, which ended the war in Bosnia. It was a coup preceded and followed by his peacekeeping mission to the tinder box of ethnic, religious and regional conflicts that was formerly Yugoslavia …

And

> Mr. Holbrooke played a crucial role in establishing full diplomatic relations with China in 1979 …

---

27 See Jeff Coulter (1979) "Beliefs and Practical Understanding", in G. Psathas, *Everyday Language*, p. 181, New York: Irvington Publishers, Inc.

28 Holbrooke held many positions of power from the 1970s until his death in December 2010: Assistant Secretary of State for President Carter [1977–1981], Wall Street years [1981–1993], Ambassador (to Germany [1993–1994] for President Clinton and to the United Nations [1999–2001] for Presidents Clinton and Bush, and 'point man' to Afghanistan for President Obama [2009–2010].

The *right* to education **29**

And

> [he] wrote his own widely acclaimed memoir, "*To End a War*" (1998), about his Bosnia service ...[29]

However, when one pays closer attention to what Holbrooke was up to all those years, one could learn that what he was involved in may not have been exclusively about 'peace-making'. For example, among several other reports in the independent media:

> probably more than any U.S. diplomat since Henry Kissinger ... Richard Holbrooke has represented the utter militarization of what is called U.S. diplomacy. He was also at the center of the nexus of U.S. militarists, of aggressive, hawkish, quote-unquote, 'diplomats', and the elite, white-shoe media culture. And that's why you see people like Joe Klein [political columnist for *Time* magazine] and others falling over themselves to engage in revisionist history about Richard Holbrooke. They only tell one part of the story ... that [he] was a peacemaker. He was a war maker ...

And

> Richard Holbrooke was a central player in the disintegration of Yugoslavia in the 1990's ... What never gets talked about is that what Richard Holbrooke and other U.S. officials were doing was supporting Croatian ethnic cleansers that were trained by U.S. private military company MPRI [Military Professional Resources Inc.] to engage in the single-greatest ethnic cleansing in the war against the Serbs in Krajina ...[30]

The reason I explicate these contrastive media versions of what Holbrooke has done in his diplomatic career is to demonstrate that, while Holbrooke may have been legitimately a 'peace-maker' (witness his involvement in the Dayton peace accords) at one time, he was also a 'war-maker' (witness his involvement in the ethnic cleansing of Serbs in the Republic of Serbian Krajina in Croatia) at another. Hence, to the *uncritical* observer, categorizing Holbrooke as a 'hero' or 'peacemaker' can be seen as the 'truth'; as well, categorizing him as a 'villain' or 'warmaker' can also be seen as the 'truth'. In Coulter's terms, the disjunctive categories are 'hero'/'villain' or 'peace-maker'/'war-maker'.

One last, very contemporary example: the lingering Confederate era icons.

---

29 Robert D. McFadden (2010) "Strong American Voice in Diplomacy and Crisis", *The New York Times*, December 13. Also see Richard Holbrook (1999) *To End a War*, New York: Modern Library.

30 See *Democracy Now!* December 15, 2010; Amy Goodman interview with Jeremy Scahill, co-founder of TheIntercept.com and John Pilger (not quoted); see his documentary film entitled *Death of a Nation*, about the genocide in East Timor, 1976–1979.

30 Left Behind

Monuments and statues were erected all over the south of the United States after the Civil War. After the Confederate Flag was removed (July 10, 2015) from the Statehouse in Columbia, South Carolina, a small group known as Take 'Em Down NOLA emerged. Their work has been to purge the south of monuments and statues that praise and honor Confederate leaders. In May 2017, New Orleans removed four such statues. Many more Confederate reminders are scattered throughout the city, including the names of some 30 schools. At the same time the Louisiana State Legislature passed a law making it more difficult to take down these statues and monuments. Mayor of New Orleans Mitch Landrieu:

> The historic record is clear: Robert E. Lee, Jeff Davis, PGT Beauregard statues were not erected to just honor these men, but as part of a movement which became known as the 'cult of the lost cause'. This cult had one goal and one goal only: through monuments and other means, to rewrite history, hide the truth, which was that the Confederacy was on the wrong side of humanity ... These monuments that we took down were meant to rebrand the history of our city and the ideals of the Confederacy ... These statues are not just stone and metal; they're not just innocent remembrances of a benign history. These monuments celebrate the fictional, sanitized Confederacy, ignoring the death, ignoring the enslavement, ignoring the terror that it actually stood for. And, after the Civil War, these monuments were part of that terrorism, as much as burning a cross on someone's lawn. They were erected purposefully to send a strong message to all who walked in the shadows about who was still in charge in the city.[31]

Malcolm Suber, who has worked with Take 'Em Down Nola for the last two years, drives home the point I want to make here:

> These memorials all across the south, in every courthouse, in every county throughout the south, they've got a Confederate soldier's monument; and they don't teach our kids in school that these people were indeed traitors ...[32]

To Suber's point, children who are not made aware of the meaning of these statues will not develop a criticality that they will so desperately need in today's world. False heroes indeed; people who wanted to maintain slavery, engender 'white' supremacy and carry out violence against the 'black' population in the United States.[33]

---

31 Part of Mayor Landrieu's speech about the removal of statues of Confederate leaders in New Orleans; carried on *Democracy Now!*, May 23, 2017.

32 Part of remarks by Malcolm Suber, interviewed by Amy Goodman and Juan Gonzales on *Democracy Now!*, May 17, 2017.

33 Most recently, August 11, 2017, the planned removal of the Robert E. Lee statue from Jackson Park

The *right* to education **31**

The point here, for our children, is that we want them to be *critical* observers, who are taught different versions of events and issues. Only from a critical standpoint can they have a balanced appreciation of their surroundings (and the people involved therein). Our children have a right to be told the *whole truth*, as best can be provided, about what they are being taught, not only a regurgitation of what the political or military or mass media pundits express. Teachers and parents must develop and maintain a level of criticality that will ensure that students in classes in say 'current events' will be provided with as full a story as possible about the matters discussed. In doing so, we are preserving the right of our students to decide for themselves what is going on, who the 'players' are and what the consequences/implications are, as a result of a fulsome understanding of those events and issues.

The particular versions of events and issues that news purveyors and government officials lead with in reports and statements seamlessly 'bleed' into narratives in schools, often through Channel One[34] and via the 'smart phones' most students constantly carry with them. When schools follow this kind of lead, and they routinely do, they fall into the trap of ideological discourse. When the narrative that is delivered to our children in classrooms of our public schools is uncritically imported from the mainstream, corporate media, we are not preserving their right to high quality education. We are parroting the voices of the powerful and ignoring the voices of those who do not have access to the megaphone, the 'bully pulpit', and other mechanisms of mass propaganda. Our children have the right to have access to the full spectrum of information, not only that which is most loudly expressed, so that they have the opportunity to decide for themselves what makes most sense to them. Of course, this can only be possible in an overall environment of criticality, something that is overwhelmingly absent in the public schools, indeed in virtually all schools, in the United States.

The right to education is clouded by such machinations from those who would have our children understand the world in ways that would benefit a small group of people, allowing them to control our children's thinking about matters from which those in power would profit. This is no less than a violation of their right to education that would inform them fairly about the world. Our children deserve much better than this. They rely on the institutions that confront them; they do this, because, when they are 6 and 7 years old, they know no better. Even when they are graduating from high school, many still know no better. That is why it is so easy to entice them into volunteering for the military, especially if they are poor and 'black' or brown. Post-graduate options are not bright for them; so, often reluctantly, they opt to enlist because they will be guaranteed a pay check, room and board and maybe some education. Has their right to education been fulfilled? Do we not owe them the proper infrastructures (economic, political, *etc.*) that can

in Charlottesville, VA, drew white nationalists to protest its removal. Violence ensued which left one dead and dozens injured.

34 See Chapter 2 on the press/mass media.

give rise to much better decision-making? Their lives may depend upon this decision! No, we need to do much better so that they can do much better. It is not their fault; it is ours. When our children are misled by half-truths, such as telling them a story about how wonderful the Army is, because members of the military 'help' this one or that one (which is partly true) and not make clear to them that the Army is a killing machine of massive power and, as members of this military organization, they will be called upon to kill people they do not even know and not even know why (which would be the whole truth).[35] That is not something our high school seniors should be asked to suffer. Their brains are not even fully developed, thereby impairing their decision-making capacities.

We do not have the same legal mess today that our history has shown us about the right to education. Much of *that* mess has been sorted out; save some lingering issues discussed here. In other words, no children are deprived *outright* from access to education as in the past. However, the issues today are about the quality, the openness, the inclusiveness and the honesty of that education in its presentation.

Our children have the right to be told the truth; not something that is partially true and partially false (which is the fundamental logic of 'ideology', the same logical structure of propaganda), but the whole truth, all the time. That requires a whole lot of honesty and commitment to a critical preparation of our youngsters for the complex world that confronts them. It means that our institutions, all of them, must be constructed so that we are routinely reminded of the obligation we have to deliver to all our children, *as a right*, equal, high-quality public education.

The essential message of this discussion is that the right to education does not mean that students have a right to sit in a classroom and listen to a teacher's version of the world and to accept what that teacher says. *Education is not about agreement; it is about understanding.* That cannot happen when only one side of any story is provided. The right to education means that students have the right to learn about a variety of versions of the world, to discuss and understand those versions and to make decisions about which ones, or parts of them, make sense to them and how to pursue their lives accordingly.

Bibliography

"Civil Rights Cases (1883)". (2000–2017) Infoplease. Sandbox Networks, Inc. Retrieved from www.infoplease.com/history-and-government/cases/civil-rights-cases-1883/

Carter, J. (2007) *Palestine: Peace Not Apartheid*. New York: Simon & Shuster.

Castro, A. (May 12, 2010) "Texas Education Board Approves Conservative Curriculum Changes by Far-Right". Huffington Post. Retrieved from www.huffingtonpost.com/2010/03/12/texas-education-board-app_n_497440.html

---

35 There is nothing 'wrong' with serving in the military. In fact, such a service can be very rewarding in many ways. To *defend* one's country is laudable, even necessary in today's world. However, an *offensive* military is always problematic when its members are ill-informed about what they are getting into.

The *right* to education **33**

Civil Rights Act of 1875, US Statutes at Large, Vol. XVIII, p. 335 ff, sec. 1.

Civil Rights Act of 1964, 42 U.S.C., Sec. 2000d-6, a.

Coulter, J. (1979) "Beliefs and Practical Understanding", in G. Psathas, *Everyday Language*, New York: Irvington Publishers, Inc, p. 181.

Goodman, A. (December 15, 2010) "Richard Holbrooke Dies at 69: Remembering Veteran Diplomat's Overlooked Record in East Timor, Iraq and the Balkans". Interview with Jeremy Scahill and John Pilger. Retrieved from https://www.democracynow.org/2010/12/15/richard_holbrooke_dies_at_69_remembering

Goodman, A. & Gonzáles, J. (May 23, 2017) "As Last Confederate Statue Is Removed in New Orleans, Will School Names & Street Signs Follow?" Interview with Malcolm Suber. Retrieved from https://www.democracynow.org/2017/5/23/as_last_confederate_statue_is_removed

Garrity, W.A. (1974). Decision regarding *Morgan v. Hennigan*, 375 F, Supp. 410 – District Court, D. Massachusetts.

Holbrook, R. (1999) *To End a War*. New York: Modern Library.

Hutchinson, K.A-M. (2009) *Boston Divided: Representations and Perceptions of Judge Garrity and Morgan v. Hennigan*. Master's thesis. University of Waterloo. Ontario, Canada.

Kozol, J. (December 19, 2005) "Overcoming Apartheid". The Nation. Retrieved from https://www.thenation.com/article/overcoming-apartheid/

Mackey, S. (1990) *Saudi: Inside the Desert Kingdom*. New York: Penguin Books, p. 14.

McFadden, R.D. (December 13, 2010) "Strong American Voice in Diplomacy and Crisis". New York Times. Retrieved from http://www.nytimes.com/2010/12/14/world/14holbrooke.html?pagewanted=all

Munro, D. (Producer). (1994) *Death of a Nation: The Timor Conspiracy*. [DVD].

Plessy v. Ferguson. (1896) 163 U.S. 537.

Psathas, G. (1979) *Everyday Language*. New York: Irvington Publishers.

Public Law PL 107–110. No Child Left Behind Act of 2001.

Ross, J. M., & Berg, W. M. (1981) *I Respectfully Disagree with the Judge's Order*. Washington, D.C.: University Press of America.

Shepherd, J. (September 20, 2010) "70 Million Children Get No Education, Says Report". The Guardian. Retrieved from https://www.theguardian.com/education/2010/sep/20/70m-get-no-education

UNICEF (n.d.) The "Kids in Need of Desks" Program. Retrieved from www.unicefusa.org/mission/protect/education/kids-need-desks-kind

United Nations (December 10, 1948) *Universal Declaration of Human Rights*, Article 26.

Zinn, H. (1980) *A People's History of the United States: 1492 – Present*. New York: Harper & Row.

2

THE 'FREE PRESS' – ON A CORPORATE LEASH!

> The people must know before they can act, and there is no educator to compare with the press.[1]
>
> – Ida B. Wells

> The ideas of the ruling class are in every epoch the ruling ideas.[2]
>
> – Karl Marx and Friedrich Engels

The only profession mentioned in the U.S. Constitution, albeit obliquely, is the journalist, that individual who composes stories of the day to inform the people of, not only what is going on, what to expect, what possibilities are on the horizon, but, most importantly, what those in power are doing, saying, proposing, hiding,

---

1 Ida B. Wells-Barnett (2014) *On Lynchings*, (originally published in 1892 under Ida B. Wells as *Southern Horrors: Lynch Law in all its Phases*) Mineola, NY: Dover Publications, Inc., p. 27. Born a slave in Mississippi in 1862, Wells fought against the lynching of black folk in the South. A graduate of Rust College, she taught school, while caring for her siblings. She wrote editorials in black newspapers and later bought a share in a Memphis newspaper and published in the *Free Speech and Headlight*, fighting for the rights of black people. In her writings, she challenged the 'rape myth' and Jim Crow and advocated for education for black children. She was a founding member of the NAACP. She died in 1931.

2 This assertion begins the section entitled "Ruling Class and Ruling Ideas" of *Part I: Feuerbach* and continues: "*i.e.*, the class which is the ruling material force of society, is at the same time its ruling intellectual force. The class which has the means of material production at its disposal, has control at the same time over the means of mental production [ideological production, the mass media of today], so that thereby, generally speaking, the ideas of those who lack the means of mental production are subject to it." Marx and Engels (1976) *The German Ideology*.

etc. At least, that was the intent. The 'Founding Fathers' were particularly committed to establishing a press that would serve the people and not those in power, political or otherwise. Those in power were there at the pleasure of the people, they argued. There were great efforts to guarantee the independence of the press, but there were also many who wanted to control this most powerful institution, because they knew that to control *the word* one could control people's conduct, their ideas and ultimately their lives. Some have argued that our fledgling democracy started out on the right foot with regard to information dissemination, but that, over the decades, we have lost our way and have fallen victim to the vagaries of capitalism and the privatization of information. I subscribe to that view. Indeed, there has been a pendulum swing from the days of the Bill of Rights until today, in which case, the media (the press) have been bought up by corporations to serve their interests and away from the service of the people. As Jeremy Scahill asserts: the two main purposes of the media are to "give voice to the voiceless and make those in power accountable".[3]

I ask for the reader's patience as I lay out some background about this most important institution and how it has become so damaged as to be unhelpful to us all and especially to the education of our children.

The fourth estate

The First Amendment states: "Congress shall make no law respecting an establishment of religion, or prohibiting the free exercise thereof; or abridging the freedom of speech, or of the press; or the right of the people peaceably to assemble, and to petition the Government for a redress of grievances."[4] Often, the interpretation of this statement is debated. For the purposes of this discussion, I want to focus upon "the press"; namely, "Congress shall make no law ... abridging the freedom ... of the press ..." These words, quite literally (that is, the "letter of the law"), mean that the press, and today that means the mass media, should be allowed to print or broadcast everything and anything, unencumbered by the government, that is "Congress" and/or the Executive branch, because of its veto power. Now, there is also "the spirit of the law" to consider; that is, the conditions under which these amendments were crafted. Remember that this new experiment, the United States of America, could not be designed in the image of the British monarchy, the 'government', which was being rejected by the revolutionaries in favor of a

---

3 This phrase of Jeremy Scahill's has been used as a quick spot between programs on Free Speech TV. Jeremy Scahill is investigative reporter and co-founding editor of TheIntercept.com. He is known for his bestselling books *Dirty Wars: The World is a Battlefield* and *Blackwater: The Rise of the World's Most Powerful Mercenary Army*.
4 Interesting how the First Amendment was about *the press* and *speech*. Why was this institution relegated to being an 'Amendment'? Surely, the task assigned to this vaunted 'independent' profession should have been accorded the status of its own 'Article' in the body of the Constitution. Curious how such an important body of practitioners was 'an afterthought'!

36 Left Behind

more 'democratic' form of self-government,[5] a form later articulated by President Lincoln in his *Gettysburg Address*, to be "of the people, by the people and for the people". Three estates of government were established: the executive, the legislative and the judicial. Because the published 'word' was controlled by the 'tyrannical' government in the British Empire, the press was naturally understood to be the word of the government. The published 'word' in a fledgling 'democracy' would have to be 'independent' of government in order to serve the people. Indeed, the responsibility of 'the press' not only had to be autonomous from the government, but also had to be aligned with the people to protect them from the government, keeping tabs on the three estates, thereby putting 'the press' on par with them; creating, therefore, the 'fourth estate'. This is part of the *spirit* of the law. As Glenn Greenwald asserts,

> The theory of a 'fourth estate' is to ensure government transparency and provide a check on overreach ... (p. 210) The idea of a 'fourth estate' is that those who exercise the greatest power need to be challenged by adversarial pushback and an insistence on transparency; the job of the press is to disprove the falsehoods that power invariably disseminates to protect itself. Without that type of journalism, abuse is inevitable. Nobody needed the U.S. Constitution to guarantee press freedom so that journalists could befriend, amplify and glorify political leaders; the guarantee was necessary so that journalists could do the opposite (p. 230).[6]

Control over the media by governments is not unique to the British Empire. The former Soviet Union was notorious for controlling information through their state operated media systems.[7] The result was that people understood that propaganda, which the Kremlin disseminated every day, expressed the voice of the powerful, in the interest of the powerful – the government. I mention this because, for four decades, during the 'cold war' between the United States and the Soviet Union, the impression, indeed the propagandized posture taken throughout the United States was that, because the media in the United States were not controlled by the government, our information was 'pure' or at least 'better' or 'unencumbered' by the political vagaries of government. While that is partly true, so is something else: in spite of the fact that our information is not strictly controlled by the government,

---

5 The concept of 'self-government' became one of the most powerful ideas to emerge from the *Enlightenment* of the 18th century, most notably from Thomas Paine, himself a journalist; see his *Common Sense* (1997; first published in 1776) New York: Dover Publications.

6 Glenn Greenwald (2014), *No Place to Hide: Edward Snowden, the NSA, and the U.S. Surveillance State*, New York: Henry Hold and Company, LLC. Glenn Greenwald is a constitutional lawyer, a journalist and co-founding editor of TheIntercept.com.

7 In Russia, this continues today even after the demise of the Soviet Union in the early 1990s; although, the emergence of 'social media' worldwide has somewhat mitigated the control of information flow.

it is, nonetheless, controlled. In our case, it is controlled by the corporations that own the media ("the press"). Unfortunately, still overwhelmingly, people believe that the media in the United States are straightforward in their dissemination of information. Sadly, this is not true. Control over media content by corporations is actually worse than government control. Because concerns of media control are directed away from the government, the uncritical impression is that there is no supreme control at all; that is, what we get is 'the truth' and not the self-serving media productions that governments rely on to protect themselves. What we actually have are the self-protecting and self-promoting media productions of the corporations, by the corporations and for the corporations. The added value to this is the fact that corporations also 'own' the government; that is, because of the overpowering ability of corporations to contribute to political campaigns,[8] they control who gets into office and what they do after in office. Government agencies and officials also contribute to distortions in information dissemination, as I discuss below. However, because corporations are the major component of the 'ruling class', the ideas of everyday life have become the ideas of corporations – the 'ruling ideas'.

We must understand that what has replaced the British or Soviet styles of government control over information flow is a cabal of corporations, whose control overshadows the government control of yesteryear.

The media monopoly

Since the 1970s, we have seen the largest and fastest monopolization in the history of the planet – the monopoly of the media. This has reduced the First Amendment's claim to "the freedom ... of the press" to an anachronism. In the late 1970s, maximizing the truth of A.J. Liebling's astute observation that "Freedom of the press is guaranteed only to those who own one"[9], corporate America began its 20-year takeover of the mass media – "the press". In 1983, Ben Bagdikian, in his seminal work *The Media Monopoly*, reported upon the 50 corporations that controlled some

---

8 The most recent evidence for this are the Supreme Court decisions *Citizens United v. Federal Election Commission* (January, 2010) and *McCutcheon v. Federal Election Commission* (October, 2013). *Citizens United* opened the floodgates for corporations to contribute virtually all they wanted by constituting them as 'people' and to establish money as 'speech'. *McCutcheon* lifted the 'aggregate limits' ($117,000) that were still in place after *Citizens United* and allowed Mr. McCutcheon *et al.*, hypothetically, to contribute up to $3.5 million, shared among candidates, political parties and PACs, with the new 'aggregate limits' of $123,200. See Andy Kroll (2014) "The Supreme Court Just Gutted Another Campaign Finance Law. Here's What Happened", *Mother Jones*, April 2.

9 A.J. Liebling (1960) "The Wayward Press: Do You Belong in Journalism?" p. 109, *The New Yorker*, May 14. Abbott Joseph Liebling (1904–1963) was a life-long journalist, known for his WWII reportage and his association with The New Yorker magazine from 1935 until his death. He was featured in the fall, 2016 issue of *Humanities*, the organ of the NEH (National Endowment for the Humanities). He was a staunch supporter of a free press and demonstrated that journalism is just as much 'literature' as any other form of writing.

38 Left Behind

67% of what we saw, heard and read every day.[10] Four years later, he updated his findings by reporting that, as the monopoly continued, those 50 corporations had dwindled to 25 corporations that controlled some 75% of what we saw, heard and read every day. In 1998, he reported that the monopoly had increased yet again; 12 corporations controlled approximately 80–85% of what we saw, heard and read every day. This seems unbelievable; however, that same monopoly still continued into the 21st century. In 2004, he deemed it necessary to revisit some of his original findings and update more fully the character of the monopoly in another book, *The New Media Monopoly*.[11] The new numbers were as follows: there are 5 corporations that control more than 87% (and into the 90th percentile) of what we now see, hear and read on a daily basis. They are Time Warner, Disney, Viacom, News Corp and Bertelsmann. This monopolization continues today, most recently with AT&T acquiring DirecTV, and Comcast merging with Time Warner Cable and owned by Charter Communications, now called Spectrum. Such developments concentrate even more control of the internet and television access; it would own CW, CNN, tbs, TnT WB, DC and HBO. At the same time, this would increase challenges to net neutrality. The 2015 FCC ruling to protect 'net neutrality' principles was upheld by the courts in 2016. With Tom Wheeler, known to be 'pro-consumer' no longer FCC Chair, new Trump appointee Ajit Pai FCC Chair is 'pro-business', giving corporate shenanigans a green light to monopolize even more. Under Pai's direction, the FCC has repealed the Internet neutrality rules (December 14, 2017).

This massive control over the mass media, from print publishing (books, newspapers and magazines) to broadcast (radio and television) to film (cellulose, magnetic tape and DVDs) to telecommunications (phones and fax) to music/audio (magnetic tape and CDs) and, yes, to the internet, has transformed our world in less than 30 years.

What the monopolies bring with them, according to Ed Herman and Noam Chomsky in their book *Manufacturing Consent*,[12] is a set of five filters, which comprise the 'propaganda model', that account for the practices behind the actual information we receive from the corporate media. They are: (1) the size, ownership and profit orientation of the mass media, *i.e.*, the monopoly control of the mass media; (2) the advertising license to do business, *i.e.*, the control advertisers have over what the content of the news, programming will be, with the threat that, if the outlet does not comply, the advertisement dollars will be pulled; (3) sourcing

---

10 The more 'linear' approximations presented here are only to illustrate the increasing control over media outlets by the ever shrinking number of corporations monopolizing ever higher percentages of our print and broadcast media. In the book, Bagdikian provides a more complex matrix of this process, e.g., Bagdikian presented evidence that the percentage of control well into the 90th percentile occurred earlier in some media in various respects. See Ben Bagdikian (1983) *The Media Monopoly*, Boston, MA: Beacon Press.

11 Ben Bagdikian (2004) *The New Media Monopoly*, Boston, MA: Beacon Press.

12 Edward S. Herman and Noam Chomsky (2002) *Manufacturing Consent: The Political Economy of the Mass Media*, New York: Pantheon, chapter 1.

mass-media news, *i.e.*, control over who is interviewed or referenced in the reports of the news – if they are not approved by this filter, journalists are either sanctioned or fired; (4) flack and the enforcers, *i.e.*, the negative responses to a media statement or program, such as complaints to the media by outsiders that can damage or cost the media; (5) anti-communism as a control mechanism, *i.e.*, this is the ultimate evil always haunting the ruling class and their property. When you combine these, you have a formidable set of constraints to the proper functioning of a media system that has as its ultimate goal, according to the Constitution, to protect the people from government and corporate power and abuse.

This monopolization of the media has virtually eliminated, for most people, any entrée into the broader spectrum of information that still exists, but that is more difficult to access. In particular, our children, who have been raised in this monopoly context, for the most part, do not know anything else. Their purview has been stunted; they do not understand that there is much more to information than what they have been bombarded with and entrained to expect and accept. Teacher training and parental awareness must become attuned to these realities so that they may introduce and maintain effective critical resources for our children. Teachers must make them aware of this perceptual fallacy and show them how to access independent sources of information and encourage them, as often difficult as it may be, to investigate how they square with the filtered diet of sound bites they are fed by the mainstream media. Moreover, parents must be as active to teach their children to be 'open minded' about everything and to pause and reflect upon what matters-at-hand mean.

The Telecommunications Act of 1996 and the FCC, FTC

The Telecommunications Act of 1996 revamped the Communications Act of 1934, deregulating major swaths of media industry rules of the past and establishing an environment of 'winner take all' on the part of corporations that were already poised to buy up their competition. One of the most egregious of changes was the removal of the ownership limits with regard to radio and television broadcasting, now allowing up to 35% of ownership in a single audience market. For example, Clear Channel Communications, which had owned 173 radio stations in 1997, owned 1,207 and 1,400 worldwide by 2004. In addition, restrictions on 'cross ownership' of media were relaxed or removed; that is, radio, television, cable and telephone corporations could own companies across industries. For example, telephone can own cable (AT&T, as of 1999; it now owns DirecTV), newspapers can own television (Murdock's FOX News, as of 1996) and so on. The expected result is that, whatever information one receives from one source, one will also receive the same message from the other(s). The Federal Trade Commission (FTC) is charged to monitor any movement toward monopolization of communication ownership in the economic/market sense. They have not met their mission goals for some decades now; witness the extreme monopolization of the media. The Federal Communications Commission (FCC) is charged with guaranteeing that

40 Left Behind

the public airways, which belong to the people, the 'commons', are not abused by the companies that enjoy free access to them; not only must their programming 'do no harm' to the public, but also 'be useful' to the public. In other words, they are charged with broadcasting 'in the public interest'. They have not met their mission goals either; witness the omnipresence of corporate messages, either in programming or advertisements and the paucity of messages that actually inform the public and are useful to us.

In June 2003, the FCC approved local and national expansions on ownership that surpassed the Telecommunications Act of 1996; in September 2003, the Third Circuit U.S. Court of Appeals stayed the implementation of the rules to comply with the requirements of the Act. In June of 2004, the same court rejected the FCC attempt to rewrite the ownership laws. The case was brought to the court by the Prometheus Radio Project,[13] challenging the FCC rules. In spite of these small victories, these government agencies continue to violate the very missions they are obliged to accomplish. In the summer of 2014, the FCC allowed a 120-day public forum and response period to encourage 'town hall' meetings across the country with regard to the proposed AT&T/DirecTV and Comcast/Time Warner Cable deals mentioned above, this only after pressure from the independent media and the public. The deals were still made.

In fact, the FCC has historically been busy telling media outlets what they cannot publish, express or say on the radio or television, in the name of 'protecting' our children from 'swearing' and recreational drug references and sexual content. The U.S. Supreme Court case *FCC v. Pacifica Foundation* of 1978 established the power of the FCC over so-called 'indecent' material in broadcasting. A child had heard George Carlin's *filthy words* routine on Pacifica Foundation radio station WBAI in New York. The father complained, and the FCC censured the station, citing a violation of the FCC regulations. The 5-4 vote in the U.S. Supreme Court case ruled that Carlin's routine was indecent but not obscene.

Instead, the FCC should be protecting our children from the obscene content that corporations bring to them, telling them what to eat, what to look like and how to act (see below). As Ida B. Wells so astutely asserted, our children's education does not only mean what we bring to them in the classroom; indeed, what they hear/view/read outside of the classroom is often more powerful than what they witness in the classroom, simply because the spectacle of the media is constant and unrelenting. Teachers cannot compete with that level of dazzle and hypnotic quality (Some have argued that the mass media *anesthetize* people instead of *awakening* them.); they operate in real time, having prepared and prepackaged all that our

---

13 The Prometheus Radio Project, founded in 1998, is a non-profit organization dedicated to building and supporting community radio stations to bring information to the people that was and continues to be taken away from us through the monopoly of the media. They focus upon building low power frequency modulated, LPFM, radio stations to bring information to local audiences; www. prometheusradio.org.

children see, hear and read. What they witness in the media is the end product of hours, if not weeks, if not months of consideration and research to get that piece of advertisement or programming or news clip "just right", whereby that media product is imbued with the exact message desired by the media company, not the logical discourse and conclusions of the teacher.

These government decisions over the past 20 years have proven to be most important in terms of the continued privatization (corporatization) of information flow, something that our children, unbeknown to them, 'consume' every day and direct their thinking in often dangerous ways. Because of the extraordinary power of the media, those messages impress our children more easily, making our job of educating them to consider various perspectives on everything that more difficult. To them, indeed to all of us to varying degrees, when more than 90% of information is monopolized information, there is seldom any thought beyond what is most easily available for our media consumption. What we get "must be the truth or they would not air it, publish it, broadcast it" as a neighbor's mother once exclaimed when I challenged her about the veracity of the mainstream media output. That is how most people think about 'the news' and, because adults do not accord it any 'pause', their children have no reason to question what they witness every day. It is the job of teachers to cut into this maze of information and help students to sort out the junk from information that is worth our attention and properly sourced, with the best journalistic practice. Without the exercise of only the highest principles of journalism, our children's minds become 'colonized'[14] with falsehoods, puffery and junk.

Channel One

One last discussion before I address some particulars of the media effects on education, in more detail. As of May 2014, after a history of several buyouts, Channel One is owned by Houghton Mifflin Harcourt, a major publisher of school textbooks. (Remember the cross-ownership of types of media that the Telecommunications Act of 1996 allowed?) From its inception in 1989, Channel One was designed to bring television into schools, under the guise of introducing students to news content, of course with commercial advertising, that could 'help' students and teachers 'interpret' the news and initiate discussion around the mass media. Unfortunately, the news 'content' is wanting, more like the fluff 'news', often found in popular culture magazines, rather than news about things that matter. For example, more newsworthy items are aired as 'headlines', which together last some five minutes; the rest of the 'news', about various topics like sunscreen or traveling on "air pods" instead of roads are allotted from two to four minutes. Just on the basis of temporal considerations, students will tend to pay closer or more attention to the feature stories rather than the more newsworthy items. However,

---

14 See Chapter 12 on Orwell, the colonization of the mind and critical thinking.

42 Left Behind

the advertising is on steroids, or at least observably taking advantage of the 'captive audience' of children in school. In fact, as part of the contract to receive Channel One broadcasts, schools plaster the walls with advertisements of all kinds, from soft drinks to clothes to electronic connections to more advertising. The "Dream Strong" program is an army recruiting tool built into the broadcasts that Channel One provides. This resonates with high school seniors, the poorest of whom will consider the military as a viable 'career' track.[15] This recruitment tool is one of many such mechanisms deployed because the U.S. no longer has the draft. These are the most vulnerable of times for our children and many are conscripted to fight in invasions of other countries or maintaining some 662 U.S. military bases in 38 foreign countries[16] to enrich multinational corporations. What is emphasized in these programs is the *schooling* or the *skill-building* our youngsters will have access to, not the *violence* of the military industrial complex.

The Channel One broadcasts are nothing more than a maximization of media messages. This phenomenon guarantees that the colonization of our children's minds is galvanized and renders the corporate mindset so ubiquitous that children cannot escape it, even in school. Teachers are subjected to further competition by this insidious machine of constant interruptions in the media from proper learning. Instead of being surrounded by images and other artifacts of education, children are visually overloaded with the products of popular culture and superficiality. The substance of education, the actual teaching, suffers such an antagonism with this programming that it has little time to deflect it. Whatever 'benefits' that may obtain from this barrage of propaganda, they wane in the face of the time spent away from proper instruction. Fruitful discussion about the media can be organized by teachers; that is, media productions can be selected by them, not by the media monopoly, to bring a critical mindedness to students about their media consumption.

The independent media

Until now, I have been discussing the character and effects of the corporate media. There are, in the midst of these monopolies, *independent* outlets of information as well. They are not typically controlled or owned by corporations, but funded by ordinary people and foundations that do work for the common good. They are somewhat less accessible than the mainstream media outlets in the sense that there are fewer of them and because people typically do not know about them; most of the media ink and air are taken up by the corporate media and, because they print and broadcast incessantly, 24/7, the presence of independent media is often unnoticed or bullied out of sight and earshot. Nonetheless, they do exist; they are available on television, the radio, newspapers, magazines and the internet.

---

15 See Chapter 9 on high school.
16 See Department of Defense, "Base Structure Report, Fiscal 2015 Baseline", www.acq.osd.mil/eie/ Downloads/BSI/Base Structure Report FY15.pdf

The 'free press' – On a corporate leash! **43**

These outlets provide information seldom seen/heard in the mainstream. They provide alternative analyses to the corporate onslaught of "junk food news" as the Project Censored organization likes to call it. Their mission: "Project Censored educates students and the public about the importance of a truly free press for democratic self-government. We expose and oppose news censorship and we promote independent investigative journalism, media literacy, and critical thinking."[17] The organization has been doing this important work since 1976. They publish an annual report on "the news that didn't make the news", compilation of the top 25 stories that the corporate media did not publish or broadcast in the previous year. Among them which still resonate today:

– civil liberties have been eroded over the last decade, most notably the Military Commissions Act of 2006, which eliminated *habeas corpus* protections;
– kidnapping by government agencies of people who are expressing dissent about government policies or actions and taken to undisclosed locations (commonly referred to as 'rendition'), without notifying families, without due process, without representation, all secret;
– in 1984, Union Carbide killed some 20,000 people in Bhopal (exposure to methyl isocyanate gas) and left another 500,000 people crippled or diseased, without prosecution, without proper compensation;
– in 2012, more soldiers were committing suicide than were dying in combat; and so on …

Most recently, Public Citizen published a report entitled "A Storm of Silence",[18] which exposes how little, if at all, the corporate media mentioned "climate change" or "global warming" in the context of reporting on hurricane Harvey. Contrary to claims that raising the existential threat of climate change in this context is not "politicizing" the hurricane; not mentioning it is.

These are not 'mistakes'; they are deliberately kept from us. These are the stories that the corporate media do not want us to know about, because they will challenge their image or reveal information that will undermine their *modus operandi*, or expose politicians' true affiliations. Instead, we get sound bites, little nuggets of this or that, without context or enough information to allow us to understand the impact of the story, something that is only possible with proper discussion. Our children must be exposed to these stories and have an opportunity to sort out, for themselves, what information is worth their attention and what is not.

---

17 See the film *Project Censored, The Movie*, www.projectcensoredthemovie.com/. It chronicles some of the stories that did not make it to the news and explains what the organization has been up to for the last almost 40 years. See Project Censored Mission Statement at www.projectcensored.org/the-fair-share-of-the-common-heritage-mission-statement/.
18 David Arkush (September 8, 2017) "A Storm of Silence: Media Coverage of Climate Change and Hurricane Harvey", Public Citizen, www.citizen.org.

44 Left Behind

Independent outlets do not have corporate or special interest constraints like corporate outlets have. Some of those independent outlets include:

On television – Free Speech TV and LINK TV on both satellite networks; these carry The Thom Hartman Program, DemocracyNow, The Ring of Fire Network (produced by Mike Papantonio *et al.*) *The Bill Press Show*, *Vice News* and many other independent reports of daily news and documentaries of ongoing events and issues.
On the radio – The Pacifica Radio Foundation, the only independent radio network left in the United States; five commercial-free, community supported stations whose programing amounts to being the substance of a 'university of the air waves'.
On the local air – many community, low FM (LFM) stations give voice to progressive ideas.
On the Internet – there are hundreds of sites, where serious journalists report the news, events and issues in a straightforward manner; among them are DailyKos.com, TheIntercept.com, ThinkProgress.com, Truthdig.com and edgeofsports.com.
In print – magazines like *The Nation*, *The Progressive*, *Mother Jones*, *In These Times* and others tackle the difficult work of investigative reporting.

These outlets challenge the status quo and bring a full spectrum of information for the consideration of the audience, something that is seldom afforded our children. Every semester over the last 30 years, I have polled my students: "Who among you has heard of the Pacifica Foundation and, in particular, their New York station WBAI, 99.5 FM?" In a population of some 6,000 students over the years, a handful of them had heard of it. This is the extent to which these independent outlets for news, culture, politics, health, education, science, *etc.*, are shunted from the public eye and ear. Yet these are the non-corporate outlets that most serve the interests of the public. Remember that the air waves belong to everybody, as part of the commons; and, when media corporations are given permission, by the FCC, to use those air waves, they must broadcast "in the public interest", not only in the interest of business. The independent media outlets overwhelmingly abide by this mandate. These are the kinds of outlets that truly help 'educate' our children, rather than distract them from their education, something Ida B. Wells fought for and would laude.[19]

Interestingly enough, those stories cited by Project Censored did see the 'light of day' in the independent press, writ large. Except that, because these outlets are

---

19 Sadly, when outlets or independent journalists do report 'the truth', or at minimum perspectives that do not square with the 'official' versions about all kinds of events, issues, matters of consequence, they are harassed or threatened or subjected to violence or death. See the global work of the Committee to Protect Journalists at http://cpj.org.

often overlooked or missed, one could still not know what is going on in the world. We should not have to rely on Project Censored to tell us about the news we did not get. Our children should be made aware of these discrepancies as a matter of course. Children can then teach their parents about having to broaden their media consumption as well, beyond the mainstream, corporate messages, a full spectrum of information. Only then will they be able to sort through what they experience and decide what makes sense and what does not. Hence, teachers must bring these matters to the attention of students, I would say, as early as the 4th grade. By reading, listening, viewing independent outlets of information, in a context of *critical thinking*, students can obtain a much broader understanding of the information spectrum and thereby be able to make much more informed decisions about how the world works. This is the way to bring media literacy to students, not Channel One.

How do these conditions impact our children and their education?

While children receive an overwhelming amount of exposure directly from the corporate media, the ideas that children typically acquire from their parents are also influenced by the dominant ideas of our culture, often at an emotional level. Edward Bernays, known as the 'Father of Public Relations', proclaimed that selling products had to be about accessing the emotional layers of people (something he likely learned from his uncle, Sigmund Freud), not about pestering people to buy this or that. He was a major figure in the Committee on Public Information (CPI), known as the Creel Commission, initially formed to influence American participation in WWI. When the tobacco companies approached him with the problem that women were not smoking enough cigarettes (in part, a result of the idea that smoking was not 'lady-like'), he organized debutantes to walk in the 1921 New York Easter Parade holding and smoking Chesterfield cigarettes. This caught the eye of women, who subsequently began to smoke more. He had captured the visual and emotional components that, when observed, resulted in the desired outcome.[20]

I am reminded of the Reverend Doctor Martin Luther King, Jr.'s sermon, in which he addresses this phenomenon:[21]

> Now the presence of this [Drum Major] instinct explains why we are so often taken by advertisers. You know, those gentlemen of massive verbal persuasion. And they have a way of saying things to you that kind of gets you into buying. In order to be a man of distinction, you must drink this whiskey. In order to make your neighbors envious, you must drive this type of car ... In

---

20 See Edward Bernays (1928) *Propaganda*, London: Routledge.
21 The Reverend Martin Luther King, Jr. sermon "The Drum Major Instinct" delivered at Ebenezer Baptist Church, Atlanta, GA, February 4, 1968. King adapted this sermon from a homily by the same title by J. Wallace Hamilton, a well-known white Methodist preacher.

46 Left Behind

order to be lovely to love, you must wear this kind of lipstick or this kind of perfume. And you know, before you know it, you're just buying that stuff ... That's the way the advertisers do it.

Those ideas are corporate ideas because those ideas have access to the mechanisms of propaganda. Corporations have the cash to buy information systems, computers, satellites, advertising time and space across the available outlets in the media; indeed, they own the mass media. They are everywhere: on household products, over the radio, on television, on billboards, on buses and taxis, woven into the programming itself (so-called 'product placement') of all kinds. This is the world of advertising – mass advertising. Corporations infiltrate every possible media outlet, affecting every domain of life, to advance their image and products, so much so that children are known to be exposed to more than 200 advertising messages every day. According to Common Sense Media, "children age 2–11 saw an average of about 25,600 TV ads per year..." (That is more than 70 daily.) And that does not include the ads they view/hear/read from 'cross-promotions', 'online advertising', 'mobile advertising', *etc.* every day.[22] These advertisements are ubiquitous and multifarious, reaching our children everywhere. I have chosen three domains of our children's lives, among the most representative of these effects: exposure to the junk food industries, exposure to the self-image industries and exposure to the desensitization of violence.

How to eat

Some of the most successful advertisements are those which have to do with food, not nutritious food, but junk food – high-calorie, low nutrition. According to the Kaiser Family Foundation, children between the ages of 2 and 17 witness from 12 to 17 such food ads per day.[23] The top networks where such advertisements proliferate, they reported, are: Nickelodeon, Fox, Cartoon Network and Disney. All have children-dense audiences. A 2009 study at Yale University[24] reported that "children consumed 45% more when exposed to food advertising" and this without the presence of hunger, leading to a culture of food consumption in the United States. In March 2013, the Center for Science in the Public Interest reported that Nickelodeon food advertisements were for junk almost 70% of the time. Is there a culture of *junk* food consumption in the United States? The Center posted a full-page advertisement in *The Hollywood Reporter* in the form of a 'Wanted' poster. With mug shot–style renditions of an older SpongeBob with a pronounced belly,

---

22 A Common Sense Media Research Brief (2014) "Advertising to Children and Teens: Current Practices", Common Sense Media, www.commonsensemedia.org.
23 The Henry J. Kaiser Family Foundation Report (2007) "Food for Thought: Television Food Advertising to Children in the United States".
24 Jennifer Harris et al. (2009) "Priming Effects of Television Food Advertising on Eating Behavior", *Health Psychology*, volume *28*, issue *4*, July, pp. 404–413.

it read, "WANTED: Nickelodeon – Nickelodeon is wanted for impersonating a responsible media company while aggressively marketing obesity to kids." The "REWARD: Healthier kids and happier, less-hassled parents."[25]

An obvious result is the growing problem of obesity in the United States. While these studies and I do not argue a 'causal relationship' between these ads and child obesity, it is clear that there is a disturbingly high correlation between the massive presence of these ads and the conduct of our children and their parents in terms of food choices. There are multiple studies that demonstrate the relationships among those food ads, the purchases parents make accordingly and the rising incidence of obesity in children in the United States.[26] This is not the case only in poor households, in which low income often means low nutritional value in diet; this problem ranges across economic status, class, race, sex, especially from the really young (ages 2–6) to teenagers in high school.[27] It is an epidemic and there are no signs of relenting on the part of fast-food chains and snack food companies in targeting children for their advertising.

This clearly means that our children are struggling throughout their school day. With that extra weight (literally) to carry, children do not move around as easily as they otherwise could. They may have a shortness of breath; their agility is reduced; they cannot participate to their potential in P.E. classes, where they exist; they become open to the threat, if not the physical then the emotional abuse, of bullying; they may be preoccupied with food and not paying attention to what is going on in their classes. Essentially, their health is impaired significantly, or, at least, sufficiently to compromise their learning. While none of these consequences obtain uniformly, they do display a tightly woven sequence of practices among the advertisers, the actions taken by children and their parents, resulting in these outcomes. As long as we allow corporations to advertise the junk that they produce, in the name of a 'free market', our children will be put at risk to consume that garbage food and become unhealthy.

As the reader knows, the 'free market' is not 'free'. This libertarian notion that the economy is free floating, that a *laissez faire* attitude benefits everyone, that 'trickle-down' economics is the way to go, has been demonstrated to be false. These economic relations do not operate with 'equivocal' impact for all who participate in them. The deck is stacked in favor of corporations. Companies practice their advertising and other activities with extreme prejudice, with extreme privilege. Especially since Citizens United (2010), when the Supreme Court decided that corporations are people, claiming that the First Amendment applied to them as well, corporations have been enjoying an overabundance of latitude with regard

---

25 See "Nearly 70% of Food Ads on Nickelodeon are for Junk" at www.cspinet.org
26 While not causal, a simple internet search will yield an abundance of evidence, showing how these are connected.
27 According to a 2013 study, 16.9% of children and adolescents, ages 2 to 19 are obese. See Papoutsi *et al.* (2013) "The Causes of Childhood Obesity: A Survey", *Journal of Economic Surveys*, volume *27*, issue *4*, pp. 743–767.

to communicating to their potential consumers. Later, with McCutcheon (2014), when the Supreme Court lifted the limits on aggregate contributions to campaigns, giving even more power to corporations to flood the election landscape with dollars to promote candidates for election, who will do the children's bidding other than the people themselves? Of course, to all fair-minded and rational people, corporations are not and never will be 'people', and their 'speech' is not free speech. The politically skewed Supreme Court will sooner or later be overruled by the only institution that can – Congress – when it passes yet another Amendment to the Constitution. The protections of the First Amendment are for real people, not artificial ones. As someone said in the midst of this controversy when the Supreme Court had just ruled on it, 'I'll believe that corporations are people when you imprison them'.

Our children's and their representatives' voices are the ones who should have free access to the airwaves, not corporations'. As long as media corporations have a free hand to do whatever they want with the privilege they have been accorded, to have access to the airwaves, our children's real freedom of speech will continue to be muffled, muted or eliminated and not be heard. Corporate advertising must be reined in and forced to comply with the promise of operating 'in the interest of the people'. Once this really happens, our children will have a better chance to think about their food choices and understand what it means to eat sensibly.

How to look

"What will I wear to the prom?" "Where can I buy that new style of dress, jeans, shirt, jacket, *etc*.?" These questions from children arise out of the daily infiltration of mass media advertisements, targeting children with flashy messages about what to wear to be 'cool' or 'rad' or 'hip'. We all know by now that these advertisements run in cycles; the styles of yesterday change for today, but become the 'latest' fashions of tomorrow, and so it goes. Hence, the idea is 'to be up to date' with ones dress according to the latest 'dress code'; and, while children insist upon 'being different or unique' they strive ever so diligently to 'fit in' and be accepted by this or that 'clique', often determined by their wardrobe. These advertisements concentrate on attracting children, who, in turn, go to their parents with 'life and death' pleas to buy this or that piece of apparel because Johnny or Sally "need" these threads to look their best according to the latest 'edict' from the fashion industry.

Of course, all of this is really about 'self-image' and 'self-esteem' and affects girls, in particular. Clothes become the 'hook' to lure kids to these or those fashions to satisfy their immediate, close circle of friends' "needs". I challenge that these are "needs". Maybe some of them are. I suspect that these are often 'false' needs, which lead to the creation of a 'false self-image' or a 'false' sense of self-esteem. The mass media dominate in this regard; they are constantly pumping out the idea that what one wears is a reflection of who one is and how important it is to 'belong', in some way, to one's *entourage*. They are notions that come to be adopted about many things that lead children to think this or that is "what I need" in order to be accepted and valued. While these matters are important to children, from very early on, they become 'hyper' important and out of proportion. In some cases, these matters overshadow other much more important matters, including their education.

This superficial aspect of life for children, and for some adults, can be consequential. The threat of bullying is also present within this context. Much of this abuse directed toward children by children is generated from the idea that what children wear 'defines' them and, if that definition is not adequate for acceptance into some group, then those children are ostracized or vilified or punched and kicked. Some particular set of ideas, often propagandized by the media, are internalized by some children, from which they assess and 'pontificate' over who will or not be accepted into the fold; everyone else is bullied, either emotionally: shunned, snubbed and ignored or physically pushed around, called names (hate speech) or beaten up. In recent times, this practice has gone 'viral' on the internet, placing photographs or video clips of classmates. Let's not forget that, in spite of some significant advances, racism, sexism and homophobia continue to plague our culture. These dimensions are often the subject of aggression on the part of some children who have missed those critical parts of their upbringing and/or education and whose parents are either bigots themselves or are out of touch with their children.

If our educational priorities were properly organized, our children would have access to analytical constructs which would, in varying degrees, mitigate the effects I am describing. If children knew about how wrong-headed all of these messages are, their lives could become unencumbered by all these false promises and distorted characterizations of life. An awareness of these kinds of media practices would immediately put them in a 'critical' mode, enabling them to think about the logic of these messages and their consequences for them in their own everyday practices and to extrapolate this kind of critical thinking to other domains of life. Maybe, just maybe, children would ask the simple question: "Can't we do better than that?" Of course, we can. However, children's ideas about virtually everything are influenced by the media; and often reinforced in the classroom (remember, much of education itself is influenced by society at large). All of that has to change along with the other, more immediate educational components.

The fashion industry has 'fashioned' our children to be preoccupied with how they look, instead of how they think and talk and write. They are distracted from learning every minute of the day in one way or another, but largely with regard to their looks. When will they be able to buy into the next fashion craze? What must they do to maintain their popularity or to create it? This is the kind of pap that occupies our children's minds on a regular basis. I can vouch for this in my own experience: whether in the classroom or on the ice when I coached girl's ice hockey. Girls/young women are talking about fashion much of the time, often in the context of attracting boys/young men. To perhaps a lesser degree, this is also true of boys/young men. Discussion about the educational matters at hand is limited to actual instruction time, or often, stolen from what is already most prominent in their minds: their looks. Now, I am not making these points because

50 Left Behind

I blame the children/young adults. No, I am trying to explicate a little bit of the huge problem this is, which is perpetrated by media advertisements and the profit motive. That is capitalism; that is how it works. And with little or no regulation, those companies run amok; they exploit any and every opportunity to drive up those profits, regardless of what it does to the society at large and to children in particular. Ida B. Wells was correct in stating that the media ("the press") have a huge influence when it comes to education. Teachers can barely compete, if at all, with the likes of the flashy, loud and mesmerizing spectacle that is the trademark of television, in particular.

Children are unaware of these facts. That is not their fault; part of the problem is that they experience very little criticality from their teachers. Their teachers, themselves affected by the same seemingly never-ending media blitz, buy into the same nonsense. There is lots of blame to go around in this regard; the *curriculum* they follow is generally devoid of critical thinking training, not even one class on the subject. If there were and if children knew about the crimes committed by the very companies they frequent to buy their clothes – most notably the exploitation of children whose age is literally the same as theirs – they might not be so frivolous about wanting this or that latest fashion item. This is how the media 'colonize' our children's minds: they flood them with drivel and omit the truth about how clothes is manufactured. These companies are never brought to account for their misfeasance and malfeasance, which cost people their livelihoods, their futures and their lives. These are real matters for consideration on their part; not a collection of 'conspiracy theories' often vaunted by the powers that be, the government, the corporations and the pundits on television. This is what I mean about the media landscaping the 'education' of our children in the wrong direction – toward complacency.

This mess does not stop there. Along with targeting our children to buy clothes so that they can 'look their best', according to artificial criteria, corporations have sexualized 'that look' kids have come to seek, that look that makes them 'sexy'; and girls are targeted overwhelmingly more than boys. Many studies and documentaries have paid close attention to these matters.[28] One sustained example is the work of the Media Education Foundation,[29] whose films have been very direct on this topic. The long running, in its four reincarnations, *Killing Us Softly*[30] addresses sexualized womanhood and childhood in advertising. Jean Kilbourne exposes the "toxic" environment of the mass media with regard to the "image" of women and girls. What the media tell us about women is that what is most important is "how women look", or, more correctly, how women *should* look. The idealized woman

---

28 See these classic studies: Erving Goffman, *Gender Advertisements* and John Berger, *Ways of Seeing*.

29 I reference these and other documentary films because the quality of such films, particularly since the tragedy of September 11, 2001, has consistently increased and because they are very powerful in their depiction of these and many other matters that occupy our minds in today's world.

30 See *Killin Us Softly 4: Advertising's Image of Women*, (2010) featuring Jean Kilbourne, Media Education Foundation.

is constantly being presented, always with the help of computer 'enhancements'; in other words, there is no such woman as portrayed in these advertisements. Even the models in these advertisements don't look like they are offered up. Because these images are fraudulent, no woman can ever achieve this look. Nonetheless, women still covet that flawless version. This also extends to girls; and this is quite disturbing – in fact, women are often portrayed to look more like girls and girls are portrayed to look more like women. Another component of this 'look' is that women become thinner and thinner. As a result, women and girls who try to achieve this look will inevitably fail, thereby often making them feel like they are themselves failures. Witness the crazy preoccupation with weight loss in the United States, not because of obesity (which should be addressed by changes in lifestyle, not 'diets'), but because people, men and women, want to look more like the people they see on TV. A result has been serious health problems as a result of eating disorders, such as binge eating (BED), anorexia nervosa, bulimia, *etc*. The reader observes correctly the very close relationship between what our children eat and how they look. Always present, fatefully, these conditions give rise to more and more violence against women.[31] That is the level our minds have been colonized through the medium still the most *gone to* for information: the television set.

These images, still or moving, instill attitudes in adults and children alike. What mom and dad are exposed to either is also witnessed by their children first-hand or is transferred to them via their practices. A most disturbing development over the last several decades is the media portrayal of women and men in sexualized contexts. One could argue that this is a matter of artistic flare and, taken in the context of adult consumption, is acceptable. Choices by parents, for themselves, are one thing; however, these kinds of representations are openly available to children and seem acceptable across the board because they are not hidden or relegated to the category of 'adult entertainment'. A perfect example of this kind of display and veiled exploitation is the 'adult beauty pageant' concept, whereby young women are paraded before audiences in the name of offering up scholarships or career opportunities, the criterion for which is 'how they look'. The reason that this is actually more dangerous than many other forms of sexism is that it is contextualized as a 'wholesome' forum for the display of youthful talent. While television, movies and music videos are often criticized for sexualizing women, even child beauty pageants are accepted as 'sensible'. Children absorb these activities as being hearty and follow in their parent's footsteps. Pornography, on the other hand, is clear in its exploitation.

Continuing with this topic of sexualizing our children, another film entitled *Sext Up Kids*[32] presents the goods on how the media impose a sexualized version of our

---

31 Witness the well-publicized comments by Donald Trump, 2016 Republican presidential candidate for the presidency and after 'elected', about women, whether journalists or beauty contestants or celebrities.
32 See LeGerrier and Hogan (2012) *Sext Up Kides: How Children are Becoming Hypersexualized*.

52 Left Behind

children. All of the trappings of our sex lives are rendered in a hyper-sexualized version of self. For example, this comment by one of the interviewees in the film seems to tell it all: "Little girls are going from toddlers to teenagers, with just about nothing in between". This means, as the film makes clear, that girls who want to be the "prettiest little girl" quickly move on to wanting to be the "hottest little girl". Children are not allowed to be kids anymore; that is, to have lives before any sexual component. I think of the concept of gender in language. For example, German has three definitizers: *der*, *die* and *dass*, masculine, feminine and neuter, respectively. Now, the concept of 'child' is rendered as *dass Kind*, the neuter gender; that is, no sexual construct is attributed to a child. This is one way to grasp what this artificial sexualization of children means. Children do not have the concepts nor the physical development to understand what it means to be 'female' or 'male'. They do not have the experience to understand sexuality as applied to the categories 'male' and 'female', categories of *sex*; television is telling them what it means to be a *man* or a *woman* and *feminine* or *masculine*, categories of *gender*, way before they discover these things on their own at the age of puberty. They receive these distorted versions of sexuality from the media, not from their education or their parents, from whom it should come.[33] Hence, the media, advertising, music videos, *etc.*, provide the visual representations of what those mean, and is how children take on and accept uncritically, how they should be, think like, act like, look like. This twisted understanding of what they should be like translates into how their actual sexuality should be expressed. Girls fall into the trap of how they think boys want girls to be and boys buy into the image of the 'idealized' version of a girl; and together they enter into relationships that are virtually dominated by these false and damaging impressions of one another.

If children were taught how to think critically about so many domains of their lives, not only would they be able to develop a strong sense of self about these sexual matters, they would also contribute to the eradication of such frivolous and dangerous expressions in the culture. That is what is missing in our schools with regard to the media; there is no concerted attempt to confront the nonsense that they are exposed to on a daily basis. They are not taught the analytical tools that they need even to address these matters as a problem in the first place, let alone how to sift through the junk and make intelligent decisions about it.

How to act

The connection between the media and violence is not as simple as it may seem. Decades of research have demonstrated that the connection between these two phenomena is not that media violence, that is, the violent actions we witness on television and in movies, makes people violent. The overwhelming majority of people who witness these same acts of violence in the media "never commit a violent act" themselves. Rather, according to George Gerbner, it is likely to make

33 See Chapter 9 on high school, the section on sex education.

The 'free press' – On a corporate leash! **53**

us scared of violence being done to us. Hence, media violence contributes to what many have called the 'culture of fear'. The violence in film and television is so diffused and ubiquitous that virtually every time we are consuming visual stimuli, someone is assaulting someone, there is a tornado or hurricane, bombs are being set off, confrontations at rallies or demonstrations are being captured on video, explosions are used to emphasize some presentation. In advertising alone, it seems that every commercial has to include an explosion of some kind in order to make the point ever more dramatically. It is ridiculous how much violence is depicted in these visual media. As Gerbner asserts,

> Today, a handful of global conglomerates own and control the telling of all the stories in the world. They have global marketing formulas that are imposed on the creative people in Hollywood; and I am in touch with them and they hate it. They say, 'Don't talk to me about censorship from Washington. I never heard about that. I get censorship every day'. I'm told, 'put more action, cut out complicated solutions'. They apply this formula because it travels well in the global market. These are formulas that need no translation and essentially image driven and speak 'action' in any language; and, of course, the leading element of that formula is violence. This is an historically unprecedented tidal wave of images and violence, inundating every home, often with expertly choreographed brutality, such as the world has never seen. This is an expansion and a mass production and the introduction into every home, a relentless, pervasive exposure to violence and brutality, many times a day.[34]

According to Michael Morgan, Professor of Communication, U-Mass-Amherst,

> The numbers are staggering. Children now see about 8,000 murders by the end of elementary school and about 200,000 violent acts by the age of 18. From movies to television shows to video games to children's programs, to twenty-four hour news channels, aggression is now routine, every day, formulaic, a staple industrial ingredient. In fact, for Gerbner, it is the routine nature of this violence that makes it so dangerous and so different from the past.[35]

However, when you add 'humor' to the mix, what Gerbner calls "happy violence", that violence is much more palatable, especially when the end results are desirable, when there is a "happy ending" to the story. The conclusion that scholars have arrived at in those many studies is that this kind of violence desensitizes people from the utter horror that it brings to real people. It is disembodied from its real effects and, while it dazzles the viewer, it numbs the senses to its real impact.

---

34 See *The Mean World Syndrome: Media Violence & the Cultivation of Fear* (Jhally & Earp, 2010), featuring the work of George Gerbner, renowned media analyst, Media Education Foundation.
35 *Ibid.*

54 Left Behind

Another angle with regard to violence is the mass media's constant message to boys and men about what 'masculinity' constitutes. Many books and articles have addressed this troublesome form of 'brainwashing'.[36] The conclusion of virtually all of them has been that mass media images are overwhelmingly responsible. While there are many sources (family, community) which advance these 'macho', 'tough', 'strong', 'powerful', 'respected', 'in control', *etc.*, false *personae* of men and disparage boys and men when they are not these kinds of men, they are referred to as 'wusses', 'wimps', 'sissies', *etc.* Far and away, it is

> the powerful and pervasive media system which provides a steady stream of images that define manhood as connected with dominance, power and control … What the media do is help to construct 'violent masculinity' as a cultural norm. In other words, violence isn't so much a deviation as it is an accepted part of masculinity … We … have to work to change the institutions that create our present choices. For example, we need to break the monopoly of the media system that we've been looking at, where mostly rich, white men dictate to the whole society the kinds of images and stories of manhood that surround us.[37]

From the culture of violence to the culture of fear, what all of this violence creates is a sense that there is much of which to be afraid. After September 11, 2001, the Bush government ramped up the rhetoric of fear, the likes of which we have rarely witnessed in the history of the United States. As you may already know, if a population is in a constant state of fear, those who are in power can do virtually anything they want 'in the name of national security', to protect those who are afraid. That is how the Patriot Act was passed and how subsequent legislation has ensued, ever more to limit our civil rights and establish a military state, one which President Eisenhower warned us about in his farewell address and one of which Donald Trump seems to be enamored.

These are the kinds of explanations that children need properly to contextualize to position what they witness in the media in order to obtain a balanced perspective on the massive media output they observe, controlled by those media conglomerates. If children were taught the kind of critical skills necessary to disambiguate and sort out these messages and images, they would no doubt understand the landscape of their lives with much more aplomb and insight, instead of from the standpoint of fear and acquiescence.

The reader may have noticed that, in the last part of this chapter, I have drawn perspectives from independent films to demonstrate that good, critical information

---

36 See, among others, Michael Kimmel (2013), *Angry White Men*, New York: Nation Books, and Kimmel (2011), *The Guy's Guide to Feminism*, Berkeley, CA: Seal Press.

37 From the trailer of *Tough Guise2: Violence, Manhood & American Culture* (2013), featuring the work of Jackson Katz, recognized for work in critical media literacy, Media Education Foundation.

is available outside of the overwhelming output from the media monopoly. I encourage parents and children to avail themselves of these myriad and diverse perspectives to enhance their understandings of the world and the immediate circumstances of their lives. The results will be, predictably, much more open and astute thinking about these issues. This broadening of ones perspectives may not 'change' much in the short run, but, over time, it will cut into the false media bubble that is constantly being enlarged as long as we do not take charge of our future.

Unfortunately, these days, no matter what the discussion is about, the media monopoly has its hands in it. It permeates our daily experiences and the educational lives of our children. If we do not challenge at every level the kind of coverage of the news and the character of entertainment we now get, we risk being doomed to become, even more than we are already, mere mediocre automatons in a global mechanism of control on every level and of every kind.

The good news is that we do not have to go down that path. Already, we have developed independent outlets, mentioned above, for a critical approach to the daily events and issues that affect our lives. More and more people use 'street-level' means to record what is going on, not to rely on what the evening news will present. The so-called 'social media' can be effective, now available just because we have cell phones, 'smart' phones, to record all aspects of daily life. These have put some of the power of 'telling stories' back in the hands of ordinary people. While overwhelmingly most people have access to these 'little boxes', our children and their children are the ones using them the most. They need to take charge of the goings on in their communities and put pressure on the establishment media to do their job, report in the interest of the public. We, the people, must regain control of 'the media' – 'the press'; this means, we must DE-privatize them and return them to the public domain, the commons and to the people. Until we do, we must (re)establish strict regulations on all owners of the media to operate in the interest of the people instead of in theirs.

Let's teach our children – not only at school, but at home too – to be bold and questioning, to be mindful of who they are and what they should do as members of collectivities of people, not isolated 'individuals', in this global reality. We do not need any more messages from the powerful; we need messages from our children, who will soon be in charge of things, that will dismiss the nonsense and enhance the truth about what life is and how to continue on with courage and dignity.

Bibliography

Arkush, D. (September 8, 2017) "A Storm of Silence: Media Coverage of Climate Change and Hurricane Harvey". Public Citizen. Retrieved from www.citizen.org/system/files/case_documents/public_citizen_storm_of_silence_harvey_climate_coverage_1.pdf

Bagdikian, B. (1983) *The Media Monopoly*. Boston, MA: Beacon Press.

Bagdikian, B. (2004) *The New Media Monopoly*. Boston, MA: Beacon Press.

Berger, J. (1977) *Ways of Seeing*. New York: Penguin Books.

Bernays, E. (1928) *Propaganda*. London: Routledge.

56 Left Behind

Center for Science in the Public Interest Report (March 21, 2013) "Nearly 70% of Food Ads on Nickelodeon are for Junk". Retrieved from https://cspinet.org/new/201303211. html

Common Sense Media (2014) "Advertising to Children and Teens: Current Practices". Retrieved from www.commonsensemedia.org/research/advertising-to-children-and -teens-current-practices

Committee to Protect Journalists. (n.d.) Retrieved from https://cpj.org/

Department of Defense (2010) "Base Structure Report, Fiscal 2010 Baseline". Retrieved from www.acq.osd.mil/eie/Downloads/BSI/Base Structure Report FY15.pdf

Jhally, S. (Producer) & Earp, J. (Director). (2010) *The Mean World Syndrome: Media Violence & the Cultivation of Fear* [Motion Picture].

Goffman, E. (1979) *Gender Advertisements.* Cambridge, MA: Harvard University Press.

Greenwald, G. (2014) *No Place to Hide: Edward Snowden, the NSA, and the U.S. Surveillance State.* New York: Henry Hold and Company.

Harris, J., Bargh, J.A., & Brownell, K.D. (2009) "Priming Effects of Television Food Advertising on Eating Behavior". Health Psychology, volume 28, issue 4, pp. 404–413.

The Henry J. Kaiser Family Foundation Report (March 1, 2007) "Food for Thought: Television Food Advertising to Children in the United States". Retrieved from www. kff.org/other/food-for-thought-television-food-advertising-to/

Herman, E.S., & Chomsky, N. (2002) *Manufacturing Consent: The Political Economy of the Mass Media.* New York: Pantheon.

Jhally, S. (Director), & Kilbourne, J. (Creator/Writer). (2010) *Killing Us Softly 4: Advertising's Image of Women* [Motion Picture]. www.mediaed.org

Jhally, S. (Producer/Director) (2013) *Tough Guise 2: Violence, Manhood & American Culture* [Motion Picture]. www.mediaed.org

Kimmel, M. (2011) *The Guy's Guide to Feminism.* Berkeley, CA: Seal Press.

Kimmel, M. (2013) *Angry White Men.* New York: Nation Books.

Kroll, A. (April 2, 2014) "The Supreme Court Just Gutted Another Campaign Finance Law. Here's What Happened". Mother Jones. Retrieved from www.motherjones.com/ politics/2014/04/supreme-court-mccutcheon-citizens-united/

LeGerrier, R. & Hogan, T.M. (Producers), & Palmer, M. (Director). (2012) *Sext Up Kids: How Children are Becoming Hypersexualized* [Motion Picture]. www.mediaed.org

Liebling, A.J. (May 14, 1960) "Do You Belong in Journalism?" *The New Yorker,* p. 105.

Marx, K. & Engels, F. (1976) *The German Ideology.* Moscow, Russia: Progress.

Paine, T. (1988) *The Age of Reason.* New York: Citadel Press.

Paine, T. (1997) *Common Sense.* New York: Dover Publications, Inc.

Project Censored (n.d.) "Mission Statement". Retrieved from www.projectcensored.org/ the-fair-share-of-the-common-heritage-mission-statement/

Project Censored (n.d.) *Project Censored, The Movie* [Motion Picture]. Retrieved from www. projectcensoredthemovie.com/

Papoutsi, G.S., Drichoutis, A.C., & Nayga, R.M. (2013) "The Causes of Childhood Obesity: A Survey". *Journal of Economic Surveys,* volume 27, issue 4, pp. 743–767.

Scahill, J. (2007) *Blackwater: The Rise of the World's Most Powerful Mercenary Army.* New York: Nation Books.

Scahill, J. (2014) *Dirty Wars: The World is a Battlefield.* New York: Nation Books.

U.S. Supreme Court (January, 2010) *Citizens United v. Federal Election Commission.* Retrieved from www.supremecourt.gov/opinions/09pdf/08-205.pdf

U.S. Supreme Court (October, 2013) *McCutcheon v. Federal Election Commission.* Retrieved from www.supremecourt.gov/opinions/13pdf/12-536_e1pf.pdf

Wells-Barnett, I.B. (2014) *On Lynchings.* Mineola, NY: Dover Publications, Inc.

3

THE BUSINESS MODEL

In our dream we have limitless resources, and the people yield themselves with perfect docility to our molding hand. The present educational conventions fade from our minds; and, unhampered by tradition, we work our own good will upon a grateful and responsive rural folk. We shall not try to make these people or any of their children into philosophers or men of learning or of science. We are not to raise up among them authors, orators, poets, or men of letters. We shall not search for embryo great artists, painters, musicians. Nor will we cherish even the humbler ambition to raise up from among them lawyers, doctors, preachers, statesmen, of whom we now have ample supply.[1]

– Frederick T. Gates

In general, the 'business model' has to do with schooling our children in ways that are amenable to the existing business climate. According to this model, so shamelessly expressed by Gate above, our children should be taught to behave and to follow the lead of their teachers, who are, in turn, following the instructions of the business elite. The idea is that, once released from the vagaries of such 'education', those graduates will have been schooled sufficiently to satisfy the needs of industry, not necessarily to satisfy their aspirations. As John Taylor Gatto asserts, "Schools are to establish fixed habits of response to authority. That is why it takes twelve years. You are to respond reflexively when anyone in a position of authority tells you what to do."[2] George Carlin also had some thoughts on this subject:

---

1 Frederick T. Gates "The Country School of Tomorrow" Occasional Papers No. 1, (New York General Education Board, 1913, p. 6). The Reverend Gates was a business advisor to John D. Rockefeller, Sr., who founded the 'General Education Board', whose philosophy was to organize children and create reliable, predictable, obedient citizens. Along with the Carnegies and Vanderbilts, Rockefeller molded society by molding children's education.

2 Cameo appearance by John Gatto in the documentary, *Thrive: What on Earth Will It Take*, by

58 Left Behind

> The big, wealthy business interests don't want well informed, well educated people, capable of critical thinking. That is against their interests. They want obedient workers, people who are just smart enough to run the machine and do the paperwork; and just dumb enough to passively accept all these increasingly shittier jobs with the lower pay, the longer hours, reduced benefits, the end of overtime and the vanishing pension that disappears the minute you go to collect it.[3]

One of the most disturbing observations across the spectrum of public education is the continued adherence to, in varying manifestations, the 'business model'. I take this to mean that schools K-12, colleges and universities are operating according to principles held by businesses, like market competition and the 'profit motive'. This may not be news to the critical reader; that is, I take it that we have known for some time now that education has become couched more and more in a 'transactional' context. What this means is that education is being *paid for* more and more. At the university level, tuition has dominated education there; and, with the recent installation of Betsy DeVos as Secretary of Education, we are likely to witness the use of public funds to pay for privately owned schools in the form of charters, vouchers and religious schools. This model is right out of the playbook of corporate aspirations to control public funds for education. In concert with this reality are some school administration attitudes, which emulate a corporate mentality, whose administrators aspire to sharing in the disbursement of these 'public' funds in their 'private' contexts. This merging of the minds is problematic. Because this *modus operandi* is something that people are quite familiar with these days, I shall not dwell upon these more obvious conditions under which the education of our children is conducted. Instead, I shall discuss some other less obvious trends, which also build upon this overall attitude. I shall address three areas of concern: architecture, language, and business partnerships and their political agenda. I shall explicate their character and demonstrate how aspects of a business mentality collide with the academic principles with which they claim to be in harmony and support.

Stephen Gagné and Kimberly Carter Gamble (2011). For more detailed insights, see Gatto's book, *The Underground History of American Education: A School Teacher's Intimate Investigation into the Problem of Modern Schooling* (2000) New York: Odysseus Group. There is nothing new about this attitude: the "Robber Barons" of the late 19th and early 20th centuries were very clear about this. Part of the mission of the National Education Association (not the current NEA) established by J.D. Rockefeller, with the Carnegie and Ford Foundations, expressed in various statements the following sentiment: that schools should deliver an obedient and docile workforce, manageable employees and eager consumers.

3 The late George Carlin's (2005) HBO comedy special *"Life Is Worth Losing"*.

Architecture

This may seem like a strange topic to address in the present discussion. I am not a traditionalist as you might have already gleaned; however, there are certain cultural trends that have emerged that manifest visually, implying certain ideas and attitudes which I cannot ignore. One such trend has been the changes in architecture for schools, the styles of the buildings that house institutions of learning. In days gone by, these buildings lent a sense of awe and wonder about the learning and research that went on inside. They were not all the same, strictly speaking, but they created a sense that what was going on in them was very particular and almost organic. These structures were most often built of red brick or limestone, covered with ivy and surrounded by well-kept grounds. When the lights shone at night through those magnificent windows, some stained glass, some just massive, what came to mind was an image of students bent over those tables in the library, studying the history of the world, contemplating the problems of the times and gleaning insight into how to solve those problems, generating a kind of solace about the future and what could become of us as a species. My nostalgia is not misplaced; such images and iconic representations are culturally organized, and have become part of what we understand about the countenance of educational institutions.

Some of the buildings that are erected today (and for some time now) destined to be schools do not have that kind of warmth. They are fashioned of steel and glass and no longer present as buildings of education and learning. They exhibit an aura more akin to the sterile, utilitarian presentation of corporate offices and board rooms. The people who populate such structures wear suits and shiny shoes, not the garb of students and their teachers. Even though campuses are generally clean, they are still energized with the hustle and bustle of students, staff and teachers coming and going. Education itself is a messy endeavor, and rightly so, presumably in the throes of interested students investigating this or that subject matter, whether language, science, art, *etc.*, or, in higher education, sorting out this or that theory or methodology or analytical approach to the many problems of the day.

Critics of this view could say that the buildings and their artistic expression are really insignificant in the sense that the buildings are not the institution; it's what goes on inside that counts. While that may be strictly true, the character of the surroundings is still important. Take, for example, edifices of worship. Can you imagine building one, even though more modern, without a significant attempt to preserve most of the identifiable components of what churches and temples and mosques look like? (They are not all the same; but they all display at least some of the iconic signposts of their histories and beliefs.) Do we not expect the limestone, the stained glass windows, the steeple, the cross or star or crescent at the peak, the Buddha, the minarets, the bell, the massive cathedral ceilings and, above all, a space that inspires those who frequent it, with benches or without? Attempts have been made by some contemporary architects to 'modernize' the appearance of these 'houses of worship'; but they cannot stray from those fundamental elements

60 Left Behind

of the structure without risking part of what makes those buildings what they are expected to be by the 'worshipers'.

For those who are religious, aren't these characteristics important with regard to their experience as practitioners? Is not part of living a religious life a matter of taking in the iconic representations of that particular religion? Is not part of the interest in subscribing to a particular religion visiting the places which connect to its history, entering those places to get closer to some of the pivotal moments of that religion? For example, doing the Hajj to Mecca for Muslims, doing a pilgrimage to Lourdes or Fatima for Catholics, praying at the "Wailing Wall" for Jews, or visiting Jerusalem for Muslims, Christians and Jews – all are manifestations of recognition of the physical components (artifacts) of faith and belief. This is true for all organized religions. Isn't there an expectation that those faraway relics should have local, physical representation too?

In the case of schools, do we not have certain expectations about what the physical plant should look like? Sure we do. Aside from the upkeep of the building, which we also want to see is up to par, we look for the welcoming qualities, those features which invite us in to partake in the learning experience ahead for ourselves or our children. We look for some sort of common sense integration between the structures of education and the promise that can and should be indicated in the organization of that space.

Choosing a college or university, while quite daunting in many ways, does still have to do with what the place looks like. Do you feel safe? Do the environs create a sense of community that is so central to the routines of educational life? Does it give you a sense of welcoming, taking you into its halls and classrooms where you hope to learn about the world and yourself? Maybe even being inspired by those luminaries who attended that particular institution, whose life work contributed significantly to this or that part of history? I know that, when I attended Boston University, I was inspired by the Reverend Dr. Martin Luther King, Jr., an *alumnus*, not because of his religious beliefs, but because of my respect for his contribution to the world.[4] There is a memorial in Dr. King's honor in front of Marsh Chapel and the College of Theology there. I remember walking by that piece of art, by Chilean sculptor Sergio Castillo, who named it "Free at Last", inspired by MLK's "I Have A Dream" speech. Through this symbol, I became connected to him, spanning time and space. Now the buildings of Boston University are in 'the city' and have limited space for sprawling lawns, like at Boston College. However, as you pass by the center of the campus, you are aware of the change in architecture

---

4 I had participated in 'sympathy' marches in March 1965, when protesters in Alabama marched from Selma to Montgomery – "Bloody Sunday" at the Edmund Pettus Bridge on the 7th until finally reaching Montgomery on the 25th. I thank my high school teachers for bringing the importance of these events to our attention and for leading us in those marches throughout the early sixties during the Civil Rights Movement and the Anti-Vietnam War protests.

The business model **61**

and recognize elements that set them apart from the buildings you passed two blocks before, whose character was not that of a school of any kind.[5]

In the early '70s, I attended the University of South Florida, taking a course or two while I worked. I remember that those buildings, typically housing the departments of this or that discipline – the humanities here, the life sciences there, the languages here and the social sciences there. All those buildings were 'modern' in character; but they were all designed to fit the grounds and the disciplines they housed. Some thought went into that architecture and the result maintained the sense that what went on there had to do with education and not business. That is what I am trying to address here. Using glass and metal does not necessarily mean that the outcome will elicit from someone the kind of sterile ambiance I mentioned above; it depends upon how those materials come together in context. There could very well be some significant benefits to using glass construction on the southern elevation of a building to take advantage of the 'green house effect' from the sun; however, doing so should not be at the expense of the fundamental concept advanced here that schools should look like schools and not like malls or office buildings or sports facilities.[6]

Indeed, some architecture can be downright 'futuristic' and still preserve a sense that, within these walls, learning takes place. Take the work of Jacque Fresco, architect/futurist. His buildings are not at all 'traditional' by any stretch; however, he manages to capture the spirit of what takes place in those buildings, whether residences, businesses, schools, houses of worship, *etc*. He understands the relationship between what people do and where they do it.[7]

For kindergarteners, spatial considerations are often foremost in the minds of parents and guardians. They want their children to feel like they are going to school as opposed to going to the mall or to worship or to work with them. The actual 'looks' of the physical plant are not the only concern for them; the building must be safe and the play yard must be fenced in. (Some of these parameters are already part of the local building codes these days.) The overall sense is that the program of activities should be isolated from the public while 'class is in session' and protected from the 'outside' world. These features of the kindergarten setting all contribute to the experience that the children who attend that school will have. These matters are not incidental either. They are planned from the very beginning, a proposal having been submitted to establish such a school, satisfying all appropriate codes,

---

5 To be fair, Boston University has many buildings, which do not 'look like' school buildings; however, they were acquired along the way as the school expanded. The original buildings do have that 'school' countenance.

6 In no way is the argument here suggesting that new ideas in architecture should be abandoned in favor of 'the way schools used to look like'. On the contrary, architectural innovations are inevitable and welcomed, but they should reflect the cultural conventions that intersect with the expectations we have about educational institutions.

7 I encourage the reader to visit Fresco's website and/or view the documentary about his work to see what I mean. The film: *Future by Design* (2006) Director/Writer William Gazecki, Open Edge Production Company; see The Venus Project: Beyond Politics Poverty and War, www.thevenusproject.com.

etc., and according to the needs of the educational professionals who will organize and operate that school. In no case will you find such educators ignoring the general parameters of how the school will look to the children.

These are not frivolous considerations; on the contrary, these visual parameters have become iconic for us, not only for schools, but for all kinds of contemporary cultural artifacts, *e.g.*, town halls, hospitals, cinemas, supermarkets, malls, prisons, fast-food chains, *etc.* In fact, people often give directions using these familiar structures: "go straight down here until you get to the town hall, then left until you see the cinema on your right across from the mosque, three hundred yards more on the left by the entrance to the mall". If these structures were not so familiar to us, they would not be relied upon to do the work of giving directions in everyday life. If we went to school in a building that looked like a residence, the education therein could be as engaging as if we took classes in the iconic buildings of Harvard or Boston College or Bard College. So, the point is not that education cannot take place in buildings that are unconventional. The point is that changing the visual impact of what schools look like can give rise to different expectations about what can go on in them. If the building looks like the corporate headquarters of some business, then the sense that business goes on in that building would not be misplaced. The reality is that much of what comprises university activities is more and more infiltrated by business and corporate concerns (more on this presently below). Schools are much more than the buildings that house them, but, without these recognizable structural characteristics, the experience students would have in them would be changed, distorted and fall short of our conventions about the whole educational package.[8]

The matter at hand here is that new schools are sometimes built in a 'corporate/business' style. That is, the visual impact that the buildings have is one that is commensurate with ones that typically house corporate headquarters or places of business. Aesthetically speaking, to each his/her own, but, in my view, the building suggests a corporate/business environment, not an educational one. In the last analysis, I offer to the reader the idea that even the architecture of our schools affect our 'ways of seeing' what our educational institutions are up to; the expectations we have of them: "Is the education taking place in those 'corporate looking' buildings about the critical education we expect or about the indoctrination of our children to the 'business model'"? The latter emphasizes transactional relationships; the former engenders more far-reaching principles of human understanding, forging the critical skills to address local and global problems and to develop social structures for peace and longevity.

---

8 One example is the downtown building which houses the Stamford Campus of the University of Connecticut. The building is very impressive – made of steel and glass – but does not look like a school in the way that I discuss here. It looks like a business location; commensurate with my claim, it houses a successful MBA Program there, while the College of Liberal Arts and Sciences has struggled over the last 30 years.

The 'customer' hyperbole

To expand upon the previous discussion, I continue here to address how it is we describe the fundamental components of the educational experience. How we talk about them, the ways in which we refer to them or categorize them is important. When we categorize people, places and things, we invoke the concept that we are using to describe them. That means that, when we use a descriptor, a word, a category, we are calling into play the concept that accompanies that category. At the conceptual level, there are rules that must be applied according to the context we are in. In order to understand, to achieve meaning from anything, the context in which it is experienced is the most indispensable component. We have a tacit knowledge,[9] common sense knowledge, of these rules, part of which is the 'logical geography of concepts'.[10] While Ryle's introduction of this construct seems somewhat technical, we can glean how he connected the use of concepts with their contextual parameters:

> To determine the *logical geography of concepts* [italics added] is to reveal the logic of the propositions in which they are wielded, that is to say, to show with what other propositions they are consistent and inconsistent, what propositions follow from them and from what propositions they follow. The logical type or category to which a concept belongs is the set of ways in which it is logically legitimate to operate with it.[11]

In less technical language, all concepts contain, at their logical base, a set of essential properties, which characterize their grammatical 'geography', allowing for their differentiation, thereby logically connecting those properties with the proper use of categories of description in specific contexts in everyday parlance. We, as users of language in our cultural settings, have a tacit knowledge of these 'properties' (that is, we have acquired them, but we are not necessarily wittingly aware of what they are), allowing us to apply correctly this or that concept in different contexts. Some of this is acquired through 'trial and error' (especially early on, we will make mistakes in our descriptive competence), giving rise to the opportunity to 'learn' the differences among different categories and their use, once we have become

---

9 Tacit knowledge refers to that knowledge we have absorbed during language acquisition, largely in the first two years of life, but throughout the socialization process, which continues our whole lives. As we acquired the words of the language of our culture, we also absorbed the essence of those words and the rules of proper application in the real contexts we encounter in everyday life. See the work of the social phenomenologist Alfred Schutz (1967) *The Phenomenology of the Social World*, Evanston, IL: Northwestern University Press.

10 Ryle was a colleague of Ludwig Wittgenstein's, the preeminent 'analytic, ordinary language' philosopher, the most renowned member to the Vienna Circle of the 1950s. He advanced the discussion of the logic of concepts and its interaction with the actual, everyday 'use of concepts' by cultural members. See Gilbert Ryle (1963) *The Concept of Mind*, London: Huchinson & Co.

11 *Ibid.*, p. 8.

64 Left Behind

linguistic (able to talk). As a result, we are able to use the correct category to describe some phenomenon in a specific context. Of course, we may, on occasion, apply an 'incorrect', 'inconsistent' category; however, the recognition of the error will rely upon the interface between the category used and the actual parameters of the context at hand. Corrections of such usage typically follow. In other words, when we make mistakes in category selection, we are not 'confused' about how to categorize our world; we simply correct them.

For example, if I take two chairs that have been mass produced to certain dimensions and characteristics, I can say of them that they are 'the same'. I do not mean 'identical' in every way; there may not be any such thing, except in mathematics. I mean that, for all practical purposes, these two chairs are the same – their shape, how many legs they have, their color, *etc*. On the other hand, if I take two chairs crafted by two different furniture makers which display other interpretations of the concept of 'chair' and whose physical appearance (number of legs, whether they have arms, whether they lean back or swivel) is different, I can say of them that they are 'similar', not 'the same'. They are both 'chairs', but different from each other. In other words, we use the categories, the terms, that correctly describe them as chairs, but describe them according to the essential characteristics which correspond to the logical properties of the concepts – 'same' or 'similar'.

As competent members of the culture, we manage this practice without notice and without difficulty. We do not have a list of the logical properties of every concept we come to use in our everyday encounters. The 'intuition' in the language we enjoy is what is responsible for this ability. With very few exceptions (physical challenges that interfere with that acquisition, *e.g.,* hearing impairments, brain damage, accidents, unusual social deprivations), all of us develop these abilities with little to no effort and use them all our lives.

Let us move to the subject at hand, one of the most fundamental concepts in education: the concept of 'student'. I ask the reader to observe that there is a difference between a *concept* and its *category*, which bears the same name. For example, based upon the discussion above, which 'logical properties' belong to the concept 'student'? Without much ado, I am confident that all of us, as members of our culture (and, actually, I would expect, cross-culturally as well), will be able to describe what kind of essential properties, characteristics such a person would be observed/expected to have, *e.g.,* activities, engagements or practices. There are no 'intrinsic' properties that we can observe (as in the case of the chairs in the example above), just by looking at a person who is a student, that is different from any other person, *i.e.,* one cannot glean directly which category of person someone belongs to (save uniforms or other insignia that provide that information). Rather, we can identify the category of person someone belongs to by what they do, who they are with, where they are, that is, their contextual information (these are different kinds of properties). 'Students' go to school; that is, they attend classes, listen to teachers present educational materials, interact with other students, discuss a myriad of topics, do homework, play scholastic sports, go on field trips, take examinations, *etc*. They are *learners*; that is, their daily 'job' is to undertake courses of instruction with qualified teachers. These are the kinds of activities they engage in routinely as members of that *category of persons*. Further, these categories of activities are said to be "category-related",[12] that is, they are related to the category of persons 'student'. In other words, it is the activities that students engage in that allow us to identify them as 'students'. When they cease to do those activities, they are open to recategorization, such as 'son'/'daughter', 'worker', 'soccer player', 'brother'/'sister' and so on, due to the recontextualization. Furthermore, recognizing what/who a 'student' is does not require any specialized knowledge on the part of ordinary members of the culture, only some exposure to that culture sufficient to make the logical connections between what people do and how we categorize them.

As this is such a common sense and routine achievement on the part of virtually everybody in any culture – that is, no one is confused or bemused when someone uses the category 'student' to refer to someone who is going to school, *etc.* (and I assert that this is unproblematic) – how curious to discover that some colleges and universities have performed a 'categorial transformation' by referring to 'students' as 'customers'. What does it mean to do this? What could the purpose be for such a transformation? Let us take a closer look at the category 'customer'. What could the logical properties of this concept be? Again, without any confusion at all, the accustomed member of our culture will provide an answer to this query of the following kind: a 'customer' refers to someone who engages in activities having to do with commerce, specifically having to do with buying objects or services within the economy. So, the context for such a person is most different from that of a 'student'. Customers 'go to stores' or on the internet to 'purchase goods' and 'hire services' from others who provide them; these activities are 'category-related' to the category 'customer'. The activity of 'going to school' is not included in the list of activities for the category 'customer'. Changing the category 'student' to the category 'customer' implies that students 'buy' education. Students do not *buy* education; at least, the logical properties of 'student' do not include such an activity.[13] But wait! Do not students pay for education in the United States, at least post-secondary education? Sure. They pay plenty, for tuition. (Which was not always the case; early on, public institutions were 'free', paid for through 'land grants' to residents of that state or commonwealth.[14]) Paying tuition is what gives rise to this misapplication of the concept. If, based upon this fact – that students pay tuition – one can categorize 'students' as 'customers', the very nature of being a 'student' is distorted beyond recognition. If students are forced to pay tuition to attend college/university – and they are in the United States – then, their

---

12 Harvey Sacks (1974) "On the Analyzability of Stories by Children", a classic analysis of the workings of categorization practices, in Roy Turner, *Ethnomethodology*, New York: Penguin Press.
13 Schools are not the only institutions in which the category 'customer' has been assigned: in many social services, such as the care for mentally-challenged people; they too are referred to as 'customers' as opposed to 'clients'.
14 See Chapter 4 on a political economy of education.

relationship with the educational institution changes along with the change in their assigned category.[15]

Changing the way students are categorized changes their relationship to the university: they now are placed into a distorted transactional relationship, in which they are seen as being paying 'customers' instead of 'students' who are attending classes, thereby reifying education into a commodity that is understood as being purchased by students. So, with that logic, students actually *become* 'customers'. The logic is clear, but it is an artificial logic, a distorted logic, which strips away the real relationship that students have with educational institutions. When students are required to pay for education, one could propose that they are paying for access to classrooms and other facilities and services, but not 'education' as such. They are not paying teachers to instruct them; teacher salaries are paid by tax revenue.

As soon as one introduces the element of money into the mix, the tendency is to change the relations that exist in that context. Any understanding of the relationship between students and teachers/schools should never be couched in terms of money and reduced to the monetary exchange for a service. Alas, that is what has emerged over the last 40 to 50 years, this erosion from a tax-based education to a tuition-based education.

These days, public colleges and universities are operated like businesses, not educational institutions. So, the current linguistic dilemma is almost expected. That is, the business model has become so entrenched in the mindset of ordinary people that it is not surprising that this is the perceived character of the relationship between people who go to school and the schools they go to.

This state of affairs has given rise to some discussion in the academic community and in the media. Articles, opinion pieces and letters to the editor have been published over the last few years which have raised this issue. One position expressed, by Professor Thirunarayanan at Florida International University,[16] was that students are indeed 'customers' because they pay tuition. As 'customers', they should be treated, in many ways, better than they are. As students, however, they do not 'pay' for their education, they still 'earn' it. While this distinction can be understood as 'technically' correct, on a practical level, if students fail to pay all fees the university expects from them, their degree, the accepted evidence for having completed a B.A., B.S., M.A., Ph.D., *etc.*, will be held back until those fees are paid, which emphasizes the customer side of this rather false relationship. In other words, the category 'customer' is the one that counts in the end, not the category 'student'. If students are 'customers', then what is 'school'? Does not that construct change too? What is the difference between the responsibilities of a school to students and

---

15 Consider Senator Bernie Sanders' proposal that all public education should be tuition-free. This is the direction we should be traveling. However, with Betsy DeVos as Secretary of Education, those prospects may evaporate.

16 M.O. Thirunarayanan (January 6, 2012) Letter to the Editor, entitled "Students Are 'Customers,' but Not in the Classroom", *The Chronicle of Higher Education.*

those of a business to customers? Businesses are expected to deliver quality goods and services, however, they are engaged in those businesses to generate profit, not to ensure that their customers are of sound mind and body, safe and happy. Contrastively, the mission of schools is to provide educational services to our children, without regard to any 'profit-making'.

The preoccupation of referring to students as 'customers', while based upon an artificial logic, lays waste to the notion that degrees are 'earned' instead of bought and paid for. To be clear, categorizing students as 'customers' does not verify that students are 'customers', it only provides insight into the logic for the incumbency of that category and the logical consequences for its use. That logic provides the legitimization for charging tuition to students by changing the way they are categorized. It is a corrosion of the very ideas of school and learning.[17]

A very closely related theme became the subject of a study,[18] in which the question of 'entitlement' on the part of students was investigated. If students 'pay' for their education, then they are entitled to their degrees, through the transactional context that 'paying for something' invokes, regardless of the intervening complexities of the educational experience. I have encountered this attitude over the years from students who have consumed and digested the notion that they pay the salaries of their professors and for "their education" and, as such, are empowered to *demand* their "good" grades and their degrees. Professor Thirunarayan was correct about students having to "earn" their degrees; however, that should never take place in the context of money changing hands.

However, this does not go to the heart of the matter. The whole idea that education should be in any way a reflection of the 'market economy', itself a distorted system of profit and greed, begs for an even more distorted version of what education constitutes. We know that the economic institution in any society is most influential in all respects. However, the distorted influence that the profit motive has had, and is having, upon education has generated a most disturbing set of problems, mostly emanating from the idea that schools of all kinds must conduct themselves as corporations do, following the same kinds of directives, undertaking daily educational activities accordingly and subscribing to the ideological mindset that goes along with it: profit. Teachers are supposed to create contexts of collective learning without 'selling' or 'pushing' or 'peddling' anything. Subscribing to a business frame of reference to understand who students are constructs a distorted caricature of the relationship they have with their teachers and professors and the institutions themselves. As long as school policies

---

17 This has given rise to 'online' colleges and universities; people pay their money and they get a degree. To be fair, I am not arguing that those people don't learn anything; I am suggesting that it emphasizes the 'transactional' relationship, not the educational one. See Chapter 7 on the teaching profession.

18 Stephany Schings (n.d.) "Are Students Customers of Their Universities?" Society for Industrial and Organizational Psychology (Division 14 of the American Psychological Association and Organizational Affiliate of the Association for Psychological Science); see www.siop.org.

muddy the waters of the true commitments of the educational partners in this way, students and parents will be inclined to view education as part of the 'consumer' mentality we in the United States are so fond of and place above so many other considerations. In other words, the relationship between teachers and students is not one of 'exchange' in the economic sense; it is supposed to be one of nurturing, guidance and cooperation.

If the economic activities of our society were to change to be in harmony with the fundamental forces of being human, which embrace cooperation and sharing among all parties to those activities rather than the exploitation of labor and the expropriation of the fruits of those activities, then we might be able to see how education really benefits everybody and not just the individual who attends school. Rather than thinking that individual children benefit from education, we would understand that educating our children is a collective insurance for the future. The combined knowledge of our children gained through education is not 'bought' or 'paid for' or 'owned' by the individual; it is provided for by the society. It becomes embodied in them, who then implement what they have learned for the benefit of the whole society. Participating in economic activities which enfold these principles reflect upon the other institutions, including education. They allow us to realize that no one should have to pay for this essential component of society, without which society itself would wither and die. Our children's education is an investment, but not one from which we should expect 'profits', in the economic sense. The 'profit' is realized in the social benefits that arise out of solid, critical education.

So, students are not customers; they need guidance to understand the past, energize the present and forge the future. Education is a requisite cultural form, provided by those of us who came before them and who must rely on the knowledge, the insights and the wits of our past and who must guarantee the proper transmission thereof to the next generation. There is no price one can accord such a necessary set of requirements. Education that is unencumbered by economic and political pressures can be preserved as one of the most essential parts of the commons.

Corporate relationships and the *quid pro quo*

School administrators, teachers and students seek out and engage in 'partnerships' (the preferred euphemism these days) with local and national corporations to help fund this or that physical plant construction, new program, 'community' project, specific research, *etc.* Cooperation as such between universities and non-educational institutions is not at issue here. What *is* at issue is the character of that 'cooperation'. Admittedly, because of the paucity of financial support that education has in the first place (and, if education were properly funded, schools might not be so predisposed to 'take' corporate money), these partnerships are often a means to raise money for the developments schools presumably could not otherwise enjoy. To the extent that those projects are realized, the schools are better for them. Or are they? The funds are not necessarily offered as a totally altruistic expression of

The business model **69**

support for those projects, for the benefit of students, teachers and the community. Whenever that happens, it is most appropriate and acceptable. However, often, something else is going on.

As the concept of 'partnership' holds in its set of logical properties, there is something to be gained by both sides: not only the school but the corporation too. What could that be? As I alluded to earlier, some contributions/partnerships could be *bona fide* and *pro bono* in that the contributors are helping 'in the common good'; namely, that funding education in whatever way can only benefit the town/city, the state and society at large. This is laudable and desirable. However, this is not always the motivation.

In the case of construction funds, the school dedicates a room or a hall or a special high-tech facility in the name of the corporation, thereby creating the impression that corporation X is on board with the mission of the school and is being a 'good community citizen' by 'donating' monies to this or that 'public' institution. Part of the result of this 'giving' is that corporations can be seen as caring about something other than their bottom line, profits for their stock holders and supporting the community (not to mention the substantial tax break they receive for their 'generosity'). This seems fair enough if that was all that was going on, until the CEO of the corporation contacts the college president to 'request' some space on the university premises to hold a business meeting or conference, for free of course. On the face of it, this seems reasonable. A gesture of this kind by the university would demonstrate, on its part, that it appreciates the original 'donation' and that it supports local business activities and projects. This actually could be seen as fair and, in some settings, desirable, but this is the minimalist scenario.

Sometimes projects are named after corporations when whole additions are built onto existing school buildings. What this essentially amounts to is a significant savings on the part of the corporation to establish some lab or working space, for which they may have otherwise had to erect a whole building. Yes, they paid for that section of the building, but they are also using it for their exclusive purposes (sometimes that space is shared with the university community), free – no rent, no heating or electric bill! They even install special access systems to keep others out; this on public university property? *Cui bono?* As already expressed, both sides of the 'partnership' benefit; that is, without the funding from the corporation, the new building or addition may not have been realized. However, the college actually relinquished the space to the corporation for its sole use. Where is the partnership there? Is the university to benefit by the fact that the corporation has its name posted all over the place? Or, will the 'prestige' of the corporation attract students or faculty onto the premises? Maybe that's it! Maybe the whole point of the 'partnership' was/is to establish some kind of credibility with that corporation (and maybe others) to instill in the minds researchers broadly speaking that, with the support of this or that corporation, they may have an 'in' with it and move to this or that research and development opportunity. This arguably contributes to the

70 Left Behind

movement toward business-oriented aspirations.[19] Or, maybe the point is to create a veneer of respectability for the corporation. These are matters worth serious consideration. However the reader views these relationships, they can give rise to real dangers when contemplating their effects upon our educational institutions and children.

Corporate funding for research

We all know that much of the research done by faculty in universities is done at the behest of and through corporate grants. When faculty members are attracted to this or that university as a result of the grants provided by a corporation, conducted in their space, what kinds of findings should we expect to see come out of that research? Let us not be naïve. Corporations, under the guise of supporting higher education, move into university space, because they funded it, and conduct their business, employing faculty members, to do the research for their projects, product development, *etc.*

There is a belief that private universities can choose to do this because there is not even a perceived conflict of interest: all funds to the university are 'private', thereby not violating any public trust. No so fast! Maybe, maybe not. The formation of such 'trusts' inevitably result in advantages for the businesses involved. They could also benefit that university. However, they can also compromise the mission of the educational institution and raise questions about the viability of the programs not directly connected to the corporate grants they receive. Furthermore, the use of faculty in universities to do research and development, say in the pharmaceutical industry, compromises the integrity of those university programs, when the findings of that research and development favors the corporations that funded it, only in part; the other part is provided for by the university. The corporations reap the profits, but do the universities? Do those corporations write checks to those educational institutions?

In the case of 'public' institutions taking grants of this kind, again, there is a clear perceived conflict of interest between the goals of the school and those of the corporation. Still, public colleges routinely take 'grant' money from corporations of all kinds. This is a huge mistake! Private money should not enter a public institution for several reasons, some of which have been explicated here. Public education should stay public and not be subservient to the goals of private interests.

I have presented three major areas in which problems arise when business influence enters the educational arena. While I do not expect that these pressures will relent by themselves, I do hope that, by becoming aware of their influence and

19 To be clear, I am not against the establishment of 'businesses' as such. I support the cooperative structures of 'business': that shared ownership of the business and the shared returns of that business among its owners. Businesses of the kind that are corporations are not like that; and, as such, should not 'partner' in this way with public colleges and universities.

effects, more people will act toward reestablishing the proper separation between the corporate world and our public universities.

Bibliography

Carlin, G. (Writer). (2005) *Life Is Worth Losing* [Motion Picture].
Gates, F.T. (1913) "The Country School of Tomorrow". New York General Education Board. Occasional Papers, No. 1, p. 6.
Gagné, S. & Gamble, K.C. (Directors). (2011) *Thrive: What on Earth Will It Take* [Motion Picture].
Gatto J.T. (2000) *The Underground History of American Education: A School Teacher's Intimate Investigation into the Problem of Modern Schooling*. New York: Odysseus Group.
Gazecki, W. (Director/Writer). (2006) *Future by Design* [Motion Picture].
Schutz, A. (1967) *The Phenomenology of the Social World*. Evanston, IL: Northwestern University Press.
Ryle, G. (1963) *The Concept of Mind*. London: Huchinson & CO.
Sacks, H. (1974) "On the Analyzability of Stories by Children", in R. Turner, *Ethnomethodology*. New York: Penguin Press.
Thirunarayanan, M.O. (January 6, 2012) "Students Are 'Customers,' but Not in the Classroom". Letter to the Editor. *The Chronicle of Higher Education*. Retrieved from www.chronicle.com/article/students-are-customers-but/130254
Schings, S. (n.d.) "Are Students Customers of Their Universities?" *Society for Industrial and Organizational Psychology*. Retrieved from www.siop.org/Media/News/customers.aspx

4

A POLITICAL ECONOMY OF EDUCATION

> The law locks up both man and woman who steals the goose from off the common, but lets the greater felon loose who steals the common from the goose.
>
> — Edward Potts Cheyney (1861–1947)[1]

A comprehensive discussion of the political economy of anything is a massively complex undertaking. A whole volume would be necessary to do justice to *the* political economy of education. This is not possible for the present investigation. However, some discussion here allows us to understand some of the connections between political and economic parameters that influence the reality of education in the United States. Consider the following connections.

The 'commons'

The concept of 'the common'[2] is very old. It first had a central place in public discourse more than 800 years ago, made popular by the signing of the *Magna Carta*

---

1 Edward Potts Cheyney (1901) *An Introduction to the Industrial and Social History of England*, (reported as doggerel from the time of the fencing of the commons). The "time" (mid-1700 to mid-1800) was during England's 'Enclosure Movement' at the end of feudal relations and the beginning of capitalist relations of production. This saying was brought to my attention by Peter Linebaugh in an interview conducted by Mike McCormick on program "Community Forum", Seattle channel 77, March 19, 2009. See Peter Linbaugh (2008), *Magna Carta Manifesto: Liberties and Commons for All*, Berkeley and Los Angeles: University of California Press. A slightly different version of this loosely written verse, "The fault is great in man or woman who steals a goose from off a common; but what can plead that man's excuse who steals a common from a goose?" was published during the purging of people from the land, in *The Tickler Magazine*, February 1, 1821.

2 In the singular or plural, "the common" and "the commons" refer(s) to the same concept: that

(June 15, 1215). The *Magna Carta Libertatum*[3] ("the Great Charter of the Liberties") was an agreement, a document of peace, a treaty, between the common people of England and King John, signed at Runnymede, near Windsor. Authorship of the Charter is unclear, but is attributed mainly to the Archbishop of Canterbury at the time, Stephen Langton. This was accomplished amid complicated struggles among the Archbishop, the Barons and Pope Innocent III in Rome. That signing, however, was soon revoked by the Pope, as the Crusades continued. It was not until September 11, 1217, with the signing of the *Great Charter of the Forest*, that commitment to the principles of the *Magna Carta* was revitalized. The two Charters were 'published' (*viva voce*, first in Latin and later in the vulgates: English and French).

The *Magna Carta* truce addressed this most fundamental condition: the relationship between the common people, who had grown tired of land relations under feudal rule, and the monarchy. The *Charter of the Forest*, signed by King Henry III, King John's 10-year old son, acting under the tutelage of William Marshal, 1st Earl of Pembroke, also recognized that common people had common rights. It proclaimed that common people were to be guaranteed access to the commons of the forest – to forage for berries and nuts, but predominantly for the wood to build housing, to repair farming tools and, most importantly, to burn as a source of heat. According to Peter Linebaugh, "Certainly, they [commoners] are represented in it, very powerfully in Chapter 7 of *Magna Carta* [Chapter 9 in the *Great Charter of the Forest*], which grants to the widow her reasonable estovers in the common, where 'estovers' means subsistence access to wood"[4]. For centuries, the commons were preserved for the people; they had the right to appropriate the bounty of the forest, because it was considered to be public and common to all to assure them their subsistence, even though some of it was actually owned by the rich – until the rupture of feudalism and its replacement by capitalism. That is when the new class system replaced the caste system, enclosing common people from the land and the forest, rights that had been secured for them by the *Magna Carta* and the *Great Charter of the Forest*.

The separation of the peasants from the land was a direct violation of the *Magna*

---

which should be accessible to everyone (commoners), regardless of ownership relations, e.g., water, forests, *etc.*

3 Perhaps the most salient component, for modern times, of this Charter was the contents of Chapter 39, in which were outlined principles, which foreshadowed some of the text of the United States Declaration of Independence, and later, of the United States Constitution in the Bill of Rights, most notably the Fourth and Fifth Amendments. However, "There are important differences between Magna Carta and the Declaration of Independence. The purpose of the declaration is to justify the powers of the state that relate to war, peace, alliances and commerce. The purpose of the Magna Carta is to curtail the powers of the sovereign. Magna Carta put an end to a war; the Declaration of Independence intended to win allies and stiffen the resolve of soldiers to fight ... Magna Carta is a document of reparations ... whereas the Declaration is a document of acquisition." *Op. cit.*, Linebaugh, p. 124.

4 *Op. cit.*, McCormick interview of Linebaugh.

Carta and the *Great Charter of the Forest*. Precipitated by the 'Enclosure Movement' in England, also experienced in France and other European countries, enclosure created dire conditions for the former 'serfs', as capitalism emerged from feudal relations of production. Land, which had been used to produce food, was transformed into 'sheep walks' to serve the textile manufactures, controlled by the bourgeois, former aristocrats of the manorial system. This separated the masses of people from the means of production – the land – resulting in the horrors of displacement, famine and death depicted most astutely in Charles Dickens's *A Tale of Two Cities* and Victor Hugo's *Les Miserables*.

Moving to the experience of more 'modern' times, the 'New World', we observe the same spirit of the commons. The commons are what the indigenous peoples of Turtle Island (North America) called the 'first LAW' – Land, Air and Water[5] – those resources that are the basis for all life and to which all forms of life have access according to their need, with the proviso that all preserve and not waste. The phrase 'tragedy of the commons' has arisen to refer to the depletion of these shared resources. The overfishing of the oceans and the pollution of our rivers, lakes and air by big business demonstrates how powerful entities take for themselves without concern or respect for 'the people' to whom these resources belong. This view of the fundamental necessities of life is in harmony with the theme of 'subsistence' articulated in the text of the *Magna Carta*. For thousands of years, not only 800, as in the case of the *Magna Carta*, those early peoples preserved the commons for the people with skill and love. However, since the late 15th century, from the colonial period to the present, this preservation has already been compromised and, today, we live in a global reality that represents a serious deterioration of that first LAW. For example, the area we now know as Oklahoma was once covered with grasses. The Indigenous peoples, most notably, among many others, the Apache, the Chickasaw, the Pawnee and the Seminole, preserved these lands for thousands of years, thereby maintaining the integrity of the soil for cultivation of crops. In less than 100 years, these tracts of land were devastated by overgrazing of cattle and sheep and plowing too deeply into the land, thereby destroying the topsoil, reducing the land to desert. While some of that land has been rehabilitated through the implementation of preservative practices, it will never be the same.

Clearly, one of the major themes of the *Magna Carta* and the *Great Charter of the Forest* was the 'subsistence' of common folk, which primarily means the preservation of life in the physical sense. However, the concept of 'subsistence' encompasses much more than that. The commons include many more facets of life other

---

5 See the work of Tiokasin Ghosthorse, a member of Cheyenne River Lakota (Sioux) Nation of South Dakota and the bands of Itazipko/Mnicoujou and Oglala. He is host of "First Voices Indigenous Radio"; see www.wbai.org. I have had the pleasure of meeting and spending some time with this most gentle and wise gentleman. Upon my invitation, he held a program for my students, who gained countless insights into his way of life, his ancestry and his hope for the transformation of U.S. policy with regard to so-called 'reservations', which continue to plague his and other indigenous peoples in the Americas and throughout the world.

A political economy of education **75**

than life preservation, strictly speaking. All reasonable people agree that police and fire protection are among the most basic components of the commons. While the commons are owned 'by no one and everyone', most people do not object to paying taxes as long as services from these institutions are rendered accordingly. Wasn't that one of the reasons ("no taxation without representation") the American Revolution was waged against England in the 1770s? Sanitation services provided by cities and towns represent, like police and fire protection, are basic forms of cooperation between an elected government and the people; they are the 'public works'. When people pay taxes and do not receive the services they are told will be provided thereby, *e.g.*, when snow is not removed from people's streets after a storm, preventing them from getting to work and from being delivered emergency services, they get angry. Paying taxes does not remove this or that public works service from being part of the commons; these services cost money to maintain. The people share that cost in order to guarantee their delivery. These are all considered 'essential services' and their delivery is 'guaranteed' in accordance with the construct of the 'public trust'. As a sidebar, many still do not understand that health care falls in this same category; hence the tedious debates over health care in the United States. It is simple; health care is a right and part of the commons and, as such, should be 'universal'.

Also included in the concept of 'subsistence' are the socio-cultural forms of the commons, namely, the norms and beliefs and values that characterize a society. Among them is the 'form' this book is about: education. Yes, education is a mode of subsistence and a part of the commons; it is of fundamental import for the subsistence of all people who enter into the fold of any ethnic group, any polity. Even though these forms change and hopefully improve, their fundamental status remains at the level of the commons, a resource that should be accessible to everyone at any time. They belong to everyone and must be maintained by everyone. Education is no less foundational to a society than other 'essential services'. All of these forms of the commons, whether physical or socio-cultural, are identifiable at the common sense level.[6] Any 9-year-old, with a moment's pause, knows this.

Education is part of those necessary activities all societies establish and practice, whether in communal contexts of bygone days or in contemporary societies. I take the position that education, after the first LAW, is the most fundamental activity

---

6 Not that you would notice, though. These too have been stolen from us with the privatization of water and the pollution of our air, all part of the extreme form of industrialization that Capitalism has brought to us, globally. In a timely and disturbing article by Dahr Jamail, entitled "Sixth Mass Extinction Event Begins; 2015 on Pace to Become Hottest Year on Record", published in Truthout.org, June 29, 2015, Jamail reports that "If current rates of ACD [anthropogenic climate disruption] continue [quoting lead author, Gerardo Ceballos, of article in *Science Advances*, June 19, 2015, entitled, "Accelerated Modern Human-Induced Species Losses: Entering the Sixth Mass Extinction"], 'Life would take many millions of years to recover, and our species itself would likely disappear early on'". Predictably, the year 2016 was even hotter and so too for 2017. This is about water, the beginning of all life.

76 Left Behind

of any society. Education is an activity that *must* be performed by all societies for their very existence and so that their members may survive and thrive. It is a public activity required to teach new members what the society is about, how it works and how they can contribute to its history. Children do not come 'prepackaged' and ready to participate in any society; they must be nurtured and educated so that they can become competent members. It has been part of the responsibilities of any society to apprise its membership of all necessary information, from the technical to the practical to the artistic, to render all into viable members of their communities. This has always been at the root of all forms of enculturation and socialization.

If that part of the commons – education – is separated from the people, pulled apart by the forces of the powerful and mandated to operate in their interests and not in the interests of the people, that is tantamount to a socio-cultural 'enclosure movement', separating people from the subsistence of their education, no less impactful than the Enclosure Act in England in 1845. Unfortunately, that separation, as for many other forms of the commons, has already happened: education has become taken over by corporate ideals and has taken on the rubrics of instrumentalist exigencies. It has become controlled by the powerful for purposes of profit, virtually always resulting in the plunder and waste of the essential subsistence of life. Education has been co-opted, stolen and distorted in the image of capitalist enterprise to such an extent that it is virtually unrecognizable as the institution of socio-cultural subsistence necessary for the nurturance and enlightenment of our children toward their life-long potential and achievement. In the process, it has commodified our children, something that is unacceptable.

We must reverse this set of realities and reconstruct our educational commons. We must resolidify the essence and substance of this fundamental institution to serve our children, to inform them about their conditions of life locally and globally in ways that allow them to develop control over their own thinking in order to make intelligent decisions and, accordingly, to afford them the space, time and opportunity to go beyond becoming knowledgeable about their world and become enlightened to consider options outside of their immediate circumstances.

Public expenditure vs. profit?

Keeping in mind the discussion in the last chapter about how our schools are operating under the auspices of a 'business model', the discussions in this chapter focus upon ways of thinking about education that confuse us about how educational practices are talked about and implemented. How is education, as part of the 'commons', understood? – in terms of its funding, in terms of how we understand who goes to school and their relationship to their participation in school work, in terms of the 'cost' of education on the part of students and in terms of what constitutes 'success' once 'educated'?

These all have political ramifications for our understandings of what education constitutes in the United States. Everything is political in some sense. However, when institutions are transformed to serve the purposes of the powerful (the political class, the managerial class, the rich), instead of those of the public, the people lose their bearings in terms of what 'knowledge' constitutes and the society is diminished in any democratic forms it might have previously established. Political institutions in the United States have been controlled by economic interests for quite some time (though not completely; the political class continues to wield its own particular influence, *e.g.*, the FCC, the FDA, the CIA, the NSANED) and, as a result, they have lost much of their ability to maintain the original pledges that made them so fundamental to our democratic experiment. If this hallowed institution of education has been taken over by the 'business' mindset, the profit-oriented mindset, and I argue that it has, then the goals have changed. The experience has changed, indeed, the reasons for educating our children in the first place have become even more than were stated by the 'Founding Fathers', *i.e.*, to serve the purposes of the economic game, something which is *anathema* to the true mission of teaching. This does not bode well for a population that claims to honor the principles of democracy. This must be challenged and not allowed to continue unabated.

Education has been institutionalized since the very beginnings of literacy. It was never understood as a service for which payment was required nor as an opportunity to profit from its delivery – that is, until the concept of 'class' gained ascendancy over the concept of 'caste',[7] some 220 years ago, when capitalism became the mode of production of dominance. As the reader knows, the main purpose of this economic activity is to extract 'profit' at the expense of everything else, most notably of labor, but also of the environment, common sense and the commons. Hence, education in a capitalist environment becomes limited and focused according to the needs of capitalist development, not of human development.

One of the ways that the relationship between the economy and education is created is by understanding that education is expensive and that its access is dependent upon the affordability of those who seek it, instead of something that is provided by the society, something that is necessary for the very survival of that

---

7 In early societies, education meant that all members became intimate with all that they needed to function effectively in that society. No one was left out and everyone benefitted from universal participation. In rank and stratified societies, education was limited to the upper echelons of the caste system, such that only certain members had access to the comprehensive knowledge of the society. Certain strata had access only to that knowledge that was useful and necessary to the 'function' that member fulfilled in the society. Plato's *Republic* described such a stratified society. It was not until the Enlightenment (beginning roughly in the late 17th century and ending roughly in the early 19th century) that education for the masses was addressed in more detail, because of the democratic principles introduced by *les philosophes* (Jean-Jacques Rousseau, Francois-Marie Arouet [Voltaire], Mary Astell, John Locke, Thomas Hobbes, Thomas Paine), which led to the American and French revolutions. Ironically, those revolutions also galvanized the emergence of capitalism, a system that stands counter to democracy. Democracy requires a citizenry that is literate and educated, capitalism does not. Instead, capitalism only requires that a population be versed in what is necessary to function in the workplace, a population of pliant and acquiescent workers, whose labor is expropriated by the capitalist. Therefore, limited education leads to limited access to the socio-economic rewards generated in that society.

78 Left Behind

society. Because, in capitalism, everything is reduced to the transactional relationship, one becomes 'educated' (after elementary and secondary) only if one pays for it, as in all socio-cultural interaction is reduced to buying and selling, hence, to its commodification.

It is curious, however, that among so-called advanced, industrialized (largely 'capitalist') societies, such as the Scandinavian countries, most of the European countries, Australia, Japan, China as well as the United States and Canada, this notion does not seem to have encroached upon the delivery of education to its youngsters, except in the United States. In those countries, in elementary and secondary, education is predicated upon simply being present in the society. For university, it is predicated upon merit; none of it costs the student a penny. In the United States, education, in elementary and secondary, is also predicated upon simply being present in the society; however, for university, it is predicated upon money.

The public treasury is supposed to fund public education, K–12, to the level at which all children will have access to the learning they are entitled to, as a matter of public trust. Unfortunately, our system falls way short of delivering on that promise and, hence, a violation of that public trust. We are told one thing – that education is paid for – and we suffer the reality – that not enough funding is allotted to pay for high-quality, equal public education for all our children. So, while families do not technically pay extra for their children's education (beyond what they already pay in taxes), the education which is delivered in their community is only commensurate with the actual funding that is provided that school district, thanks to either the tax base available to that community, which varies widely according to income levels[8] or the partisan decisions made by their politicians or both, from the local to the state to the federal levels. As a result, more and more families today do not receive the educational 'bang for the buck' they pay in taxes. I am not suggesting that the only parameter for the proper delivery of education is money; many other factors influence good education. Those are discussed throughout this book. However, funding is at the root.

It is one thing to suffer poverty and not be able to participate in the society to a significant degree (and that is a growing problem in the United States); it is another thing not to receive the educational experience, promised to our children. Because the needed funding is not made available to all school districts in such a way as to guarantee that all our children receive equal, high-quality public education, no matter where they live and no matter what their financial condition, any claim that education in the United States is 'the best in the world' is simply false. Funding lies at the fulcrum of the delivery of proper public education.

---

8 As discussed in the chapter on poverty, schools in wealthier communities receive more funds and resources than poor communities, because of the higher taxes collected from the homes of much higher value, resulting in huge disparities in the delivery of education among school districts across the country.

A political economy of education **79**

What is wrong with this picture, and how can we work to change the practices that bring us to this state of affairs? The first thing to do is to realize that education cannot be an institution from which we should expect to extract any profit. It is a socio-cultural necessity, not an entrepreneurship or business from which it is expected to amass sums of money. It is not a practice from which we should expect to ingratiate ourselves financially or otherwise; it is a service that is culturally based and necessary, provided to the public, at the expense of the public through their taxes. It is not something that should appear in the *credit* column of a balance sheet; it occupies exclusively the *debit* column.[9] There is nothing to collect from recipients of education; all components of a solid education must be provided for; *no child should ever be left behind* or ever want in terms of educational needs. The benefits of education are observed in the livelihoods of those children and the future that they can build, hence the 'payback' is in how the society and the world will thrive as a result of solid and thoughtful educational practices.

In a society such as the United States, the wealthiest nation on the planet, we should be enjoying nothing short of the best education, period. Unfortunately, that is not the case. Too much of federal discretionary funds are spent on war and 'defense'. Including the allotment for the Veterans Administration, of the total discretionary budget of $1.11 trillion for fiscal year 2015, military spending was $663.81 billion or 59.57% and the total spending for education was $69.98 billion or 6.28%.[10] This indicates a gross imbalance in the appropriation of federal tax dollars. Along with significantly decreasing the military budget, the allotment for education should be immediately quadrupled.

Take, for example, the K-12 districts across the country; the solution, in theory, is very simple: spend more money on education and manage that allotment correctly to achieve what I am advocating. Arrange a system of expenditure from the local to the state to the federal on the basis of need, not on how much money there is in the local community 'pot'.[11] While current disbursement practices are somewhat sensitive to these disparities, the poorest communities continue to receive insufficient funding. This results in deficiencies, in this or that community, while expecting the same level of educational delivery, the same standard of educational

---

9 I advocate the development of a different form of economic reality, one which respects the concept of 'economy' itself, one which means to develop a relationship with the resources available in any given area (resource-based economy) and use them prudently, according to our needs, economizing, thereby creating a sustainable ecological reality for the many, not one of exploitation for the present and for the few and to the detriment of the future, as a money-based economy does. This kind of global economy will take many years to achieve; in the meantime, other intermediary steps must be taken. See *op. cit.* Fresco.

10 Based upon the data from the Office of Management and Budget (n.d.), www.whitehouse.gov/omb/. The National Priorities Project (n.d.) compiled government data and provided these percentages; see www.nationalpriorities.org/budget-basics/federal-budget-101/spending/.

11 For the purposes of providing for the commons and education in particular, 'the pot' should be bottomless. Of course, I do not advocate waste; I mean that whatever is needed should be provided, ultimately from the federal level, where the biggest 'pot' of funds resides.

80 Left Behind

excellence. A 9-year-old can figure this out in minutes; she understands the flaws in the current way of thinking and the logic in what I propose here, which has been proposed by many others before me.

Each district should be assessed in real terms, based upon the conditions on the ground. What is the student population? What are the real taxes that a community can collect, based upon who lives in that community and what value housing and property is assessed?[12] At the same time, no city or town should be forced to expend so much of their budget at the expense of other needs in the community. Many townships and smaller/poorer communities often spend too large a portion of their budget for school expenses than they can really afford, leaving other important funding needs impoverished.[13] And, in other cases, schools suffer because of the urgency to spend on other municipal needs. Those details are a simple matter of balancing the needs against the availability of funds at all levels. Other, local needs short of funds should also be supplemented from the state and federal coffers. Some local communities spend the vast majority of their tax revenue on schools; that's not right either. For example, "The biggest bite of ... property tax dollars is used to fund education. The average Maine community uses 60% of its property taxes for that purpose".[14] Funding from the feds is effectively a fixed rate of the individual district's allotment for education.[15] The state's funding for K-12 is, on average, 25% of a state's budget.[16] However, these sources of funding are not always able to fulfill the actual needs of each of those districts; the wealthier districts seem to do well, while the poorer districts suffer. Whatever is left to fund is often left unfunded, because the local communities fall short of what they need. The way this must be understood is from the 'bottom up', not from the 'top down'; that is, once the level of contribution a locality can afford is determined, the state steps in to fill the gap, to the extent it can, then, the federal dollars must top off the needed funding to support the best facilities, teachers, programs, *etc.*, in every district so that all those children will be afforded the reality of an education that is truly equal, no matter

---

12 There are problems in this part of the puzzle too: based upon location of homes and the parameters of evaluation, appraisals of homes are often disproportionately devalued or inflated, creating a system of housing worth that 'floats' and does not always reflect the real value of a home, resulting in erroneous levels of tax revenue therefrom.

13 See "Does Local Tax Financing of Public Schools Perpetuate Inequality?" by Jaj Chetty and John Friedman (2011) of Harvard University and the National Bureau of Economic Research. Their findings suggest that the quality of education in school districts reflects the funding that the local communities can muster. Sadly, the 'quality' is measured in terms of test scores.

14 See Matthew Stone (April 20, 2013) "School Funding at Heart of State Local Spending Debate over LePage Budget". *Bangor Daily News.*

15 Total federal funding has hovered around 9% between 2002–2003 and 2010–2011 with averages of 46% to 49% from local sources through 2012–2013. See Lauren Musu-Gillette and Stephen Cornman (January 25, 2016) "Financing Education: National, State, and Local Funding and Spending for Public Schools in 2013".

16 According to the Center for Public Education (2008), states allot a disproportionate percentage of their budgets to education: from 31.4% in Nebraska to 89% in Hawaii. See www.centerforpubliceducation.org and www.census.gov.

A political economy of education **81**

where they live and no matter what their economic strength might be. As a rule of thumb, my research suggests that the allotment for education should be no more than 20% of the treasuries at each level: local, state and federal. That would not burden budgets at any level and go a long way to wresting our education delivery from the disaster that it currently suffers.

This is a scheme that must be developed and maintained from kindergarten, to elementary, to secondary, to post-secondary (college, trade school, technical school, *etc.*) and to post-graduate training of all kinds, tuition-free throughout. It is not like we do not have the funding to do this; it is that our major institutions have become slaves to the "military-industrial complex" that President Eisenhower talked about in his farewell speech. In whatever way(s) possible, that hold on our institutions of learning must be broken or anything discussed in this book will not have a chance to work. The question is: what kind of society/world do we want to live in – one that subjugates us to the vagaries and whims of corporations, that diminishes our humanity and dignity, that takes from us and gives little in return,[17] or one that recognizes that human beings and our needs and aspirations are what we must spend our energies and wealth on to preserve and enjoy and advance us to our full potential?

Only the collective movement(s) of people on the ground can create the necessary conditions to support the kind of education that all our children deserve: equal, high-quality public education.

Public funding and the student loan industry

There is a popular commitment which maintains in the United States, in concert with the United Nations 1948 Declaration of Human Rights, expressed in the following way: education, at least for elementary and secondary, should be provided by local, state and federal government dollars, funded by the tax base. While public university education also formally followed this scheme, more recently, in large measure because of Senator Bernie Sanders' 2016 bid for president, there has been a call for reinstating tuition-free public college/university. Often referred to as 'free education' (of course, nothing is 'free'), we know that the cost of that education is massive, requiring much more than the 6% currently being allotted from the federal discretionary budget and subject to cuts all the time. In other words, while our budget is more than adequate properly to support our educational needs, the political will to do so is sparse, leaving all of our poor children and most of the rest wanting for high quality education.

The Morrill Act of 1862 (named after Congressman Justin Morrill of Vermont,

---

17 Because corporations are steeped in 'the bottom line' or profit, they actually stand in opposition to what I argue in this book. We do not need corporations. They are anti-democratic and operate only for the benefit of their owners/shareholders and to the detriment of those of us who work for them. They should have nothing to say about educating our children.

who sponsored it), also known as the Land-Grant College Act of 1862, signed into law by President Abraham Lincoln on July 2, 1862, established affordable (tuition-free) college education, mostly for agriculture and mechanic arts, A&M programs. It granted all states acres of land for each of their congressional seats and funding for the new public schools was provided by the federal and state governments. This policy proposed that it would make post-secondary education accessible to all children, regardless of their financial condition.

In 1794, the *Ecole Normale Superieure* was established in Paris, France, to institute training for teachers. In the United States, the 'normal' school was also established first in Vermont (1823) and Massachusetts (1839) for teacher training, at first for elementary. These schools were either tuition-free or subsidized by local and/or state treasuries. They were all public schools.

Land-grant institutions, whose initial purpose was to provide programs for agriculture and mechanic arts, eventually included other disciplines of knowledge to afford people, who would otherwise not be able to attend post-secondary schools, a tuition-free opportunity to get a college education. That sound practice has been in trouble for quite some time now. In the case of the University of Connecticut, a land-grant institution (1881), the premier agricultural school in Connecticut, tuition-free education for residents of Connecticut ended in 1972. The only costs to students before that were room and board, university fees and books. Now, students pay tuition to a public institution.[18] While there is still a fee differential between residents of Connecticut and students from other states and other countries,[19] every student pays tuition. For the academic year 2017–2018, full-time residents pay $11,998 (~$3,000 increase over the last five years) and out-of-staters pay $44,066 (~$10,000 increase over the last five years). Including room and board and all fees, the cost rises to $27,354 and $49,422, respectively. These are costs that very few students can afford, even if they are residents of Connecticut and who live at home.

As a result, many students choose to attend community colleges located throughout the state for their first two years of college. In Fairfield County, CT, many students attend Norwalk Community College (NCC) or Housatonic Community College (HCC), where tuition is significantly lower and students live at home (There are no school housing costs). For the 2017–2018 school year, NCC's full-time tuition (including all fees) is $4,336 (~$1,000 increase over the last five years) and HCC's is $4,336 (~$1,300 increase over the last five years). While, by contrast, these costs are less, they still represent a substantial cost for students to continue their education beyond high school; and, because they are two-year institutions, students are forced to leave and enter another four-year institution, always costing more. This scheme is repeated, with some variations, throughout the country.

---

18 This means that they pay twice: they pay in taxes and again in tuition.
19 Out-of-country students have no access to grants or loans.

A political economy of education **83**

While tuition (for post-secondary, either college or trade school) has increased over the last 40 years, income has not. That is, at best, income has leveled off. Overwhelmingly, real income has declined. Since the recession of 2007, "median wealth for middle-income blacks fell ... 47% ... Hispanics ... 55% ... [and] white families ... 31%." Meanwhile, "the median wealth of upper-income white families in 2016 was 25% greater than its pre-recession level ..."[20] Most recently, everybody has suffered the rapacious folly of Wall Street and 'Casino Capitalism' in the 2007 'crash', from which we are all reeling. While affording education is still a struggle for 'whites', it is almost impossible for other 'racial' groups. Do schools recognize this trend? No. They continue to raise tuition and fees, because their operations are predicated on the 'bottom line', just like businesses, even in public institutions. If education were truly financed by the state, as was proclaimed in the spirit of the Merrill Act, we would not be in this kind of regressive mode. The claim to a tax-based education system has been compromised and distorted because of shifting political priorities, resulting in improper funding of equal, high-quality public education for all our children.

The unfortunate outcome of insufficient funding for school is that either youngsters do not attend post-secondary education or they are forced to apply for loans or grants or borrow money from someone or some combination of these to help them meet the costs of higher education. There are state grants awarded to institutions for disbursement (and these do support some needy students) and competition grants, those which are disbursed to students whose achievements are high enough, whose scores on standardized tests are the 'best'. This is by no means a true 'measure' of any student's achievement. In other words, the criteria for the award of a grant are predicated upon the current system of test-taking.[21] Applications for grants are often themselves tests. This is most disturbing and unfair, as this book describes in a variety of ways. If higher education were to be tuition-free again, grants would be awarded for room and board, not tuition.

During the 2012 presidential campaign, former Governor Mitt Romney suggested that students borrow money from their parents (and, by logical extension, from relatives) for college. The myopic character of that comment was immediately recognized by all. Virtually all parents cannot afford to finance their children through university. Only the very rich can do that, maybe 10% of the U.S. population. Hence, potential students borrowing money from relatives and friends is not realistic because chances are very good that those people are just as strapped for cash as they.

Not surprisingly, the overwhelming majority of students must opt to apply for loans and, if approved, assume tremendous debt to attend college. There are

---

20 See Rakesh Koshhar and Anthony Cilloffo (November 1, 2017) "How Wealth Inequality Has Changed in the U.S. Since the Great Recession, by Race, Ethnicity and Income". *Pew Research Center.*
21 See Chapter 8 on the mismeasure of our students.

84 Left Behind

subsidized loans, which the federal government guarantees and, as a result, for which the interest is less.[22] For unsubsidized loans, interest rates are higher, thereby making repayment even more difficult and prolonged.

It is not unusual for graduates from a four-year college or university to have tens of thousands of dollars in student loan debt (the average is between $40,000 and $70,000). When students attend private colleges and universities, that debt is more likely to be between $150,000 and $200,000, and typical state institutions are not exempt from these numbers, depending upon the programs of study. This means that, because the low-paying jobs they are likely to obtain cannot sustain the burden of this high debt and unnecessary interest, graduates will be paying off those loans for decades to come (typically beginning some six months after graduation), preventing them from engaging in their lives with some confidence that they will succeed at something. Instead, they will be shackled to those loans, often unable even to pay anything on the principal, paying only the interest, if that. For example, loans amounting to $20,000 will typically require a payment of some $300 per month. That is way too much for recent graduates, most of whom will be working for minimum wage or not much more. There are options to reduce the monthly payment, but this means that students will be extending the payments into the future, because the principal will not pay down unless the payment is more than the interest (and fees) on the loan at that time. Meanwhile, interest continues to accrue monthly. So, not only are students forced into this vortex of indebtedness, but they are also victims of prolonged payment schedules because of an unreachable principal pay down; and, to add insult to injury, students will have to pay something more like a 'compound interest' on those loans.

Those students who have the good fortune to 'know somebody' in this or that industry or business or profession, who could help them with a job, will fare much better than those whose experience has always been 'working class' and not 'connected' to those who own the means of production in those businesses, industries and professions. Based upon the enormous numbers of young graduates

---

22 An interest increase on Stafford Loans from 3.4% to 6.8% was slated for a vote on July 1, 2012. It failed. Congressional Republicans and Democrats agreed that such an increase should not obtain at that time; however, they disagreed on how to finance the current rate: Republicans wanted to expropriate funds from the Affordable Care Act and the Democrats wanted to change the law with regard to individuals free of paying SSI and Medicare taxes beyond their $113,000 income. During the summer of 2013, however, as a result of mean-spirited rhetoric on the part of reactionary forces, Congress passed a measure to double the interest rate for Stafford Loans, returning it to 6.8%. There was an effort on the part of several senators and Congress members to reverse that decision, but Congress recessed on August 2 without having made any corrections or changes. On June 11, 2014, Senate Bill 2432 denied any relief for almost 40 million students who have loans, the total of which now is estimated at $1.3 trillion. This remains a most disturbing state of affairs. As of the 2015–2016 school year, rates for federal student loans fall between 4.29 and 6.84%, depending upon the program. See S. 2343-112 Congress (2011–2012). The rest of the information is available by going to the Congressional Record and entering the topics and dates included in this footnote at www.congress.gov.

A political economy of education **85**

holding these loans, our newest generation will be relegated to a poverty they never thought possible.

The problem here is that students are told that, in order to obtain a 'good job' – presumably one that pays 'well' and one in which the conditions are 'good' and one in which the benefits are 'good' – they must attend college and get a degree. Without this dubious inducement, I wonder how many youngsters would embark upon this expensive journey. The promise of that 'good job' is massively unfulfilled; however, those who would presumably supply those jobs are not unfulfilled. They are the corporations, whose coffers are awash with cash, thanks to the 'bailout' of 2008, and whose inclination is to engage in more global *chicanery*, looking for even cheaper labor overseas (*e.g.*, the TPP[23] and other existing trade agreements), rather than make good on the explicit pledge of making 'good jobs' available to those who completed college. Instead, they are stingingly offering up the lowest-paying jobs in decades, without benefits, often part-time and no steady pay check, a result, in part, of the increased migration of good jobs overseas. The result is that students are subsidizing the banks instead of the government subsidizing them. What a scam! This is outright exploitation of our youngsters, guaranteeing for them an economic liability into their extended future.

Along with the increase in tuition has come the decrease in educational funding by local, state and federal budgets. Predictably over the last few decades, education, along with social services in general, has been targeted for decreases in funding. This is always contextualized by presidents, governors and mayors as necessary because the budget cannot sustain the same level of support due to the rise in cost of services. For example, on June 26, 2011, Republican Governor Scott Walker of Wisconsin signed into law the state budget,[24] cutting "$800 million from public schools" and "$250 million from the University of Wisconsin"[25]; this while supporting private, charter schools through voucher schemes, bowing once again to his corporate masters, the Koch brothers. This kind of action on the part of governors (it is not only Walker who has decreased educational spending, but governors across the country) is most disturbing, especially when they do this in the name of making a better world for children and against the common will of the people. The real reason money is not made available to education (and social services) is because

---

23 The Trans-Pacific Partnership is a proposed secret agreement to cooperate with 12 countries in Asia, North and South America and New Zealand, purporting to provide multiple jobs for people throughout the region, including U.S. workers. However, the agreement (portions of which were released by WikiLeaks) also corporatizes even more of decision-making, very much in the area of lowering regulatory protections for workers, safety and the environment, often trumping sovereign laws of the nation states involved, often corporate 'rights' v. peoples' rights. This would be a further step toward global oligarchy. For curious reasons, Trump backed away from the TPP: one reason he offered was that he would rather make 'unilateral' trade deals, not multilateral ones, thereby maintaining more control over the ensuing trade.

24 See Wisconsin State Budget Act of 2011, Assembly Bill 40.

25 *Ibid.* K-12 cuts, p. 20; higher education cuts, p. 25.

86 Left Behind

so much of the federal budget is 'earmarked' for war and war machines, that for the country that spends more on war than all other countries combined.

In the 1940s, every tax $1.00 paid by individuals was matched by a corporate tax of $1.50. This paid for lots of social services, including education – remember, public, post-secondary education was overwhelmingly tuition-free in those days, so the tax base picked up the tab. Currently, for every $1.00 individuals pay in taxes, corporations pay $.25. Yes, that is twenty-five cents.[26] Between 1953 and 1961, an individual or corporation paid as much as a 91% tax rate for an annual income above $200,000[27]; that translates, in 2015 dollars as some $1.7 million in annual income. However, there is no 91% income tax rate any more for income above any amount. In fact, corporations just got a huge tax break when the GOP passed a $1.5 trillion tax cut bill, 70% of which will help the top fifth economic group.[28]

With the controversial changes in tax policies, favoring the wealthy, it is difficult to predict what poor and working class people will suffer. These numbers are likely to change during fiscal year 2018 as the Republican House of Representatives consider new tax law legislation. Mega corporations have access to mega 'loop holes', allowing them to deduct so much sometimes as not having to pay any taxes at all. From 2008 to 2011, 30 corporations paid zero tax. Among them were: DuPont, Verizon, Boeing, Wells Fargo, Honeywell and General Electric, all with more than $160 billion in profits over those three years.[29] When people talk about 'welfare', they usually mean the funds made available to people in financial trouble, through this or that government social program. People are largely unaware that most of the welfare dollars go to corporations. Corporate welfare far surpasses all of the social programs for people.

For example, Thom Hartmann reports that a family earing approximately $50,000 a year pays $42.00 to support the social welfare net and $6,000 in corporate welfare.[30]

It is not unusual for a city to issue a corporation tax-free certificate to attract it to settle in for ten years. Some, at the end of those ten years, move to another city

---

26 See Richard Wolff (September 19, 2011) "The Truth About 'Class War' in America". *The Guardian* at www.theguardian.com/commentisfree/cifamerica/2011/sep/19/class-war-america-rep ublicans-rich.

27 Depending upon the strength of the state's economy and the number of school districts they need to fund, states can be required to provide a larger percentage of their budgets to education, e.g., 31.4% in Nebraska and 89% in Hawaii. See www.cbpp.org/research/state-budget-and-tax/policy-basics-where-do-our-state-tax-dollars-go.

28 See Golshan, Tara (December 22, 2017) "4winners and 4 losers from the Republican tax bill" at http://www.vox.com/2017/12/20/16790040/gop-tax-bill-winners.

29 See Think Progress report, November 3, 2011, citing the Citizens for Tax Justice Report, 2011, at: https://thinkprogress.org/30-major-corporations-paid-no-income-taxes-in-the-last-three-years-while-making-160-billion-ed305efc3fa3/. Also, see the October 4, 2016 Citizens for Tax Justice Report updating how companies used tax havens to avoid paying taxes at: www.ctj.org/offshore-shell-games-2016/-executive.

30 See The Thom Hartmann Program Op Ed (November 5, 2013) "Food Stamps Are Affordable; Corporate Welfare is not" Free Speech TV.

A political economy of education **87**

or country, not having contributed to that community, other than employing some people, whose pay was well below a living wage, and enjoying the infrastructures that the city had to offer. At least, when people receive a helping hand, they have already contributed to the community in taxes.

The reason I take this space to highlight these facts is to punctuate how the economic policies in the United States favor the rich and corporations. All students who have student loans (the rich do not need loans) are not only caught in the throes of paying them back, but they also have to deal with the unequal treatment they suffer when it comes to paying their taxes on the paltry wages they earn. Economic democracy dictates that tax revenue, among many other parameters, would be fair and not be collected in such disparate ways.[31] Accordingly, tax revenue would look more like it used to in the 1950s. We do not experience 'economic democracy' in the United States. We have certain originally established, and later fought for and won, forms of 'political' democracy, but not 'economic' democracy, because Capitalism is not a democratic form of economic means of production. For example, political rights in the form of the Constitution and Bill of Rights, reproductive rights for women, some LGBTQIA rights and people with disabilities rights have been won. While these protections are currently in place, they are constantly being challenged by reactionary forces in our society. We have not made any gains like these in economic terms.

Corporations have held our economy hostage[32] by demanding 'tax breaks' to entice them to stay in the U.S.[33] instead of moving their operations overseas, where even cheaper labor is in abundance, whether it be China, Taiwan, the Philippines, Mexico, all of Central America, *etc*. This was made possible particularly since the early 1990s and after when NAFTA and CAFTA and the WTO began dominating the trade policies of the United States. The results are that jobs have been taken to other countries by corporations who pack up and leave workers in the U.S. unemployed, hurting and unable to contribute to the tax base. In 2015, the official unemployment was at 9.5%; the actual rate was more like 16 to 18%, when you count those who have stopped looking for work for whatever reason(s) or not working full-time, not counted in the official numbers.[34] When unemployment is high, as it has been since the 'depression' of 2007, tax contributions are negatively correlated; that is, they are very low, thereby diminishing the funding that social services and education rely on properly to be supported.

---

31 See Richard D. Wolff (2012) *Democracy at Work: A Cure for Capitalism*, Chicago, IL: Haymarket Books.
32 Deregulation has put corporations in such an advantageous position as to be dictating economic policy to Congress, instead of the other way around.
33 Tax policy should include *penalties* for leaving the country.
34 In 2015, the official rate dropped to about 5%, with the real rate at 9.8%. Editorial (April 1, 2016) "Sorry, But The Real Unemployment Rate is 9.8%, Not 5%". *Investor's Business Daily*, Politics Section, www.investors.com and the Bureau of Labor Statistics, www.bls.gov.

While university education could be funded in the present context by cutting funding for the war machine (some 60% of discretionary federal budget spending) and rerouting some of that to an increased funding for education, the people (and corporations) the least in need are the ones still paying the least in taxes. Increasing tax rates for corporations and wealthy individuals should be reestablished. This would go a long way toward the elimination of tuition; as a result, fewer students would be forced to take out loans. With further advancements in this direction, eventually, tuition could be eliminated[35] and the student loan numbers would become a fraction of what they are now.

On the private institution front, I remember learning, when I was in high school, that Dartmouth College, sensitive to their logo – the head of an indigenous man – would offer, free of charge, a college education to any and all "American Indians".[36] I remember thinking that this was the right thing to do. I wanted to think that they recognized the genocide that had been perpetrated upon them by one colonial band of brigands or another for centuries and because of the conditions they continued to suffer on those 'reservations',[37] that maybe this was a kind of 'moral imperative'. Unfortunately, nothing is forever. The language now used by Dartmouth, as of 2005–2006 and holding, to identify "American Indians" and (they have added) Alaska natives is: "a person having origins in any of the original peoples of North America [and particularly for the Abenaki Tribe, part of which lived where what is now Hannover, New Hampshire, where Dartmouth resides] and who maintain cultural identification through tribal affiliation or community recognition." However, as of 2008, Dartmouth's web site states that "All of Dartmouth financial aid is granted [to students] solely on the basis of financial need ... regardless of their ethnicity ..." While some students may still receive "free tuition" (paid by grants or scholarships from other sources) that indigenous waiver of tuition is no longer in place – so much for a 'moral imperative'.[38]

35 Senator Bernie Sanders is behind a growing effort to eliminate tuition in all public schools, either to eliminate the collective student loan debt or at least to restructure the interest on existing and new loans. President Obama announced his "College Promise Initiative" on January 9, 2015. As an effort to lessen or eliminate tuition for community college attendance, this program is tied to Pell Grants and requires a 25% pay out by the states. As of this writing, 186 states/colleges have signed up. See https://collegepromise.org and 'Fact Sheet' from the Office to the Press Secretary at www. whitehouse.gov. Most recently, due to the installation of Betsy DeVos as Secretary of Education, the likelihood of achieving tuition-free college education is slim.

36 The reason for quotes here is to highlight the fact that the indigenous peoples of the North American continent are neither American nor Indian. They have always been members of tribes and nations that have populated this continent for at least 15,000 years.

37 To be clear, indigenous peoples have a right to hold their ancestral lands to preserve their cultures and traditions. The problem is that the lands alloted to them by the U.S. Government are not adequate and, under the "reservation" construct, their lives are controlled more than set free. I invite the reader to read and think about how the "reservation", as historically and currently managed, has served to separate indigenous peoples from us, instead of bringing us together.

38 See https://admissions.dartmouth.edu/visits-program/dartmouth-bound/native-american-commu nity-program

Fort Lewis College in Durango, CO,[39] is the only institution in the country, as of this writing, that offers a tuition waiver for any and all "qualified Native Americans". This means that these students "must be 1/4 Native American OR enrolled in a federally recognized tribe OR a direct descendant of a tribal member who lived on a reservation prior to June 1, 1934." There are a few other states (California, Maine, Massachusetts, Michigan, Oklahoma, Utah and Washington) which have tuition waivers, scholarships or grant programs; however, they are financial aid packages, from which the colleges actually receive funds for those students. Some of these states recognize only residents of their state or neighboring states. Some only accept state-resident indigenous students. Maine also provides room and board scholarships for historical Maine tribe members. While these efforts on the part of some states are laudable, the reality is that most states do not practice these kinds of policies, resulting in ever-mounting tuition fees and overall costs for indigenous students to attend college. Ultimately, this means that indigenous students are *left behind*. The back-peddling from policies that favored indigenous peoples and the policy changes in tuition for land-grant institutions create, for public institutions, a regressive position when it comes to affordable college education.

The accumulated debt that students have at the present is more than $1.4 trillion. That is more than all the credit card debt in the United States. All student loans should be 'forgiven' and all public and private colleges and universities should return to a tuition-free format. Loans for room and board should be interest-free, with a payback plan that is no more than 1% per month of the cumulative loan debt for the first few years until the student earns a living wage and can increase payments on her/his own, even then, according to what is commensurate with their income. This means that students cannot earn a 'minimum wage', still $7.25 per hour, and afford the kind of payback that student loan banks want. As of 2016, Washington D.C. has the highest minimum wage of $11.50 per hour. The next highest per-hour rates are: Washington and Massachusetts, $11.00 per hour; California, $10.50; Connecticut, $10.10; Vermont and Arizona, $10.00; Alaska, $9.80; Oregon, $9.75; New York, $9.70; rates in all other states are below that.[40] The problem is with the concept of 'minimum wage'; the operative concept should be 'living wage'. Wages must be commensurate with the cost of living where people live. While this varies somewhat, mostly because of the cost of housing, newly graduated students cannot make ends meet and afford to repay education loans unless they are making at least $20.00 per hour. Banks should be doing their part in investing in our youngsters, not gouging them with interest payments and penalties.

In a nutshell, we must recognize that education is a most fundamental right, along with the right to health care and housing and food and water ... all part

---

39 See www.fortlewis.edu under the search title: Native American Admissions.
40 See Doug Whiteman (January 2, 2017) "The 10 states where the minimum wage is highest" at www.bankrate.com/finance/jobs-careers/states-with-highest-minimum-wage-1.aspx#slide=1.

90 Left Behind

of the commons.[41] The financial apparatuses of the society should be organized accordingly. That is, these rights must be funded such that everybody is taken care of, not only the privileged. And, as education is the beginning of everything we do in life, it should hold a hallowed position in our minds and in our budgets. Only with sustained pressure on our elected officials and a commitment on our part to take action directly to those officials can we achieve a level of educational support toward the expressed goal of equal, high-quality public education for all our children.

The education to success mythology

In keeping with our economic theme and how it intersects with politics, I want to make a few further comments about the promise of a 'good job' once our children graduate from the schools they were told would be necessary to obtain gainful employment.

I can still hear the echoes of the slogans of the 1960s expressing how important getting a good education was/is in life and that not finishing high school would follow us all our lives. By the time I graduated from high school, the slogans changed to how we needed a college degree in order to get along in life. As soon as I finished college, the slogans change yet again to assert that we needed a master's degree in something in order to be competitive in the market place for jobs. For those of us who were contemplating teaching in university, the bar was set even higher to require a doctorate. I'm not certain where these cries came from specifically; but whoever it was/is must have been selling education because earning those diplomas and degrees does not guarantee anyone a job, especially since the current 'depression' of 2007[42] and, most significantly, those levels of education cost plenty. Moreover, the old adage that "it is who you know, not what you know, that will get you somewhere in life" still tells the story.

I am not arguing against going to school and pursuing education of all kinds. Indeed, education, as I have argued in this book, is necessary, not because of some slogan, but because it is fundamental for life. The point here is that, while having

---

41 In unguarded form, former governor Mitt Romney was proud to express that he does not subscribe to this tenet. In a speech (May 17, 2012) to very wealthy supporters, during a fundraiser for his candidacy for president, he said, "There are 47 percent of the people who will vote for the president no matter what. All right, there are 47 percent who are with him, who are dependent upon government, who believe that they are victims, who believe that government has a responsibility to care for them, *who believe that they are entitled to health care, to food, to housing, to you name it. That that's an entitlement. And the government should give it to them...*" (italics added). Included in his comment "you name it" is education. This is the kind of position that is shared by many Republican and Tea Party officials and elected Congress members. See "Full Transcript of the Mitt Romney Secret Video" by The Mojo News Team (September 19, 2012) at www.motherjones.com/politics/2012/09/full-transcript-mitt-romney-secret-video/; also see David Corn "Secret Video: Romney Tells Millionaire Donors What He REALLY Thinks of Obama Voters (September, 17, 2012).

42 See Paul Krugman's *End This Depression Now* (2013).

a 'good education' should better position our youngsters to get good paying jobs (and I appeal to the reader to consider that *having a good education* has been in doubt for a long time now and is getting worse as I write these words), the fact is that simply having one does not hold the promise that it once may have.

It is true that, in many contexts, a certain level of education does bode one well to be considered for certain kinds of employment. That is, the education itself, the 'training' puts one at an advantage for those jobs – say computer skills, the trades, *etc.* Overwhelmingly, though, this is not the case. Most jobs do not have that kind of one-to-one relationship with the education completed; hence, the actual education achieved will not necessarily have prepared anyone for a particular job. The 'requirement' of a certain level of education in most cases has to do with the demonstration that, if a person has completed college, s/he is able to be trained in the job position/post in the offing. Not to be misled here, though, having that level of education does not guarantee that job, nor the interview for it. In fact, someone else, without the same level of education, announced to be required for this or that job, may well get that job in spite of that deficiency because s/he knows the employer through his or her parents, corporate acquaintance or social/religious political organization.

However, there is a type of education that provides the kind of information that is directly related to a future job: the vocational trajectory. I am not arguing that even here one is guaranteed a job in the chosen trade (those same nepotistic practices are in place there too); however, the actual learning, the training, is targeted to that particular trade (plumbers, electricians, mill wrights, carpenters, computer technicians, *etc.*). With some on-the-job training, an apprenticeship or the like, one can move incrementally into a career with some confidence. Of course, we are invoking the premise 'all things being equal'. The current economic conditions (2007–present) have distorted these relationships even more.

I remember when I was about to enter high school, there were different programs or tracks of instruction that students could choose, *e.g.*, general, college, business and industrial arts (the trades). There were required courses that all students had to take, *e.g.*, English, mathematics, science, history and gym. There were also elective courses that were intermingled that could be taken instead of or partly instead of other more fundamental courses, *e.g.*, music, foreign languages. It was not clear to us how decisions were made with regard to these 'choices', but we do know, in retrospect, that 'tracking' was practiced, based upon those pesky IQ tests.[43] The higher scoring students were tracked into the 'business' or the 'college' program and the lower scoring students were tracked into the 'general' or the 'industrial arts' program. The logic was that the higher scoring students were 'smarter' and

---

43 I do not know how I scored on these. Judging, though, on how poorly I did on tests of any kind, I was probably tracked accordingly. However, the expectations that I presented in this reification ceremony did not prove to be correct. I learned much more than I recorded on those tests. I am certain that I am not the only one who can make that claim.

good candidates to move on to college, where they could pursue further education in those areas and presumably secure better paying jobs because, the promise goes, the more education one has, the better chances are of landing a stable and secure economic future. Those lower scoring students would not be able to handle the college *curriculum* and would be better suited to the more 'hands-on' programs in the trades or other 'professions' such as factory workers or office workers or other kinds of workers, whose income would be relatively low by comparison and maybe not as secure. Turns out that those trades pay better than most jobs that college graduates enter into, after all those years of college and all that debt. What is more, the manufacturing in the first half of the 20th century in the United States was a model for the world, whereby workers enjoyed very good pay in relationship to the cost of living and came to expect that their wages would increase along with the increases in the cost of living; and they had pensions. That ended in the 1970s and we have not seen anything like it since.[44] Students who attend trade schools may still have to take out loans, but the programs are relatively shorter, thus not requiring as much debt.

That is the issue here: income levels of future employment were being decided by teachers and administrators on the basis of a score on an IQ test,[45] administered in the elementary years. Over the past 60 years, educational tracking has been responsible for the kinds of education youngsters have had access to and, arguably, the kinds of jobs available to them once graduated. That has played out and, when one investigates the results, one finds that 'success' has been realized by very few, those who have inherited wealth or businesses, not by those whose reality has been a constant struggle to survive, living from pay check to pay check, trying to make ends meet and often failing. Is this what 'success' means?

The jobs that are made available to our youngsters, upon graduating from high school, are overwhelmingly minimum-wage jobs (unfortunately, this is also true for college graduates), which exacerbate the problems they now have when considering further education of whatever kind. One of the reasons they are trapped in this largely unforeseen predicament is that much of their daily educational fare had to do with tests and the preparation for them. They are not prepared for the real world. Curiously, one of those tests that is administered during the sophomore year – the ASVAB (Armed Services Vocational Aptitude Battery) – predisposes many high school students to consider military service, because they are not well

---

44 There still exists the occasional pension. I was delighted to realize that the State of Connecticut continued to offer a pension program in the 1980's, partially securing retirement years for us. It still does, but who knows for how much longer, with the growing political/economic insecurities we face.

45 The interested reader can learn about how these IQ tests, in particular, fueled the Eugenics Movement in the United States in the 1920s. See, among several other works, evolutionist biologist Richard Lewontin's (1970) critique of Arthur Jensen's, educational psychologist, work on IQ and intelligence in the *Bulletin of the Atomic Scientists*, volume 26, issue 3; also see *The IQ Controversy* (1976) edited by N.J. Block & G. Dworkin, New York: Pantheon.

prepared to face the vagaries of the employment search, often resulting in dead-end jobs at fast-food or retail stores. Is that what 'success' means? Even though information about this test (at www.military.com) claims that it is designed to help students decide their career paths, whether college, vocational or military routes, it is clear that this test is designed to encourage young people to "join the military"; viewed as 'necessary' because there is no longer conscription, the draft, in the United States. For whom? For what purpose? More and more, the answer to that question is not to protect one's nation from foreign attack; it is to participate in foreign wars that make money for corporations. Is that what 'success' means?

The point here is that the military institution is recruiting our young people as early as the sophomore year of high school. This instills in those young minds one of the major options available to them upon graduation. While there is nothing wrong, in principle, with contemplating a career in the military, it is curious that there would be such a test in the sophomore year of high school to 'help' students make such decisions. This is too early for such decisions! However, planting that thought at that early stage in one's life tacitly directs students to realize that the military option is on par with others that they could consider. The concern is that joining the military in these times is tantamount to going to war. All the students I have taught in the last 15 years have grown up in a world racked by war the United States either instigated or participated in; they have known nothing else. Joining the military is not becoming part of a 'defensive' institution to 'protect' our shores from foreign assault, *etc.* (Although, the rhetoric from government and media outlets continually propagandize that very fear.) On the contrary, it is virtually guaranteed that those who 'sign up' will see combat somewhere in the world. This is a particularly stark reality when we observe that the United States is engaged in military operations all over the world. Is fighting around the world for corporate gain the meaning of 'success'?

We are propagandized daily about the 'American Dream' and what it takes to achieve it. "If you work hard, you will achieve the American Dream"; or "My father came to the United States with one dollar in his pocket and he built a business through hard work; and if you do that, you will succeed as well". This is the tired Horatio Alger story. These claims are always made to emphasize the 'individual', not the collectivity of a neighborhood or a community, where 'success' in that context, means that the whole corpus of people participate and benefit. All of those kinds of claims, some true, some 'urban legends', cloud the reality of what is possible in a capitalist economy. Those claims are tantamount to equating 'success' with 'becoming a capitalist'. Of course, capitalism does not work that way; it requires many workers for each capitalist to engage the production process that is capitalism. Not everyone can become a capitalist, by definition. So, not everyone can achieve the American Dream. George Carlin expressed it well: "The reason they call it the American Dream is because you have to be asleep to believe it". Let's wake up and help develop real economic change so that the economic institution is in harmony with the real public and collective goals of education.

To recapitulate, our discussions about a political economy of education have

94 Left Behind

focused upon four topics that lend themselves to unpacking the confusions about the relationships education has with the access people have to it, the way language has changed to accommodate the business model which has engulfed it, to the horrors of student loans necessary to afford it and to the question about how we fare employment wise after we have obtained it.

As addressed in these pages, we face many problems along several parameters of the political/economic kind. Because our society is money-based, everything becomes interpreted and pursued through that myopic lens. Until we recognize that money, that is, its pursuit to the detriment of everything else, is the root of many of our educational problems, we will not be able to establish and maintain any semblance of an educational system proposed here. Another main obstacle to our children being able to achieve 'success' has to do with how the very concept is contextualized: it is couched in the context of the 'individual' instead of in the context of the collectivity, the neighborhood, the community, the society. Successes that our children achieve are successes for all of us; but we do not talk about it that way. Our efforts in encouraging our children to succeed must include the provision of an economic context in which they will have opportunities to do so. 'Success' cannot be the empty promise that it is today, one that cannot be delivered to them. It has to include the real conditions which provide the infrastructure to make 'success' a reality: the economic, political, social, cultural and ideological dimensions must be in harmony and predisposed to offer the array of necessary components for such success. The whole society must change to accommodate our children in their quest for the success they all deserve and upon which we rely for the continuation of worthwhile life on this planet.

Bibliography

Block, N.J. & Dworkin G., Eds. (1976) *The IQ Controversy*. New York: Pantheon.

Ceballos, G. (June 19, 2015) "Accelerated Modern Human-Induced Species Losses: Entering the Sixth Mass Extinction". *Science Advances*, volume *1*, issue *5*. Retrieved from http:// advances.sciencemag.org/content/1/5/e1400253

Center for Tax Justice (October 4, 2016) "The Use of Offshore Tax Havens by Fortune 500 Companies". Retrieved from www.ctj.org/offshore-shell-games-2016/-executive

Center on Budget and Policy Priorities (April 24, 2017) "Policy Basics: Where Do Our States Tax Dollars Go?" Retrieved from www.cbpp.org/research/state-budget-and-tax/policy-basics-where-do-our-state-tax-dollars-go

Chetty, R. & Friedman, J.N. (2011) "Does Local Tax Financing of Public Schools Perpetuate Inequality?" *National Tax Association Proceedings*, volume *103*, 112–118.

Citizens for Tax Justice. www.ctj.org

Corn, D. (September 17, 2012) "Secret Video: Romney Tells Millionaire Donors What He REALLY Thinks of Obama Voters". *Mother Jones*. Retrieved from www.motherjones.com/politics/2012/09/secret-video-romney-private-fundraiser/

Dickens, C. (2011, originally published in 1859) *A Tale of Two Cities*. Mineola, NY: Dover Publications.

Garofalo, P. (November 3, 2010) "30 Major Corporations Paid No Income Taxes in The Last Three Years, While Making $160 Billion". Retrieved from https://thinkprogress.

org/30-major-corporations-paid-no-income-taxes-in-the-last-three-years-while-making-160-billion-ed305efc3fa3/

Ghosthorse, T. (Producer). (n.d.) *First Voices, Indigenous Radio* [Radio show]. New York: Pacifica Foundation Radio Station.

Hugo, V. (2016, originally published in 1862) *Les Miserables*. London: Penguin, Random House.

Investors Business Daily Editorial Board (April 1, 2016) "Sorry, but the Real Unemployment Rate Is 9.8%, not 5%". *Investor's Business Daily*. Retrieved from www.investors.com/politics/editorials/sorry-but-the-real-unemployment-rate-is-9-8-not-5/.

Jamail, D. (June 29, 2015) "Sixth Mass Extinction Event Begins; 2015 on Pace to Become Hottest Year on Record". *Truthout*. Retrieved from www.truth-out.org/news/item/31612-sixth-great-mass-extinction-event-begins-2015-on-pace-to-become-hottest-year-on-record

Koshhar, R. & Cilloffo, A. (November 1, 2017) "How Wealth Inequality Has Changed in the U.S. Since the Great Recession, by Race, Ethnicity and Income". *Pew Research Center*. Retrieved from www.pewresearch.org/fact-tank/2017/11/01/how-wealth-inequality-has-changed-in-the-u-s-since-the-great-recession-by-race-ethnicity-and-income/

Krugman, P. (2013) *End This Depression Now*. New York: W.W. Norton & Company.

Lewontin, R. (1970) "Race and Intelligence". *Bulletin of the Atomic Scientists*, volume *26*, issue *3*, 2–8.

Linbaugh, P. (2008) *Magna Carta Manifesto: Liberties and Commons for All*. Berkeley and Los Angeles: University of California Press.

McCormick, M. (March 19, 2009) Interview with Peter Linbaugh. "Community Forum", Seattle Channel 77.

The Mojo News Team (September 19, 2012) "Full Transcript of the Mitt Romney Secret Video". *Mother Jones*. Retrieved from www.motherjones.com/politics/2012/09/full-transcript-mitt-romney-secret-video/

Musu-Gillette, L. & Cornman, S. (January 25, 2016) "Financing Education: National, State, and Local Funding and Spending for Public Schools in 2013". National Center for Education Statistics. Retrieved from https://nces.ed.gov/blogs/nces/post/financing-education-national-state-and-local-funding-and-spending-for-public-schools-in-2013

National Priorities Project (n.d.) "Federal Spending: Where Does the Money Go". Retrieved from www.nationalpriorities.org/budget-basics/federal-budget-101/spending/

Office of Management and Budget (n.d.) "Budget". Retrieved from www.whitehouse.gov/omb/budget

S.2343-112 Congress (2011–2012).

Stone, M. (April 13, 2013) "School Funding at Heart of State Local Spending Debate over LePage Budget". *Bangor Daily News*. Retrieved from https://bangordailynews.com/2013/04/20/uncategorized/school-funding-at-heart-of-state-local-spending-debate-over-lepage-budget/?ref=relatedBox

The White House. www.whitehouse.gov

Whiteman, D. (January 2, 2017) "The 10 States Where the Minimum Wage Is Highest". Retrieved from www.bankrate.com/finance/jobs-careers/states-with-highest-minimum-wage-1.aspx#slide=1

Wisconsin State Budget Act of 2011, Assembly Bill 40. Retrieved from https://docs.legis.wisconsin.gov/search/

5

POVERTY: THE PERENNIAL PROBLEM

It is not easy for men [women] to rise whose qualities are thwarted by poverty.
— Juvenal (Decimus Junius Juvenalis)

The ravages of poverty are well documented, globally. Philosophers and social commentators have observed and researched and analyzed the genesis of poverty. To all honest investigators, the causes are obvious: the implementation of political policies, informed by economic exigencies, enacted by elites which guarantee that some people reap social rewards and others not.[1] George Bernard Shaw's preface to his play, *Major Barbara*, expresses incisively: "The greatest of our evils and the worst of our crimes is poverty."[2] In my view, this is not at all overstated.

Aside from early societies, communal in organization – whose driving constructs were sharing and cooperation, thereby creating an egalitarian experience – all stratified societies, having instituted a ranking or hierarchical scheme, from the caste systems to feudal monarchies to the so-called 'democracies' in the modern era, have established foundational criteria to limit access to the wealth of a society to the few and to the detriment of the masses. The emergence of capitalism and class society, the new mode of social division, in the late 18th century, galvanized that

---

1 For a classic discussion about poverty, see Frances Fox Pivin and Richard Cloward (1971) *Regulating the Poor: The Functions of Public Welfare*, New York: Vintage. Also, for the ramifications of poverty, see Tavis Smiley and Cornel West (2012) *The Rich and the Rest of Us: A Poverty Manifesto*. Carlsbad, CA: Hay House.

2 Shaw's play *Major Barbara* was first performed in 1905 and first published in 1907 by Dover Publications, Inc. The quote is taken from the first section of the Preface entitled "First Aid to Critics", p. xii.

template and developed into what we see today as the *epitome* of disparity between rich and poor.

Capitalism

Before I discuss the impact of poverty on education, I want to describe the parameters of an economic system which predisposes, indeed guarantees, the sustained presence and proliferation of poverty. Poverty, under global capitalism, arises out of the antagonistic relationship between workers and employers. From the perspective of the employers, those who own the business agree to pay workers so much money for so much labor. As work gets done, workers go home with a pay check, and that's it. From the perspective of the workers, the owners make all the decisions – what the activities of the business are, where to do them, how to do them and what to do with the proceeds from the business. Overwhelmingly, what this means is that the owners extract wealth from the labor of the workers, while not sharing it with them. Accordingly, and this is the crux of the matter, owners of that production process, whether it be a manufacture or a service, benefit handsomely from that process, while the workers, according to the 'contract' (so much pay for so much work) receive only what the owners will allow according to their calculus regarding the least possible wages for the most possible work, guaranteeing them *profit*. As a result, employers, owners of business, reap more and more wealth from workers' labor and workers are less and less able to make a living, setting the stage for *poverty*. This is the general *modus operandi* of capitalism.

We also know that not all businesses succeed; their owners can also experience dreadful losses, as well as the loss of work for the employees. That is the nature of capitalism; the incentive continually to grow no matter what and, if not, to fail. According to Richard Wolff, all of this contributes to a rollercoaster character of the economy over the decades (some 11 crises since the Great Depression of 1929), thereby creating more unemployment and more poverty.[3]

Income

The problem is that, overwhelmingly, the pay that workers receive is not commensurate with their contribution to the production process nor with the cost of living where they live. That is, workers do not receive adequate compensation for the work they perform. This contributes to the creation and maintenance of poverty, not having enough money to pay for all the goods and services that people need to live properly – being able to put food on the table, afford safe and adequate housing for the family, clothing, the delivery of health care, education, recreation, vacations, a retirement with dignity, *etc.*

---

3 See Wolff's (2009) *Capitalism Hits the Fan: The Global Economic Meltdown and What to Do About It*, North Hampton, MA: Olive Branch Press.

The *minimum wage* concept sets a standard that is decided upon independently of people's real needs and conditions of life. It is a lazy way to 'settle' the matter of wages, whether at the state or federal level. Setting such a minimum might be sufficient in some communities and not in others, no matter what the hourly wage is proposed. The *living wage* concept, on the other hand, addresses the specific needs of people in different areas of the country, commensurate with their cost of living.

In the summer of 2013, Senator Bernie Sanders proposed a $10.00/hour minimum wage in support of 'fast food' workers. This would still not be enough. These workers themselves protested in July and August, 2013 for a $15.00 minimum. In the best of these cases, all workers would still occupy a place just above the poverty line (and in very little less danger than their fellows at or below that line) at approximately $32,000 a year – not considering if those people would be allowed to work a 40-hour week consistently nor what their benefits would be.

People are poor because of these structural relationships, not because they are lazy or ignorant or inept. When the last census was taken, 2010, the poverty threshold was at $22,107 for a family of four; in 2013, it was $23,624, not adequate; In 2016, it was at $24,336, still not adequate. Using the 2010 annual income poverty threshold to demonstrate how unrealistic this threshold was/is, some researchers doubled that amount to $44,628, what they called "double poverty", and discovered that the level of material deprivation and the poverty rate was a stunning 33.9%. They also found that 44.3% of those poor lived well below either threshold, in deep poverty, at $11,057 for a family of four;[4] that is less than $1,000/month, $250/week, gross income. That level of income for an *individual* is not viable. No matter where you live in the U.S., that kind of income does not afford anyone economic security. Indeed, in the most affordable communities in the U.S. (I am thinking of rural communities all over the country and in some urban neighborhoods like Biddeford, Maine or Ansonia, CT), in order to live with any kind of security, simple arithmetic tells us that such a low income level would have to be increased a magnitude of between 3 and 5, making that annual income between $55,000 and $75,000 for a family of four. Overwhelmingly most of us cannot even imagine the level of poverty that the people of the Lakota Nation on the Pine Ridge Reservation in South Dakota suffer at an average annual income of less than $3,800. This constitutes the second poorest nation in the western hemisphere, after Haiti.[5]

4 Figures provided by the Economic Policy Institute's State of Working America Data Library "Poverty Level Wages Series", sample ages 18–64 (2010). See these and updated numbers at www.epi.org/data/ - ?subject=povwage.
5 See "First Voices, Indigenous Radio", hosted by Tiokasin Ghosthorse, member of the Lakota Nation, Pine Ridge, South Dakota; Pacifica Foundation Radio Station WBAI 99.5 FM in New York; also streaming at www.wbai.org.

Employment

Virtually everybody is willing to work and in possession of skills commensurate with the requirements of a full range of jobs. There is no mystery here. We know why people are poor and how it happens. We know that some 20% of our nation's implements of production along with some 20% of our nation's labor force lay fallow.[6] All we have to do is to connect the two, thereby creating work for millions of people, who are desperate to work. That would take political action, spending public money to create the jobs that the private sector, the corporate sector, refuses to do. Our current political representatives do not understand the efficacy of this argument and have no political will to correct the causes of unemployment and to establish policies and economic mechanisms to create public work, thereby eliminating much of poverty and its consequences. Truthfully, capitalism thrives on the fact that there are unemployed people, providing leverage against strikes and protests for the low wages employed workers suffer, guaranteeing it access to the unemployed who are willing to work for even less.

When people are faced with the reality of dire circumstances across the board in their lives, the most urgent needs are addressed first: food and water, then shelter and so on. These conditions leave little, if any, room for people to ponder the other necessities of life: health care, participation in the political arena, education, *etc.* The safety net, which is supposed to guarantee some level of economic support to people who are in need, has been attacked by the reactionary politics of the last 40 years, with significant success, thereby limiting, if not eliminating, many of the protections that have been in place since FDR in the 1930s. President Roosevelt, in the midst of the most devastating depression the world has witnessed, established Social Security, Workmen's Compensation and other safety net programs which secured benefits to unemployed people and those of retirement age, guaranteeing for them some economic protection against poverty and a level of dignity in their time of need. Those protections have been eroding since the early 1970s due to the efforts of reactionary forces in Congress, most notably the Republican party, the *American Legislative Exchange Council* (ALEC), whose purpose is to write legislative policy for representatives and senators in Congress and corporate entities, not least among them are the Koch Brothers and their *Americans for Prosperity* and *FreedomWorks*, reactionary organizations linked to the Tea Party Movement.[7]

---

6 The details of this argument are explicated by Richard Wolff (2012) in his *Democracy at Work: A Cure for Capitalism*, Chicago, IL: Haymarket Books.

7 We just suffered another 'depression' since 2007; however, we have not seen similar efforts to take care of the poor, the elderly, the sick and the disabled. Instead, we have seen the systematic dismantling of those FDR long-standing programs. See Paul Krugman (2012) *End this Depression Now*, New York: W.W. Norton & Company.

Taxes

The more unemployment there is, the fewer income taxes can be collected for the commons, resulting in fewer social protections. These protections are not only about unemployment benefits, food stamps and Medicaid, they include police, fire and education. These are all public services that require public funds to be maintained. Without the funds, these services are routinely cut or eliminated, leaving those most in need without that safety net that is so fundamental to the democratic principles that are so oft vaunted by political candidates, but forgotten once elected into office. Taxes are in immediate need of transformation. Perhaps the most egregious state of affairs is that fact that the rich and corporations do not pay their fair share of taxes. The vast majority of taxes are paid by people in the lower middle class. Tax cuts for the rich are constantly being proposed by the rich through their predominantly Republican Congressional members. They appear in the least expected places: currently (September 2017) in the latest proposal to 'repeal and replace' Obamacare. Tax breaks for the rich are more important than providing healthcare to millions of people, who stand to lose it in the Graham-Cassidy bill.

The rich already enjoy huge tax breaks: for example, social security taxes (6.2% paid by both employer and worker) are not levied after someone earns more than the $127,200 per year cap.[8] For all others, who earn below that amount, every dollar is taxed. All those tax dollars that could be collected are not, in favor of the rich and to the detriment of the social security system and all those retirees who worry about not receiving their social security checks after 2030, when some 'predict' that Social Security will be in trouble. There is a simple solution to this: lift the cap and tax every dollar no matter how high the income. However, there is little political will to change the tax laws, because representatives and senators are 'owned' by big oil and gas, thereby will likely do their bidding and their own. (All congressional members make more than the cap.) Changing the laws as I suggest would not be in their interest, but it would not only secure the system, it could be expanded to fund retirement at age 55 instead of 65–67, and fund Medicare for everyone. That would mean that poor people would also be covered, making their lives much better; they may still be poor, but, at least they would presumably be healthier.

If people are unemployed or underemployed, they will not be able to afford to buy a house for their family. That means less revenue from property taxes. Much of the social net is funded by these taxes. Without an adequate tax base to raise funds for the social welfare that people expect from a state whose leaders continually tell them is a part of the responsibilities of a democracy, the delivery of such services will not reach those in need. To witness these shortcomings in a country that is so wealthy is evidence of a discrepancy between political promises and economic reality. This fact is partially responsible for the Occupy Wall

---

8 Social security taxes are not spent on education as such, but this point exemplifies how the system is skewed in favor of the wealthy.

Street movement which began September 17, 2011, in Zuccotti Park, New York City. Subsequently, 'occupy' protests and demonstrations took place in over 95 cities in some 80 countries and more than 600 communities in the U.S. There has been a lull in such broad scope activities in the last few years, but rekindled since the Trump Administration moved into the White House.

Understanding these economic matters allows us to consider the effects of the discrepancy between the rhetoric around the promises regarding education and the fact that it is one of the most under-delivered services in our country. The newborn is immediately a member of the species, but is not immediately a member of the culture. To become a member of the culture requires an enculturation process that takes place over the course of many years. Parents (or their surrogates) are central in this process; indeed, they are necessary. As children move along in their maturation, parents continue to be the most important figures in their lives. If those parents are unemployed or underemployed, the impact on their children is transformed from having the ability to nurture them, in the presence of the tools necessary to achieve the proper influence, to being unable to deliver even the most fundamental of needs for them, the basic tasks of providing food, shelter, let alone the next level of care for them in terms of health and education.

Poverty and education

Parental participation

Being poor affects all domains of life, including access to the opportunity for and the delivery of education. We hear complaints that 'those' parents do not involve themselves in their children's education, help them with their homework and participate in school activities, *etc.* This comes from a profound ignorance of what being poor means. Struggling parents don't lose sight of their responsibilities because they are poor: their condition of diminished economic capacity puts them in such dire circumstances that they spend an inordinate amount of time trying to satisfy the more basic needs of food and shelter and less time on assisting their children with some of their other needs, health care and education suffering the most. Wealthy parents are also known not to involve themselves in their children's education, but they have the means to make choices. Therefore, when discovered, such latter cases of nonparticipation are found to be even more egregious.

The importance of parental participation in their children's education has taken on a new twist in Tennessee. Tennessee Republicans, co-sponsored by Republican Senator Stacey Campfield, are calling for a 30% reduction in welfare benefits to parents whose children have low grades or do not pass the state exams or are held back a grade level. What sense does it makes to take away some of what is already insufficient? Campfield did not have a clause in the bill that called for a 30% reduction in pay for the wealthy parents whose children have low grades or do not pass the state exams or held back a grade level. The measure already cleared committees of both chambers. Campfield stated that "We have done little to hold [parents]

102 Left Behind

accountable for their child's performance." This is a stunning example of how some ignorant and mean-spirited legislators demonstrate their contempt for the poor; they exploit the flawed system of testing further to exacerbate the misery suffered by those families.[9] Campfield withdrew the bill after her own party refused to support it.

Free education?

We often hear that education is free in the United States until 12th grade. Not so; pre-school is not 'free', imposing an extra burden on parents to pay for this essential year of learning, which gives children a tremendous 'jump start' in their education. President Obama, in his 2013 State of the Union Address, pledged to establish pre-school education for all children in the U.S. Skeptics do not have much hope that such a boost in our educational culture will become a reality. However, there has been some movement in this direction: headway has already been made, most notably in New York City, under Mayor Bill de Blasio, who has instituted free pre-school. We can only hope that other cities and towns will follow suit. That is what puts pressure on the federal playing field to force this to happen countrywide.

Getting back to 'free' education, nothing is 'free', not even lunch. Somebody has to pay for this, one of the most expensive parts of the commons. We know that public education is paid for by tax dollars. Those dollars are collected by governments, federal, state and local. One might think that, because these monies are collected from these different sources, all children are treated the same with regard to access to and delivery of education. I wish that were true. The manner of disbursement of funds is where the trouble lies. If we consider that the mission of education (building the necessary tools of teaching, the teachers, everything required to affect a well-rounded education) is the same, no matter where the schools are, no matter which children attend those schools, then it should be relatively easy to determine what kinds of funding will be necessary to support that mission. While it is true that land and construction costs vary all over the country, it is also true that a committed educational policy would/could provide whatever funds are necessary to support all communities. This means that disbursement of funds would be different for different communities, but the end result would/should be that all schools would possess all the same necessary tools to take on the challenge of providing the education that all our children deserve, no matter what their economic circumstances.[10]

Unfortunately, funds are not disbursed in that manner. Instead, funds from the state and federal governments tend to be lump sums that are distributed relatively equally across the array of schools in a given state, with some exceptions.[11] That

---

9 See Amy Goodman (April 4, 2013) "Tennessee Measure Would Cut Welfare for Children's Low Grades".

10 If poverty is not addressed in a serious way and eliminated, the proposals here are moot. They do not have a chance to develop without comprehensive legislation and political power to make them work. In a context of poverty, education will always be compromised and stunted.

11 For example, in the case of extraordinary poverty or special education or physical plant upgrades,

Poverty: The perennial problem **103**

leaves the balance to be provided by local cities and townships. Therein lies the problem. Funding should be provided by the local communities to the best of their ability and according to the percentage I have suggested as a starting point, 20%; then, the state provides the next round of funding that is necessary in the various disparate communities, also at 20%; then, the federal monies top off the funding, providing whatever is left to bring all communities up to par across the board with staffing, physical plant, programs, *etc.* Then, and only then, will poor families gain equity in education.

Some communities are wealthy, some are not. To the extent that a community can raise taxes is to the extent that it can allot funds to support public education, among many other goods and services that it is required to provide. Priorities become established, often influenced by political wrangling. Because of conflicting needs, funds can be funneled here and there, away from the requirements of education. Often, these communities cannot raise enough funds from their tax base to meet their responsibilities, forcing them to beg and borrow, resulting in debt. Regularly, funding to education is cut or eliminated, resulting in the curtailment or abandonment of this or that program in the schools, often the humanities: language, art and music programs. Because these cuts hurt low-tax–revenue communities the most, poor children suffer the most. Sometimes, public schools are closed in favor of private charter schools, thereby compounding the problem, because they are organized *for profit*[12] and the cost of education increases. That means that public funds are funneled into private schools, thereby depleting monies tagged for public education.

School closings

During the last week of March and the first week of April 2013, announcements of school closings by Chicago mayor Rahm Emanuel, resulted in 54 closures at the end of the school year.[13] The reasons cited for the closings are that there has been, over the last few years, a decline in population in this district, the third largest in the nation, and a poor performance record. Curious how these closings were almost exclusively located in the third largest district in the country, affecting some 400,000 students, overwhelmingly populated by black and brown low-income families. School board members responsible for the plan argued that these schools were underutilized and/or the ratings were below par. Demographics are one parameter that may be a legitimate concern when planning school utilization.

---

etc., states and federal funds have been increased. Incentive funds are predicated upon test scores in those schools.

12 Closing public schools and replacing them with *charter* schools, sometimes partially privately and partially publicly funded through 'vouchers', brings us closer to the politically motivated goal of privatizing all public schools, resulting in taking decision-making from the people and relegating it to corporations and businesses, either local or national.

13 See Steven Yaccino and Motoko Rich (March 21, 2013) "Chicago Says It Will Close 54 Public Schools", *The New York Times*, Education Section.

104 Left Behind

However, keep in mind that the measure for performance continues to be those pesky standardized tests. They are not only meant to 'measure' the performance of the students, but also the teachers, something teachers are increasingly challenging, including teachers in the Chicago school system. The fear is that Arne Duncan, the then-Secretary of Education from Chicago, was a supporter of the charter school concept and may have been making a play to establish a foothold for them in Chicago.[14]

This is wrong-headed. Schools 'fail' primarily because there isn't enough funding for them, not because of the teachers and students. I am not arguing that there are no 'bad' teachers. I have had such teachers, and that is part of what must be addressed and solved. However, in my view, virtually all teachers are competent, committed professionals who want only the best for their students. Part of the problem is that they are not allowed *to teach*; they are forced into a predetermined mindset about standardized testing and compelled, by administrators who must demonstrate that their school will achieve the right score, to spend an inordinate amount of time instructing students on how to take tests, instead of teaching them the content that would prepare them, not for the test, but real life. New methods of evaluation must be put in place to assess teaching and student achievement other than testing.[15] Because of the reasons I have outlined above, poor children suffer the most from these practices. Instead, one-on-one evaluation would monitor their skills, their insights and their analytical capacities, necessary to lead an 'examined life'.[16]

What results is that schools in poor communities receive fewer funds and wealthy communities receive more. This can happen from township to township, from city to city or from neighborhood to neighborhood within the same township or city. It is well documented that the level of education provided in poor communities is lower than that provided in more affluent communities.[17] This is not because poor people are not as smart as rich people. It is because the facilities that are in place in poor communities are far less adequate for the purposes of engaging in learning. This discrepancy is obvious to any reasonable and honest observer. What is also obvious, once anyone becomes apprised of the ways money is spent, is

---

14 As problematic as having Duncan at the education helm was, the recent installation of DeVos, as Secretary of Education, is like Duncan on steroids. After having caused significant mischief in Michigan, this billionaire education interloper wants to privatize all of public education in the forms of charter schools, vouchers and religious schools, creating a constant flow of dollars from public into corporate coffers.

15 See Chapter 8 on the mismeasure of our students.

16 Socrates cautioned that "the unexamined life is not worth living" as he was being tried for heresy. He was on trial because he encouraged his students to challenge their teachers and the dominant beliefs of the time. He advocated that they think for themselves. He was sentenced to death with the option to live if in exile and in silence; he chose death because such a life would not be worth living.

17 See the classic study by Jonathan Kozol (1991) *Savage Inequalities: Children in America's Schools*, New York: Crown Publishers, Inc.

Poverty: The perennial problem **105**

how practices in the allocation of funds could be changed so that an equal amount of funding could reach the end-users an equal amount of funding could reach the end-users? with the following words: "the delivery of education can be equalized in any school no matter where it is and no matter what constitutes the economic reality of the people in that community.

Food insecurity

Many children go to school, anticipating the meal they will receive, however inadequate, once they arrive, because food is scarce at home. The stark reality that many poor children go hungry much of the time is something that most of us do not think about. Apart from the health dangers, when children are hungry, no education can take place. Here are a few statistics: currently in the United States, almost 49 million people suffer "food insecurity",[18] more than 16 million of them are school-age (18 years or under) children; one out of five children is hungry – that is 22% of all children in 2011; also that year, more than 31 million children received school lunches during the school year, but only 2.3 million children participated in the summer food program; of the families receiving food stamp (SNAP) benefits, some 47% are children; and 9 out of 10 teachers assert that nutrition has a huge effect on how children perform in school and that a healthy breakfast is key to their health, academic achievement and probability of graduation.[19]

The lack of nutrition for our children is not a result of a shortage of food; it is as a result of the cost of food, consistently increasing because of the politics of food. Huge corporate monopolies control the production and distribution of food, thereby controlling the third element of any economy: consumption. They control the price, based upon the profit that they decide they want to extract from this or that food stuff. This is done without any concern about who will be able to afford it.[20]

---

18 "Food insecurity" refers to the condition that people suffer when they experience limited or uncertain access to nutritionally adequate and safe foods. This construct is often reported in terms of the percentage of availability of such food over the period of a year.

19 See Feeding America's Child Food-Insecurity Reports from 2011 to 2014 at www.feedingamerica. org/research/map-the-meal-gap/child-food-insecurity-executive-summary.html. They also report that "In September of 2016, the Economic Research Service at the United States Department of Agriculture (USDA) released its most recent report on food insecurity, indicating that 41 million people in the United States are living in food insecure households; 13 million of whom are children." See www.ers.usda.gov/topics/food-nutrition-assistance/food-security-in-the-us/.

20 Whether grains, meats or vegetables, the cost of food is souring due to two main influences: profits for agribusiness, which are determined according to corporate dictates and without regard to consumers, and global climate change, responsible for, at least, the increase in the intensity of conditions such as wind and heat and storms such as hurricanes and cyclones or earthquakes and their resulting tsunamis. These conditions place the best food choices out of reach for people who suffer poverty at any level, resulting in poor nutrition and its consequences, including those related to the education of our children.

106 Left Behind

If we have an ongoing condition of poverty as expressed by these statistics, and it is verifiably obvious that we do, then the complaints about low or under par academic achievement of our children has to do with poverty and not with test scores and 'disruptive students' and 'unmotivated trouble-makers'. This is the old nonsense of 'blaming the victim'. No, the conduct of our children, while important, is not the problem; their conduct is a consequence (the symptom) of their real material conditions, their access, or lack thereof, to their fundamental needs, mostly based upon their economic circumstances. Drive out poverty and you drive out the major cause of negative educational outcomes, from attendance to attention in class, to problems with conduct to incentives to learn to take pride in one's education, to graduation rates.

What to do?

So, what can be done about poverty? That is the central question. There is no one answer. First, we have to understand how poverty is created, as suggested above. Then, policies that tackle its genesis must be adopted and enforced. Then, those policies must be maintained and updated to remain current with the changing times. The decisions that have to be made with regard to this must be made by people across the country, from the ground up. The people must demand of their elected officials the kind of decision-making that is in the interest of the people and not solely in the interest of the corporations. One such issue which is central is the matter of the 'minimum wage'; this language has to change in favor of the 'living wage'. All manner of policies will have to be considered and ameliorated, from bottom to top. When we consider that some 60% of all federal discretionary funds is spent on war, defense and veterans, and only 6% of those funds is spent on education,[21] balancing that lopsided practice would be a perfect place to start. Quadrupling the allocation of funds to education would be an excellent first step toward solving the funding part of the problem. If we open our minds and are driven by guaranteeing education for our children, there is a tremendous threshold of opportunity to increase funding for education straight away. Establishing these kinds of 'reforms' would do much to correct the path that we are on. If this does not change fundamentally, we are not going to be able to institute and sustain the equal, high-quality public education that everyone wants for our children. In short, capitalism is already in decline; it can die peacefully by working to replace it with a system that respects all people and not only those at the helm of economic and political power.

So, specifically in terms of education, here is what could happen. Given the proper political and economic commitments needed to follow through, and this

---

21 These kinds of percentages have been in place for several years; see www.oneminuteforpeace.org/budget for ongoing monitoring of military spending versus other spending from the discretionary budget. The 2013 military spending represents almost $1 trillion or 57%.

Poverty: The perennial problem **107**

is only possible when people in all of those communities are engaged in the politics of their schools (action by elected officials has proven to be abysmal in this regard; they must be pushed and challenged by the people), a full assessment of the resources needed to provide equal, high-quality public education for all our children must be compiled by educators in any given community. That assessment must be commensurate with a standard established for all schools. In other words, all such actors, from philosophers to teachers to parents to students from all communities and regions and states, must construct a template for the delivery of education – a standard which takes into account all of the myriad requirements such as the physical plant, the books, the library, the sports facilities, the computers, *curricula* that truly identify what students should learn at a given level[22] and the trained teachers[23] required to put that education into action.

Depending upon the particular circumstances of any given school, the local assessment must detail the particular needs so that it can meet the standard. Once the details have been agreed upon and documented, funding must be allotted across the board, implementing and maintaining the standard throughout the country. If the local community falls short of providing the funds to meet the standard, funding from the state and federal governments must be provided over and above that which the local community can provide so that all communities will meet and sustain the standard. This means that only the best facilities will be available to all children across the country, regardless of their economic conditions. If poverty were addressed in a serious manner society wide, presumably there would be much less poverty and its effects would be greatly diminished, thereby reducing the level of necessary funding, while maintaining the commitments to our children. This will require a true 'transformation' of our economic system, not random 'changes' here and there. While local remedies will be necessary, they will have to be adopted in the context of a national rebirth to reconstruct all those elements that will influence all those regional, state and municipal changes. Once these conditions are created and maintained, no child will be deprived of that high-quality public education, which every one of them has a right to and deserves.

There are no delusions about how difficult creating these conditions will be. Certainly, there will be many political and economic discussions and disagreements. There will be much apprehension and disappointment. However, as in all struggles, outcomes will obtain either for or against the principals enunciated here. It is up to all of us to get this on our agenda. Let's get started!

---

22 This is an ongoing problem, particularly of late. While politics are always involved in the delivery of education, particular conservative, and sometimes reactionary *curricula* have been adopted, *e.g.*, Texas, South Carolina and others; see Chapter 7 on teaching.
23 Currently, teachers are taught in the traditional 'banking' system of education. Teacher training must move away from the standardized testing mode to the critical and 'dialogical' mode argued for in this book. See Preface.

108 Left Behind

Bibliography

Bilmes, L.J. & Stiglitz, J.E. (2008) *The Three Trillion Dollar War: The True Cost of the Iraq Conflict*. London: W.W. Norton and Company.

Economic Policy Institute (February 13, 2017) *State of Working America Data Library*. Retrieved from www.epi.org/data/ - ?subject=povwage

Feeding America (February 13, 2017) "Food Insecurity Executive Summary". Retrieved from www.feedingamerica.org/research/map-the-meal-gap/child-food-insecurity-executive-summary.html

Ghosthorse, T. (Producer). (n.d.) *First Voices, Indigenous Radio* [Radio show]. New York: Pacifica Foundation Radio Station.

Goodman, A. (April 4, 2013) "Tennessee Measure Would Cut Welfare for Children's Low Grades". *Democracy Now!* Retrieved from https://www.democracynow.org/2013/4/4/headlines/tennessee_measure_would_cut_welfare_for_childrens_low_grades

Juvenal (Decimus Junius Juvenalis). (A.D. c. 55–c. 130) *Satires*, III. 1. 164.

Kozol, J. (1991) *Savage Inequalities: Children in America's Schools*. New York: Crown Publishers.

Krugman, P. (2012) *End this Depression Now*. New York: W.W. Norton & Company.

One Minute for Peace (n.d.) "Budget Details". Retrieved from www.oneminuteforpeace.org/budget

Pivin, F.F. & Cloward, R. (1971) *Regulating the Poor: The Functions of Public Welfare*. New York: Vintage.

Shaw, G.B. (1907) *Major Barbara*. Mineola, NY: Dover Publications.

Smiley, T. & West, C. (2012) *The Rich and the Rest of Us: A Poverty Manifesto*. Carlsbad, CA: Hay House.

Wolff, R. (2009) *Capitalism Hits the Fan: The Global Economic Meltdown and What to Do About It*. North Hampton, MA: Olive Branch Press.

Yaccino, S. & Rich, M. (March 21, 2013) "Chicago Says It Will Close 54 Public Schools". *The New York Times*. Retrieved from http://www.nytimes.com/2013/03/22/education/chicago-says-it-will-close-54-public-schools.html

6

DISCRIMINATION: SOME STRUCTURAL SUSPECTS

God helping me I do my best to hasten the day when the color of the skin be no barrier to equal school rights.

– William Cooper Nell (1816–1874)[1]

When our parents told us, as fledgling members of our culture, to go to these places and not those, to associate with these people and not those, or to engage in these activities and not those, they were teaching us to 'discriminate' between and among a multiplicity of relationships that were potentially in our best interest and those which were not. That kind of discrimination is one of the fundamental skills we must develop and master in life so that we can make correct decisions about the kinds of interactional contexts that could help us develop relationships that could keep us safe, healthy and happy. For example, it is perfectly reasonable to decide to pursue contact with that person or that place or that activity based upon the activities of that person, in that place. In other words, the lesson is that we should discriminate based upon what people do and say, the places they frequent and who they are, not by what they 'look like'. The Reverend Dr. Martin Luther King, Jr. expressed it this way in his "I Have a Dream" speech: "I have a dream that my four children will one day live in a nation where they will not be judged by the color of their skin but by the content to their character."[2] This should be part of the critical

---

1 As a 13-year old student at the African Meeting House School in Boston, MA, in 1829, Nell, because of his race, was denied the Franklin Medal for Scholarship (an honorary award for the encouragement of scholarship in the free schools of Boston, it derives its name after Benjamin Franklin, Boston's greatest and most famous of native-born sons); he later worked to desegregate Boston's schools.
2 Speech delivered August 28, 1963, on the steps of the Washington, DC, Lincoln Memorial.

110 Left Behind

thinking arsenal we develop over the course of our learning experiences, with the help of our parents and teachers, in order to get along in the world, something that is poorly missing in our present educational practice.

The discrimination that is properly part of enculturation and socialization is not the kind I address in this chapter. In what follows, I take 'discrimination' to be an act, either in word or deed, either in favor of or against people, based upon the characteristics they display, independent of their actions. I remind the reader that discriminatory practices arise out of 'ignorance' and sometimes out of 'greed' or 'vengeance' or 'hate' or their permutations.

In broad terms, discrimination arises out of the misunderstanding of many different forms of human characteristics: sex, gender, 'race', ethnicity, national origin, age and species. It targets black and brown people, women, the elderly, the disabled, children and LGBTQIA[3] people. Addressing all of these would require its own volume and would direct our discussions too far astray. I contend that, while not *exactly the same*, many of the different categories of people who suffer discrimination will recognize the practices I discuss in their own experience. I think that it is fair to assert that, while the forms of discrimination vary somewhat among the different people 'targeted' for discrimination, the end result is always the same: it is either a matter of favoring a person of a more dominant group in society or disfavoring a member of a group that has been subordinated in society.

Accordingly, I shall limit my discussions here to the form of discrimination we know as 'racism' and follow through with regard to three major issues: economic racism and the funding of our public schools, the so-called 'school to prison pipeline' and the reactionary decision-making around *curricula* – all facets of discriminatory decision-making that influence what our public schools bring to our children all over the country.

'Race'

In the interest of beginning with a clear set of concepts, I ask the reader to bear with me while I lay out some considerations. People's understandings of these matters, I have learned, do not exhibit a consensus; and most fundamentally, the concept of 'race' is often misunderstood in the United States by laypeople. I have asked my incoming college students about what 'race' is for a long time and the responses I have received have not changed much over years. Here are some: "geographical location"; "language"; "country of origin"; "culture"; "religion"; "clothes" and so on. What did they learn in high school?[4] Not often, a student in the class would venture a guess that it had something to do with the 'color of one's skin'; still erroneous, but closer to what some 'experts' still want to claim. This kind of conceptual

---

3 LGBTQIA are letters representing, in order, Lesbian, Gay, Bisexual, Trans, Queer, Intersex and Asexual.
4 See Chapter 9 on high school.

Discrimination: Some structural suspects **111**

muddle of 'race' has been consistent for almost 40 years in my experience. How can we understand what racism is, a particular kind of discrimination I am interested in discussing here, if we have no operational idea of what 'race' is? We cannot.

A discussion of 'race' can be tricky though. It was Johann Friedrich Blumenbach,[5] an anatomist, who invented the concept of 'race'. He delineated (in an expanded edition in 1795), through messy conjectures and subjective methods of analysis and judgments, five principle varieties of mankind: Caucasian, Mongolian, Ethiopian, American and Malay. Of course, for Blumenbach, the Caucasian (the 'white') variety was the "primeval one" (para. 81), the 'first' one, the 'purest' one, the one, some have claimed since, which is the 'superior' one. That was the beginning of this troublesome concept, the kind which Orwell would claim was constructed out of "pure wind".[6]

Most honest scholars[7] take the position that the concept of 'race' is at least problematic, that it does not mean much, that it is confusing, and that it is not helpful when discussions of racism arise. Here's why: on a technical level, researchers who have investigated the concept of 'race' have sought to make definitive statements about it to appeal to a 'scientific' protocol, rendering their claims warranted and logical. They claim that there are physical characteristics that are different among 'races': melanin pigmentation in the skin, color of eyes, shape and size of the cranial vault, length of the arms, absence or presence of the fold in the upper eyelid, the propensity for this or that disease, *etc.* In other words, if these same 'experts' look for differences among people, they will find them and use them to claim that they are the 'evidence' that 'proves' the existence of 'race'. Tim Berard has argued that these "physical differences fall along a continuum instead of in neat categories". That is, the differences cannot be neatly mapped upon members of 'races' and, conversely, nor can the claimed 'races' be understood as "pure" and "distinct" categories of racial characteristics. Indeed, the traits that are attributed to certain 'races' do not "co-vary with each other neatly".[8] *A fortiori*, there are no 'pure races' and no mutually exclusive categories of physical characteristics that can, once and for all, be attributed to this or that 'race' of people. The fact is that any discussion of 'race' like this presupposes its existence. Candidly, 'race' is a mythological construct.

---

5 See Johann Friedrich Blumenbach's (1865) "On the Natural Variety of Mankind", in *The Anthropological Treatises of Johann Friedrich Blumenbach.*

6 See George Orwell's (1946) "Politics and the English Language".

7 See Ashley Montagu's (1997; originally published in 1942) *Man's Most Dangerous Myth: The Fallacy of Race,* 6th edition, Lanham, NC: AltaMira Press; Richard Lewontin *et al.* (2017; originally published in 1984) *Not in Our Genes,* Chicago, IL: Haymarket Books; Steven Jay Gould (1996; originally published in 1981) *The Mismeasure of Man,* New York: W.W. Norton & Company.

8 Personal communication with Associate Professor of Sociology Tim Berard, Ph.D., at Kent State University. See his "On Multiple Identities and Educational Contexts: Remarks on the Study of Inequalities and Discrimination", (2005) *Journal of Language, Identity and Education,* volume 4, issue 1, pp. 67–76.

Racism

> "On Racism"
> Racism rose so cleanly off the tongue.
> One would need be ignorant to not be moved.
> It fuels the world economy; gives funk its groove.
> Keeps the rich in good standing and the poor in their place,
> Without science or fact or evidence or reason.
> It was all the rage in 1663 and still fits so well in all seasons.
> Civil Rights could cost you your life, but racism is free.
>
> *– Lynn Gentry*[9]

If, as I have established, 'race' is a myth, then how can we have racism? Logically, the concept of 'racism' is related to that mythological concept, but, unfortunately, it is very real. The practice of racism in the United States is about discrimination *against* someone (non-'white'[10]), acts (deeds or words) that are falsely predicated upon physical differences among people. The incorrect and erroneous understanding is that people with these or those physical characteristics embody these or those traits and, because of them, one is justified in this or that discriminatory practice: the calling of names, the blame 'game', exclusion from certain contexts, opportunities and locations, violence of all kinds (including killing). Racism also includes practices of discrimination *in favor of* certain people, typically 'white' people in the United States, to the detriment of non-'white' people. While racism has no color (that is, anyone, 'white', 'black', brown, *etc.*, people *can be racist*), the preponderance of racist discrimination is 'white' racism, that racism overwhelmingly practiced by 'white' people against non-'white' people. This constructs a set of conditions that favors 'white' people, *'white' privilege*, thereby providing 'white' people an unfair advantage in life over non-'white' others.[11]

Indeed, the foundations of this country are built upon a racist ideology which

---

9 Poem by 'street poet' Lynn Gentry "On Racism"; read by Gentry in a video clip run by VICELAND TV in between parts of season 2, episode 8, entitled "Rivals: Battle of Algiers", in their series "Vice World of Sports".

10 Something that has always amused me is this business of color, the degree of melanin production in people's skin. The reference to 'colored people' is problematic: everybody is 'colored'; that is, no one is without color. Moreover, I have encountered (or seen in photographs, *etc.*) very few people who could correctly be categorized as 'black'. Overwhelmingly most black people are not 'black'; they are of varying shades of brown, some darker, some lighter. Same goes for 'white' people; I have encountered very few people who could correctly be categorized as 'white'. Overwhelmingly most white people are not 'white'; they are of varying shades of red/pink, orange, brown, some darker, some lighter. The only 'white' persons are referred to as 'albino', people who lack the capacity to produce melanin pigmentation. So, why are the categories of 'black' and 'white' being used to talk about people, when (virtually) nobody is either? Hence, I use scare quotes around the categories 'black' and 'white' in these discussions.

11 While the last 30 years has seen a decline in some overt forms of racism, more subtle forms have persisted. See *op. cit.* Berard (2005).

Discrimination: Some structural suspects **113**

legitimized the extreme exploitation of people who displayed more melanin in their skin, that is, 'black' slave labor. So much of what we enjoy as infrastructure in the United States was fashioned through the toil, sweat and blood of *'black' slaves* (actually this phrase is redundant: slaves were, by definition 'black' and vice versa). In fact, racism was born out of the colonial experience in the Americas in the form of *chattel slavery*, that form in which 'white' people *owned* 'black' people, slaves. Slavery, as a mode of production, was established centuries ago in Egypt, Rome, Persia and other empires. Those forms of slavery were based upon one's status *vis-à-vis* the result of a conflict, invasion or war; that is, the conquerors enslaved the conquered. The skin color of those conquered peoples was irrelevant.

However, the type of slavery practiced in the 'new world' was associated with the color of the skin: 'black' folk were slaves, 'white' folk were free. 'Black' people were slaves because they were 'black', and no other reason. The plantation system of production, predominantly in the southern states, is what created the demand for the kind of labor 'white' people either did not want to do or was too demanding to do. (This continues today, with immigrants.) This is a very specific kind of slavery, never before seen in human experience. This is when racism was born, about 525 years ago, when the African slave trade was established by 'white' Europeans.[12] Along with that Atlantic slave trade, mythologies were developed by white European colonialism to justify the horrible treatment of those slaves. White and Cones distill the most fundamental myth in this way: "they were deemed inferior beings, sub-humans who deserved to be treated as property."[13] This continues today in the form of racism to justify the discriminatory treatment that the children of those slaves suffer today. Those mythologies have been institutionalized across the board in the United States, in all major dimensions from the economic to the social to the cultural to the political to the ideological and institutions subsumed under them, including education.

Institutional racism

Broadly speaking, we can distinguish between 'individual' racism and 'institutional' racism. Individual racism is when someone discriminates, in actions, word or deed, in favor of or against a member(s) of a particular racial[14] group. A 'racial group' refers to people who display similar physical characteristics, *e.g.*, melanin pigmentation, *etc.* When we observe discrimination against a 'black' man/woman/child by someone who is 'white' and it is clear that the attack is racially motivated, we can identify that as 'individual' racism. When we hear racial epithets directed

---

12 See John Henrik Clarke (1992) *Christopher Columbus and the African Holocaust: Slavery and the Rise of European Capitalism*, Alameda, CA: A & B Distributors & Publishers Group, Part 3.
13 See Joseph L. White and James H. Cones III (1999) *Black Man Emerging: Facing the Past and Seizing a Future in America*, New York: Routledge, p. 18.
14 I use the categories 'racial' or 'racially' in their *vernacular sense*; not in any *pseudo-scientific* sense as I have discussed.

114 Left Behind

toward 'black' people in general, that is individual racism. On the other hand, when we observe discrimination against 'black' people, that is generated from, say, zoning laws in a particular community, resulting in 'red lining' or from a state law that requires photo IDs in order to be able to vote, that is 'institutional' racism because the discrimination that targets 'black' folk is generated from the "official" or "established" institution, not from an individual.[15]

A glance back at institutional racism in education

I will not revisit the whole history of how black folk were prevented from going to school. Arguably, the worst oppression that slaves suffered was the tremendous physical abuses of all kinds, from being pushed around, to being assaulted in all manner of violence, to rape of women and children, to being murdered. However, perhaps the most egregious of nonphysical violence slaves suffered was to prevent them from learning how to read and write.[16] This virtually eliminated the possibility of their participation in any democratic forms and discovering, independently of what their masters told them, what their true circumstances were; obviously, they knew of their enslavement. However, they knew very little about possibilities there might be for contact with other slaves, about how other slaves elsewhere were being treated, about cooperating with other slaves to affect any change or to strive for their freedom. Slavery meant not only the hard work that never ended, but also meant that black folk and their children were destined to illiteracy until they died.

Of course, slaves did, nonetheless, connect with other slaves around them and eventually with slaves in different parts of the United States, often resulting in slave revolts, large and small, most of which were put down by the overseers and plantation owners. One notable revolt was the Louisiana Rebellion. Inspired by the Haitian Revolution of 1781, and its independence in 1804 (not that you would notice with the continued pillaging of that 'Pearl of the Antillies' by the imperialist relations of the U.S. and France that have been long established there), slaves revolted on a plantation and moved to New Orleans, January 8, 1811, recruiting other slaves along the way. While the significance of such rebellions is controversial, "Rasmussen asserts that the following reign of 'white' terror and militarization not only made New Orleans *American* [as opposed to *French*, the dominant power

---

15 See Tim Berard's (2010) "Unpacking 'Institutional Racism': Insights from Wittgenstein, Garfinkel, Goffman and Sacks", *Schutzian Research, A yearbook of Lifeworldly Phenomenology and Qualitative Social Science*, volume 2, pp. 111–135.

16 Some slaves did learn to read and write, most notably those who were 'house slaves' as opposed to 'field slaves'. House slaves spent time around the white plantation owners and were exposed to some literacy, however by chance. See Malcolm X's speech, January 23, 1963 at Michigan State University, East Lansing, MI, "Message to the Grass Roots" in which he draws differences between the "house negro" and the "field negro". http://rcha.rutgers.edu/images/2016-2017/1960s/ Documents/12.-RCHA-2016-The-Culture-of-the-Sixties-Malcolm-X-Message-to-the-Grass-Roots-condensed-1963.pdf

Discrimination: Some structural suspects **115**

there, PLJ] but also prepared the city to take victory during the Battle of New Orleans during the War of 1812 over the British".[17]

The exclusion of 'blacks' from access to education continued throughout the 19th century, with few exceptions. Massachusetts was a pioneer in education in the United States. In 1852, the state of Massachusetts passed a law requiring attendance in schools. The Massachusetts School Attendance Act of 1852 specified that:

> Every person who shall have any child under his control between the ages of eight and fourteen years, shall send such child to some public school within the town or city in which he resides, during at least twelve weeks, if the public schools within such town or city shall be so long kept, in each and every year during which such child shall be under his control, six weeks of which shall be consecutive.[18]

In 1855, Massachusetts desegregated public schools, something that foreshadowed the struggles as a result of Plessy v. Ferguson, forty years later. In the meantime, the U.S. Supreme Court decided, in Dred Scott v. John F.A. Sandford (March 6, 1857), that black people could not be citizens and, therefore, could not benefit from a "citizen's" right to education.[19] Predominately southern states hunkered down against educating 'black' people, something that had been provided in the north for decades.

The Emancipation Proclamation (January 1, 1863) announced that slaves could be free of their shackles, at least physically. During Reconstruction (1865–1877), many African Americans were elected into political office in the South as a result of alliances with white Republicans, working together to make political changes, among which was to rewrite state constitutions to guarantee free public education for 'blacks' and 'whites' (albeit substandard and unevenly established). Cooperation like this was not novel, but sparsely experienced; such alliances continue to manifest today, but are not highlighted. As a result, people tend not to recognize these ongoing coalitions, in the face of the need for such associations. As Kenneth Bancroft Clark asserted, "A racist system inevitably disrupts and damages human beings; it brutalizes and dehumanizes them, black and white alike."[20] The struggle

---

17 Wendell Hassan Marsh (2011) "The Untold Story of One of America's Largest Slave Revolts", *The Root*, www.theroot.com. Marsh is quoting Daniel Rasmussen (2010) *American Uprising: The Untold Story of America's Largest Slave Revolt*, New York: Harpers.

18 The 1852 Massachusetts School Attendance Act, Chapter 240, Section 1.

19 Later overturned by the Thirteenth and Fourteenth Amendments to the Constitution.

20 Dr. Clark (1914–2005) was the first African American to receive a doctorate at Columbia University and the first African American to receive tenure in the CUNY system. His 1950 report "Effects of Prejudice and Discrimination on Personality Development" influenced the 1954 *Oliver Brown v. Board of Education of Topeka*, Kansas Supreme Court decision. This was a fact-finding report Mid-Century, White House Conference on Children and Youth, Children's Bureau, Federal Security Agency (mimeographed).

116 Left Behind

to bring education to 'blacks' was entering a new stage and proved not to be any easier than it had been under slavery.

In 1896, separate facilities for' blacks' and 'whites' were established under Plessy v. Ferguson; some southern states understood that to be a 'green light' to separate the delivery of public education between' black' and 'white' children as well, using the same language of Plessy "equal but separate" education. It wasn't until 1954, under Brown v. Board of Education, that such a practice was declared unconstitutional based upon the 'Equal Protection Clause' of the Fourteenth Amendment (July 9, 1868).

For every advancement 'blacks' made in the struggle for any education at all, it seemed that the established institutions, legal, economic and political, were determined to foil their efforts and maintain ignorance as the order of the day. Even today, with many of these obstacles out of the way, 'blacks' continue to suffer structural hurdles in their quest for equal, high-quality public education.

Economic racism

Access to education for our children is predicated upon the income a family earns and where that family lives. Income and wealth disparity in the United States is worse than ever. The reader will be familiar with references, especially in the last decade in public discourse, to people belonging to either the 1% or the 99% of the U.S. population. The old categories were 'the haves and the have nots'. In those days, the disparity was still significant, but nothing like what has developed over the last 40 years. Today, the spread between the rich and the poor is unprecedented.

As discussed in Chapter 5, according to the U.S. Census,[21] in 2013, there were 45.3 million people living in poverty (approx. 14.5% of the population); "poverty" being defined as an annual income of $23,624 for a family of four.[22] Not surprisingly, using the Census Bureau categories, a disproportionate number of African American and Latino families populate this group. Of the 313,395,400 people in the U.S., 37,782,700 are African American, 54,253,200 are Latino/Hispanic and 195,398,700 are 'white'.[23] Expressed differently, 'black' people form 12.3% of our population, 14.4% of whom are poor, 1 in 5, or 10,312,400. Latino people make up 17.5% of our population, 23.1% of whom are poor, 1 in 3, or 12,853,100. The U.S. 'white' population comprises 75.1%, 9.6%[24] of whom are poor, approximately, 1

---

21 I leave out the other populations of people, not because they are unimportant, but because their inclusion would only complicate the points I want to make. Obviously, similar points can be made with regard to those populations of indigenous peoples, Asian Americans and peoples from other locations. www.census.gov/content/dam/Census/library/publications/2014/demo/p60-249.pdf.

22 In 2013, these were the average incomes of the following groups: 'whites' − $58,270; 'blacks' − $34,598; Hispanics − 40,963; Asians − 67,065. U.S. Census Bureau, 2013.

23 Based upon U.S. Census Bureau, 2014.

24 Percentages based upon U.S. Census Bureau, 2010.

Discrimination: Some structural suspects **117**

in 10, or 19,027,400.[25] While numerically, there are more 'white' people living in poverty than any other group, the proportions for 'blacks' and Hispanics represent *a much higher percentage of those groups, living in poverty*. The gross lopsidedness in these figures, among these groups, must be obvious to the reader. Moreover, these figures do not obtain by accident; structural/institutionalized racism is embedded in all of our institutions. This means that where people live and the income they are able to cobble together are connected to discriminatory housing and labor practices throughout the country. Among the multiple consequences of this reality is the hard fact that 'black' and brown children are afforded much less in the form of quality education.

★★★

A reminder: the racism that I am trying to unpack here is not the overt kind of yesteryear; it is far more sophisticated and subtle. That is, virtually no one is coming out and saying any more that this child cannot attend school because s/he is 'black' or brown. There is no need; the institutionalized versions of racism are in place and successful. So, economic parameters serve to do the work of discrimination to keep those 'minorities' in check and 'in their place'. The racism has become less 'personal' and more 'structural', thereby masking its operational features.

★★★

To bring these numbers to life in a more manageable way and in the context of education, consider the following case: the state of Connecticut and, more specifically, the circumstances of two neighboring communities. Both are in Fairfield County, Connecticut, the so-called 'gold coast': the city of Bridgeport and the adjacent town of Fairfield. In 2013, statewide, there were 189,700 'white' people living in poverty out of 2,478,900; there were 84,900 'black' people living in poverty out of 383,000; and 100,900 Latino/Hispanic people living in poverty out of 401,200.[26] Stunning! True to the national averages, poverty among 'black' and brown people, both in Connecticut and these two municipalities, is severely disproportionate. That poverty means that the children who attend school in those two communities will have very disparate educational experiences.[27]

Let us consider the racial makeup of the public school children in both municipalities. In Bridgeport, in 2013, there were 69,655 'white' students, 49,525 'black' students and 52,653 Latino/Hispanic students, while in Fairfield, there were 54,335 'white' students, 916 'black' students and 2,584 Latino/Hispanic students. Notice the much higher population of 'black' and brown students in Bridgeport. When

---

25 Figures based upon U.S. Census Bureau, 2014. Even for the Census Bureau, I issue a *caveat* here: these numbers are in constant efflux and are difficult to pin down accurately. These are the best approximations at this writing.

26 See U.S. Census Bureau, 2014.

27 See Chapter 5 on poverty.

118 Left Behind

yearly household family income is ranged from "less than $10,000" to "more than $200,000" in $5,000 increments (2012), we observe again a stunning disparity in that distribution between the two municipalities. In Bridgeport, of 50,824 households, the lower the income category, more families apply (lowest income: 6,591 families); the higher the income category, fewer families apply (highest income: 826 families). By contrast, in Fairfield, of 20,227 households, the lower the income category, fewer families apply (lowest income: 567 families), the higher the income category, more families apply (highest income: 5,432 families). While there is some variation in the ascending and descending number of families in between these income extremities, the increasing or decreasing trends are consistent throughout. The 'color line' is clear.[28]

What this means is that we have two communities that are as different racially and income-based as any two communities anywhere in the U.S. What would you expect the education outcomes to be in each of these locations? Well, when we add a couple more parameters to the mix, like the property tax base and the rate of graduation for these communities, we can begin to understand the relationship between school funding and the success of our children. In terms of income tax, we observe the disparity of average income of both communities: $105,059 in Fairfield, $42,687 in Bridgeport;[29] this, with fewer children to fund in Fairfield and with the higher mil rate for property taxes in Bridgeport at 54.37 and 25.46 in Fairfield.[30] My purpose here is to make absolutely clear that the cash base in these two adjacent communities from which funding is drawn, from both the municipality and the state, for public schools, is grossly disparate. Disparate in terms of per capita funding. Actually, Bridgeport receives more dollars from the state because its population is larger than Fairfield's; however, that fact still translates into an abundance of resources in Fairfield and a paucity of resources in Bridgeport.

Not surprisingly, the educational experience for the children in those communities is like 'night and day'. One parameter to demonstrate that fact is the difference in the 'success rate' of the children in each. Unfortunately, the high school graduation rate (2015) in Bridgeport is much lower than in Fairfield: 63.6% vs. 94.1% respectively.[31] Overall rate statewide was 87.2%. There is a positive correlation between graduation rate and school funding. This is not difficult to understand. It's not the number of students; it's not the teachers; it's not all those other 'reasons' critics hurl at the problem, while some of these can apply in the mix. It is a matter of the kind and amount of financial infusion schools receive.

The reason that this picture is racist is because the financial status of poor people, disproportionately 'black' and brown, cannot sustain the cost of education; and,

---

28 These calculations are based upon the data at the following websites: www.city-data.com/city/Bridgeport-Connecticut.html and www.city-data.com/city/Fairfield-Connecticut.html.

29 *Ibid.*

30 These rates are reported as Fiscal Year 2015 for Bridgeport and as Fiscal Year 2017 for Fairfield. See http://www.ct.gov/opm/cwp/view.asp?a=2987&q=385976.

31 See www.sde.ct.gov for details.

Discrimination: Some structural suspects **119**

whatever is done to attenuate these circumstances from the outside, is not enough. That racism in the economic domain feeds the racism in the educational domain. Education is so expensive that the taxes generated in poor communities cannot support what is required to provide high-quality public education for their children. All across the country, those communities, despite the state and federal grants (which often have 'strings attached'[32] and are inadequate) are simply left to plod along on their own.

As I was completing this work, an astute Professor Jensen published an essay on *Common Dreams*, one paragraph of which struck so true and commensurate with what I have been arguing. The essay is about how to "transcend white supremacy" and an example of how to begin to address that monumental question, he writes:

> Here's one easy example: Raise taxes, primarily on the upper middle class and wealthy, to fund public schools equally. De facto racial segregation in housing means school segregation, and racialized wealth disparities mean racialized inequality in education. So get serious about giving every school the funding needed, channeling extra resources to struggling schools until they reach parity. Assign the most experienced teachers to the schools that have been neglected; let the new teachers handle the rich kids. Raise taxes, and no whining.[33]

The only way to level off this scenario is to pump funding from outside those communities that are 'poor'; not funding from the state and the federal with strings attached, funding that supports the same level of resources that those wealthy communities enjoy. What we need immediately is to quadruple the federal allotment for education from 6% to 20%.[34] That way, all public schools would benefit from proper physical plants, high-quality teachers, the best learning resources, reasonable teacher/student ratios, foreign language instruction, music, art, sports … all of it, for all our children, regardless of racial categories. They are our future and must be afforded only the best possible to do better than we did. We must begin this now; we must get off our couches and activate.

Mass incarceration

Racial oppression continued throughout the late 19th and most of the 20th centuries in the United States; but the Jim Crow Laws plagued black people even more

---

32 Funds are often predicated upon the 'success' of this or that incentive program, measured in test scores, *proficiency*: if successful, more funds; if not, less funds. Because of the myriad of infrastructural deficiencies in predominantly 'black' schools, in which *proficiency* may fall below expectations, they receive less funds.

33 See Robert Jensen (August 17, 2017) "When will the United States transcend white supremacy?" *Common Dreams*, www.commondreams.org.

34 See Chapter 5 on poverty.

120 Left Behind

in the South. That oppression took the following forms: 'blacks' could only obtain low-paying and back-breaking jobs, along with many poor 'whites'; poor 'blacks' and 'whites' were separated to prevent them from coalescing in their struggles; segregated public spaces and accommodations, including schools; 'blacks' could not use libraries; 'blacks' could not vote; 'blacks' received bogus trials with all-'white' juries; 'black' witnesses could not testify against any 'white' person; and 'blacks' suffered sustained oppression from the likes of the Ku Klux Klan with their cross-burnings and lynchings.

Effectively, because capitalism and racism are so inextricably bound, even though slavery was abolished, something else had to be created in order to keep 'black' and brown people from thriving. Yes, this was a conscious effort! One way to accomplish that is to afford them the least of what education has to offer, thereby limiting the jobs that might otherwise be available to them. This guarantees that they remain in the lowest of the low sectors of society and, therefore, become the poorest of the poor. Capitalism is best served by such a workforce because, the lower the wages, the more profit can be expropriated by the capitalist. Does this read like a conspiracy? It *is* one.

What is worse is the systematic 'criminalization' of 'black' and brown people for being poor and/or jobless. When they are seen as not conducting their lives in ways other sectors of society do, those who can afford to undertake a life that is, even if they are also poor on some level, more in the mainstream, they are vilified by those around them and by authorities, who are in the mindset of 'blaming the victim'.[35] Tolerance is in short supply and they suffer the brunt of racially charged institutions, the police, the judicial system and the 'correctional' system.

Even though Jim Crow was abolished in the 1960s (due in no small part to the Civil Rights Act of 1964 and the Voting Rights Act of 1965), we still witness the continuation or reintroduction of old, tired conditions, including 'voter ID cards',[36] purging voter rolls of African American voters because of false claims that they are 'felons' in Florida (2000) and Ohio (2004), or because they did not respond to a mailing by the election board, having moved since the last election, *etc.*[37]

These newly conjured assaults are referred to by Michelle Alexander as the "New Jim Crow".[38] Part of her argument is that the substance of renewed oppression

---

35 This phrase has become ageless; see William Ryan's classic essay (1971) *Blaming the Victim*, New York: Vintage Books.

36 Seventeen states require voters to present photo identification, nine of which require those without ID to cast provisional ballots. Fifteen states require voters to present non-photo identification, 12 of which require those without that ID to cast provisional ballots. See www.ballotpedia.org/Voter_identification_laws_by state. Experience has shown that provisional ballots are largely not counted. This is tantamount to poll taxes. See www.gregpalast.com.

37 See Greg Palast (2012) *Billionaires & Ballot Bandits: How to Steal an Election in 9 Easy Steps*, New York: Seven Stories Press.

38 See Michelle Alexander (2012) *The New Jim Crow: Mass Incarceration in the Age of Colorblindness*, New York: The New Press.

Discrimination: Some structural suspects **121**

against 'black' folk is in the draconian mass incarceration that has taken place over the last forty years. Indeed, this problem is so severe and obvious that its magnitude is not in dispute. Grace Wyler reported that the mass incarceration problem in the United States is staggering.

> The United States has an enormous prison problem. A more-than-2.4-million-prisoner-sized problem, to be precise, locked up in the archipelago of federal penitentiaries, state corrections facilities, and local jailhouses that form the nation's thriving prison-industrial complex ... Today, more than one out of every 100 Americans is behind bars, and the US has the largest prison population in the world, both in terms of the actual number of inmates and as a percentage of the total population ... In fact, the US is home to nearly a quarter of the world's prisoners, despite accounting for just 5 percent of the overall global population.[39]

Unprecedentedly, President Obama, on July 16, 2015, visited the Federal Correctional Institution in El Reno, OK, and talked to some of the inmates about what brought them to prison and what their lives are like and what their expectations are. His visit was planned as part of his commitment to reform the incarceration practices and release nonviolent prisoners, whose sentences are away and beyond any relationship to their offenses.[40] Beginning in October 2015, federal inmates were being released; some 6,600 planned in the short run and another 8,850 by the end of 2016; many of those were pulled out of school to be imprisoned.[41] While this is a most important gesture on the President's part, our children continue to be placed in situations in schools that give rise to the threat of incarceration.

As I write this, I reflect upon the numerous incidents of police violence against 'black' people, a reminder of the onslaught of brutality that has been perpetrated upon them from the very beginning of the colonization of this, the North American, continent.[42] In June 2014, we witnessed the beginning of yet another surge of assaults upon African American men and women. With dozens of police killings of unarmed 'black' men and women in between, the latest litany began[43]

---

39 In a graphic, her article represents that the incarceration rate average is 716 in 100,000 people in the U.S. compared to 155 in 100,000 people in the rest of the world. See Grace Wyler's "The Mass Incarceration Problem in America" at *Vice News*, July 26, 2014; www.vice.com.

40 The reader may want to investigate the difference(s) between violent and non-violent offenders in light of the fact that they are all subject to the same racist policies still present in police agencies. See Maya Schenwar's (2014) *Locked Down, Locked Out: Why Prison Doesn't Work and How We Can Do Better*, San Francisco, CA: Barrett-Koehler Publishers, Inc. Also, view interview of Maya Schenwar at www.democracynow.org, July 17, 2015.

41 As of this writing, it is unclear how these releases are going.

42 I do not forget, here, about the genocidal brutality indigenous peoples suffered at the hands of Europeans.

43 I remember well the brutality meted out to Rodney King, March 3, 1991, by Los Angeles police, Abner Louima in August 9, 1997, by New York police, the 41 shots that killed Amadou Diallo,

122 Left Behind

with the murder of Sean Bell, November 23, 2006, New York, NY. This murder was followed by these notable murders:

Kenneth Chamberlain Sr., November 19, 2011, White Plains, NY;
Trayvon Martin, February 26, 2012, Sanford, FL (not by police, by George Zimmerman; but with the protection of police);
Kimani Gray, March 9, 2013, New York, NY;
Eric Garner, July 17, 2014, Staten Island, NY;
John Crawford, August 5, 2014, Beaver Creek, OH;
Michael Brown, August 9, 2014, Ferguson, MO;
Ezell Ford, August 11, 2014, Los Angeles, CA;
Dante Parker, August 12, 2014, Victorville, CA;
Tamir Rice, November 22, 2014, Cleveland, OH;
Walter Scott, April 8, 2015, North Charleston, NC;
Samuel DuBose, July 19, 2015, University of Cincinnati police;
Sandra Bland, July 21, 2015 arrested – July 24, 2015 found dead in Waller County Sheriffs' custody, Hempstead, TX.

They continue. These were the incidents that were lavishly exploited in the corporate media; the other dozens of cases, which were not, are equally important to know about and understand as a part of the disturbing trend to violate 'black' people's rights by all manner of violence, including fatal shootings. It is in this context that we can couch the whole business (and it is a *business*) of incarcerating our children. When these children, overwhelmingly 'black', are killed or sent to jail by authorities, there is no education for them. This is what I mean by education being subject to racist practice.

The 'school to prison pipeline'

The delivery of education requires skill, commitment and perseverance if our children are to learn anything. The last thing students should have to suffer is the constant, misguided surveillance that many school boards and administrators think they need to create a safe and orderly environment for their district's schools.[44]

This preoccupation with 'surveillance' of our children is nothing new, I am sad to report. While it is true that Massachusetts led the cause of free public education in many ways, it also was the first state to institute the 'reform school'. The Lyman School for Boys (1848–1971) in Westborough, MA, had been a 'State

---

February 4, 1999, by New York police and the many others in between and since. See http://gawker.com/unarmed-people-of-color-killed-by-police-1999-2014-1666672349.

44 To be clear, I am not arguing that our children should not be protected while in school, especially with the violence that has visited our schools over the last twenty years, from Columbine to Sandy Hook and, most recently, Parkland.

Manual Labor School' since 1846. It was where school age boys, who refused to attend public school, were sent.[45] The concept of the 'reform school' combined the educational and criminal justice systems into a 'penal colony'. Literally, this school, and many others after it, was a mini-town unto itself; there was little to no contact with the outside. Many 'boarding schools', while not 'reform schools' *per se*, followed a similar model. I attended such a school and the 'penal' quality was definitely preserved, in the interest of 'shaping the character' of the boarding students. The feeling was at times more like we were 'inmates' in a place where we were being 'programmed'. Of course, we were not placed there by authorities like those placed in reform schools; however, the level of discipline was maximal.[46] Our days were regimented as to leave very little time that was not organized in some way ("Idle hands are the devil's workshop"[47]) to yield some particular set of predetermined outcomes. Many of these 'outcomes' were, admittedly in the end, identifiable as 'desirable' for young men to develop, but the methods used at times included humiliation, ostracism and guilt, practices which were reminiscent of the time I had spent in orphanages as a small boy. As mischievous as we were, we did not have police officers on campus, nor were we carted off to the local jail to 'teach us a lesson' in proper comportment. All punishments were meted out in-house.

Many progressions of this model developed over the decades and, in my view, the practices that have been adopted in schools today harken back to those days of 'reform schools'. Today, however, we speak about these circumstances as necessary measures to 'protect our children' from the vagaries of social violence, personified in their classmates. Instead of our children in school being treated from a per-spective of 'disciplinary actions' for infractions, like *absence, unruliness/fighting and rule-breaking,* they are treated from the perspective of 'criminal justice' for those infractions, understood by officers in schools as violations of the law, like *truancy, assault and law-breaking.* Disciplinary actions taken by school officials range from suspension to incarceration. Not uncharacteristically, those children who are sus-pended, some 'indefinitely', require intervention by legal organizations, from local attorneys to the ACLU, in order to be reinstated in their schools. Those incarcer-ated face much more draconian circumstances, often involving bail they cannot pay or legal representation they cannot afford or extended jail time for something that should have been taken care of 'in-house'.

Take Dontadrian Bruce, for example. This 'black', 15-year old from Olive Branch, MS, was 'indefinitely suspended' for wearing a T-shirt with the number "3" on the front, the principal took to represent a 'gang' based in Chicago, the "Vice Lords". The administrators were acting to comply with the so-called "zero

---

45 See the detailed description of the Lyman School at www.abominablefirebug.com/lyman.html.
46 To be fair, on balance, I look back on my years in that school as beneficial.
47 See Bible (The Living Bible version), Proverbs 16:27.

124 Left Behind

tolerance", a policy which grew out of the Gun-Free Schools Act of 1994. Only after the help of the ACLU, was he reinstated after 21 days.[48]

Or take Kiera Wilmot, a 'black' Bartow High School student in Bartow, FL. Her science experiment, involving toilet cleaner, water and aluminum foil inside a bottle, created a minor explosion (something that was expected). She was arrested and charged with "possession and discharge of a weapon on school property and discharging a destructive device". Charges were dropped later; however, the felony charge still haunts her.[49]

The Roanoke Times carried a story about an 11-year-old boy at Bedford Middle School who was suspended in 2014 for having a "pot leaf" in his backpack, with a lighter. The 11-year-old was a 6th grader in the gifted and talented program at the school in Virginia. His story is most emblematic of this ongoing practice in the United States.

> Some schoolchildren claim another student bragged about having marijuana. They inform school administrators. An assistant principal finds a leaf and a lighter in the boy's knapsack. The student is suspended for a year. A sheriff's deputy files marijuana possession charges in juvenile court.[50]

One might think that the authorities would have verified that the "leaf" was indeed marijuana.

> There was only one problem: Months after the fact, the couple [the parents] learned the substance wasn't marijuana. A prosecutor dropped the juvenile court charge because the leaf had field-tested negative three times.[51]

The parents – both teachers – had filed a civil rights lawsuit against the school administration and the sheriff's office for engaging in "malicious prosecution". If this reads 'absurd' to you, you are smarter than both the school officials and the sheriff's deputy. This is not only absurd, it is criminal on the part of these institutional officials in whose care we entrust our children.

> The school's and sheriff's lawyer, attorney Jim Guynn, has reportedly moved to dismiss the suit because he claims that, under the school board's anti-drug policies, it may not matter whether the leaf was marijuana or not.[52]

---

48 See Nona W. Aronowitz (2014) "School Spirit or Gang Signs? 'Zero Tolerance' Comes Under Fire", *NBC News*.
49 See William E. Gibson (2015) "Vindicated Florida Teen Goes to the White House", Washington Bureau of *SunSentinel*.
50 See Dan Casey (March 15, 2015) "Not-Pot Leaf Gets 6th-Grader in Big Trouble", *The Roanoke Times*.
51 *Ibid.*
52 *Ibid.*

Discrimination: Some structural suspects **125**

On top of the 'legal' charge and the suspension, the boy has suffered emotionally, exacerbating what was already a deplorable litany of malfeasance.

> The full story by Dan Casey ... goes into the fact that every single thing about this situation is terrible and stupid and indicative of an awful cultural shift in attitudes towards not only drugs, but children and the jobs of the adults charged with the duty to protect these children. The evidence, from the beginning was dubious, and when you are meting out huge suspensions, you'd better know exactly what you are doing – and none of these people seem to. Because of this suspension, the Bays' child would be sent to a more problematic school and so they tried schooling him from home, but don't worry, nothing like this could have adverse effects on an 11-year-old, right?[53]

The school system also required the boy be evaluated for substance abuse problems. So the Bays took him to his longtime pediatrician in Lynchburg, who referred them to a pediatric psychiatrist.

They said the psychiatrist told them he didn't believe their son had a substance abuse problem. But by then, the boy had other problems. After the disciplinary hearing, "he just broke down and said his life was over. He would never be able to get into college; he would never be able to get a job," Linda Bays said.[54]

Now their son is skittish about going out in public, suffers from panic attacks and is depressed. The psychiatrist is treating him for that. The child is finally coming back to school because his psychiatrist says it's the best thing for him. But, like any grossly incompetent authority figure who has completely blown it, the child will be on *strict probation*. Somebody *should* be on strict probation, and it's not an 11-year-old! These examples are selected out of dozens, if not hundreds, of such incidents, taking school children away from schools and inducting them into the world of incarceration.

According to the Dignity in Schools Campaign, there is a "disproportionate number of suspensions and arrests of African American and Latino students as well as harsh penalties against students with disabilities." In the last school year (2012–2013), "52 percent of suspensions involved African American students, who make up just 27 percent of the public school system."[55]

---

53 Based upon the original *Roanoke Times* article by Walter Einenkel (September 18, 2015) "11-Year-Old Gifted Student Suspended 1 Year for Having a Pot Leaf That Wasn't a Pot Leaf", posted by the *Daily Kos*; this was the posting that brought this case to my attention.

54 *Ibid.*

55 The Dignity in Schools Campaign (DSC) challenges the systemic problem of pushout [excessive "zero tolerance" adherence, routine 'law enforcement' instead of 'in-house discipline' PLJ] in our nation's schools and advocates for the human right of every young person to a quality education and to be treated with dignity. The DSC unites parents, youth, advocates and educators to support alternatives to a culture of zero-tolerance, punishment and removal in our schools: See Amy Goodman interview with Manny Yusuf, April 16, 2013 at: www.democracynow.org/2013/4/16/headlines/students_officials_condemn_school_to_prison_pipeline_in_nyc.

126 Left Behind

These troubling practices become even more vexing when we observe that 'black' and brown students are disproportionately paraded through the criminal justice system for conduct that could have/should have been addressed and resolved in the schools. In light of the disturbing statistics that have been gathered, one could complain that schools are providing, for 'minority children', a direct path to the courts and incarceration.

> U.S. Department of Education data shows that in most states Black, Latino and special-needs (disabled) students get referred to police and courts disproportionately. The volume of referrals from schools is fueling arguments that zero tolerance policies and school policing are creating a 'school-to-prison pipeline' by criminalizing behavior better dealt with outside courts.[56]

Because I have highlighted the presence of racism in Connecticut, let us consider the rate of referrals to police and the courts there. According to the 2011–2012 figures, Connecticut schools referred more than 5 students per 1,000 to police and the courts. Of those, 61.1% of students were 'white', almost 4 students per 1,000 were referred; 19% of students were brown, almost 8 students per 1,000 were referred; 12.7% of students were 'black', more than 11 students per 1,000 were referred. These rates are replicated in most of the United States. In states where there is a low 'black' and brown percentage of residents, more 'white' students are referred. In states where there is a high 'black' and brown percentage of residents, many fewer 'white' students are referred.[57]

A relatively recent wrinkle in these practices involves a categorial differentiation between students who are referred to the courts as either 'criminalized' or 'medicalized'. According to a new school discipline study, "using a large data set containing information on over 60,000 schools in over 6,000 districts",[58] David Ramey asserts:

> The bulk of my earlier research looked at how, for the same minor levels of misbehaviors – for example, classroom disruptions, talking back – white kids tend to get viewed as having ADHD, or having some sort of behavioral problem, while black kids are viewed as being unruly and unwilling to learn.[59]

---

56 See The Center for Public Integrity (winner of the 2014 Pulitzer Prize); posted April 10, 2015 by Chris Zuak-Skees and Ben Wieder. www.publicintegrity.org/2015/04/10/17074/state-state-look-students-referred-law-enforcement.

57 *Ibid.*

58 From Abstract of David Ramey's (2015) "The Social Structure of Criminalized and Medicalized School Discipline", *Sociology of Education*, volume *88*, issue *3*, pp. 181–201.

59 Public release quoting Ramey, *op. cit.*, in "Schools with higher black, minority populations call cops, not docs", American Association for the Advancement of Science (AAAS) *EurekAlert!* released, July 22, 2015.

Discrimination: Some structural suspects **127**

And,

> When we are thinking of making schools safe, we are using police officers, metal detectors, uniforms, so the importance of the criminal justice system is reproduced in school.[60]

And, comparing school districts, Ramey reports:

> This is where you see race really mattering. The predominantly black schools in advantaged districts have much higher levels of suspension than predominantly white schools in advantaged districts. Conversely, predominantly black schools have much lower rates of [mental health program] enrollment than predominantly white schools in advantaged districts.[61]

These racist attitudes and practices of today are the same as those of yesteryear; the only difference is that their institutionalization has been updated and modernized. For many reasons, including 'gentrification', 'ghettoization' and 'redistricting'/'gerrymandering', 'black' students are still prevented from attending schools or given no choice but to attend substandard schools, improperly funded, not to afford them equal access to education. These are all well documented conditions and are at the base of what I want to focus upon now: how the curriculum is skewed away from including the history, the social reality and the struggle of 'black' folk.

Distorted curricula

The reader will recall that I invoked the work of Thomas Kuhn in the Introduction to provide a context for what I am advancing in this book: the need for a "paradigm shift" in the way we conduct education. Kuhn's comments about "normal" science are addressed in Popper's work, highlighting the dangers of such science. He puts us on notice:

> 'Normal' science, in Kuhn's sense, exists. It is the activity of the non-revolutionary, or more precisely, the not-too-critical professional: of the science student who accepts the ruling dogma of the day ... in my view the 'normal' scientist, as Kuhn describes him, is a person one ought to be sorry for ... He has been taught in a dogmatic spirit: he is a victim of indoctrination ... I can only say that I see a very great danger in it and in the possibility of its becoming normal ... a danger to science and, indeed, to our civilization. And this

---

60 *Ibid.*
61 Jack Holmes quoting Ramey, *op. cit.*, in "White Kids Get Medicated When They Misbehave, Black Kids Get Suspended – or Arrested", *New York Magazine*, August 6, 2015.

128 Left Behind

shows why I regard Kuhn's emphasis on the existence of this kind of science as so important.[62]

I want to expand the context of Popper's cautionary statement to include *all of education*; that is, no matter what the subject matter may be, science, history, sociology, *etc.*, we must challenge "indoctrination" and broaden our view of these disciplines, individually, and create a path to multidisciplinary education. Such a *curriculum* would not only enhance the investigation of each subject matter individually, often artificially separated, paying attention to the interrelationships that exist and develop between and among them, but also give rise to an awareness of the 'organic' nature of all of them taken together.

When we think about public education, aside from the funding, the physical plant of the schools and reasonable access to those schools, we think about the *curriculum*. How well have our teachers crafted what our children will be taught? What is the character of the academic (reading, writing, arithmetic, language arts, foreign languages, science, history, social studies like sociology and civics [which is no longer taught!]), and nonacademic art (like drawing and painting and pottery, *etc.*), music, sports, *etc.*, programs decided upon and implemented? Unfortunately, there is ample evidence that the decisions about what our children will learn are overwhelmingly made by people who stand to gain by advocating a certain kind of program of instruction and who are not teachers.

In early 2016, I conducted a mini investigation of all state departments of education in the U.S. with regard to their membership to see what that make-up looked like. The findings are dreadful, if we expect that academic decisions should be made by people who have had training and experience in teaching children. There are 136 state-level members of boards of education nationwide.[63] Of those, there are 34 teachers,[64] 28 educational bureaucrats,[65] 8 politicians,[66] 16 lawyers[67] and

---

62 See Sir Karl Raimund Popper (1902–1994) "Normal Science and its Dangers", in Imre Lakatos and Alan Musgrave (1965), Proceedings of the International Colloquium in the Philosophy of Science, London, volume 4, *Criticism and the Growth of Knowledge*, Cambridge, UK: Cambridge University Press, pp. 52–53.

63 Member information was unavailable for the following states: Alaska, Arizona, Montana, Vermont and Wisconsin. Apparently, these states do have departments of education; however, it is curious that there are no bios of their members. Alaska has a 'commissioner' and 'deputy commissioner', both of whom are former teachers (it is not clear if these people are part of the board structure or not); there are no details. None of these states' board of education members are part of the figures cited in this discussion.

64 'Teachers' are those who have taught school at any level, from K to college, for a prolonged period of time; do not include those who have had a 'brush' with teaching and those who have been 'educational bureaucrats'.

65 These members are those who are not teachers, but who have been involved in school boards and the like; some have been, or are, involved in education at large, but not in the classroom.

66 These members are involved in various political entities, such as state legislature or municipal service.

67 These lawyers' practices range across the legal spectrum; one is a jurist.

Discrimination: Some structural suspects **129**

36 business men and women.[68] The remaining 14 are from varied fields, such as medical, religious, social/community work, one pilot and one lobbyist.

These figures raise a 'red flag' in my view. When we think about the details of a *curriculum*, we expect that what our children learn will be organized according to certain criteria and as a result of significant experience on the part of those who make those determinations. When only 25% of those who make *curricula* decisions in all of the United States are seasoned teachers, I should think that people would take note and try to address this lopsided condition. How long has this been the case? Difficult to tell. For some reason, this kind of current information is very difficult to obtain, let alone historical documents. As the reader will realize, such state memberships are in efflux and will change from one year to another. I do not trust that these numbers have, or will, change. However, the point here is that the paucity of *teacher* participation in *curricula* decision-making is unacceptable and is conducive to the "indoctrination" that Popper alerts us to.

Some of the most outrageous manipulation of history in textbooks, most notably since *circa* 2010, has come from the members of the Texas School Board of Education (SBOE), fundamentalist Christian, reactionary individuals.[69] To be fair, Texas is not the only board of education that 'meddles' in the materials our children study. What makes Texas so important in these matters is that "No matter where you live, if your children go to public schools, the textbooks they use were very possibly written under Texas influence."[70] That is because Texas has some 5 million school children reading those textbooks. (Texas buys some 50 million textbooks annually.) That means that decisions made in Texas emanate throughout the United States. The sheer number of textbooks required in Texas influences decision-making at the publishing houses that print them. They are not interested in printing 50 different textbooks on the same subject to satisfy the diversity of *curricula*; hence the pressure to adopt Texas textbooks. The decisions made by the board members of the SBOE[71] are effectively imposed upon the students of almost every other state in the union.

For example, Thomas Jefferson, because of his role in establishing the separation of church and state, has been eliminated from World History and replaced with St. Thomas Aquinas and John Calvin. The concept of 'capitalism' has been purged from the pages of textbooks; replacing it is the concept of 'free enterprise'.

---

68 These members range from banking, to finance, to the trades, to real estate, *etc.*
69 The state of Texas has been noticed more in the last few years and written about because it has moved in quite reactionary directions with regard to decisions about *curricula*. So, I am not 'picking on it', only carrying through with some observations that will resonate with the reader.
70 See Gail Collins (2012) "How Texas Inflicts Bad Textbooks on Us", *New York Review of Books*, June 21.
71 Incidentally, you should know that Texas has 15 districts, the SBOE members of which have the following biographies; there are six educational bureaucrats, two politicians, one businessman, one attorney, one politician/businessman, one lobbyist, one social worker and two teacher/educational bureaucrats. The SBOE does not have one career teacher on the board. It is clear that the 'business model' and 'religious belief' thrive among these board members.

130 Left Behind

The word 'slavery' has been ejected and replaced by the 'Atlantic triangular trade' and 'states' rights and sectionalism caused the Civil War. It is claimed that Senator Joseph McCarthy's 1950s blacklists are defensible because 'communists' posed a real threat during the 'cold war'. Hip hop music was deemed "irrelevant' and replaced by country music. In science, "evolution is hooey" has been the slogan advanced by the SBOE. According to the language adopted by the SBOE, any mention of 'evolution', "should identify it as only one of several explanations of the origins of humankind" and should be treated as "theoretical rather than factually verifiable". Evolution is replaced by the concepts of 'creationism' and 'intelligent design'. Even though this 1974 language was repealed by the state, efforts continue in the same vein. Effectively, these decisions are made based upon beliefs, not science nor history. These beliefs are backed by political action, which creates the conditions for the adoption of erroneous claims and distorted information, fed, *en masse*, to our children.

> Five million public school students in Texas will begin using new social studies textbooks this fall based on state academic standards that barely address racial segregation. The state's guidelines for teaching American history also do not mention the Ku Klux Klan or Jim Crow laws. And when it comes to the Civil War, children are supposed to learn that the conflict was caused by 'sectionalism, states' rights and slavery' – written deliberately in that order to telegraph slavery's secondary role in driving the conflict, according to some members of the state board of education. Slavery was a 'side issue to the Civil War,' said Pat Hardy, a Republican board member, when the board adopted the standards in 2010. 'There would be those who would say the reason for the Civil War was over slavery. No. It was over states' rights.'[72]

These discussions portray some of the more subtle forms of discrimination as well as the more noticeable ones. I have chosen these to give some 'voice' to forms of discrimination often overlooked or set aside for programmatic purposes. These conditions that characterize our present state of affairs with regard to the *curricula* decisions that are made, for me, are fundamentally important that we understand them as a threat to a critical set of criteria for the education of our children; indeed, for our 'black' and brown children, who are not afforded insights into their own historical impact upon our country. Furthermore, our children do not learn well under the constant surveillance by law enforcement officials in their schools, arguably generative of the disturbing rate of incarceration of our children, all of which is predicated upon the lingering racist institutions we seem to protect more than our children and their learning experiences.

There are significant ongoing efforts to address this state of affairs. Speaking about the February, 2018 bicentennial celebration of Frederick Douglass' birth,

---

72 Emma Brown (2015) "Texas Officials: Schools Should Teach That slavery was 'side issue' to Civil War", *The Washington Post*, July 5.

Kenneth Morris, Jr., the great, great, great grandson of Frederick Douglass describes one of the goals of the celebration:

> We want, in the same way that Frederick Douglass heard his master say "education will unfit him to be a slave", we want to "unfit" young people to be oppressed, to look at how media shape their consciousness of who they are and how these systemic issues affect them and issues of lack of opportunity and lack of education; we want to inspire and uplift one million 'Frederick Douglasses'.[73]

In the interest of not allowing the most important point of this chapter to get lost in the several historical and contemporary points made here, impediments to education for 'black' and other minority children in the present context are not directly part of the rubrics of law, as in Jim Crow Laws, nor are they a result of overt violence against them as in slavery and in the years from the beginning of Reconstruction to the middle to the 20th century; those have been largely altered for the better. They arise from the institutionalized forms of racism that afford them disproportionately less in economic terms, *e.g.*, hiring practices for living-wage jobs, access to housing, access to health care, access to safe and viable school facilities and access to their own histories and traditions denied them in flawed *curricula*.

Racism will not evaporate overnight. However, until it is stemmed in its tracks, we will continue to lament these outcomes. Fighting the *spectre* of racism wherever it resides is mandatory. In the context of education, it is a major obstacle to the free, equal, high-quality public education we desire for all our children. We must pledge now to work to destroy this menace and work to build structures that are open, embracing the diversity of our country for the benefit of all now and in the future.

Bibliography

Alexander, M. (2012) *The New Jim Crow: Mass Incarceration in the Age of Colorblindness.* New York: The New Press.

Aronowitz, N.W. (March 9, 2014) "School Spirit or Gang Signs? 'Zero Tolerance' Comes Under Fire". *NBC News.* Retrieved from https://www.nbcnews.com/news/education/school-spirit-or-gang-signs-zero-tolerance-comes-under-fire-n41431

Berard, T. (2005) "On Multiple Identities and Educational Contexts: Remarks on the Study of Inequalities and Discrimination". *Journal of Language, Identity and Education*, volume 4, issue 1, pp. 67–76.

Berard, T. (2010) "Unpacking 'Institutional Racism': Insights from Wittgenstein, Garfinkel, Goffman and Sacks". *Schutzian Research, A Yearbook of Lifeworldly Phenomenology and Qualitative Social Science*, volume 2, pp. 111–135.

Bible (The Living Bible version) Proverbs 16:27.

Blumenbach, J.F. (1865; originally in 1775) *On the Natural Variety of Mankind, in The Anthropological Treatises of Johann Friedrich Blumenbach.* London: publisher unknown.

---

73 See interview by Amy Goodman at www.democracynow.org, February 3, 2017.

132 Left Behind

Bridgeport, CT student population at www.city-data.com/city/Bridgeport-Connecticut. html and Fairfield, CT student population at www.city-data.com/city/Fairfield-Connecticut.html

Brown, E. (July 5, 2015) "Texas Officials: Schools Should Teach That Slavery Was 'Side Issue' to Civil War". Education section, *The Washington Post*. Retrieved from https:// www.washingtonpost.com/local/education/150-years-later-schools-are-still-a-battle-field-for-interpreting-civil-war/2015/07/05/e8fbd57e-2001-11e5-bf41-c23f5d3face1_story.html?utm_term=.bec77586663b

Casey, D. (March 15, 2015) "Not-Pot Leaf Gets 6th-Grader in Big Trouble". *Roanoke Times*. Retrieved from http://www.roanoke.com/news/casey-not-pot-leaf-gets-th-grader-in-big-trouble/article_67dc2868-0f0a-53c0-96ad-595a88391aa3.html

Census Bureau (September, 2014) "Income and Poverty in the United States: 2013". Retrieved from www.census.gov/content/dam/Census/library/publications/2014/demo/p60-249.pdf

Clark, K.B. (1950) "Effects of Prejudice and Discrimination on Personality Development". White House Conference on Children and Youth, Children's Bureau, Federal Security Agency (mimeographed).

Clarke, J.H. (1992) *Christopher Columbus and the African Holocaust: Slavery and the Rise of European Capitalism*. Alameda, CA: A & B Distributors & Publishers Group: Part 3.

Collins, G. (June 21, 2012) "How Texas Inflicts Bad Textbooks on Us". *New York Review of Books*. Retrieved from http://www.nybooks.com/articles/2012/06/21/how-texas-inflicts-bad-textbooks-on-us/

DeNavas-Walt, C. & Proctor, B.D. (September, 2014) "Income and Poverty in the United States: 2013". Retrieved from www.census.gov/content/dam/Census/library/publica-tions/2014/demo/p60-249.pdf

Description of The Lyman School (1886–1971) Retrieved from www.abominablefirebug. com/lyman.html

Einenkel, W. (September 18, 2015) "11-Year-Old Gifted Student Suspended 1 Year for Having a Pot Leaf That Wasn't a Pot Leaf". *Daily Kos*. Retrieved from https://www. dailykos.com/stories/2015/9/18/1422548/-11-year-old-gifted-student-suspended-1-year-for-having-a-pot-leaf-that-wasn-t-a-pot-leaf

EurekAlert! (July 22, 2015) "Schools with Higher Black, Minority Populations Call Cops, Not Docs". Retrieved from https://www.eurekalert.org/pub_releases/2015-07/ps-swh072215.php

Gentry, L. (April 8, 2017) "On Racism" recited on Viceland TV during a telecast between 10:30 and 11:00 a.m.

Gibson, W.E. (October 20, 2015) "Vindicated Florida Teen Goes to the White House". *SunSentinel*. Retrieved from http://www.sun-sentinel.com/news/education/fl-polk-honors-student-arrest-20151020-story.html

Goodman, A. (April 15, 2013) "Students, Officials Condemn School-to-Prison Pipeline in NYC". Retrieved from www.democracynow.org/2013/4/16/headlines/students_officials_condemn_school_to_prison_pipeline_in_nyc

Goodman, A. (July 17, 2015) interview with Maya Schenwar. Retrieved from www. democracynow.org

Goodman, A. (February 3, 2017) interview with Kenneth Morris, Jr. Retrieved from www. democracynow.org

Gould, S.J. (1996; originally published in 1981) *The Mismeasure of Man*. New York: W.W. Norton & Company.

Holmes, J. (August 6, 2015) "White Kids Get Medicated When They Misbehave, Black

Kids Get Suspended – or Arrested". *New York Magazine*. Retrieved from https://www. thecut.com/2015/08/white-kids-get-meds-black-kids-get-suspended.html

Jensen, R. (August 17, 2017) "When Will the United States Transcend White Supremacy?" *Common Dreams*. Retrieved from https://www.commondreams.org/views/2017/08/17/ when-will-united-states-transcend-white-supremacy

Juzwiak, R. & Chan, A. (December 8, 2014) "Unarmed People of Color Killed by Police, 1999–2014". Retrieved from http://gawker.com/unarmed-people-of-color-ki lled-by-police-1999-2014-1666672349

King, M.L., Jr. (August 28, 1963) "I Have a Dream" speech. Retrieved from www.archives. gov/files/press/exhibits/dream-speech.pdf

Lewontin, R. with Rose, S. & Kamin, L.J. (2017; originally published in 1984) *Not in Our Genes*. Chicago: Haymarket Books.

Malcolm X (January 23, 1963) "Message to the Grass Roots". Michigan State University, East Lansing, MI. Retrieved from http://rcha.rutgers.edu/images/2016-2017/1960s/ Documents/12.-RCHA-2016-The-Culture-of-the-Sixties-Malcolm-X-Message-to-the-Grass-Roots-condensed-1963.pdf

Marsh, W.H. (February 25, 2011) "The Untold Story of One of America's Largest Slave Revolts". *The Root*. Retrieved from http://www.theroot.com/ the-untold-story-of-one-of-americas-largest-slave-revol-1790862932

Montagu, A. (1997; originally published in 1942) *Man's Most Dangerous Myth: The Fallacy of Race*. Sixth edition. Lanham, CA: Alta Mira Press.

Brown, O. v. Board of Education of Topeka, Kansas (May 17, 1954) Supreme Court decision. Retrieved from https://supreme.justia.com/cases/federal/us/347/483/case.html

Orwell, G. (1946) "Politics and the English Language". Retrieved from www.orwell.ru/ library/essays/politics/english/e_polit/

Palast, G. (2012) *Billionaires & Ballot Bandits: How to Steal an Election in 9 Easy Steps*. New York: Seven Stories Press.

Popper, K.R. (1970) "Normal Science and its Dangers", in I. Lakatos & A. Musgrave, eds. *Criticism and the Growth of Knowledge*. pp. 52–53. Cambridge: Cambridge University Press.

Ramey, D. (2015) "The Social Structure of Criminalized and Medicalized School Discipline", *Sociology of Education*, volume *88*, issue *3*, pp 181–201.

Rasmussen, D. (2010) *American Uprising: The Untold Story of America's Largest Slave Revolt*. New York: Harpers.

Ryan, W. (1971) *Blaming the Victim*. New York: Vintage Books.

Schenwar, M. (2014) *Locked Down, Locked Out: Why Prison Doesn't Work and How We Can Do Better*. San Francisco, CA: Barrett-Koehler Publishers, Inc.

The 1852 Massachusetts School Attendance Act, Chapter 240, Section 1. Retrieved from www.mhla.org/information/massdocuments/mglhistory.htm

White, J.L. & Cones, J.H. (1999) *Black Man Emerging: Facing the Past and Seizing a Future in America*. New York: Routledge.

www.ballotpedia.org/Voter_identification_laws_by_state.

www.dignityinschools.org.

www.eds-resources.com.

Wyler, G. (July 26, 2014) "The Mass Incarceration Problem in America". *Vice News*. Retrieved from https://news.vice.com/article/the-mass-incarceration-problem-in-america

Zuak-Skees, C. & Wiedere, B. (April 10, 2015) "A State-by-State Look at Students Referred to Law Enforcement". Retrieved from www.publicintegrity.org/2015/04/10/17074/ state-state-look-students-referred-law-enforcement

7

THE TEACHING PROFESSION

... For rigorous teachers seized my youth,
And purged its faith, and trimmed its fire,
Showed me the high, white star of Truth,
There bade me gaze, and there aspire ...
  — *Matthew Arnold: "Stanzas from the Grande Chartreuse"*

Teachers

Teachers are public servants. They populate a profession of individuals whose purpose is to help liberate the forces within people, overwhelmingly children, to understand themselves and the world around them. Within whatever culture, they are also entrusted with passing on to its newest members the best of what that ethnic group has created in its collective history. Education is messy. It is not messy because this teacher or that makes it messy. It is messy 'by nature'. Teachers cannot enter into the practice of teaching thinking that it is a matter of 'transferring' information, a simple 'process' of telling students about this and that and be done with it. No, it is much more. It is not enough that teachers know their academic area; they must understand the context of their practice and must be able skillfully to manage the diverse components of that environment. That is the most messy part.

While teachers should be those who have been trained to accomplish a wide range of tasks, they must also be those who have lived, that is, who have had some significant experience in life and what it requires to survive and thrive. Teachers must be dedicated, tenacious and patient individuals, highly aware of the complicated task that it is to engage the youth of their society, for that engagement is conducted across a vast continuum of realities: economic, political, cultural, social and ideological. They must be compassionate and empathetic as they confront the

The teaching profession **135**

consequences of what the youth enjoy and endure within these realities. Teachers must be much more than 'reservoirs' of this or that corner of knowledge; they must be, depending upon the context, coaches, counselors, confidants and surrogate parents, friends, colleagues and comrades. Only if these foundational criteria are met by the prospective teacher can we discuss what particular training and specialized knowledge they should possess in order to create the context for the learning of others. Accordingly, teachers hold a very special place in any society; they are charged with the daunting and, sometimes, amorphous task of taking our children 'by the hand' and introducing them to the complexities of the culture in all of its manifestations, from academic subjects to social protocols to emotional parameters and beyond.

Teacher training

Teaching is a profession that does require training, especially in the elementary and secondary contexts.[1] Teachers must not only become theoretically astute[2] and informed about the subject matter (the academic area) of their choosing, they must also become knowledgeable about the age group they intend to *serve*.[3] In addition, teachers engage in a multiplicity of tasks attendant to classroom instruction. While children are in school (or in the extended classroom – the community, undertaking project-based education), teachers provide virtually *everything*: they must deliver the *curriculum*, presumably constructed by them and other teachers (and not by *non*teachers), they lead them in getting food and drink at breakfast and/or lunch; they must discipline them; they must listen to their personal needs and respond appropriately; they must be compassionate and understanding; they must attend to the educational needs of each individual student to ensure that s/he understands the subject matter at hand. (This is separate from presenting the material in lecture form; it requires one-on-one attention.) They must preside over any project-based educational venture and venue; they must assure their safety and wellbeing; they must provide emotional support; they must monitor the interactional reality in that particular classroom, or other context to maximize learning, to mention a few.

---

1 Teaching at the university level is different and, as such, requires a different kind of training, best provided by the mentors of the prospective Master or Doctoral candidates. It involves those candidates' acquiring "Teaching Fellowships", whereby they are assigned introductory courses, usually at the same university they are attending. The mentors visit those candidates on a regular basis, not every class, to observe and do evaluations of their classroom work: how they communicate with students, how they field questions from them, how accurate their lectures are with regard to the subject matter of that course they are supposed to relate, etc. Effectively, it has the format of 'on-the-job' training.

2 See Preface, where I discuss the proper parameters of a viable philosophy of education.

3 I select this category deliberately: public school teachers are *servants*, *public servants*. Teaching is a profession which is recipient designed, designed to pay attention to the details necessary to fulfill the needs of all our children, one whose rewards are based upon the benefits rendered to those we serve, not upon what we may gain as a result of our interactions with those we serve.

136 Left Behind

Teachers who perform these, even only adequately, are extraordinary professionals. Yet, that professional performance is not honored equal to its expectations. In the words of Jacques Barzun (1907–2012), "Teaching is not a lost art, but the regard for it is a lost tradition"[4] We also expect much of counselors and social workers, two other professions which are similarly not appreciated commensurate with their charge.

Especially, teachers in elementary and secondary education have the most 'face time' with students (being in constant close contact with them for some seven hours a day[5]), requiring of them that they 'be on' all day. The pressures are immense. No matter how well prepared teachers might be, the rigors of the day-to-day performance of teaching takes a massive toll on them. I have the highest respect and compassion for these selfless individuals, who do this, day after day, with little to no thanks, as Jacques Barzun asserts above. I assert that overwhelmingly most teachers do this; those who do not are in the extreme minority. Where they do not, action must be taken to rectify it. Where they do, which is virtually always and everywhere, those teachers should command the highest respect from their communities and the society at large.

What should teachers go through in their 'training'? There are two trajectories: *classroom* work in which the prospective teacher learns about the philosophy of education and its attendant manifestations; and, along the way, *project-based field* work (outside the classroom), actually to do teaching in the presence of seasoned teachers, their mentors or internship supervisors, to learn the multifarious skills necessary to deliver only the best education to our children. These two paths should guide the formal training that teachers receive in university.

I have talked to some teachers in training. They take courses in child development (heavily based upon psychological perspectives as opposed to say sociological ones, in my view more helpful), history of education, skills building in reading and math, *etc.* But, little philosophy, or little philosophy of education. Any reference to 'philosophy' is largely 'methodology', the mechanics of teaching rather than a way of thinking about that teaching, *e.g.*, what the assumptions are, the questions at issue, the concepts that must be deployed therein, the points of view that are available therein and, ultimately, what the purposes and goals are.[6] By 'philosophy', I mean a set of guiding theoretical principles for teaching that escort the teacher through the experience of learning.[7] Methodologies should be commensurate with these principles, as they become the means by which learning is achieved, but are conceptually separate from the principles.

---

4 Jacques Barzun, (1981, originally published in 1945) *Teacher in America*, Carmel, IN: Liberty Fund, Inc. French philosopher of education, Presidential Medal of Freedom, 2003.

5 This very long school day must be reduced to approximately five hours a day. Accordingly, the curriculum must be tightened up to be more efficient, thereby making the whole day more pleasant and less stressful.

6 See Richard Paul and Linda Elder (2016) *Critical Thinking: Concepts & Tools: The Miniature Guide to Critical Thinking Concepts and Tools*, Seventh Edition. Tomales: The Foundation for Critical Thinking.

7 See Preface.

The most salient component of teacher training that I noticed was the fact that it is precisely the same as what teachers, when released into the classroom, do with their students: they are trained, not only in how to teach to the test, but also how to study for the test(s) that they must suffer themselves in order to be certified, the requirements of licensure in one or another state. In Massachusetts, for example, all K-12 education graduates must pass the CLST (Communication and Literary Skills Test[8]). This is among many others they must successfully suffer; most usually tests in reading and math, supplemented by tests in a teacher's specific area of emphasis: social studies, language arts, writing, *etc.* They receive an inordinate number of 'strategies' to prepare students to take tests and to administer them, relatively very few 'philosophical tenets' to lead their students in their learning and how it relates to their learning and their lives. In short, teacher training should be commensurate with that which I have worked to liberate myself and others from over the years: pedagogy – the methodology that instructs through memorization and reproduction which requires *obeisance.*[9]

What do teachers do? 'Schooling vs. education'

Truly, the most fundamental problem is the fact that we do not *educate* our children, we *school* them. Schooling has to do with what we can observe taking place in our elementary and high schools, all over the country: the sequential imposition of one subject after another, meted out in predetermined time slots, regulated by bells and buzzers, routinely not allowing for the completion or logical follow through of any project, each disjoined from the other, day after day, month after month, year after year. Schooling then is a series of 'sound bites' (just like in the mass media), organized to instill in our children a regimented scheme to oblige them to obey and follow directions, reinforced by standardized testing; in other words, this, so they can learn to 'fit into' a society that is prescribed to deliver only the kind of social reality conjured by those in positions of power and who came before them. In the meantime, children have little time to develop independently from this experience and to learn how to apply what they learn to their everyday lives. Teachers are forced into a scheme that does not allow them to do what is most logical to them: to create a context of learning that is organic and commensurate with the best knowledge they have, unfettered by preoccupations with 'measurement' and score-keeping. Instead, their lives, teachers and students, become dissociated from a reality that could be, one that could connect the learning part with the practical part of what constitutes life.

---

8 Interesting how these novice teachers must pay tens of dollars for each section of this test; all provided for by the Pearson Company, the largest firm involved in 'educational assessment', which designs these tests and receive handsome compensation. I wonder how many teachers they have on staff? They do not list any on their website at www.pearson.com and, when you search "people on staff", the reply is "We're sorry, we did not find anything that matched your search". Not very reassuring when these tests hold so much sway in the lives of our children and our would-be teachers.
9 See Preface for discussion about the difference between 'pedagogy' and 'interactive' learning.

138 Left Behind

This also goes on in colleges and universities, albeit somewhat differently. There, the schooling takes the form of lectures about how the world is or should be or cannot be and the regurgitation or recitation or parroting with little the whisper of any critical thought or questioning. This is simply a more sophisticated form of 'stuffing' information into students, but a continuation of what our children got in elementary and high school. Sophisticated only in the sense that the trappings of compulsory public education have been replaced by the veneer of 'advanced', voluntary education, education that purports to be deeper and broader. However, in reality, it is all the more nefarious because students are told that they are adults now and that they are 'in charge of their education' (actually true) and that they have the false freedom to choose this or that course to satisfy this or that requirement toward their degrees. They are also told in a variety of ways that they need this education in order to have a chance at a 'good job', something that, in my view, is immoral and part of a scam to get thousands of our youngsters into debt, repayment for which will project into their middle lives. The fraud is that those who could make good on the promise of 'good jobs' are not doing so: instead, they are supporting the banks and other financial institutions secure more profits. The crime is consequential beyond the individual fraud against our children, it is a crime against our future as a society.

Face-to-face education vs. 'distance learning'

When I think of education in general, I picture the classroom and the learning project in the community and the interaction that takes place there. The teacher welcomes the students and proceeds to engage them in the subject matter at hand. All of this takes place in a face-to-face context, one in which all participants, teachers and students, interact together, taking up one component of the subject matter at a time and moving from introduction to familiarization to competence.

Sometimes, as some teachers know well, there are no guarantees of harmonious interactions in that classroom, often resulting in undesired outcomes. There are many classroom situations that do not come close to the scenario I depicted above. Some of those classroom settings can be brutal for all kinds of reasons for the teachers and the students: various disruptions, lack of respect for the context and each other; sometimes physical altercations rendering an otherwise organized situation into a nasty undertaking. These conditions should never develop, but, they do arise out of the fundamentally flawed system we continue to endure. These troublesome factors are counterproductive to already difficult work and can only properly be addressed in another book project; they deserve full treatment. However, only with the cooperation of administrators, teachers and students can solutions be found to address these unfortunate situations.

Nonetheless, even for the worst teacher and/or the worst students, the face-to-face context still allows for the opportunity to settle things down and, once dealt with, learning can resume with discussion to present, troubleshoot and galvanize the apprehension of concepts, topics and their consequences. Teaching is

The teaching profession **139**

a fundamentally intimate undertaking, one which requires acute skills and insights into what goes on in the classroom and at project locations, *etc*. Teaching, to be at its best, must be conducted *in person*; hence, face-to-face education.

When I was a young man, I remember hearing about 'correspondence' courses that were offered by companies to afford people an opportunity to study something that would not otherwise be in the offing. For many people, it was a course in a language that claimed, once completed, that people would achieve enough familiarity with the language to communicate in it in a rudimentary way. Or, a course of study in say mechanical drawing could open doors for one in drafting or some related field of employment. The company would send you some books (this was before cassette recordings) and connect you to a monitor (person), with whom you communicated. These courses were affordable and, regardless to what extent one 'succeeded' – which was really up to the student – one understood that the relationship between the individual and the institution offering the course was limited and no claims were made by that institution with regard to any 'certification' or 'accreditation' in that course of study. However, the student could demonstrate that s/he had taken instruction in this or that subject and completed it.

These days, the same concept is applied to a multiplicity of educational endeavors: 'get rich quick' schemes in real estate or some other marketing context – how to get the most out of investing in stocks and bonds or the commodities market – or some other kind of 'schooling', 'training' that is "guaranteed" to get one a job or pass this or that certification examination, including achieving higher SAT test scores. Now, these courses do have electronic aids, *e.g.*, cassettes, audio and video discs and internet access to all manner of information. All of these companies make claims that entice people to partake in something that they know little to nothing about, and that, after a few weeks of reading and trial and error, they will become conversant enough with the subject to succeed at whatever the course is claiming.

This is not an on-the-job training program or an apprenticeship. The consumer buys the materials they are sent through the mail, and that's it. There are offers of online assistance, but that might cost more. Ultimately, the relationship one has with the company is transactional: the one people have with a store from which they buy a commodity of any kind.

I do not disparage these kinds of relationships that people seek out to inquire into information that might help them cope with the complex world we live in, especially when the economic realities are so dire for most people. Also, I do not judge the success or failure of these programs. I suppose that these kinds of informational outlets could be helpful some of the time; however, people should heed the old saying, "*caveat emptor*" (consumer beware). In other words, this kind of learning experience may not always yield what is claimed.

However, the latest version of this concept, in my view, is not so easily accepted. A disturbing trend has befallen us: 'distance learning' through 'online courses', at the college level. This concept has slowly infiltrated colleges and universities, some more than others. Because of the wonders of the internet, communication between and among people is easy and timely, either in writing or, most recently, in the form

140 Left Behind

of live imaging through Skype and other formats. These communicative venues are remarkable and can supplement and complement educational efforts of all kinds.

Hence, I do not disparage this kind of technology either. What I find worrisome, however, is that, as in many other contexts, what seems benign at first can develop into something disruptive and ultimately downright destructive. For example, electronic voting machines might have seemed reasonable at first. They could 'speed up' vote-counting significantly; they are light and compact compared to the mechanical 'lever' machines we used for decades; these characteristics are, on their face, quite desirable. Unfortunately, these are superficial advantages. These machines have proven to be a 'Trojan horse' into the inner sanctum of perhaps the most iconic practices in a struggling democracy. Because many of those machines do not provide a 'paper record' of the votes cast, recounts and verifications are very difficult.

What is most egregious about these new machines is that they slam open the doors for hackers, who have the means to skew elections in a particular direction. This has been demonstrated by several investigative journalists and writers, most notably Greg Palast and Jonathan Simon.[10] Indeed, evidence has shown that we have not had a 'clean' election' since before 2000 and many who study these matters are skeptical about the ones before that and the upcoming ones as well.

The idea of 'online courses' also seems benign on its face. What could be nefarious about such a *modus operandi* to deliver educational information to students? Claims are made that this is only another way to conduct 'innovative' education to "keep up with the times", to take advantage of the wonders of the internet. I argue that this way of 'teaching' consists of abolishing the classroom and project-based ventures – where real education can take place because of its face-to-face character – by separating the teacher from the students and students from each other. Through the 'marvel' of the computer, which provides access to the internet, students, potentially from around the world, are able to take a course of study offered by an institution's teacher (currently at the college/university level) for credit in a matriculated program; this without ever meeting or getting to know 'face-to-face' either the teacher or the other students. Everything is 'managed' over the internet.

There are several problems underlying this model of 'education', whether partially or fully undertaken over the internet. As already indicated, there is no face-to-face interaction, a hallmark of effective education.[11] Discussion in the course is reduced to being 'text messages' or 'instant messages' to one another; and the whole undertaking is *mediated* through the computer or other devices and their

---

10 See Greg Palast (2002) *The Best Democracy Money Can Buy: An Investigative Reporter Exposes the Truth About Globalization, Corporate Cons, and High-finance Fraudsters*, London: Pluto Press, now a documentary film by the same title; and Greg Palast (2012) *Billionaires and Ballot Bandits: How to Steal an Election in 9 Easy Steps*, New York: Seven Stories Press. Jonathan D. Simon (2014) *Code Red: Computerized Election Theft and the New American Century*, Arlington, MA: www.CODERED2014.com.

11 See Preface about the dialogical encounter.

screens. The professor/teacher is relegated to being a 'manager' of the proceedings in the course, clicking here and there to navigate students' activities and maybe answering questions.

That is true only if there *is* a professor/teacher at the other end. Or, is the person at the other end a mere functionary, whose job is to manipulate prepackaged data sets, presumably prepared by the professor/teacher, *e.g.*, pat answers to predicted questions posed by students, in real time, and paragraphs of discourse predesigned to introduce foundational concepts, explain problem parts of the course, and assignments of work necessary to complete the course? All of this can be done without the sustained presence of professors/teachers. All of this kind of information is available to whomever wishes to gather it, compile it and deliver it in such a course.

Recall the work of ALEC, the American Legislative Exchange Council, a reactionary organization whose main purpose is to write legislation for members of Congress, both in the Senate and the House of Representatives. Funded by the Koch brothers, it has been demonstrated that representatives and senators have presented bills that were written by the operatives at ALEC, not by them. What appears to the citizenry as the work of our representatives in Congress is sometimes the 'lobbying' work of this kind of operation. What does that say about our representatives? Are they incompetent? Are they lazy? Are they corrupt? Why would an elected representative abdicate his/her office to anyone or any other institution? The results of such abdication is that the bills that are sent along are crafted to serve the purposes of special interests and not those of the people and are therefore fraudulent.

Is that what is going on with these 'distance learning' college courses? Is the delivery of 'education' online a 'fraudulent' enterprise? I suspect that such courses offered by faculty in established accredited universities are managed by the actual professors at that university. I know that the courses offered at the University of Connecticut are professor managed. Fair enough, even though I do not subscribe to this kind of format. The learning results may or may not be ideal. That can be determined according to some criteria to which I do not have access and is beyond the purview of this book. So, they get 'a pass' for the time being.

However, the reader may have noticed that such 'online' college programs have arisen over the last several years, *e.g.*, Capella, Strayer, Phoenix and Kaplan, all avowedly accredited. These institutions are not operating in the same way as say the University of New Hampshire, which has a well-developed online program. It has had full academic programs long before its development of the online courses. The institutions listed above are exclusively operating online. They are selling the idea that one can obtain a college degree simply by applying to the institution, paying the tuition and 'attending' the course, which amounts to reading books and articles and other assigned materials (including contact with an online professor), and taking tests, all conducted over the internet. I am not in a position to evaluate these programs. However, I do have some questions, questions that all potential attendees should pose.

These are 'for-profit' companies, which employ professionals, presumably 'professors' to conduct classes. Are those professors conducting those classes? There may

142 Left Behind

be professors on staff, but who is actually doing the online work of managing the courses? Or are the courses being conducted by functionaries who manipulate the courses 'in real time' and according to protocols from professors?

I do not know and can only speculate that these conditions leave the door wide open for the same kind of malfeasance that is going on with ALEC and our representatives. I do hope that such practices do not exist in any of these online colleges/universities; but one can only wonder about how easy it would be to set up an operation that purports to have professors on staff, but that hires functionaries instead. However, the point I want to make here is one about the validity of the methodology itself, not whether or not someone might learn something in that context.

Is this what colleges and universities in the future will look like? From a common sense point of view, just as professors in regular universities already entrust the more mundane tasks of educational activities to their student teaching fellows, isn't it conceivable that many of the routine tasks will be conducted by functionaries? Their 'training' might not be much more than an orientation to the course material and how to manipulate the computer program to accommodate the student population enrolled in that course. The obvious problem is that this challenges the survival of the teaching profession. We must preserve the face-to-face teaching context; it is tried and proven.

The STEM curricula

In 2014, the Obama Administration launched the STEM (Science, Technology, Engineering and Math) education program by investing more than $3 billion in federal programs. The programs were designed to encourage interest on the part of students to study in these areas. They range across the educational spectrum, from K–12 and post-secondary institutions. Teachers are always delighted when there is an infusion of funding, no matter what it is, but they were particularly pleased that the Department of Education deemed it important to fund the sciences, an area of concern for the United States because its world placement in science has waned in the last 50 years. According to the PISA, 2015 scores,[12] the United States posted the following rankings: mathematics – 41st in the world; reading – 24th in the world; science – 25th in the world. It is not surprising that something needs to be done about all areas of education, but the STEM program is supposed to address the void in our children's performance in these particular areas.

Judging from past experience, it does not seem that good science makes much difference when confronted by protectionist political-economic exigencies. On the

---

12 PISA (Programme for International Students Assessment) *Excellence and Equity in Education, vol. 1* (2016) is a triennial survey that reports upon 15-year-old students' achievements in terms of "knowledge and skills that are essential for full participation in modern societies". It is launched by the Organisation for Economic Co-operation and Development (OECD), Paris. See http://oecd.org.

The teaching profession **143**

one hand, lip service is paid to the notion that our future is predicated on making sure that our children not only understand how science works, but also how to discover more and more about science and open new doors that will enhance our understandings of the world around us and the surrounding universe. On the other hand, when insights in science are discovered or attempted to be deployed by scientists, they are often ignored or interrupted or halted or covered up by government shenanigans for political purposes or by corporations so that they can maximize short-term profits at the expense of destroying our planet even more, thereby putting the human species in more jeopardy. Should science be 'trumped' (pun intended) by government politics and corporate greed or should science be part of the rules by which to conduct government and business?

For example, nuclear power plants have been shown to be dangerous in cataclysmic ways. The monumental catastrophe caused by the earthquake and ensuing Tsunami in Fukushima, Japan, in March 2011, rendered two reactors, initially, and a third one weeks later, not only incapacitated, but more importantly, spreading nuclear waste water everywhere and radiation throughout a more than 50-mile radius. Hard science (*e.g.*, hydrology, nuclear physics, civil engineering, *etc.*) demonstrates how dangerous these plants are, even when they are new and when 'accidents' seem less likely. (I use inverted commas here because good science recognizes that nuclear plants are, by definition, accidents waiting to happen.) The constant production of 'spent fuel' (doublespeak for 'nuclear waste') is dumped into our waterways and the oceans, polluting them forever. Social science demonstrates that these plants are not even economically viable, requiring public monies (taxes) to allow them to continue to operate. Those tax dollars could be much better spent on solar, which has zero impact on the environment, and wind energy systems, which have virtually zero impact on the environment (save some noise, depending upon where they are installed), instead of subsidizing corporate skullduggery.

Nonetheless, nuclear plants continue to operate, even beyond their life expectancy of 30 years. At this point, most of the nuclear plants have past their life expectancy, but are still online. (Check out Indian Point just north of NYC, causing trouble for some time now; it may close down in 2021). Thankfully, there are some who see the folly in this thinking and practice and have acted responsibly: the Vermont legislature has decommissioned Yankee One (December 2014), the only nuclear power plant in the state. Angela Merkel, the Chancellor of Germany, upon the heels of the Fukushima disaster, took eight of its 17 nuclear power plants offline and has established a time line to decommission the rest of them by 2020.

Meanwhile, President Obama continued to talk about the construction of several new nuclear power plants in North Carolina and Georgia. This illogic is profound; how can STEM, and the 'good science' that it can bring to our children, compete with this kind of disregard for science? Interestingly, Toshiba, the parent company of the Westinghouse Electric Company, whose technology is used in more than half of nuclear power plant construction, has filed Chapter 11 on March 29, 2017. Due to cost overruns and the significant decrease in cost (~50%) of solar and wind power production, resulting in a decrease in consumer costs, Westinghouse will

144 Left Behind

cease the U.S. projects and concentrate on plants overseas in Europe, the Middle East and Africa (EMEA). The nuclear industry questions whether or not these plants will be completed.[13]

While this is excellent news (not for EMEA), we also learn, on the same day, that the U.S. has bully-boycotted the United Nations debate to ban nuclear weapons (120 nations attended, 40 nations did not). Ironically, it was the result of science that produced nuclear weapons, a unique technology that can destroy the planet very quickly, multiple times, if deployed. It was asserted by Professor Zia Mian that

> The news is not that the U.S. is leading a boycott. We knew that the United States was not going to participate and that it's been trying to force its nuclear/NATO allies also to not participate. The news here is that, after 70 years, the vast majority of countries in the world have decided they've had enough of waiting for the United States and the other countries with nuclear weapons to keep their promise that they would get rid of nuclear weapons and said 'enough is enough'. We are now going to create an international treaty that will ban nuclear weapons and you [nuclear countries] are going to be 'nuclear outlaws' and you're going to have to deal with this new reality.[14]

The conduct of the United States at the U.N. flies in the face of the introduction of the STEM *curricula*. I am not against the idea of the STEM program; *au contraire*, such opportunities for our children to study and understand the physical world are welcome and sorely needed. However, I think that it is hypocritical to advance 'good science', in one breath and deny it in the next. Students may well benefit from this infusion of funds for science; however, they will also have to realize that, no matter how studious they are, they will be confronted with the formidable power of reactionary politics and greed.

More, on the same day:

> A supervisor at the Energy Department's International climate office told staff this week not to use the phrases 'climate change', 'emissions reduction' or 'Paris Agreement' in written memos, briefings or other written communication, sources have told POLITICO.[15]

---

13 See report on Trump's executive order to dismantle several climate rules, established by President Obama at www.democracynow.org/shows/2017/3/29, March 29, 2017.

14 *Ibid.* Professor Mian is a physicist, nuclear expert and disarmament activist; he is also the co-director of the Program on Science and Global Security at the Woodrow Wilson School of Public and International Affairs at Princeton University. He is co-author with Harold A. Feiveson, Alexander Glaser and Frank N. Von Hippel of *Unmaking the Bomb: A Fissile Material Approach to Nuclear Disarmament and Nonproliferation* (2014) Cambridge, MA: MIT Press.

15 See "Energy Department Climate Office Ban Use of Phrase 'Climate Change'". www.politico.com/story/2017/03/energy-department-climate-change-phrases-banned-236655.

The teaching profession **145**

As I have pointed out elsewhere, the struggle for a sane society does not only take place on the economic and political battlefields, it takes place on the *ideological* battlefield, in the very way we use language, particularly generated by the mass media, resulting in the ways we think about what is going on.

Another example: in light of a multitude of nasty polluting outcomes from hydraulic fracturing (aka 'fracking') in Pennsylvania, New York and in Canada, which science has demonstrated to be very dangerous,[16] this method of extracting petroleum from tar sands and areas deep in the ground continues to take place. The latest controversy about this dirty oil has been the construction of the Dakota Access Keystone XL Pipeline (DAPL), contracted to be built by Energy Transfer Partners, L.P. Their permit to proceed had been denied under Obama, after months of protest by the Standing Rock Sioux Tribe in Canon Ball, ND. However, Trump re-permitted the project in Presidential Memoranda, January 24, 2017.[17] The rationale, according to Trump, is that this project will create "28 thousand jobs".[18] Ellen R. Wald Ph.D. (historian and scholar of energy industry) writes:

> Construction of the pipeline would require thousands of short-term construction and related service jobs. These jobs would most likely number fewer than 10,000 and would only last a short time, and an even shorter duration in any single location. The long-term operation and maintenance of the pipeline would not create a meaningful number of jobs, because pipelines are simple to maintain once built.[19]

The pipeline would take fossil junk oil from Alberta, Canada, to the Koch Brothers' refinery in Corpus Christi, TX. It is estimated that it takes as much energy to produce this petroleum as it will provide once extracted from the ground. Here, mathematics tells us that this is not viable, and, the pollution, mostly of ground water, that it will create makes it most undesirable.

Since Donald Trump has been in the White House, the hope for a scientifically empowered society is in jeopardy. The Trump team is populated with climate change deniers and overall science skeptics of all kinds. Witness the defunding of the EPA, the gutting of the NIH and this re-permitting of the Dakota Access Pipeline, which is, as of the third week in June 2017, again being stalled because of an incomplete

---

16 See the HBO documentary film *GasLand* (2010) by writer/director Josh Fox, in which is documented the pollution of water supplies with methane gas flowing out of people's kitchen faucets, residents witnessing flame coming out once ignited.

17 This pipeline has already leaked some 5,000 barrels of oil near Amherst, SD, November 16, 2017. See Steven Mufson and Chris Mooney (November 16, 2017) "Keystone Pipeline spills 210,000 gallons of oil on eve of permitting decision for Trans Canada".

18 Amy Harder (January 24, 2017) "Trump Takes Action to Revive Keystone, Dakota Pipelines". *The Wall Street Journal*.

19 See E.R. Wald (2017) "Here Are the Jobs the Keystone XL Pipeline Would Create under Trump's Executive Order". *Forbes*.

'environmental impact' study. Let's hope that it will be permanently cancelled, as the environmental, especially water, risks of oil pipelines are well documented.

Yet another example: most people remember the horrific accident (predictable outcome based upon information demonstrating that safety regulations were not followed) at the BP Deepwater Horizon oil rig in the Gulf of Mexico in April 2010. This explosion killed 11 workers and spilled millions of gallons of crude oil from Texas to Florida. We watched daily for months while slow progress was made to cap the drilling hole at the bottom of the Gulf. This 'accident' savaged the coastal waters and killed innumerable plants and animals, destroying the livelihoods of thousands of people. The promise of some $20 billion in compensation only began to flow a year later; this in the light of second quarter profits (July 2011) for BP of $5 billion. Full compensation has not been disbursed. Yet, in spite of a brief moratorium on drilling imposed by President Obama, operations have resumed in the Gulf.[20] The industry has a very bad record for spilling oil all over the planet, mostly in the transportation of the oil. While oil spills have decreased in recent years, one spill is too many.[21] Science tells us that these operations should cease, especially now when global climate change is so evident; corporations tell us that there are no dangers, that the damage is minimal or that they have things under control, so that they can continue to exploit the planet, pollute the atmosphere and destroy the future of the species of this planet, including human beings. Those industries should be banned immediately and required to retool and start advancing solar and wind turbine technology and manufacturing. That would bring economic activity in line with the science.

All of the industries in these examples have a special relationship with universities: much of the R&D is done at universities by professors, whose expertise is exploited by those corporations. The distorted relationship between their science and the practices of the corporations reflects the disjointedness I have been discussing between the corporations and what we know about safety, conservation and the correct path we should take to produce energy without polluting the planet.

Here is a very poignant case in point.

Dr. Rick Steiner of the University of Alaska had been working, for the past three decades, in Sea Grant ocean studies with the National Oceanic and Atmospheric Association (NOAA), a function of the Department of Commerce. In the spring of 2009, NOAA terminated his funding and wanted the U of A to discharge him from his position at the university. Why? Dr. Steiner had been an 'advocate' of the environment, expressing concerns about drilling for oil and gas in Bristol Bay and, more recently, the Obama-sanctioned exploration drilling by Shell in the Beaufort

---

20 See Katy Reckdahl (April 15, 2015) "Five Years After the Deepwater Horizon Oil Spill, BP's Most Vulnerable Victims Are Still Struggling". *The Nation.*

21 According to The International Tanker Owners Pollution Federation Limited (ITOPFL), the number of large oil spills (>700 tonnes [mega tons ~2,204.6 pounds]) in the 1970s was 246; in the '80s, 93; in the '90s, 78; in the 2000s, 33. In the 1970s these represented 55% of all spills; in the '80s, 21%; in the '90s, 17% and in the 2000s 7%. See itopfl.com for details.

The teaching profession **147**

Sea in the North Aleutian Basin, and explicating the potential 'dangers and damage to the environment'. This means that Professor Steiner was not being an 'unbiased and neutral educator', according to Leon Cammen, director of the National Sea Grant Program. In other words, if your reports on your research findings square with the political whims of the funders, you are 'neutral'; if not, you are engaged in 'advocacy'.

The university refused to fire Dr. Steiner and made up the difference in his salary to finish out the academic year. The AAUP affiliate union has pursued his grievance through several levels and General Secretary Roger Bowen expressed deep concern about his case. Dr. Steiner has since resigned, [quoting]

> The message here is that if you say the wrong thing, especially about controversial issues, you can lose your grant funding—or worse. It's exactly the wrong message for the faculty to get, and for the state. If Sea Grant can tell the University of Alaska that their grant comes with such stipulations [as restrictions of faculty free speech], then why can't Shell or Exxon?[22]

The University of Alaska is heavily funded by the oil and gas industries, to the tune of some 85%, by Conoco Phillips and BP in particular. These companies are not interested in the science that could foreclose any movement towards drilling. In fact, regardless of the science, they want to proceed for short-term gain at long-term cost to the environment.

The way they want to deal with any challenge is to do away with it. Dr. Steiner is a nuisance; he is telling people something they do not want people to know, so they take the necessary steps to silence him. Not only is this an issue of ignoring science, it is also an issue of academic freedom. The assumption that underlies this STEM education effort is that good science is what we need to guide our decision-making to hedge our bets with regard to our future on this planet. The collusion among our political, economic and ideological dimensions has made it clear that they are not interested in the science if it challenges the overall agenda they have been shown to protect: the perpetuation of 'profit' over everything.[23]

Is that the way to deal with truth-sayers about the devastation of our global waters? Have we not learned from the worst oil *spill* (and this is doublespeak when we are talking about an act of neglect, and not a mistake), the Exxon Valdez incident?

On March 24, 1989, the Exxon Valdez poured 11 million gallons of crude oil across 1,300 miles of shoreline in Prince William Sound. Since then, only ten of

---

22 Doug Lederman (May 6, 2009) "A Battle for the Sea (Grant)". *Inside Higher Ed.*

23 See Gramsci on 'hegemony'; Antonio Gramsci (1989 reprint; originally published in 1971) *Prison Notebooks*, New York: International Publishers Co. Written between 1929 and 1935, after being imprisoned by Mussolini in 1926, Gramsci warned about hegemonic dominance leading to brutal force (*e.g.*, fascism) in times of crisis.

148 Left Behind

the 30 species of wildlife have returned to 'normal'.[24] The clean-up has never been completed and the people whose lives were destroyed by this catastrophe were never compensated. Initially, they were supposed to receive from Exxon some $500 million in compensation. After 25 years of court filings, Exxon whittled that number to less than $5 million and, to date still has not provided full compensation to all concerned.[25]

Is the stark reality of the science brought to us by Dr. Steiner to be ignored because the oil and gas industries want to continue their reckless explorations? I am an advocate of bringing 'science' to our students; however, what is the point of having our professors and researchers do that science and then have that same science denied by corporations and political policies? What kind of message does that bring to our students/children when political and economic power overrules the power of science?

Public institutions are funded by the public. What goes on in those schools is subject to the purview of the public. When private, corporate interests and political ideological hardliners get involved and contribute to the development of *curricula* and violate the very premises of academic freedom and education free form the goals of capitalist exploitation, conflicts of interest ensue; questions arise about public monies being expropriated to support private projects, however minor or according to whatever 'the rubric of the partnership' may be. These are legitimate questions and this kind of relationship is inappropriate and fundamentally contrary to the spirit of the public service these schools should be providing our students. They should not be part of the public education experience. If education were properly funded by the public, with the oversight of the people, there would be no 'need' to solicit or accept funding from corporations.

In the broader context, I leave this section with Denis Hayes's[26] *Earth Day* speech:

> Hey, this is a science march; so, I assume you all knew there was going to be a quiz. This is about last November's election. Did America somehow vote to melt the ice caps and kill the coral reefs and acidify the oceans? [march participants respond] No! Did we vote to reduce EPA's research budget, by a whopping 42%? No! Did we vote to defund safe drinking water by one third? No! Did we vote to eliminate environmental work in Chesapeake Bay and San Francisco Bay and Puget Sound and the Gulf of Mexico and the Great Lakes? No! Well, that's what we got. Forty-seven years ago, on the first Earth Day, 20 million regular, everyday Americans, including millions of angry

---

24 See Joanna Walters (March 23, 2014) "Exxon Valdez: Animal Populations in Prince William Sound, Alaska". *The Telegraph*.

25 See Kiley Kroh (July 15, 2013) "25 Years After Exxon Valdez Oil Spill, Company Still Hasn't Paid for Long-Term Environmental Damages". *Think Progress*.

26 Denis Hayes was the national coordinator of the environmental teach-in, on the first *Earth Day*, in New York City, April 22, 1970, then the largest demonstration ever, some 20 million people, in the United States. See www.youtube.com/watch?v=diuHs28AR2w.

The teaching profession **149**

students, rose up and stormed the political stage and demanded, demanded a clean, just and resilient environment. Forty-seven years later, to my astonishment, we're back in the same spot. We've got a president, a vice-president, a cabinet and the leadership of both houses of Congress, who are all climate deniers. They are scrubbing 'climate change' from federal websites and ordering federal employees not to use the words 'global warming' in any communication. This is not conservative politics. This is an inquisition, gunning for Galileo. It's now crystal clear that the man who lives right there [pointing at the White House] did not come here to 'drain the swamp'. He's filling the swamp to overflowing with conflicts of interest, with a White House that wreaks of greed and sleaze and mendacity. America has had 45 presidents, but we have never before had a president who was completely indifferent to the truth. Donald Trump makes Richard Nixon look like Diogenes. We are racing now toward a climate cliff and our coal-loving president is punching the accelerator; and so, millions of you are marching across America and around the world. Our job is clear: today is the first step in a long-term battle for scientific integrity, a battle for transparency, a battle for survival. So, don't leave here thinking that you came out in the rain, all of you, this awesome crowd, standing in the rain, freezing and thinking … now you've done your part, because you haven't, not yet. Like that first *Earth Day*, this *Earth Day* is just the beginning. And, in that battle, losing is not an option; because, if we lose this fight, we will pass on a desolate, impoverished planet for the next 100 generations. I'm old enough that I can remember when people all over the earth saw America as the world's best hope, Today, right here, right now, all of you, let's commit ourselves to becoming the world's best hope again.[27]

Direct influence from political leaders

Consider President Obama's appointment of Arne Duncan to the office of Secretary of Education. He is a well-known figure in the Chicago School System. He is the son of Sue Duncan, a longtime operator of a tutoring center, which has helped many inner-city youths get their homework done and develop learning skills often not properly provided in the local schools. After serving some time as Chief of Staff in the Chicago school system, in 2001, Chicago Mayor Daley appointed him CEO (not the superintendent, not the dean, not the president, but the CEO) of the Chicago Public Schools. How telling is this title in the context of this discussion? Let us not forget the power of language. Evidently, this category is actually quite fitting for the kind of educational policies Duncan has espoused over the years.

He led the Renaissance 2010 Plan, which was created for Mayor Daley by the Commercial Club of Chicago – an organization representing the largest businesses

---

27 Speech by Denis Hayes at the "March for Science", *Earth Day*, April 22, 2017, Washington, D.C., across from the White House.

150 Left Behind

in the city. The purpose of the Renaissance 2010 was to increase the number of high quality schools that would be subject to new standards of accountability – a code word for legitimating more charter schools and high stakes testing in the guise of hard-nosed empiricism. Chicago's 2010 plan targets 15 percent of the city district's alleged underachieving schools in order to dismantle them and open 100 new experimental schools in areas slated for gentrification.

On March 1, 2010, President Obama addressed the U.S. Chamber of Commerce, praising Colin Powell and his wife, Alma, for setting up, since 1997, America's Promise Alliance, an organization dedicated to targeting the American high school dropout problem. Obama asserted that it was fitting that education be addressed in the context of the Chamber of Commerce because the economic success of Americans is "tied to the level of education achieved". He went on to note how more than 1 million students drop out of high school each year, nearly 1 in 3, over half being black or Latino. (This tone is almost one which 'blames the victim' because he declares that students who drop out don't only hurt themselves, but their families, their communities and their country; note the placement of agency.) As dropouts, they earn $10,000 less than graduates and, during the recession of 2010, are three times more likely to be unemployed than someone with a college degree. Obama proclaims that a high school diploma is an "economic imperative", probably "the best reason to get a diploma".[28] So, the solution, in part, has to do with targeting the 5,000 lowest performing schools over the next five years. He posits that performance has to do with test scores, citing an example in Rhode Island the previous week, where the board of education saw fit to fire the principle and many of the teachers because only 7% of the 11th graders had passed the state math test. While he did not advocate this kind of move in all cases, his view about how to address these problems does include it. His comments run the gamut from identifying the problems and working with the existing staff, to replacing principals and teachers, to closing down schools either temporarily or permanently and replacing them with 'charter' schools, which, he asserts, have provided many opportunities to students, not only to finish school but also to afford them courses which are college level and prepare them better for life. Obama announced a $900 million commitment to efforts directed at solving this dropout problem.

Knowing the kinds of priorities Duncan has with regard to education, will those targeted schools be corrected or will they be replaced by 'charter' schools, often private ones whose *curricula* are conceived as adjuncts to business and commerce? Is all this rhetoric about saving our schools a smoke screen behind which lies a plan to rid our communities of public schools altogether? Not one word was uttered addressing the possibility that our public schools are underfunded in the first place. These $900 million will not go far to ameliorate the condition of our schools. Only through a comprehensive drive to reestablish schools as our own, not those of corporations and businesses, can we regain control over what goes on in them.

---

28 See www.whitehouse.gov and search for speech to Chamber of Commerce on March 1, 2010.

The teaching profession **151**

Most recently, as a result of Trump moving into the White House, many dubious appointees have been installed in the Presidential Cabinet. Again, a corporate-leaning Education Secretary has been empowered: Betsy DeVos. Her experience with education has been as a billionaire lobbyist, not an educator; this in Michigan for decades as Stephen Henderson writes:

> This deeply dysfunctional educational landscape – where failure is rewarded with opportunities for expansion and 'choice' means the opposite for tens of thousands of children – is no accident. It was created by an ideological lobby that has zealously championed free-market education reform for decades, with little regard for the outcome. And at the center of that lobby is Betsy DeVos, the west Michigan advocate whose family has contributed millions of dollars to the cause of school choice and unregulated charter expansion throughout Michigan.[29]

Apparently, DeVos is gearing up to repeat much of the same at the federal/national level. She is a staunch supporter of vouchers for private and religious schools and an advocate for charter schools (which DeVos calls "choices"), both types of schools taking public dollars and funneling them into private contexts. The charter schools are operated like corporations, whose *principals* are CEOs, not principals. No one in her family has attended a public school and she does not support teachers' unions. She does not support free tuition for college and waffled when asked about reporting sexual assault on campus to local police. When asked by Senator Maggie Hassan (D-NH) during the Senate Confirmation Hearing about vouchers, she did not avow supporting the Individuals with Disabilities Education Act, when students with disabilities receive vouchers to attend a school. That act supports those children's right to education in any context; however, some students have had to sign away their rights to accept the vouchers.

One of the most telling interchanges at those hearings was the one with Senator Al Franken (D-MN), when he asked DeVos about the difference between 'proficiency' and 'growth' in the evaluation of students. She did not demonstrate any familiarity with this debate.

> Franken: No, I'm talking about the debate between proficiency and growth and what your thoughts are on that.
> DeVos: Well, I was just asking to clarify, then …
> Franken: Well this is a subject that has been debated in the education community for years. And I've advocated growth, as the Chair and members of this committee knows, because, with proficiency, teachers ignore the kids at the top, who are not going to fall below proficiency and they ignore the kids

---

29 Valerie Strauss (2016) "A Sobering Look at What Betsy DeVos Did to Education in Michigan – And What She Might Do as Secretary of Education", *Washington Post*, December 8, quoting Stephen Henderson Op Ed in *The Free Press*, Detroit, MI.

152 Left Behind

at the bottom, who, no matter what they do will never get to proficiency. So I've been an advocate of growth. But, it surprises me that you don't know this issue ... I was kind of surprised, well, I'm not that surprised that you did not know this issue.[30]

As I address in Chapter 8 about the mismeasure of our students, this *is* an important issue. Proficiency assessment operates within quantitative parameters of testing and growth assessment operates in the realm of qualitative evaluation that moves away from 'measurement' and toward one-on-one mentoring, which requires close, weekly if not daily, monitoring of students and their improvement. This is the only way to eliminate the scourge of test scores. This requires more teachers who are well trained and committed to their craft. If teachers are well paid and supported by institutions that understand the worth of this kind of assessment, our children would not only survive the vagaries of education, they would thrive and surpass those expectations.

Since the unprecedented tie-break by Vice President Mike Pence, installing her as Secretary of Education, DeVos has made some disturbing comments about several matters pertaining to education. I cite one here:

HBCUs are real pioneers when it comes to school choices. They are living proof that when more options are provided to students, they are afforded greater access and greater quality.[31]

What a strange way to describe these 'black colleges/universities'. As the reader knows, these institutions were established because slaves, and black children during Reconstruction and the establishment of Jim Crow Laws, were not allowed to go to school. To characterize these schools as "choices" is to deny the experience of black folks in our history and to install the concept of 'choice', where there was none. This demonstrates DeVos's, either ignorance of racism in the United States or a mean-spirited streak in her character. Either, in my view, is egregious. Taken as a whole, her presence in a position of power with regard to education is completely *anathema* to what is highlighted and proposed in this book.

Here are a couple more developments in the Department of Education under Trump and DeVos:

The potential change surfaced in a scathing resignation memo sent late Tuesday night by James Runcie, the head of the Education Department's

---

30 The first day of Senate confirmation hearings for Betsy DeVos, Education Secretary nominee, January 17, 2017.

31 This DeVos tweet was reported everywhere on March 1, 2017. HBCU is the abbreviation for historically black college or university; they were referred to this way by The Higher Education Act of 1965. Such colleges/universities' main mission was the education of black Americans.

federal student aid program … He cut short his term, which was slated to run until 2020, after clashing with the Trump administration and Betsy DeVos, the education secretary, over this proposal and other issues … Mr. Trump's proposed budget for 2018 slashes funding for the department by nearly 50 percent. Moving one of its core functions [student loan program] to Treasury would significantly diminish the agency's power. It could also alter the mission of the student loan program. [32]

What this transfer of authority would do, most notably, is give the Treasury oversight of these loans and, very likely, put students at a disadvantage, because their protections could devolve, *i.e.*, the Treasury may take on a more hardline stance on 'collections' of loan repayment.

The U.S. Department of Education has an Office for Civil Rights, whose mission "is to ensure equal access to education and to promote educational excellence through vigorous enforcement of civil rights in our nation's schools."[33] It has come to light that DeVos "believes in a limited federal role in education. She has signaled that her office is 'not going to be issuing any decrees' on civil rights and that those should come from Congress or the courts."[34] This announcement means that the Department will be reducing inquiries into civil rights violations in the public schools and universities in the United States. The 'decree' will have a particularly disruptive effect upon the already flawed practices involving minority student treatment and sexual assaults on college campuses. I believe that these moves by DeVos are designed eventually to eliminate the Department of Education, an agency that was supposed to protect the rights and opportunities of our youngsters, not create contexts of even further stress and injustice. I fear that public education may be put on 'life support' following these reactionary moves by Trump and DeVos. We cannot allow these destructive policies to take our education system away from the commons and out of reach of reasonable people, who are working to build a viable form of public education. DeVos wants to destroy public education and replace it with everything private and/or religious.[35] These pronouncements only serve to eliminate the Department of Education, the public schools, teachers/professors and install a cloning system that rivals Orwell's Oceania.

---

32 See Jessica Silver-Greenberg, Stacy Cowley and Patricia Cohen (May 25, 2017) "Trump Administration Considers Moving Student Loans from Education Department to Treasury". *The New York Times*.

33 See www2.ed.gov/about/offices/list/ocr/index.htm.

34 Erica L. Green (June 16, 2017) "Education Dept. Says It Will Scale Back Civil Rights Investigation". *The New York Times*. Trump and DeVos want to cut the education 2019 budget by 5%; see Valerie Strauss, Danielle Douglas-Gabriel and Moriah Balinit (February 13, 2018) "DeVos seeks cuts from Education Department to support school choice". The Washington Post.

35 After the 2001 state take over of the Philadelphia school district and efforts to privatize it, the state has returned control over to the city, after some 22 schools were privatized, described as a "failed effort". See Katie Steele, (January 11, 2018) "Pa. government will give control over Phila. school district back to the city", *The Daily Pennsylvanian*.

154 Left Behind

Teaching and *research; why both?*

As I have just expressed, the professoriate may well be under attack by these reactionary forces. Assuming that we will still have a viable means to bring critical instruction to our youngsters, there is one policy modification that would make a huge difference in the delivery of university education: change the current structure of responsibilities for professors in 'Research 1' institutions, ones that have doctoral programs and whose faculty members engage in extensive research. Currently, the responsibilities of faculty members in such institutions are three-fold: they are required to take on a significant research load in their area of expertise, teach a full load of courses – typically two courses per semester (sometimes less) – and be involved in service (administration) to their department, their school, the university and the public.

In my experience observing how things really happen 'on the ground', setting 'service' aside for the moment, I have noticed that faculty members who are committed to research, and who do lots of it, are not the best teachers. Conversely, teachers who are committed to teaching, and who do lots of it, are not the best researchers. These comments will no doubt bring opprobrium to my doorstep, but I do not mean this in an accusatory tone. *Au contraire*, I sympathize with their predicament; indeed it was mine as well. No one can devote 100% of their efforts to two separate and distinct tasks, both fundamental to higher education – teaching and research. Teaching requires 100% of one's efforts and so does research. There are few faculty members I have encountered over the more than 50 years I have spent in academia as a student and a teacher, who have delivered at that level, in both areas. Those who have are truly exceptional.

The skill sets of faculty members do not always live up to the required degree that is expected by these universities in these two areas. One problem that arises is that really good researchers, faculty members who are dedicated to their research, can fall short in the classroom, not because they plan to do, but because their time and energies are stretched. The idea is that those faculty members can bring their research findings to their graduate students, thereby providing them with 'cutting edge' results, conclusions and discoveries. Fair enough; however, here is the problem: these universities pressure faculty members to treat their research as their primary goal.

In fact, tenure policies are replete with emphasis upon research: actually, with the number of research articles faculty members publish in a given year, from one to three, depending upon the institution, teaching and service falling way behind in importance. By definition, this virtually exclusive emphasis upon research puts faculty members in a frame of mind in which teaching becomes less important and that, if they want to achieve tenure, they had better do research. Once they achieve tenure, say, in some six years, the pressure relents somewhat, but their fate has been cast and priorities typically remain the same. I think that this set of conditions is detrimental to faculty members in both of these professional trajectories. Whichever professional *penchant* a professor has, teacher or researcher, should be maximized, not high-jacked by the imposition of other major responsibilities that distract them from their passion.

If faculty members had only their research to do, that might not be unreasonable. And, if other faculty members had only their teaching to do, that might not be unreasonable either. However, as explained above, that is not all they have to do. In fact, in order to do justice to teaching, research must be of a secondary concern. And there are those committees and community outreach to consider too. Moreover, many faculty members, who are happy to do some research but maybe not that much because they are teachers first, do not want their classroom responsibilities to suffer. By the same token, many researchers, who are happy to do some teaching but maybe not that much because they are researchers first, do not want their research to suffer. This is a real conundrum in the academy. However, the solution is quite simple.

Why not separate them? Why not allow teachers to teach and researchers to do research? The university accreditation standards would still be satisfied and, *a fortiori*, the status of 'Research 1' would be intact; both areas would be covered, except now by different faculty members. In such a context, researchers can concentrate on their research and give the occasional lecture on their findings, say, once per semester, and the teachers can concentrate on their instruction and publish a research paper, say, every other year. Faculty members would do better work because of the decrease in stress and they would be happier. This is not pie-in-the-sky; it is a reasonable and viable alternative strategy to the current undesirable one.

Some institutions support only research, so-called 'think tanks' and others require only teaching, *e.g.,* colleges that concentrate on instruction and do not require intense research, typically community colleges and some four-year institutions. The insistence upon requiring these two major responsibilities is detrimental to faculty members. It bifurcates their professional lives. The pressures are enormous and, I don't care how skilled any faculty member purports to be, something suffers. So, if a teacher wants to write a book, that book will take a lot longer to write than it would if a researcher wrote the same book. Accordingly, if a research wants to improve her/his teaching performance, the effort will be much greater than it would if a teacher required the same upgrade. The reason is because each has a different professional emphasis/agenda. They are both torn between these two necessary professional programs.

A personal note: I taught at a 'Research 1' institution and suffered the scenario I describe. I have always been a teacher first and did research as a secondary pursuit. This was unacceptable to the university and, for this short fall, I was rewarded with having to increase my teaching load. I could have finished this book in two years had I not had to teach ten courses per year; my course load, three courses per semester, and four extra courses per year because my salary, and that of many others, fell way short of the cost of living. Instead, I spent ten years on this project. The upside of that time frame is that I was able to bring several more struggles regarding education to the reader.

156 Left Behind

Teachers' unions

The AAUP organization is a union. It has protected college and university professors for more than 100 years. Its mission statement is as follows:

> The mission of the American Association of University Professors (AAUP) is to advance academic freedom and shared governance; to define fundamental professional values and standards for higher education; to promote the economic security of faculty, academic professionals, graduate students, post-doctoral fellows, and all those engaged in teaching and research in higher education; to help the higher education community organize to make our goals a reality; and to ensure higher education's contribution to the common good. Founded in 1915, the AAUP has helped to shape American higher education by developing the standards and procedures that maintain quality in education and academic freedom in this country's colleges and universities.[36]

I include this statement here because I want the reader to understand that teachers/professors need to be represented in the labor context just like plumbers, carpenters, air traffic controllers, hotel and restaurant workers, migrant workers, nurses, *etc.* While there may be differences in the circumstances among all professions/trades/services, the basic relationship is all but the same: the structurally antagonistic relationship between the employee and the employer. All unions, whether national or local have similar statements of their missions.

As you know, in capitalism, the fiscal power overwhelmingly rests in the hands of the employer. And, as such, each worker needs to be represented by something bigger than her/himself. Without this protection, the worker is left to confront the employer alone and this is not a fair 'confrontation'. With a union, the employer must confront the whole union and its contractual elements, not only the individual employee. Without union protection, the worker would be at a disadvantage. This is exactly what happens when workers do not have union protection.

Teachers/professors are no different in this regard; they require the same kind of protection, even though their work is different from other professions/trades/services. They, like all workers, need protection from unsafe working conditions, from unfair work relations, from being denied a living wage, from frivolously losing their jobs and from, once retired, from living their last years in substandard conditions, *etc.* These are the protections and contractual guarantees that a union brings to the conditions of work for its members.

There are two major national unions for teachers: the American Federation of Teachers (AFT), founded in 1916, the more powerful of the two, and the National

---

36 https://www.aaup.org/about/mission-1

Education Association (NEA), founded in 1857: both serve K-12 teachers, the AFT with ~1.6 million members and the NEA with ~3.2 million members.

There are several other state and local/city unions, mostly affiliated with these national unions, serving millions of teachers across the United States.

Tenure

Tenure is another misunderstood component of teaching. Many who like to blame teachers for the mess we are in invoke this most important protection of academic freedom, barring dismissal of elementary, secondary and university teachers on frivolous grounds. Tenure does not mean that teachers, no matter what they do, are protected. No. However, when challenged, teachers must be afforded, much like the legal protections of due process, guaranteed by the Fifth Amendment of the Constitution (although the USA Patriot Act put a big dent in that) and a fair hearing by his/her peers, the Sixth Amendment According to the American Association of University Professors (AAUP),

> After the expiration of a probationary period, teachers or investigators should have permanent or continuous tenure, and their service should be terminated only for *adequate cause* [italics added], except in the case of retirement for age, or under extraordinary circumstances because of financial exigencies.[37]

This does not mean that teachers 'cannot be dismissed', as claimed by those who want to point at this necessary protection as a significant cause of our educational problems. One of the fundamental issues about tenure has always been around what teachers teach. Political actors should never have a say about what the content of education should be; that is the job of teachers. That is the rub. Politicians do, more and more these days, want to control what our children are taught.[38]

Obviously, tenure is designed to protect full-time teachers, not 'adjunct' teachers. These are *part-time* teachers. I was an adjunct for several years and the experience I had is very much like what teachers must continue to suffer today. They teach one or two courses in this institution or that at a time; often they must weave several of these courses together in order to make a living. And, these courses are scattered across a significant geographical landscape, requiring many hours of travel from home or between institutions. They are not in good shape, not only with regard to the protections that tenure affords, but also in terms of salary. These teachers are paid very poorly, and they seldom have any 'benefits', most notably healthcare.

---

37 See the *1940 Statement of Principles on Academic Freedom and Tenure*, section headed by "Academic Tenure". www.aaup.org/file/1940 Statement.pdf.

38 See Chapter 6 on discrimination and Katherine Mangan (May 23, 2010) "Ignoring Experts' Pleas, Texas Board Approves Controversial Curriculum Standards", *Chronicle of Higher Education* at www.cronicle.com/article/Texas-Board-Approves/65661.

158 Left Behind

They are not guaranteed their teaching position the next semester or year at that same institution. So, they are constantly scouring the job listings for teaching positions, often in locations that are really too far to be practical. Nonetheless, they pursue doggedly on to make a living. Some eventually find a full-time post; others, and more and more these days, continue as adjuncts for decades. This because institutions are not replacing their full-time, tenured retirees with full-time tenure-track professionals; so much so that the ratio between full-time and part-time faculty is at an all-time high. According to *Inside Higher Ed*,

> More than half the nation's most vulnerable college students are in courses taught by part-time, adjunct faculty members who lack the job security, credentials and experience of full-time professors – as well as the campus support their full-time peers receive ... Part-time faculty teach more than half (53 percent) of students at two-year institutions.[39]

According to a study by the AAUP,

> By 2007, almost 70 percent of faculty members were employed off the tenure track. Many institutions use contingent faculty appointments throughout their programs ... Faculty serving on a contingent basis generally work at significantly lower wages, often without health coverage and other benefits, and ... the full range of faculty rights and responsibilities.[40]

We must reverse these numbers and reestablish the tenured faculty as the overwhelming majority of teachers not only in university, but also in K–12.

If we want to discover the root causes for the disarray of our educational institutions, we have to look somewhere else. I discuss many areas which we can identify as problematic in this book; but the teachers, in spite of the fact that there are some 'bad' teachers, are not the problem. Rather, it is what they are forced to implement in the classroom that is a big part of the problem.

The blame game

Teaching is hard work. I asserted this fact at the outset of this discussion because there has developed a false attitude in the United States that suggests that it is not

---

39 Paul Fain (April 7, 2014) "Low Expectations, High Stakes", *Inside Higher Ed*. While this comment is basically correct, I disagree with the part that states that adjunct faculty members "lack ... credentials". Overwhelmingly, these professionals are very well credentialed; they suffer from discrimination of one kind or another and/or the unwillingness of colleges and universities to hire full-time faculty.

40 AAUP Report "Tenure and Teaching-Intensive Appointments" (2010) updated (2014), section 1. "The Collapsing Faculty Infrastructure", based upon original AAUP data (2007) "Trends in Faculty Status, 1975–2007", www.aaup.org.

The teaching profession **159**

hard work and that the teachers must be lazy or don't know what they are doing, because why else would we have the troubles with education that we have? Here are some of the comments that have become all too common: "Teachers have it good; they only work six-hour days and they have the whole summer off." or "My kid is not getting a good education; who are they hiring these days to teach?" or "What are they teaching our kids; we had to do that when we were in school?" or "I can't help my kid with homework; I never saw that stuff before." In virtually every complaint, the teacher is at least partially to blame in some way, and this before any insight into what the problem is.

Everyone knows that there is no profession in which we do not find the occasional case of fraud, misfeasance, malfeasance, laziness, incompetence, *etc.* What we do not find, as a rule, is the wholesale characterization of a profession as somehow problematic. Parents, school boards, politicians (mayors, selectmen/women, *etc.*) are responsible for much of the negative 'press' we have seen about teachers: the parents who are interviewed on the evening news and complain about what the teacher is teaching their children; the members of the school board who call a press conference to address the troubles with education in their district and suggest that their teachers are not held accountable because of the unions; the politician who vaunts his/her devotion to education in the halls of the state house or Congress and laments how the *curricula* are not being taught 'to the letter'.

Education *is* in trouble and, apparently, many people have found a scapegoat. They can't blame the parents – they entrust their children to the schools, even though they must partake in that education – they are not in the classroom; they can't blame the school board members – they only hire and fire school personnel and make up the *curriculum* – they are not in the classroom; they can't blame the politicians – they make the rules/laws that affect how education will proceed – they are not in the classroom. Who *is* in the classroom and responsible for the day to day delivery of education? Teachers. They must be the ones who are causing all the problems. No. To be fair, it is not altogether surprising that this is the kind of rhetoric we hear; teachers are positioned between the decision-makers about education, the school boards and political figures on the one side and the actual delivery of education, face-to-face with the children on the other. Children, because they don't have any say in what they receive educationally, are 'silent' targets in educational decision-making, relying upon their teachers. Teachers are dictated to by members of the school board and/or the political leaders in their school district and often have no voice in the policies that they have to implement in the classroom. Overwhelmingly, boards of education are populated by people who are not teachers, have never taught and will never teach. I remind the reader of the survey I conducted about state departments of education in the U.S. – Chapter 6, page 128 – which showed that only 25% of all the 136 members across the country are/were teachers.

The lack of input by teachers in policy decision-making is a chronic problem across the country. One teacher at the Education Nation Teacher Town Hall

Meeting complained, "Those who can, teach; those who can't, pass laws about teaching!"[41] That sentiment was expressed as the fundamental problem teachers have in delivering the education they know our children need. The message was clear. It did not matter from which state or school district, teachers repeatedly expressed the lack of input they have in policy decision-making in their schools. They are made by people who are not teachers. This nonteacher/professor configuration is replicated at the college/university level as well. Therein lies a fundamental problem.

Consider the notion that a board of directors or trustees of some corporation or institution were to be made up of people, whose experience was unrelated to the mission of that enterprise: say, a restaurant having automobile mechanics making decisions about what food to buy, how to prepare it, plate it and serve it to customers; or a law office having artists making decisions about what cases to accept, how to defend or prosecute them. All reasonable people would be shocked at these scenarios. In many school districts, members of school boards are appointed by the elected superintendent of schools. Sadly, some of those appointments are of people who are from all walks of life other than education. Why aren't we just as shocked when it comes to education?

Or, to be more specific to the setting I am describing, take the institution whose bureaucrats make the decisions about what protocols or 'Standardized Operating Procedures' (SOPs; this is a favorite categorial phrase of functionaries) will be followed 'down the line' or 'in the field' or 'on the ground'. The reason these constructs exist in the first place is because those bureaucrats do not occupy those contexts 'on the ground' *etc.*; indeed, they are removed from them altogether. Whether the institution is a social services agency, a university, or one of any kind in which the people who actually do the work, provide those services, teach the students are not allowed to constitute their own conditions but dictated to by those who have no idea what the real intervention with the public constitutes; in those contexts, there will always be a disjunction between policy and delivery of services.

Indeed, if teachers were making decisions about the *curricula* and other fundamental educational policies and we were faced with the 'failures' we are seeing across the country, maybe we could 'blame' them for the mess we are in. However, that is not the situation we have. Those decisions are made by people who are blinded by, for example (but not the only criterion), the quantification of education through standardized tests, thinking that 'success' can be measured, instead of evaluated and assessed. Hence, 'failure' is a result of that quantification, scoring below some pre-determined and artificial level.[42]

41 View or read NBC News Education Nation Summit, October 6–8, 2013, at www.nbcnews.com/feature/education-nation/.
42 See Chapter 8 on the mismeasure of our children's education.

There are actually several problems with our education system and its delivery, as I argue in this book. However, we are looking in the wrong direction when we want to blame teachers; until we broaden our scope, until we take a closer look at many more components of learning, we will never identify what and where our problems lie so that we can address them properly. *It's not the teachers!*

Bibliography

AAUP (1940) Statement of Principles on Academic Freedom and Tenure, section on "Academic Tenure". Retrieved from www.aaup.org/file/1940 Statement.pdf

AAUP Report (2007) "Trends in Faculty Status, 1975–2007". Retrieved from www.aaup. org

AAUP Report (2010, updated 2014) "Tenure and Teaching-Intensive Appointments", section 1 of "The Collapsing Faculty Infrastructure". Retrieved from www.aaup.org

Arnold, M. (1855) "Stanzas from the Grande Chartreuse", Stanza 12. Retrived from www. poetryfoundation.org/poems/43605/stanzas-from-the-grande-chartreuse

Adlesic, T., Gandour, M., Fox, J., & Roma, D. (Producers), & Fox, J. (Director). (2010) *GasLand* [Motion Picture].

Barzun, J. (1981, originally published in 1945) *Teacher in America.* Carmel, IN: Liberty Fund, Inc.

Department of Education Office of Civil Rights (n.d.) "Mission Statement". Retrieved from www2.ed.gov/about/offices/list/ocr/index.html

Editorial Board (March 1, 2017) "Ms. DeVos's Fake History About School Choice". *The New York Times.* Retrieved from https://www.nytimes.com/2017/03/01/opinion/ms-devoss-fake-history-about-school-choice.html

Education Nation (2013) NBC News Education Nation Summit, October 6–8. Retrieved from www.nbcnews.com/feature/education-nation/

Fain, P. (April 7, 2014) "Low Expectations, High Stakes". *Inside Higher Ed.* Retrieved from https://www.insidehighered.com/news/2014/04/07/part-time-professors-teach-most-community-college-students-report-finds

Feiveson, H.A., Glaser, A., Mian, Z., & Von Hippel, F. (2014) *Unmaking the Bomb: A Fissile Material Approach to Nuclear Disarmament and Nonproliferation.* Cambridge, MA: MIT Press.

Goodman, A. (March 29, 2017) "Trump Dismantles Climate Rules". Retrieved from www. democracynow.org/shows/2017/3/29

Gramsci, A. (1989 reprint; originally published in 1971) *Prison Notebooks.* New York: International Publishers Co.

Green, E.L. (June 16, 2017) "Education Dept. Says It Will Scale Back Civil Rights Investigation". *The New York Times.* Retrieved from https://www.nytimes.com/2017/06/16/us/politics/education-department-civil-rights-betsy-devos.html

Harder, A. (January 24, 2017) "Trump Takes Action to Revive Keystone, Dakota Pipelines". *The Wall Street Journal.* Retrieved from https://www.wsj.com/articles/trump-set-to-take-action-on-keystone-dakota-pipelines-1485270333

Hayes, D. (April 22, 2017) Keynote oration at the 'March for Science', Earth Day. Retrieved from www.youtube.com/watch?v=diuHs28AR2w

Henderson, S. (December 3, 2016) "Betsy DeVos and the Twilight of Public Education". *The Free Press.* Retrieved from http://www.freep.com/story/opinion/columnists/stephen-henderson/2016/12/03/betsy-devos-education-donald-trump/94728574/

ITOPF (2016) "Oil Tanker Spill Statistics 2016". Retrieved from www.itopf.com/knowledge-resources/data-statistics/statistics/

162 Left Behind

Kroh, K. (July 15, 2013) "25 Years After Exxon Valdez Oil Spill, Company Still Hasn't Paid for Long-Term Environmental Damages". *Think Progress*. Retrieved from https://thinkprogress.org/25-years-after-exxon-valdez-oil-spill-company-still-hasnt-paid-for-long-term-environmental-damages-b5a325b28ee1/

Lederman, D. (May 6, 2009) "A Battle for the Sea (Grant)". *Inside Higher Ed*. Retrieved from https://www.insidehighered.com/news/2009/05/06/alaska

Mangan, K. (May 23, 2010) "Ignoring Experts' Pleas, Texas Board Approves Controversial Curriculum Standards". *Chronicle of Higher Education*. Retrieved from www.cronicle.com/article/Texas-Board-Approves/65661

Mufson, S. & Mooney, C. (November 16, 2017) "Keystone Pipeline spills 210,000 gallons of oil on eve of permitting decision for Trans Canada". *The Washington Post*. Retrieved from https://www.washingtonpost.com/news/energy-environment/wp/2017/11/16/keystone-pipeline-spills-210000-gallons-of-oil-on-eve-of-key-permitting-decision/?utm_term=.415ddd0f424d

Palast, G. (2002) *The Best Democracy Money Can Buy: An Investigative Reporter Exposes the Truth About Globalization, Corporate Cons, and High-finance Fraudsters*. London: Pluto Press.

Palast, G. (2012) *Billionaires and Ballot Bandits: How to Steal an Election in 9 Easy Steps*. New York: Seven Stories Press.

PISA (Programme for International Students Assessment) (2016) *Excellence and Equity in Education, vol. 1*. Paris: Organisation for Economic Co-operation and Development (OECD). www.oecd.org/education/pisa-2015-results-volume-i-9789264266490-en.htm

Reckdahl, K. (April 15, 2015) "Five Years After the Deepwater Horizon Oil Spill, BP's Most Vulnerable Victims Are Still Struggling". *The Nation*. Retrieved from https://www.thenation.com/article/five-years-after-deepwater-horizon-oil-spill-bps-most-vulnerable-victims-are-still-st/

Silver-Greenberg, J., Cowley, S., & Cohen, P. (May 25, 2017) "Trump Administration Considers Moving Student Loans from Education Department to Treasury". *The New York Times*. Retrieved from https://www.nytimes.com/2017/05/25/business/dealbook/trump-administration-considers-moving-student-loans-from-education-department-to-treasury.html

Simon, J.D. (2014) *Code Red: Computerized Election Theft and the New American Century*. Retrieved from www.CODERED2014.com

Strauss, V. (December 8, 2016) "A Sobering Look at What Betsy DeVos Did to Education in Michigan – And What She Might Do as Secretary of Education". *Washington Post*. Retrieved from https://www.washingtonpost.com/news/answer-sheet/wp/2016/12/08/a-sobering-look-at-what-betsy-devos-did-to-education-in-michigan-and-what-she-might-do-as-secretary-of-education/?utm_term=.525e5f661c9c

Strauss, V., Douglas-Gabriel, D., & Balinit, M. (February 13, 2018) "DeVos seeks cuts from Education Department to support school choice". *The Washington Post*. Retrieved from https://www.washingtonpost.com/news/education/wp/2018/02/12/devos-seeks-massive-cuts-from-education-department-to-support-school-choice/?utm_term=.fa6435de0306

Wald, E.R. (January 24, 2017) "Here are the Jobs the Keystone XL Pipeline Would Create under Trump's Executive Order". *Forbes*. Retrieved from https://www.forbes.com/sites/ellenrwald/2017/01/24/here-are-the-jobs-the-keystone-xl-pipeline-would-create-under-trumps-executive-order/#22e781e4773d

Walters, J. (March 23, 2014) "Exxon Valdez: Animal populations in Prince William Sound, Alaska". *The Telegraph*. Retrieved from http://www.telegraph.co.uk/news/worldnews/

northamerica/usa/10717533/Exxon-Valdez-Animal-populations-in-Prince-William-Sound-Alaska.html

Wolff, E. (March 29, 2017) "Energy Department Climate Office Ban Use of Phrase 'Climate Change'". Retrieved from www.politico.com/story/2017/03/energy-depart ment-climate-change-phrases-banned-236655

8

THE MISMEASURE OF STUDENTS[1]

> Social physics is that science which occupies itself with social phenomena, considered in the same light as astronomical, physical, chemical, and physiological phenomena, that is to say as being subject to natural and invariable laws of discovery of which is the special object of its researches.[2]
>
> — Auguste Comte (1798–1857)

Positivism: A brief retrospective

The present evaluation system deployed by our public schools, standardized testing, has its roots in the roughly 170-year-old idea that, in order to study human beings, one must quantify them; that is, reduce them to manageable forms to fit mathematical models. This perspective is known as 'positivism'. The idea is that, in order to make the study of social phenomena (social interaction, politics, economics, culture, education, *etc.*) as certain (positive) about its findings as those of natural phenomena (astronomy, physics, geology, chemistry, *etc.*), one must use those same experimental, mathematical, statistical and formulaic methodologies. Known as the 'father' of modern sociology, Auguste Comte advanced the idea that the study of society could be as 'positive' (certain) in its findings as the study of natural phenomena had been demonstrated to be. He asserted that "Men are not allowed to

---

1 I borrow from Steven Jay Gould's excellent book title, *The Mismeasure of Man* (1981), New York: W.W. Norton and Company.

2 As quoted from Comte's *Social Physics*, Book 6 of *Cours de philosophie positive* (2012). Georg G. Iggers (1959) "Further Remarks About Early Use of the Term 'Social Science'".

The mismeasure of students **165**

think freely about chemistry and biology; why should they be allowed to think freely about political philosophy?"[3] Comte argued that advances in science had enlightened us about the physical world, animal, vegetable, *etc*. What we needed, he proposed, was a 'physics' of the social, *importing into the study of society the same conceptual constructs and methodologies, experimental and statistical, deployed by the natural sciences.*[4]

Such methodologies require that each piece of the analytical puzzle be reduced to its component parts in order to allow for the investigation to proceed. For example, in physics, to understand motion, one must reduce its elements, such as 'force', 'friction', 'inertia' and 'acceleration', to numerical values. When this methodology is applied to the study of social phenomena, it requires investigators to proceed in the same way. To understand human beings, one must reduce us to our 'elements', such as 'race', 'sex', 'age', 'status', 'class', 'income', *etc.*, to numerical values, identified as 'variables'.

The determination and selection of variables has often been problematic and sometimes specious, thereby rendering the investigation of the study at hand absent of relevant rules for the proper conduct of the analysis. For example, are the variables correct categories of the phenomena they propose to represent? Is there not 'interpretation' involved and decision-making to arrive at such determinations? These questions are particularly relevant when the study at hand is dealing with 'abstract categories' such as emotions, intentionality, ethics and morality. This, unlike in the case of natural phenomena, means that people and their interactional components become reified. While this facilitates the operationalization process (the requisite procedures or steps to take to allow for the analysis to go forward) of the experimental model, it separates people from our 'group life' or contexts in which we operate. This allows the researcher to focus upon one or two, sometimes multiple, variables (multi-variate analysis), thereby isolating what is to be investigated. These variables are then assigned 'codes' which the formula (the statistical program) can accept. The results are an array of numbers, now assigned values, which represent the 'findings' of the analysis. All of this work is done absent the context in which people live, the 'here and now' of the interaction which engages people.

This methodology has yielded many insights about the human condition (*e.g.*, studies to identify how many people live in this or that neighborhood, town, city, state, how many people work in this or that industry, how many women vs. men hold this or that position in this or that profession, the census, *etc.*, a process often referred to as 'counting beans'). However, those insights have often been flawed in that there is much lost in the process (most notably, contextual information), without which we cannot attain the breadth and depth of understanding that is possible. The reduction of human interaction (and all socially constructed components

3 Alan Lindsay Machay (1991) *A Dictionary of Scientific Quotations*, New York: CRC Press.
4 See August Comte (2012), *op. cit.*

166 Left Behind

of life) into a collection of 'variables', instead of maintaining human action within its contexts, has proved to be problematic. Wittingly or unwittingly, this results in the virtual elimination of the person and the context of whatever is being investigated.

As Herbert Blumer asserted in his succinct essay on the 'variable',

> The statement of the variable relation merely asserts a connection between abbreviated terms of reference. *It leaves out the actual complexes of activity and the actual processes of interaction in which human group life has its being* [italics added]. We are here faced, it seems to me, by the fact that the very features which give variable analysis its high merit – the qualitative constancy of the variables, their clean-cut simplicity, their ease of manipulation as a sort of free counter, their ability to be brought into decisive relation – are the features that lead variable analysis to gloss over the character of the real operating factors in group life, and the real interaction and relations between such factors.[5]

The continued practice of this type of analysis only mystifies further who we are and what we do every day. We are much more than variables in a matrix of numbers and, no matter how the numbers are manipulated; we deserve much more in terms of the study of social phenomena. To avoid this necessary outcome when proceeding in the positivistic mode, a reestablishment of the context and of the myriad components of everyday life into the analysis of human action is necessary. According to Blumer,

> The scheme would be based upon the premise that the chief means through which human group life operates and is formed is a vast, diversified process of definition. The scheme respects the empirical existence of this process. It devotes itself to the analysis of the operation and formation of human group life as these occur through this process. In doing so it seeks to trace the lines of defining experience through which ways of living, patterns of relations, and social forms are developed, rather than to relate these formations to a set of selected items. It views items of social life as articulated inside moving structures and believes that they have to be understood in terms of this articulation. *Thus, it handles these items not as discrete things disengaged from their connections but, instead, as signs of a supporting context which gives them their social character* [italics added]…This procedure is to approach the study of group activity through the eyes and experience of the people who have developed the activity. Hence, it necessarily requires an intimate familiarity with this experience and with the scenes of its operation. It uses broad and interlacing observations and not narrow and disjunctive observation. And, may I add,

---

5 Herbert Blumer (1956) "Sociological Analysis and the 'Variable'", *American Sociological Review*, volume *21*, issue *6*, p. 689.

The mismeasure of students **167**

that like variable analysis, it yields empirical findings and "here-and-now" propositions, although in a different form.[6]

This was proposed in the 1960s, with some success, but the social sciences continue to be ravaged by this way of investigating, evaluating, indeed 'measuring' human beings and their sociality.

Standardized testing

The positivist approach to the study of social phenomena was enthusiastically adopted into the evaluation of educational performance and potential. This was achieved in 1926 by launching the maiden administration of the Scholastic Aptitude Test (SAT *post hoc*) in high schools and to the freshmen at Princeton University. The eugenics movement in the United States, which had based its racist claims upon the results of IQ testing, applauded the use of the SAT as another form of continued surveillance over students and to afford higher education only to the 'best of our students'. While it might be more cumbersome to claim racial bias in the current SAT tests, many have successfully argued bias in cultural terms and certainly in relation to native languages other than English of students who take the test, thereby continuing to weed out 'undesirable' students and prevent them from access to higher education.

The SAT was the grandchild of the College Entrance Examination Board Test of 1901, essay format, to help establish a uniform *curricula* in high schools. In 1905, French psychologist Alfred Binet (1857–1911) invented the first IQ test, a test that was supposed to 'measure' the intelligence of individuals. His idea was not all that wicked; he was only interested in determining the 'mental age' of students, thereby assisting educators to construct proper *curricula* to help students learn. Unfortunately, his testing ideas were co-opted by Robert M. Yerkes[7] and were implemented as 'intelligence' tests for army recruits to determine who were the most suitable in society, not for the purposes of enhancing education. In the 1920's, Carl Brigham (1890–1943), the inventor of the SAT, wanted to use this test to forestall the decline of American education, which was, in his view, proceeding at

---

6 *Ibid.* Thanks to the initial challenge to positivism by the Chicago School (among whose members are G.H. Mead and H. Blumer) in the 1950s and later in the 1960s and '70s, the formulation of qualitative methodologies by H. Garfinkel and H. Sacks, we can investigate social phenomena without numbers and formulae.

7 Yerkes (1876–1956) was a psychologist at Harvard University and President of the American Psychological Society in 1917. The same year, he worked with Henry Goddard at the Goddard Training School in Vineland, New Jersey, administering the so-called Army Alpha written test and the Army Beta pictorial test, presumably designed to detect 'mental acuity'. Results indicated that 'white' men had a mental age of 13, Russians 11.34, Italians 11.01 and Poles 10.74. "Negroes registered a mental age of 10.41. These results fed the eugenics movement. See Stephen Jay Gould (1981), *op. cit.* pp. 194–232.

168 Left Behind

an "accelerating rate" because of "racial mixture", based upon his belief in a biological relationship between race and intelligence, which, of course, is nonsense.[8]

As in the investigation of people without context, standardized testing also deletes the subject – the student. It deploys a methodology of numbers that separates what the student has learned from what the student happens to respond to on a given item of the test on a given day. The test scores become the phenomena to pay attention to rather than the actual learning the student has achieved. This is a fundamentally misguided approach to the evaluation of our children and presents one of the most basic of problems we face in our educational practice.

In terms debated in the educational community, this is what is known as 'proficiency', that form of assessment that posits that an arbitrary matrix will yield a quantified and reliable measuring percentile of any student's achievement. The other side of the debate advances a different mode of assessment known as 'growth', that form of assessment that advances a methodology that requires much closer, ongoing, weekly if not daily, evaluation of students in order to understand how each student is doing, how each student is progressing, based upon a set of standards of excellence.[9] As the reader is discovering, I endorse forms of this latter methodology of evaluation and assessment of students, from kindergarten through graduate study.

Not only is the practice of administering these tests one of our enduring obstructions to real education, it is exacerbated by the fact that they are administered in our schools *ad nauseam*. Preparing our students for these tests has become the *modus operandi* of the *curricula* and is a waste of time; 'teaching' our students to master the skills necessary to score higher on these tests takes away time and effort from the real practices that yield knowledge, understanding and insight into our world, local and global – the real task of education. Telling our students in subtle and overt ways that, unless they do well on this or that test, they will not amount to much or be able to pursue higher education or even be able to embark upon a viable life in this world is not only a lie, it is a language of oppression that is contrary to the very core of education. Testing does not allow us to determine how our children are learning or to decipher where the problems are in our educational progress; testing *is* the

---

8 Carl C. Brigham (1923) *A Study of American Intelligence*, London: Oxford University Press.
9 The distinction between these two constructs: 'proficiency' versus 'growth' was the subject of Senator Al Franken's questioning of Betsy DeVos, the then nominee for the Secretary of Education post. DeVos displayed a profound ignorance of the debate and had no position on it. In his own words, on this issue "In the hearing, I made sure that I gave her as much context about this issue as possible before asking for her thoughts. She had none. In fact, she had no idea what I was talking about. It was shocking in a hearing full of them (for example, she had no idea that disabled children's right to a quality education is protected by a federal law, and she suggested that schools might want to keep guns around in case of grizzly bear attack)." See Al Franken (2017) *Al Franken, Giant of the Senate*. Boston, MA; New York: Hachette Book Group, Inc., p. 381. Also see Congressional Hearings on the confirmation of DeVos as Secretary of Education. In a tie vote, broken by Vice President Mike Pence, DeVos was confirmed and is now the Secretary of Education; many troubles to follow.

problem. In order to solve some of the problems in education, one step toward that end is to eliminate this kind of testing and replace it with proper student/teacher evaluations which require attention to the details that learning itself requires, the specific needs of each student and what means can be implemented to ensure that students and teachers are treated fairly.

Apart from the obvious revolution in the technology available to us now across all institutions, the most influential change in education is how testing has become a fetish. The preoccupation with this unnecessary practice has transformed what was once a more 'organic' experience into one which is dominated by the standardized test. We had exams 60 years ago, but nothing like today. What used to be only a relatively limited element in the evaluation of students, testing has become *the* mode of evaluation, virtually eliminating the ongoing daily or weekly assessments that were always more important. I am not suggesting that testing 60 years ago was unproblematic; testing has always been misleading. I am only pointing out that the practice of testing has exploded into an unnecessary preoccupation. Properly constructed testing has its place for specific fact-finding for, say, reading levels in order to develop a learning plan to help students (the idea Binet had to start with), not to penalize them and hold them accountable to a prescribed set of mechanical *criteria* that could plague their educational experience and the very lives upon which they are embarking; today, testing dominates the learning day.

Testing and the scores that are meted out have been so immersed in the consciousness of our students, from elementary to graduate studies, that their response to questions about how they are doing in school invariably include a report upon the 'grades' they are receiving. For example: "I got an 'A', a 'B' on my test" or "I have a 3.1 GPA". Curious (or is it?) that they do not launch into discourse about how interesting this or that has been to study; or how they did not know how rewarding it has been to learn about this or that; or how challenging this or that was to investigate and that, while it took some time, they have achieved a significant level of understanding, *etc.* Students have been forced into a paradigm of scores and percentiles that have distorted for them, and for the rest of us, the true understanding of what the results/outcomes of education should be. This also means that, when teachers are asked about this or that student's performance, the answer is also invariably in terms of grades, *e.g.*, "He is a 'C' student" or "She is an 'A' student" or "She is trouble; she is barely making it with 'Ds'". Hence, our children become what they are 'documented' to be, not who, taken more holistically, they really are.[10]

Every teacher I have talked to about this over the years, and especially since the passing of the No Child Left Behind (NCLB *post hoc*) Act, has expressed frustration

---

10 I was first introduced to this construct by Dorothy Smith's work, most notably her 'The Social Construction of Documentary Reality", in which she demonstrates that persons are reified into what someone else 'documents' them to be. Hence, their reality becomes the document, not the person. Also see her "K is Mentally Ill".

170 Left Behind

over the fixation that school systems have developed: the distorted quantification, and thereby the reification, of students and teachers; that is, the reduction of human beings to a percentile entry on a matrix. This obsession with measurement, a direct outgrowth of 'positivism', has led to the mismeasurement of teachers, of our children and, all the more, of the very institution of education.

The late Senator Paul Wellstone (1944–2002) had the right idea:

> Making students accountable for test scores, talking about putting an end to social promotion is bumper sticker slogan politics. Well, politicians can thump themselves on their chests and say we are all about responsibility and high standards, about ending social promotion, but far from improving education. As a United States Senator, I would argue high stakes tests marks a major retreat from accuracy, from fairness, from quality and from equity.[11]

And because testing is mandated, instruction has moved away from the presentation of concepts and the demonstration of processes, across the span of subject matter from science to languages to social science and so on. Instruction then becomes dominated by 'what is on the test' and not by the deliberate presentation of materials, from which students can grasp either the concepts, the methodologies, the practices that they can actually use in their lives. This dialogue from *Star Trek: The Next Generation* captures this point:

> PICARD: There is no greater challenge than the study of philosophy.
> WESLEY: But William James won't be in my Starfleet exams.
> PICARD: The important things never will be. Anyone can be trained in the mechanics of piloting a starship.
> WESLEY: But Starfleet Academy [...]
> PICARD: It takes more. Open your mind to the past. Art, history, philosophy. And all this may mean something.[12]

(We have many "Wesleys" to protect against the onslaught of thinking that the 'test' is the goal of education.) 'Teaching to the test' takes away the spirit of learning and reduces it to memorization or unreliable knee-jerk recognition, which does not rise to the level of understanding.[13] These practices masquerade as educational assessment, offering only surface and cursory observations rather than the deep

---

11 Paul D. Wellstone (March 31, 2000) Excerpt from speech delivered at Columbia University Teaching College, conference on high stakes testing, www.wellstone.org/legacy/speeches/education-speech. In addition, check out www.cloakinginequity.com/category/high-stakes-testing/.

12 Gene Roddenberry's *Star Trek: The Next Generation*, Stardate: 42779.1; originally aired: May 15, 1989.

13 See Nerida J. Spina (2017) *The Quantification of Education and the Reorganization of Teachers' Work: An Institutional Ethnography*. Ph.D. theses, Queensland University of Technology. QUT ePrints. ttps// eprints.qut.edu.au/104977/.

and broad discovery that we need to have if we are actually going to educate and, hopefully at some point, to enlighten our children.

In a context in which some on the far right, and others on the not so far right, have advocated that the Department of Education[14] be abolished, this kind of 'dumbing down' is not surprising. What this mindset and the attitudes which have grown out of it have done is to interject a most frightening set of practices for teachers and hence for students. Teachers are unable to present the varied and challenging components of a *curriculum*; they are forced to become almost robotic in their daily activities and, by logical extension, drive their students in the same direction. Because of time constraints or the unwillingness of administrators to allow real learning to take place because they are preoccupied with the test scores that have become fundamental to the funding of their schools, this becomes the norm.

Content is not taught anymore; content is reified into questions and answers about isolated phenomena. Literature-based education has been replaced (more than 2 to 1) by 'information-based' education.[15] This results in the decontextualization of the content being investigated in the full range of inquiry. Furthermore, there are more tests these days: we have had the PSAT and the SAT, but they have been joined by this 'state aptitude test' and/or that 'state achievement test' (administered at every age, beginning in elementary), the ASVAB (military), *etc.* These are touted as necessary tools to determine promotion to the next grade or into which avenues students should be steered (college, vocational school, *etc.*) once they graduate from high school. (If only that *was* what they did/do; instead, they frighten students and stress them out, while reducing them to a number in a percentile matrix.) They constitute an extreme version of the intermediary tests and quizzes they suffer every week to obtain 'grades' to establish a 'scientific' or 'positive' expression of their performance.

In a world of quantification, this is what matters, not actually knowing how students are doing by having a chat to them and discussing how they understand the materials of inquiry at hand. Education becomes a matter of a 'GPA' instead of having the ability to think clearly about something, to express it either verbally or in writing and to be able to defend the claims that are made. Instead,

---

14 In 1980, President Jimmy Carter created the Department of Education, which President Ronald Reagan immediately challenged, supporting its termination and the deregulation of public education. Today, the Republican Party continues to call for its termination in the voices of Former House Speaker Newt Gingrich, Minnesota Rep. Michele Bachmann, Texas Gov. Rick Perry, New Mexico Gov. Gary Johnson and many others.

15 Literature-based education is practiced by using classical novels or contemporary works to develop discussion about important issues students should be aware of and construct understandings about. Information-based education is practiced by accessing internet sites and other sources that provide bits of information that 'fit' what the student 'needs' for the moment. Often, what is accessed is out of context and without any discussion. With literature-based education, at least there is a chance that the student will have an opportunity to think about something of import; with information-based 'education', the student is caught up in a mechanism to 'plug in' the correct missing element in the task.

their admission to any college, university, or trade school relies on the scores they receive on those tests.

It doesn't end there; for those who want to pursue graduate school after college, they are faced with the GMAT or the GRE or the LSAT, depending upon what career they are aspiring to. Because these tests are so important for admission to whatever program, high school becomes a training school for test-taking. Students are constantly plagued by the threat of these tests and learn that failure means lost opportunity. As a result, students spend an inordinate amount of time and energy 'studying' (inside and outside of school) how to take tests instead of spending that time trying to understand the principles and logic behind what they observe in the world every day, something that should be at the core of their education.

One part of the logical remedy to this set of circumstances is for colleges and universities to abolish this quantification system and, instead, require interviews and essays of prospective students.[16] At least, teachers in high schools would have to spend time with students to develop good interview conduct and prospectus writing, skills well worth the effort and still not taught in high schools.[17] Meanwhile, teachers are forced into a system that evaluates them too, one by virtue of how many students pass the tests and move on to the next level. They are constantly 'under the gun' to 'produce'[18] students who can achieve good test scores. The quantification of a traditionally more 'organic' practice of teaching will give us the likes of 'graduates' who are myopic and ill-prepared to tackle the complexities of life. The only thing that can be achieved by teachers under these circumstances is to repeat sound bites to students, correlational properties to be memorized for a test. In such a context, no discussion can take place, no explanation can ensue, no thinking for one's self or applying critical constructs to decision-making, solutions and just plain figuring something out can be established.

Alfie Kohn cites in his powerful little book, a common complaint, that jaded attitude among so many expressed as follows: "[standardized tests...are] so incredibly pervasive that I wonder whether there's really anything we can do about them."[19] I was disappointed to learn that some of the master's level classes students attended actually advocated 'teaching to the test'. When the training of teachers is dominated by the concept of 'standardized testing', the wrong mindset is established in the prospective teacher, which, expectedly, serves to perpetuate this

---

16 To be fair, some colleges and universities are already placing less importance on these tests and moving in the direction of a more qualitative evaluation of prospective students; however, because these attitudes and practices have been so institutionalized, 'the damage is already done' and too many still make 'first cuts' based upon these scores.

17 See Chapter 9 on high school

18 I use the concept of 'production' wittingly here; this test-taking system reduces education to a 'manufacture/business' model.

19 Alfie Kohn (2000) *The Case Against Standardized Testing: Raising the Scores, Ruining the Schools*, Portsmouth, UK: Heinemann, p. 50.

The mismeasure of students **173**

bankrupt practice. Alfie Kohn lays out five 'fatal flaws' of the so-called "Tougher Standards" movement:

It gets motivation wrong ... a preoccupation with performance often undermines interest in learning, quality of learning, and a desire to be challenged...

It gets pedagogy wrong ... [advocates] the sort of instruction that treats kinds as though they were inert objects, that prepares a concoction called 'basic skills' or 'core knowledge' and then tries to pour it down their throats...

It gets evaluation wrong ... 'excellence,' 'higher standards,' and 'raising the bar' all refer to scores on standardized tests, many of them multiple-choice, norm-referenced, and otherwise flawed...

It gets school reform wrong ... 'Accountability' usually turns out to be a code for tighter control over what happens in classrooms by people who are not in classrooms – and it has approximately the same effect on learning that a noose has on breathing...

It gets improvement wrong ... the dominant philosophy of fixing schools today consists of saying, in effect, that 'what we're doing is OK, we just need to do it harder, longer, stronger, louder, meaner and we'll have a better country.[20]

In spite of all these problems, President Barack Obama sadly endorsed the flawed concept of 'testing': "I don't want to see a student get a diploma and not be able to read that diploma. We just need better tests..."[21] The idea of 'tougher standards' is also part of the Common Core program that has already been adopted by some 44 states and the District of Columbia. The program does advocate critical thinking and problem-solving, skills which were part of the *curriculum* decades ago, but ignored since and replaced by memorization and regurgitation. However, testing remains at the center of what education looks like in the United States.

Randi Weingarten, President of the American Federation of Teachers asserts that:

Teachers don't want to spend valuable time endlessly preparing for "the test." They want to guide their students to ask insightful questions, offer well-reasoned opinions, and work diligently until they master content... Test-based

---

20 For more on these and other "flaws", see Alfie Kohn (1999) *The Schools Our Children Deserve: Moving Beyond Traditional Classrooms and "Tougher Standards"*, Boston, MA: Houghton Mifflin.

21 Obama's speech to the Urban League at their Centennial Conference, Washington, D.C., July 29, 2010, on education, teachers and the Race to the Top campaign.

174 Left Behind

> accountability is out of balance… Nations that outperform the United States have gotten this balance right—emphasizing teaching and learning versus testing and blaming.[22]

It is very important to hear comments like these from prominent people who are in the fray around standardized testing. Even though these sentiments are shared by the overwhelming majority of the members of the teaching profession and by parents and students, it is seldom that they/we have the opportunity to express them in the mainstream/corporate media; leaders do sometimes have that opportunity and we appreciate when it happens. With Betsy DeVos at the controls of the Department of Education, we can only expect more of the same or worse. Just what we need: another billionaire with a privatization mindset in charge of public education!

Here is another problem which arises out of this preoccupation with standardized tests: basing the success or failure of public schools upon test scores[23] is not only myopic but also misdirected. When schools fail *bona fide* (and I base that determination upon criteria which can be demonstrated with evaluation that does not delete the students and their contexts), we discover that the most prominent component of that failure is educational funding. Without addressing the underlying conditions of failure, the blame game accords that failure to be because those schools are 'public schools'. To those who want to destroy public education, this is all they need to propose unceasingly that privatizing the schools will solve the problem. Those who want to privatize public schools don't care about education, at least not the type I am arguing for in this book; they only see dollar signs, actual dollars moving from public coffers into theirs. Hence, public funds are just fine, but much better when they are spent to support 'private' education that virtually guarantees that our children will never have the opportunity to witness education without standardized tests. However, if we address the fundamentally unequal method of educational funding and see that some schools are well funded and others are not, some abysmally so, then we can come up with a different reason for 'failure', one which has nothing to do with test scores or that the schools are 'public' (or 'private' for that matter), but one which has to do with not having a nationwide bottom-line policy to fund all schools so that they all have what they need to educate our children.

---

22 See Randi Weingarten (February 19, 2012) "Fixing the Fixation on Testing", *New York Times*. www.aft.org/sites/default/files/wysiwyg/download021912.pdf.

23 'Success' means high scores and no critical thinking and 'failure' means low scores and no critical thinking. With standardized testing as the tool to evaluate and monitor education, our children lose no matter what the score.

Alternatives to standardized testing

Many investigators (academics, policy analysts, journalists) have already delved into what could revamp or replace standardized tests. Before the NCLB Act, many sought to change student assessment practices and move away from standardized testing because they realized how detrimental such testing was for students. After NCLB, critics found the proverbial rug pulled out from under them; that is, testing became 'chiseled in stone' as the official evaluative tool. However, attempts continue to be made to change this misguided policy. According to the National Center for Fair and Open Testing (FairTest), there are several alternatives to testing which minimize the effects of the current 'evaluation' practices in the United States. They range from administering essay assignments, to emphasis upon knowledge, to routine contact with students. These kinds of evaluation techniques are not really 'tests', but modes of assessment that do not include 'bubble sheets' and 'multiple choice' formats. Many teachers and educational organizations have been thinking about this drag on learning for quite some time and every small victory that brings us closer to abolishing standardized testing is a welcome event.

The so-called 'opt out' movement recommends that schools "say no to the test".[24] In May of 2013, the teachers of Garfield High School in Seattle, WA, refused to administer the MAP (Measures of Academy Progress) test and began a campaign called Scrap the MAP on many grounds, including:[25]

> the test is not aligned with the state-mandated *curricula*; test does not serve the needs of students, in particular students whose first language is other than English; too much class time is spent on test preparation, taking time away from needed instruction in language arts and math; computers are taken up by this preparation, taking time away from students' projects that require computer time.

In their resolution condemning the MAP test, they state:

> Whereas testing is not the primary purpose of education ... Whereas the MAP was brought into Seattle Schools under suspicious circumstances and conflicts of interest ... Whereas the SEA [Seattle Education Association] has always had the position of calling for funding to go to classroom and student

---

24 See The Bartleby Project, named after the protagonist in Herman Melville (1853) "Bartleby, the Scrivener: A Story of Wall Street". The connection is as follows: later in the short story, when Bartleby is asked by the lawyer to examine a document, he responds: "I would prefer not to". This is the response that teachers and students are adopting as their mantra: "I would prefer not to administer/take the test". John Taylor Gatto initiated this project; read his statement at www.bartlebyproject.com/gatto.html or in the Afterword to his (2008) *Weapons of Mass Instruction*.

25 Valerie Strauss (January 11, 2013) "Teachers Refuse to Give Standardized Test at Seattle High Schools – Update". *The Washington Post*.

176 Left Behind

> needs first … Be it Resolved that … the MAP test should be scrapped and/or phased out and the resources saved to be returned to the classroom.

The teachers developed an alternative to the standardized model which includes three major criteria: "process, validity and creation/review". Assessment should include

> classroom work, teacher/students choice, integrated with curriculum, demonstrate student growth as well as standards achievement, [freedom from] gender, class, and racial bias.[26] Then, valid measurements should reflect actual knowledge and learning, not test-taking skills, be educational themselves, be differentiated to meet students' needs, allow opportunity to go back and improve, have tasks that reflect real world thinking and abilities.

And thirdly,

> the creation and review of assessments should include community input, undergo regular evaluation and revision by educators and be graded by teachers collaboratively.[27]

Jesse Hagopian, a history teacher at Garfield, asserted that the idea can be captured in the manner that Ph.D. candidates are evaluated: they undergo a research program and are accountable to a panel of faculty members who evaluate their progress and achievement. This is a qualitative approach that does not employ any quantitative 'measurements'; rather, the comprehensive and collaborative nature of this kind of evaluation lends itself to considering all circumstances of each candidate and giving weight to all components of the student's achievements.

Students do not learn in the same ways nor at the same pace. Teachers should be trained to monitor these differences in the classroom. In my own experience, evaluation of students has been much more 'organic'. First of all, I have never given exams, as such. All evaluation/assessment has been by allowing students to express what they have learned either in writing or verbally. Overwhelmingly, with very few exceptions by students who self-describe as being "good test takers" (and, accordingly, they would prefer to take tests) or who are not particularly good writers or who are not verbally blessed, students welcome the opportunity to demonstrate their progress in other ways than examinations. My experience has been that, once those students grasp the idea of evaluation without tests, they become convinced of its efficacy. Students are more relaxed about 'performing'

---

26 See Anna Mundow (October 21, 2007) "The Advocate of Teaching Over Testing", *The Boston Globe*, interview with Jonathan Kozol, who asserts that "NCLB widens the gap between the races more than any other piece of educational legislation I've seen in 40 years … [Its] gains aren't learning gains, they're testing gains. That's why they don't last."

27 *Op. cit.*, Valerie Strauss (January 11, 2013).

The mismeasure of students **177**

and do much better. This means that evaluation on the part of the teacher requires that time be taken to read and comment upon papers that students write and pay attention to what they say, either in class or in conference. It also means that more care must be taken when 'grading' papers; students must understand where they are going wrong and where they are correct in their thinking and understanding. This takes more time, it requires a deep commitment to the profession, and it is more difficult. However, in my view, this is a necessary component of teaching.

For example, engaging students about their learning, checking on them about this or that presentation they just witnessed, outright asking them how they are doing and following up with a plan to correct misunderstandings and redirect their compass. By 'correct', I do not mean to insist upon one or another way of understanding that the teacher may present, that is 'agree with the teacher'. No, real education is a matter of understanding, not agreement. I mean students should have the opportunity to monitor their understandings with the help of the coach/ teacher against universal intellectual standards[28] proposed in a good critical thinking scheme. If this kind of contact with students were practiced routinely, amazing results in performance, in understanding, indeed, in education follow, virtually as a matter of course. Because of the qualitative character of these kinds of evaluative parameters, a teacher can glean much more about what a student has learned than a score on a test. This kind of evaluation includes the subject, the student, and the context that is created by the student and the teacher. Testing deletes both of these, reducing evaluation ('measurement') of student achievement to a test score, thereby practicing positivism again. Proper and qualitative evaluation takes time, time that is well spent, time often stolen from teachers and students by multiplying more and more test-practice sessions.

The most important components that will enable the achievement of what I broadly propose here are threefold:

1   Standardized testing must be abolished as a 'measure' of student performance. It should be relegated to the specific task of determining deficiencies in learning programs to enhance them and render them more efficient and effective in delivering the best education to our children.
2   Teachers must be retrained to emphasize qualitative evaluation of our students, as we abolish the overwhelming overuse of the standardized test.
3   Teachers must be evaluated by their peers, not by the results of standardized tests their students take, nor by students, but based upon the level of performance in the classroom and in project-based efforts, the parameters for which are abundantly available to the profession.

I am plagued by the question: why haven't we moved beyond the internal-combustion engine and the required-by-design use of fossil fuels to run them? Is it

---

28 *Op. cit.* Paul and Elder (2016) p. 8.

178 Left Behind

simplistic of me to speculate that maybe an answer (aside from the extraordinary lobbying from the fossil fuel corporations) is that we do not encourage our youngsters to think critically and for themselves? What if the format for learning were open and welcoming of new ideas, however odd they may sound in the beginning? What if we allowed our students to 'think outside the box' and to develop their own ways of seeing and challenge themselves and all of us, and not constrain their thinking to what is on the test? Maybe the electric car would be a reality today, one that would be affordable for the masses of people instead of being one that only 'maverick' rich people can 'show off' in? Of course, huge corporations must go as well. Could they not be challenged in the same way by the same kind of education? Challenging the *status quo* is necessary for change. If our children are only provided with the ideas dictated by the powers that be, the ruling class, we have no hope for the future. Of course, we already have the technology to produce electric cars for everyone straight away. Our children need to understand that it is the politics of that production which stands in the way. That is the part that is missing in their thinking, because the *curricula* do not include a critical analysis of our society, something that is impossible to achieve in a context of standardized testing and the privatization of schools. There is no room for that in such a scheme.

Given the recent challenges to the entrenched thinking about student evaluation, we can hope to see some changes toward a truly effective set of tools properly to evaluate our children. Those changes will likely come 'hard' with our new Secretary of Education, Betsy DeVos, in office. As always, those tools of change will be developed at the grass roots of communities, not by politicians and pundits in the media. As engaged members of our communities, it is up to us to make the changes necessary to restructure our school policies better to serve our children.

Bibliography

Binet, A. (1916) "New Methods for the Diagnosis of the Intellectual Level of Subnormals" in E.S. Kite, Trans., *The Development of Intelligence in Children*. Vineland, NJ: Publications of the Training School.

Blumer, H. (1956) "Sociological Analysis and the 'Variable'". *American Sociological Review*, volume *21*, issue *6*, p. 689.

Brigham, C.C. (1923) *A Study of American Intelligence*. London: Oxford University Press.

Comte, A. (2012) *Cours de Philosophie Positive*, vol. *6*. (French Edition). Charleston, SC: Nabu Press.

Franken, A. (2017) *Al Franken, Giant of the Senate*. Boston, MA; New York: Hachette Book Group.

Garfinkel, H. (1967) *Studies in Ethnomethodology*. Englewood Cliffs: Prentice-Hall, Inc.

Gatto, J.T. (2008) *Weapons of Mass Instruction*. Gabriola Island, BC, Canada: New Society Publishers.

Gould, S.J. (1981) *The Mismeasure of Man*. New York: W.W. Norton and Company.

Iggers, G.G. (1959) "Further Remarks About Early Use of the Term 'Social Science'". *Journal of the History of Ideas*, volume *20*, pp. 433–436. In: *John Stuart Mill: Critical Assessments*, Volume *4* (Ch. 80, pp. 154 ff). Edited by John Wood.

Kohn, A. (1999) *The Schools Our Children Deserve: Moving Beyond Traditional Classrooms and "Tougher Standards"*. Boston, MA: Houghton Mifflin.

Kohn, A. (2000), *The Case Against Standardized Testing: Raising the Scores, Ruining the Schools*. Portsmouth, UK: Heinemann.

Machay, A.L. (1991) *A Dictionary of Scientific Quotations*. New York: CRC Press.

Mead, G.H. (1967) *Mind, Self and Society*. Chicago, IL: University of Chicago Press.

Melville, H. (1853) "Bartleby, the Scrivener: A Story of Wall Street". *Putnam's Magazine*, volume *2*, issue *12*, pp. 609–616.

Mundow, A. (October 21, 2007) "The Advocate of Teaching Over Testing". *The Boston Globe*. Retrieved from http://archive.boston.com/ae/books/articles/2007/10/21/the_advocate_of_teaching_over_testing/

Obama, B. (July 29, 2010) speech to the Urban League Centennial Conference in Washington, D.C. on education, teachers and the "Race to the Top" campaign.

Roddenberry, G. (May 15, 1989) *Star Trek: The Next Generation*, Stardate 42779.1. "Samaritan Snare". www.imdb.com/title/tt0708768/mediaviewer/rm1582022912

Sacks, H. (1992) *Lectures on Conversation, vols. I & II*, edited by Gail Jefferson. Cambridge: Blackwell.

Smith, D. (1974) "The Social Construction of Documentary Reality". *Sociological Inquiry*, volume *44*, issue *4*.

Smith, D. (1978) "'K is Mentally Ill': The Anatomy of a Factual Account". *Sociology: The Journal of the British Sociological Association*, volume *12*, issue *1*.

Spina, N.J. (2017) *The Quantification of Education and the Reorganisation of Teachers' Work: An Institutional Ethnography*. Ph.D. thesis, Queensland University of Technology. QUT ePrints. https//eprints.qut.edu.au/104977/

Strauss, V. (January 11, 2013) "Teachers Refuse to Give Standardized Test at Seattle High Schools – Update". *The Washington Post*. Retrieved from www.washingtonpost.com/news/answer-sheet/wp/2013/01/11/teachers-refuse-to-give-standardized-test-at-seattle-high-school/?utm_term=.1713efdb4900

Weingarten, R. (February 19, 2012) "Fixing the Fixation on Testing". *New York Times*. Retrieved from www.aft.org/sites/default/files/wysiwyg/download021912.pdf

Wellstone, P. (March 31, 2000) Education Speech at the Columbia University Teaching College. Retrieved from www.wellstone.org/legacy/speeches/education-speech

9

WHAT OUR CHILDREN DO NOT LEARN IN HIGH SCHOOL, BUT SHOULD

The teacher, child, and environment create a learning triangle. The classroom is prepared by the teacher to encourage independence, freedom within limits, and a sense of order. The child, through individual choice, makes use of what the environment offers to develop himself [herself], interacting with the teacher when support and/or guidance is needed ... students learn to think critically, work collaboratively, and act boldly – a skill for the 21st century.[1]

– Montessori Method

Arguably, we did not really learn everything we need to know in kindergarten.[2] Fulgham made a compelling argument which resounded quite effectively and we accepted the spirit of his argument; however, we could never only rely upon what our teachers taught us in the sandbox. So, what should we be learning after kindergarten? Not an easy question to answer; not because it is so complicated, but because no one seems to agree on what the elementary or the secondary *curricula* should comprise.[3] Some guidelines may be agreed upon, however, because many decisions are made largely without a national comprehensive set of principles,[4]

---

1 Taken from the Introduction to the Montessori Method; http://amshq.org/Montessori-Education/ Introduction-to-Montessori. I invite the reader to look into the components of this methodology; some of them are also proposed in this book.

2 Robert Fulghum (1986) *All I Really Need to Know I Learned in Kindergarten: Uncommon Thoughts on Common Things*, Ballantine Books: New York.

3 I remind the reader that there are countless variations on how students learn and at what rate they achieve understanding in this or that subject matter. This means that more direct student-teacher attention must be paid.

4 Practical decisions should be locally made by teachers 'on the ground'; however, better national

What our children do not learn in high school **181**

there is much left to be desired. Often, these decisions are made by school boards, whose members are not even educators, but politicians or businesspeople, routinely influenced by their own agendas and not necessarily in the interest of our children.[5] Such influence sometimes leads to the banning of books.

For example, in July 2013, the Associated Press obtained emails between state education officials (February 9, 2013), including then-Superintendent of Public Instruction Tony Bennett, that demonstrated that former Indiana Governor Mitch Daniels sought to remove Howard Zinn's work, most notably his *A People's History of the United States*, from state classrooms less than two weeks after Zinn's death on January 27, 2010. In an email to Indiana education officials, Daniels wrote,

> This terrible anti-American academic has finally passed away.[describing *A People's History* as a] truly execrable, anti-factual piece of disinformation that misstates American history on every page … Can someone assure me that it is not in use anywhere in Indiana? If it is, how do we get rid of it before more young people are force-fed a totally false version of our history?[6]

His comments gave rise to outrage in the academic community, especially since the former governor is now president of Purdue University.

This attempt to politicize and remove any diversity of perspective from the view of our students with regard to versions of American History is not unique. In 2012, Arizona's HB 2281 banned Zinn's *A People's History* as part of sacking the Mexican American Studies Program in Tucson. Paulo Freire's *Pedagogy of the Oppressed* was also banned.[7] This kind of censorship continues today: on March 2, 2017, Arkansas HB 1834 was introduced by Republican Representative Kim Hendren to ban Zinn's *A People's History*, claiming that it was "too scary for children". Texas and Nevada have also been known to censor books for school children's reading. Banning books and censoring this or that perspective on issues and events cannot be the path to take if we want our children to understand how the world works and how they can live in it. This is not how/what we want our children to learn in high school.

When I was a student in elementary school, we spent most of our time on language skills (grammar, the voices, the cases, the accord between the relative pronouns and their antecedents, and lots of actual writing to practice those skills, often copying passages from books to 'witness' the way language should be expressed and to practice 'penmanship', something ignored today – no more cursive, on

---

guidelines must be established to eliminate (1) the huge disparity among the *curricula* across the nation, (2) the myopic decision-making on the part of local small-minded people and (3) the varied criteria that teachers must satisfy to become 'certified'.

5 See Chapters 6 & 7 on teaching and *curricula*.
6 See Scott Jaschik (July 17, 2013) "The Governor's Bad List". www.insidehighered.com/news/2013/07/17/e-mails-reveal-mitch-daniels-governor-tried-ban-howard-zinn-book.
7 See Preface of this book for discussions about Freire's work.

182 Left Behind

arithmetic (mostly the basic operations: addition, subtraction, multiplication and division) and not so much on reading. There were reading assignments and some reading aloud in class, but most of the reading was left to us at home with the help of our parents (when that was possible, not so in my case and many others). Reading consisted largely of reading the 'lessons' we were assigned rather than stories or poems. As a result, many reading problems (*e.g.*, dyslexia, hyperlexia[8]) went undetected and unaddressed. In my case, dyslexia was undetected, resulting in my being plagued with troubles in reading throughout my elementary and secondary school experiences. Commensurate with these reading deficiencies, my grades were only average, leading to poor SATs and achievement tests. Curiously, however, my grades did not match what I was actually learning – a surprisingly deeper understanding of many academic subjects and life. I did not realize this until I started to take classes at a teacher's college and found the material relatively easy, as long as I did not take too many classes at once. Nonetheless, my reading deficiencies persisted. Many children suffer this today, even with the heightened awareness of these conditions.

Today, some precautions are taken, though those and other learning deficiencies are still plaguing students into high school and college. For example, we hear a disturbing number of cases of attention deficit disorder (ADD) and attention deficit/ hyperactivity disorder (ADHD); it is not clear, to my satisfaction, what these are, what causes them and what definitive symptoms characterize them. Nonetheless, psychopharmacological intervention is often prescribed in the form of stimulant medications like methylphenidate or dextroamphetamine. The assumption on the part of these orthodox practitioners is that children are inattentive and/or disruptive because they suffer some kind of psychological dysfunction. There is such a tendency on the part of the medical and pharmaceutical industries to 'medicalize' all kinds of conduct and conditions. However, research at the Pfeiffer Treatment Center[9] has discovered, among other findings through nutrient therapy and analysis, that some 75% of children/people 'diagnosed' with ADD or ADHD are deficient in zinc. They have been delivering health care through nutritional methods with notable success.[10]

My elementary and secondary education also required other subjects, such as:

---

8 Dyslexia is a learning disability with regard to reading which demonstrates problems with word recognition, reading fluency and comprehension. Hyperlexia is an ability that surpasses age-appropriate expectations; however, most, if not all, children demonstrating this ability fall short in the area of speech recognition, virtually always suffering from autism.

9 The Pfeiffer Medical Center Health Research Institute is located in Warrenville, IL, www.hriptc. org/pdfs/ADHD Cu Zn SOD Copper Paper.pdf.

10 I juxtapose these here because there doesn't seem to be any clinical evidence for these 'disorders', as the conduct observed is known to be 'caused' by a multiplicity of factors: physical, emotional, familial, interactional, nutritional. Our children are often violated by the orthodox medical profession in the United States (allopathy) because its practitioners are either ignorant of or have contempt for alternate therapies like nutritional remedies. There is another possible understanding for children's conduct: they just may be acting like children.

What our children do not learn in high school **183**

science, history, foreign languages, music, civics (yes, that was part of the curriculum back then) and recess (the opportunity to move around at play, which today has morphed into 'physical education', another area that needs attention; see below). With a number of variations and some improvements, elementary and secondary education still operate along the same lines. These years were all supposedly designed to prepare me, from K through 8, for high school, where I would be challenged with more of the same, presumably at a higher level, but not always. I suppose there was some achievement there (in spite of the organized parroting and regurgitation that we were required to master), but high school was proposed as a kind of 'proving ground' for what would become of us in life. Not much talk of that in elementary school. But, in high school, discussions about 'work' and 'making money' and 'success' and 'postpubescence'; these were the overarching concerns above and beyond the academic ones.

What should high school be about, and what kinds of skills and knowledge should we be achieving? Well, to start with, there should be an academic program that is properly taught and monitored.[11] That should include all of the usual suspects just mentioned. I may have missed something (my purpose here is not to lay out an alternate *curriculum*, revamped from top to bottom), but I want to argue that the *curriculum* is missing a lot more than I may be. If we take at face value the notion that high school should be doing more than preparing students for college (and I know first-hand how inconsistently that is going, having witnessed the disparities among entering college students), because many high school graduates are not meant to go in that direction, we find that there are several skills and/or knowledge sets that the overall system of education does not include in the *curriculum*.

In the pages that follow, I shall introduce and discuss several areas not included in middle and secondary *curricula* – not an exhaustive list – to illustrate the kinds of preparation that the vast majority of young people are not getting; preparation that, in my view, is fundamental to education at these levels and that would transform the quality of graduates, who would then move on to higher education *of all kinds*. Please note that the following offerings do not eliminate or de-emphasize the need to teach youngsters all of the accepted subjects already in place, but redefine and replace existing methodologies, thereby creating a more holistic approach to their delivery. Some of them are academic in nature and some are practical in nature.

I have heard it said (I may have said it myself) at one time or another, in a context in which an adult expected a youngster to understand something and did not: "What did they teach you in high school?" I think that we all expect that high school graduates have achieved a certain level of academic achievement in

---

11 I have discussed these matters in the Preface. However, I want to emphasize here one of those discussions: learning should be a cooperative practice, project driven, involving teacher and student, one in which the broad *curriculum* mandates (which should be guidelines and not hardline prescriptions) are fleshed out, altered, enhanced, changed by the practitioners themselves to maximize the organic character of learning and not to 'box in' students and teachers into sterile and decontextualized directives. The Montessori Method shares some of these.

184 Left Behind

overall general knowledge (which has yet to be established in the United States, *viz*, the expectations of achievement vary widely from state to state, community to community). However, the poser of that question was very likely referring to some kind of practical, common sense knowledge which, in his/her view, should have been solidified by the time graduation came along. In other words, the adult is expecting some kind of practical knowledge s/he learned in high school, but, apparently, is no longer being taught or reinforced. Well, that adult is correct.

There were many skills, as opposed to academic subjects, that used to be part of the *curricula* in those days; such as diction, problem solving, public speaking, shop (various types, ranging from woodworking to metal to automotive to printing to sewing and many others), driver education, personal financing, civics, *etc*. Some of these may still be part of *curricula* here and there in the country, but they are no longer a consistent part of the requirements that all students must meet to graduate. This is partly why high school graduates today lack certain insights into the real world. Depending upon which part of the country children grow up in, there may be some other skills which are still taught because they are skills that are practiced in their whole community, often seasonally, most notably *farming*.

Upon little investigation, we discover that there are many other skills not included in most high school *curricula,* ones we hear characterized as those 'we were born with'; not possible, but the point is well taken. Those skills are at the level of 'common sense knowledge', that type of practical knowledge that should be reinforced in a systematic way, that kind of knowledge that is part of the wits students have about them in terms of how things are done, or the expectations they have of each other on an ongoing basis, or the recurring patterns of everyday life that have become part of who they are as competent members of the culture.

Critical thinking

> For myself, I found that I was fitted for nothing so well as for the study of Truth ... gifted by nature with desire to seek, patience to doubt, fondness to meditate, slowness to assert, readiness to reconsider, carefulness to dispose and set in order; and as being a man that neither affects what is new nor admires what is old, and that hates every kind of imposture.[12]
>
> – Francis Bacon, in Herman and Rishards (1920)

Even though Bacon did not use the words 'critical thinking', what he described captures some of the elements of this important skill. Arguably, most of the practical education that we were provided in the middle of the 20th century has either disappeared or is waning. Before I discuss some of those 'practical' skills our current

---

12 Quoting Francis Bacon's Novum Organum, (January, 1920) *The Reformed Church Review*, Fourth Series, Volume XXIV, Chapter II "The Novum Organum of Francis Bacon".

educational institutions have allowed to erode, I want to consider perhaps the most fundamental of all skills: critical thinking (*post hoc* CT). It has an 'academic' quality because there are several concepts that must be identified and understood to operate when taking charge of our thinking, but it also has a 'practical' quality because its deployment, its applicability allows us to solve a problem, to make a decision or to figure something out, *in any domain of life*.

I have polled incoming college students for 20 years to determine how many had received any instruction in critical thinking. No significant experience was reported. No students have ever had a course in CT; no students have had a 'mini' course in CT (maybe a short course lasting an hour); no students have had a sustained discussion about CT in whatever context. The only reports, a handful, of any exposure to CT were occasioned, in passing, comments in different contexts, *e.g.*, in physics, English and social studies classes. These responses were expected, but disturbing. Expected because education is not set up in the United States to encourage any kind of critical mindedness at all; instead, what is systematically endorsed is the notion that our society's responsibility is to 'educate' our children for the workforce, to instill in them compliance and acquiescence to the demands of the global money-based society. Disturbing because, one would think that, by the late 20th century, we might have discarded this way of thinking and replaced it with the notion that society should be maintained by each next generation of educated, yes, but also enlightened, empowered and collectively motivated people, working together toward a 'sustainable' mode of living. That is impossible without the paradigm shift I am advocating here.

The fact is that my generation, the 'baby boomers', has not moved far beyond the mindset that what our teachers tell us should be taken 'at face value', that, if the teacher/professor 'said so', it must be correct. A parallel attitude is when people say "I heard/saw it on the television news; if it wasn't true, it wouldn't be on TV". This is not only naïve, it is precisely why we go to school in the first place: to learn how to read and write and think for ourselves so that we do not have to rely on what other people say. We can figure it out for ourselves. What makes something 'true' is not because the teachers say so; it is not because someone in the media said or wrote it; it is because what they say is verifiable and can be discovered independently. If we cannot read and write adequately, if we are not taught how to take charge of our thinking, we are severely limited in our ability to develop criticality.

Something which is often confused about education is that in order to understand what is being addressed in any classroom, from elementary to post-graduate study, it must be correct, and, as such, students must *agree* with the teacher. No. *Education is not, and should never be, a matter of 'agreement'; it is a matter of 'understanding'.* I know that some teachers posture themselves in ways that can be intimidating and, because of their (well-earned) positions in those institutions of learning, they present an air of authority that is difficult for students to question. Students then think that they have to agree with the teacher. I am not suggesting that students challenge everything teachers say; I am advising students to think beyond what the teacher says and come to understandings based upon more than what the teacher says.

186 Left Behind

I am not suggesting that teachers mean to mislead students or feed them non-sense, but teachers are people too. They can be wrong about something. They are just as subject to sets of beliefs and values that may not be properly supported by facts. Accordingly, they could, with the best of intentions, advance ideas that are only partly true. How do students know to what extent something they are told by their parents, teachers, mass media purveyors, *etc.*, is true? They must engage their thinking so that it satisfies a set of 'universal intellectual standards',[13] which operate as a 'checking system' for their thinking.

I have been teaching a course in CT since 1996 to incoming university freshman.[14] In my view, this is too late to be introducing critical thinking concepts to our youngsters. They should have been trained, for the best results, by the 4th grade. This is when they have access to most of the concepts that are necessary to engage in fruitful critical thinking. Accordingly, by the time students reached high school, they would have been well versed in CT and it would have become regular fare. Unfortunately, this is not happening; however, 'better late than never'.

In the summer of 1996, I spent ten days training to teach 'critical thinking' with Dr. Richard Paul,[15] co-founder with Dr. Linda Elder, of the Foundation for Critical Thinking in California. I had looked into a few different approaches to the teaching of CT and decided that Paul's approach was the best to introduce those concepts to students. What convinced me that Paul's methodology was the best was the fact that all the concepts he uses are common sense concepts that students are already aware of, if not experts in, by the 4th grade. The training afforded me a framework through which I was able to address the fundamentals of CT from a conceptually grounded set of principles and relational analytical constructs. One of the slogans is about what CT constitutes seems banal, but one has to think about in order to realize that CT is an active endeavor that can be routinely a part of one's thinking. It is: "Critical thinking is thinking about you're thinking while you're thinking". So, it is about 'paying attention' to what we are thinking about, in the making, so that we can monitor it. This allows us to, as Paul asserts, "self-assess and self-correct" the trajectory of our thinking. At the heart of instruction in CT is an analysis of 'reasoning', a breakdown of the different "elements of CT", from assumptions to purpose to questions asked to evidence found to concepts

---

13 These are the universal intellectual standards: clarity, accuracy, precision, breadth, depth, relevance, logic, significance and fairness. See *Op. cit.* Paul and Elder (2016), Universal Intellectual Standards, pp. 8 & 9.

14 Some 20 years ago, I looked into the possibility of teaching at the high school level. My thinking was that students, if they are not taught critical thinking in the 4th grade, high school would be the next best scenario. I was not suited to teach in elementary; my patience with the little ones is not abundant. It turned out that I would have had to retrain to such an extent, getting 'certified', etc., that it became impossible because of my family responsibilities. So, I was trained in teaching 'critical thinking' and began teaching CT straight away.

15 Richard Paul is author of (1993) *Critical Thinking: What Every Person Needs to Survive in a Rapidly Changing World*, Foundation for Critical Thinking.

What our children do not learn in high school **187**

implemented to points of view taken to decisions made, solutions arrived at and consequences and implications of what has been figured out. Along with these elements are the "traits" one must develop toward taking charge of ones thinking, *e.g.*, intellecutal integrity & humility, perseverance, *etc.* The three modes of operation involved in CT are "identification, analysis and evaluation".[16]

My purpose here is not to go through all of the components of CT, but rather to indicate the kinds of discussions that are involved in the presentation and practice of CT. Teachers can easily train to do this and to pass on these insights to their students.[17] Once students are exposed to these concepts, they are given assignments to verify their understanding of and to practice CT. With some practice, they begin to incorporate these analytical skills into their schoolwork and into their lives. At a time when our world is crying out for people to understand the complexities of a global experience, we do not need students who are acquiescent and docile; we need our people to be prepared to challenge the old ideas and replace them with ones that help move us in directions that will make the world viable for their children and grandchildren, a world that is safe from wars and from the toxic mess left behind by corporations and the military.

This kind of instruction can either be a stand-alone course or one which is incorporated within another course, like I did, and its relevance made clear to students. It should be given in the elementary schoo as early as possible, and reviewed every year thereafter, so that students may employ insights they gain in these early years in future projects and assignments (in subsequent years in elementary, high school and on to college or other post-secondary education). Along the way, they also learn to implement CT in their everyday lives, thereby affording them the tools to make better, more informed decisions about how the world works and how they operate in it. Good Critical Thinking skills are indispensable to everyone these days, in the context of rising global discord and violence.

Little boxes

Part of that 'competence' in everyday life is to know how to conduct oneself in various contexts encountered daily. Certainly, one interactional observation these days is that children pay more attention to the 'little boxes' they have with them constantly, *e.g.*, internet phones, gaming consoles, tablets, *etc.*, than to their interlocutors. Many students don't seem to know what the appropriateness rules are for different settings. While annoying, this is not the worst of it.

Our youngsters are perpetually bombarded with technological innovations, platforms and devices. The technology, *per se*, is not the problem; the ubiquity with

---

16 See www.criticalthinking.org for details about these tools to build criticality. I use quotes in this paragraph to highlight that these concepts are advanced by Paul and Elder in their approach to critical thinking. See Paul and Elder (2016) pp. 13–15.

17 The Foundation for Critical Thinking offers Annual International Conferences on critical thinking.

188 Left Behind

which it is perpetrated is. Everywhere we turn, computers and other electronic devices are dominating the landscape. Children don't seem to be able to communicate with each other without doing so through some kind of device. Books are being replaced by 'e-books'. People are forced to do banking through the internet. Software systems are constantly being changed to satisfy this or that new criterion. Courses are moving from the classrooms to the 'online' format.[18] Our lives are being mediated through the likes of computer programmers, software developers and cyberspace functionaries.

I like the advertisement where the dad is coming home and looking around to see where his family members are. His children are on the computer together, presumably playing a game, his wife is paying attention to another electronic device and yet another member of the family is doing something else involving another device. Everyone is separated from one another through the use of these devices. He turns off the power to the house and all members come together because their devices are not operating. One child asks, "What happened, daddy?" He answers, "The power went out," and offers him a hot dog. The family is shown sitting around a table eating hot dogs and talking to one another. I do not like this ad for the 'hot dog'; I like it because it underlines the absurdity of our daily practices, which do not involve face-to-face interaction. People today, not only children, are walking around with their noses in an electronic device of some kind. People, especially children, do not talk to one another enough.

Another example is the Microsoft advertisement in which people are depicted as walking around a street, each engaged in the new Microsoft phone. They bump into each other and disregard one another and never look up from this phone. A car has crashed into a telephone pole (ironic) and the street is strewn with debris, indicating that no one cares about anything else. This scenario is very emblematic of our preoccupation with the latest technology, but, in this case, it is touted as a desirable scenario, because Microsoft wants to sell these phones and that is more important than social interaction. Yet another example is the advertisement in which family members are texting each other to announce that it is time to have dinner and they continue to use their devices even after they have gathered at the dinner table.[19]

These 'little boxes' are not going away any time soon. However, they must be purged from the classroom and other contexts of learning, unless they are part of the matters at hand and monitored to be used only for that purpose. The use of these 'boxes', admittedly itself a skill, serves to distract students from the learning they are charged to achieve. More realistically, the skills I am emphasizing here are the ones that can position our youngsters in much better stead in the society we live

---

18 See Chapter 7 on teaching and *curriculum*.
19 See Jean Twenge's (2017) spot-on book, *iGen: Why Today's Super-Connected Kids Are Growing Up Less Rebellious, More Tolerant, Less Happy – And Completely Unprepared for Adulthood – And What That Means For Us*, New York: Atria Books.

What our children do not learn in high school **189**

in, that give them confidence about who they are and what is required/expected of them in post-secondary-school life.[20]

Project-based education

If we can institute a comprehensive program for CT and do away with the little boxes, and we can, then the best trajectory for education is to establish far-reaching project-based programs to educate our children *in context*. These are the kinds of 'projects' that students in elementary through high school and, yes, college and other post-secondary education, should have available to them. Think about it for a moment: what if part of education was exposure to the real world and not limited to the classroom? What if, say, students were to travel to one of the many Habitat for Humanity[21] sites and observe, participate in and learn from the building of houses?[22] What an excellent opportunity, not only to learn about building houses, but to make connections with the 'academic' requirements of school. For example, students learn geometry, arithmetics, architecture, cooperation and sharing, engaging in something bigger than themselves, helping to situate themselves in the community, all thanks to touching the world around them, becoming intimately involved in the real world and experiencing what it means to achieve something collectively. Geometry courses could use the context of the building site to construct exercises in geometric problems, such as the Pythagorean theorem or the determination of area and perimeter, *etc.* Mathematics courses could do the same with regard to solving special problems for the bathroom, the bedrooms and the cellar. What about the environment and studying the placement of the house at this location and not that one because of 'wetlands' laws? What about the aesthetics of the house in that location and the landscaping required to maintain the ecosystems of that location? And, after all those observations and participations, students have several writing assignments about the whole experience, either by description or compare/contrast or a poem. What about art? Students could be assigned to do a mechanical drawing of the house, based upon their measurements, or a painting or a drawing of the house. While on-site, students are moving around, not sitting in a chair in a classroom; that is worth the site visit all by itself! Some of all of this is already going on; we just need to institutionalize it and make it available throughout the country.

---

20 Of late, there are efforts by some to address this "Tech Addiction"; see the Truth About Tech Campaign, co-founded by Tristan Harris of the Center for Humane Technology and James Steyer of Common Sense Media at www.comonsense media.org.

21 While this is a faith based organization, people need not subscribe to a Christian belief system to participate and benefit from the experience, while helping our fellow human beings. There are also Habitat for Humanity ReStore locations as well, where volunteers restore furniture, appliances and organize reusable plumbing and heating supplies, etc. These are all wonderful locations for project-based education. www.habitat.org.

22 Sometimes, these sites are local, sometimes not. Schools should inquire into their project schedule to plan for this kind of extraordinary experience for their students, from elementary to post-secondary; there is something to learn for every student.

190 Left Behind

Or take a visit to the bicycle shop, where students can learn the mechanics of the bicycle, maybe how to fix or tune it up. How could that be exciting? Well, aside from the experience of touching the bicycle parts and learning how they all fit together, there is physics in the form of levers and friction and acceleration and speed and weight-to-power ratios. And, as in all cases of project-based learning, there is writing about what the student learned, either a technical piece or an essay on the wonders of bicycling.

This methodology is flexible, interesting for the students, designed to facilitate discovery and make the connections with processes, operations and procedures that abound in life and, sometimes, they will forget that they are learning and 'going to school'. Brought to my attention by a friend, Lydia Phillips, one example of this bicycle shop concept is the after-school program (ideally, such a project-based program would be part of the *curriculum*) in Biddeford, ME. Founded by Andy Greif, students from the surrounding schools drop by the Community Bicycle Center[23] where they can to learn how to repair bicycles and, eventually, to build their own bicycle. Children learn much more than the physical characteristics of bicycles; they learn how to cooperate and to interact with other students, customers and adult mentors. They learn how to work within a community and how to involve themselves in something bigger than themselves.

Other examples of project-based learning and practical skills that can be obtained are: the ability to grow food, awareness of how our own bodies work (*i.e.*, physical education and nutrition), first aid and CPR (cardio-pulmonary resuscitation), knowledge of how a house works, how to use simple hand tools, how to cook and sew, how to fix something instead of throwing it away, how to find one's way in the woods, how to balance a money account, how the economy works, how the political system works, how information is disseminated (*e.g.*, via the mass media) and many others. Some of these were part of instruction in school when I came up. To be fair, many of them were augmented by my parents and relatives – that was because *they* had been taught by somebody, either in school and/or by their families and because we lived in a context that had maintained the solidarity of a community.

The 'community' has waned over the last 60 years for many reasons, perhaps the most salient of which is the centralization of jobs in metropolitan areas. As a result, familiarization of knowledge sets of these kinds have not been passed down to children for some time. That does not mean that they are no longer relevant or necessary. I can already hear complaints from some that "times have changed and we don't need that anymore". Really? To be sure, much has evolved over the years; some economic or political or cultural processes replacing others, ones of times past that are obsolete or less relevant today, *e.g.*, the rotary dial phone, the ribbon magnetic audio and video tape recorders/players, the typewriter, banking in person, *etc.* Times have changed; but with change should come the means to understand more fully what has changed and how to deal with it. Without the skills I am referring to

---

23 See www.communitybike.net.

What our children do not learn in high school **191**

here, we move ahead without a purchase on the real, on the ground, characteristics of daily living. Yes, things have changed, but they have not become ephemeral; our need to interact with the daily practicalities has not gone away.

My purpose here is not to discuss every knowledge set, but to address some of my favorites, some of the most fundamental knowledge we should all still have obtained by the time we graduate from high school. For example, once a house is built, how does it work?

How does a house work?

This is an area of profound ignorance, save perhaps for the youngsters whose parents are trades workers (similar to farmers' children) and from whom they almost automatically learn several things about how a house is put together and what makes the house the container/provider of so many of our needs. Most students I have spoken to have not thought about this at all before or, at least, during the last four years they spent in secondary education. They have no idea, for example, what a circuit breaker is and how it works. They do not know what happens to waste water when they flush the toilet. They do not know how the heating system works, both for domestic water and for warming the premises. They do not understand the physics of how the house is put together – that there are pipes and wires in the walls; that the foundation is made of stone or concrete; why the roof has this or that pitch, *etc.* Because they do not know these things, they do not know what to do if something 'goes wrong', if there is a water leak of some kind, if the electricity or heat is lost, if the sink overflows and so on. What about the dangers related to the appliances and systems in the house: the washing machine, the range, the heating, the air conditioning? What about the forces which act upon the house in terms of weather and temperature? How can one keep the house cool when it is hot or warm when it is cold; this, without heating and air conditioning? What about the concept of 'convection'? Solar panels? Wind power?

There could be a course (and some of these topics may already be touched upon 'in passing' in this or that course in some schools) that takes these topics and explains just what each one does and how it works and how to monitor and repair (at the most basic level) the service that it provides us. Either a 'spec house' or a house being built by local contractors at which students could report to observe and participate in the building of that house. If such a house is not available in the area that semester, mock-ups of parts of houses could be built (at very modest expense) so that students could have a 'hands-on' experience, thereby developing an understanding of all these parts of the house, how they work and how to maintain them.

I am not proposing that all students become carpenters, plumbers and electricians at the end of this course. The training of these and other trades people at the post-secondary education level continues to be necessary and most rewarding for many young graduates. I am proposing that students have a working knowledge of the mechanisms and functions of a house, any house, thereby empowering them to use the house correctly and know when something is not right and how to address

192 Left Behind

the problem in ways that can forestall the development of any really dangerous circumstances as well as to avoid dangerous (ill-informed) 'thinking'. Such a course would not have to take up more than one semester during any high school year.

All of us can grow our own food!

This is perhaps the most important practical skill youngsters should have obtained in high school. Some youngsters do have these skills, not because they were taught in school, but because they come from a family that works a farm. These students live in the dense farming areas of the country, where life is closely related to the cycle of growing food. Few students in these areas grow up without an intimate knowledge of where food comes from and how to grow it, either because they work the farm or because they grow up in that context. Theories and methods of farming are sometimes part of the *curriculum* there, because many students will follow in their parents' footsteps and continue growing food. They also acquire by doing, either in their own families or more generally in their communities, a way of learning that yields much more than solely by reading about something in a book. Unfortunately, this phenomenon is disappearing. With the growing monopolization of factory farming, small, family farmers are being pushed out. While there is a rise in the interest in organic family farming in some areas of the country,[24] *e.g.*, Washington, Oregon, Vermont and Maine, these efforts are difficult and seem miniscule against the behemoth of agribusiness.

Even more problematic these days is the draconian threat to our food supply in the form of genetically modified organisms (GMOs). Because these GMOs have been replacing several of our staple crops – most notably soy, cottonseed, corn, canola oil, U.S. papaya, alfalfa, sugar beets, milk and aspartame (which is found in many 'processed foods') – the otherwise 'clean'[25] food produced in the past, since the 1980s in particular, our food supply has been compromised by companies like Monsanto.[26] These companies have decided that food production is something that should be controlled by a corporation rather than by farmers, the people who actually scratch the soil to produce the sustenance of a society. Because food production has been significantly overtaken by corporate interference, the quality of that food has waned and become most problematic. In fact, unless you are buying

---

24 Farm Aid Grant Programs help families establish their farms all over the country. They have protested 'factory farming' and tried to return farming to the family for almost 30 years. See www.homegrown.org.

25 "Clean" in the sense that the genetic character of these and other foods had not been altered. Our food has already been significantly poisoned by herbicides and pesticides for many decades; not only by spraying the plants, but, because of repeated spraying, the soil now has been severely damaged and, in many instances, irreversibly so. Consequently, we must strive to grow and buy our produce and other foods from organic farms and gardens.

26 Other companies are: BASF, Bayer, Dupont, Dow Chemical Company and Syngenta. See www.sourcewatch.org/index.php/%22Big_6%22_Pesticide_and_GMO_Corporations.

What our children do not learn in high school **193**

organic fruits and vegetables, there is real confusion about what is contained in those foods (in relation to the pesticides and herbicides that were used during the growing life of those plants or the rBGH and antibiotics used with animals), because companies are still not required to include that information on their product labels, except in rare state law cases,[27] thereby hiding the truth about the quality of the food we are consuming. Even the organic foods are not 100%, because of the contamination from pesticides and herbicides that has already poisoned our soil and hence our food supply.

Something that very few people know about is the spraying of aluminum, barium and strontium in the atmosphere. Under the pretense of mitigating global warming/climate change, geo-engineers are introducing these reflective heavy metals into our skies, manifest as 'chemtrails'.[28] The verified fallout from these ongoing flights over us is a massive increase of these metals, to the tune of 61,000 times more than what is already deemed toxic, in our air, our water and our soil. This raises the pH of our water and soil up to 50% more than what is normal and poisoning the air we breathe, resulting in elevated heavy metal levels in our bodies. How can we grow 'organic' food under these circumstances?[29]

In spite of these horrific developments, what must be developed more and more is 'personal' farming, those activities of gardening and food production that all of us can do on our own and 'collective' farming in communities everywhere. The principle is that, if we observe food production from beginning to end and we know what the process requires to be organic and safe for us, we can 'guarantee' that our food will not contain poisons of various types to harm us. Hence, we take charge of what we put into our mouths, thereby reducing the harmful effects of pesticides and herbicides and GMOs. Moreover, if we observe the fundamental rule that the closer to home we procure our food, the fresher it will be, thanks to eliminating unnecessary transportation and refrigeration, and the less expensive it will be, both monetarily and in terms of the pollution of our air.

Children need to know about these things and be taught how to grow their own food. While it is true that not all children have access to land from which to yield a crop that might sustain them and their families,[30] all communities should

---

27 After several failures to pass GMO labeling laws, e.g., Prop 37 in CA (2012), I-522 in WA (2013) and Measure 92 in OR, Prop 105 in CO (both in November, 2014), Vermont was the first to pass GMO labeling laws (in effect July 1, 2016). Several other states have 'proposed' similar laws. However, they are all different. Congress passed a weak law in July, 2016, allowing companies to use QR codes, which require smart phones to read the label. See justlabelit.org.

28 See www.chemtrailcentral.com and watch the film at www.youtube.com/watch?v=q7Nn0AKFtGY.

29 See http://educate-yourself.org, http://chemtrailcentral.com, www.rense.com and the documentary by G. Edward Griffin, Michael J. Murphy and Paul Wittenberger (2010), entitled *What in the World Are They Spraying?*

30 I am reminded of the feudal serf, who, in spite of the terrible conditions he suffered under the manorial lord, still controlled a small plot of usufruct land to feed himself and his family. The emergence of capitalism in the late 18th century and the privatization of land have made this possibility even more difficult for modern workers.

194 Left Behind

be required to provide common land (remember the 'commons'?) for this purpose. Many people rent apartments or own condominiums where no land is available. If their neighborhood or community had plots of land set aside for food production (all communities have plots of land that could be used in this way), they would be able to control the most fundamental need of their existence and not have to rely on agribusiness to supply them with the food stuffs that are necessary for life. This is more a matter of political will than availability of common land.[31]

Incorporating this into the *curriculum* of any school is easy and is already being done in some schools. Whether on school grounds or down the street in the community, students can learn the principles of growing organic food, the fruits of which could be (and already are in some instances) brought to the schools to supply the on-campus breakfasts and lunches that are so in need of upgrade (something that some people complain about because of the costs related to buying food, even though some of which is already donated by community farms and businesses). Students would have the satisfaction of growing the food for the school and eating high-quality foods, instead of pizza and other prepackaged or frozen junk food like chicken nuggets or other such fare. They could be eating a healthy salad and sharing the fruits of their labor. This system could provide all the food necessary to feed students, and it would take a bite out of the food budget of all schools. In some areas of the country, such as the southern states, this program could take a big bite out of the budget, because of the extended growing time climate provides, less so for Maine and Montana and Washington, unless such food production were really funded like it should be and would take place in bio-domes year round and with the adoption of the technology of aquaponics. In the meantime, they would come to understand what it takes to grow food the correct ways and understand that having access to safe and healthy food is no more difficult than having access to the inferior quality food that has become the mainstay in the United States.

One salient example of 'garden-to-school cafeteria' food production is already happening in Berkeley, CA. As Alice Walker, founder of Chez Panisse Restaurant in Berkeley asserts,

> Good food should be a right and not a privilege. And, I think, people see it as something only for the people who can afford it. But, really, what we need to do is to bring this good food into the public school system and make it available to every child who lives in this country. Right now, we are feeding them food that isn't good for them.[32]

---

31 We do not need agribusiness or corporate control of our food supply. We should take charge of that ourselves and allow family farmers to supplement what we cannot grow locally, either ourselves, in our neighborhoods and in our larger communities. There should be municipal, state and federal subsidies to support this kind of food sustainability.

32 See the documentary *Food Fight: A Story of Culinary Revolt/Revolution Never Tasted so Good* (2008), a film by Christopher Taylor in association with November Films.

This sentiment is echoed by Ann Cooper, Director of Nutrition Services, Berkeley USD, Berkeley, CA:

> School lunch is making our children sick. The CDC has said that of the children born in the year 2000, one out of every three Caucasians and one out of every two African-Americans and Hispanics will have diabetes in their lifetime; and further, most before they graduate high school. The results are going to be, they say, for the kids born in the year 2000, they are going to be the first generation in our country's history to have died at a younger age than their parents ... Schools absolutely have to take the lead to turn this around.[33]

These innovators are making good on their claims by establishing gardens and cafeteria food programs that feed our children 'good food'. Part of that program includes the establishment of a 'project-based' component that engages the students. Alice Walker has founded The Edible Schoolyard, operating at a middle school, whose goal, according to Kyle Cornforth, a program associate, is "to get students to learn about where their food comes from and learn about sharing food as a community."[34] One of the initial parts of the program is to hold a 'taste test' at the beginning of each school year to demonstrate to incoming students (6th graders) how better corn grown in the garden is better than corn bought in the local market.

> It's unanimous that the garden corn is better ... we're teaching kids to think critically about the food choices that they're making ... when you decide what kinds of food you are going to buy, you're affecting your health ... you are also affecting the environment and the community that you live in.[35]

They also assert that funding cannot come from local sources as most communities could not afford what this kind of national project would cost. This would mean that politicians must realize how important such programs would be for our children. And therein lies the problem. Funding whose purse strings are controlled by elected officials is most difficult to obtain, because of the enormous amounts of money that control elections and campaign financing. When corporate money fills the coffers of politicians (*cf.* Citizens United and MeCutcheon), it is very difficult to advance these goals. The 'farm bill' that must be passed every year is dominated by agribusiness lobbyists, whose target senators and representatives receive millions of dollars in subsidies for their districts and states. The voices of the few in Congress, those that support vital changes toward a sustainable farm bill, *e.g.*,

33 *Ibid.*
34 *Ibid.*
35 *Ibid.*

196 Left Behind

Democrat Representative Ron Kind, 3rd District of Wisconsin, are muted amid the cacophony of corporate influenced politicians, who feed the echo-chamber of 'business as usual'. Here is Congressman Kind:

> Madam chair, the fundamental fact is that, when you have two-thirds of the subsidy program in the farm bill going to just thirty congressional districts, who are well represented on the committee, I think that [it] is unrealistic to expect that the committee is going to produce a policy statement that embraces reform and new ideas. I should know; I used to serve on the committee. My district takes a hit under this reform bill. But, sometimes, it takes a group of well-intentioned individuals to move the cause of reform forward.[36]

The bill was defeated by a 309–117 vote. Congressman Kind and others continue to advocate for a farm bill that will protect our children; however, I am afraid that the people will have to intercede and create a grassroots movement to make these changes.

I am not proposing that all students become farmers (that profession is much more complicated and requires much more training because production is for exchange into the market place and not only for personal consumption). I am proposing that they acquire the common sense knowledge that will allow them to understand what it takes to grow food and realize that, if need be, they could support themselves by scratching the soil themselves. I already know farmers, not in the farm-belt, who donate their time to supervise such projects already in process; this can be easily replicated all over the country. This course would have to be year-long and offered all the time, beginning with the spring semester of any year, freshman through senior, to prepare the soil and plant seeds and getting things started and the fall semester of any year to evaluate and harvest the crops. The summer months would be part of the course too; students would be responsible (taking turns, not constantly tied to the process) to do the weeding and watering and the appropriate care for the crops. This would allow students to experience and participate in the whole process, from beginning to end. This process could begin and end anytime using aquaponics technology.

The real bonus of this kind of learning, though, one which is 'project-based', is that students learn much more than growing food. They are simultaneously taking a course in botany, soil and water management, earth science, the use of tools, mathematics, geometry, social interaction, community participation, civics and sharing and cooperation. This one project can yield more not only in these ways, but also because they learned through experience, *in the making*, instead of solely in the classroom.

Along with the credits students earn in actually doing the work of growing

36 *Ibid.*

What our children do not learn in high school **197**

food, they also develop an understanding of what is healthy to put in their mouths, which would coincide with another course they would have to take: health – not the sort of course we are familiar with these days, which is inadequate – rather a course which would teach students how to eat and exercise and rest, all of which they can take into their adult lives during and after high school. Read on for those discussions.

'No test' evaluation

Project-based education affords teachers the opportunity to evaluate their students in-the-making because they are present; that is, while students are performing their activities and demonstrating, in action, their skills in mathematics, physics, geometry, architecture, interactional and social skills, *etc.*, teachers become witness to the proficiencies their students achieve and the progress they make. Monitoring them is observational and experiential, not a matter of digging something out of them in a test or examination.

Our assessment protocols must change. They must move away from the nonsense of standardized testing and forge new and innovative procedures that identify the performance of our children in qualitative and dynamic ways that actually do justice to the enactment of their educational progress. Of course, this evaluation/assessment *modus operandi* will require hiring more qualified teachers, thereby requiring the investment of more public funds to support our most important promise to our children.

Instead of stressing our children with tests, we could be allowing them the freedom of engaging their education, not submitting to it. As John Taylor Gatto has asserted, "Schools are intended to produce, through the application of *formulae*, formulaic human beings, whose behavior can be predicted and controlled."[37]

What I am advocating here would go a long way from how Gatto correctly characterizes our present state of affairs in education: the production of "formulaic" graduates. I trust that, if we implement some of the changes suggested in this book, we will be able to characterize our educational 'intentions' very differently, for the benefit of our children and the society at large. Changing our current *means* of education will yield very different *ends*: instead of graduates who are *docile* and acquiescent, we can engender graduates who are critical and who can challenge the status quo. In the present context, during this Trump Administration, our children must learn to 'question everything' and be able to make decisions based upon good information from across the spectrum of ideas and from a far wider range of sources.

---

37 One of John Taylor Gatto's comments upon receiving the New Your City's Teacher of the Year Award, January 31, 1990.

198 Left Behind

Health education

The health of our youngsters is seriously in trouble. Many of them do not eat right; they do not exercise enough, if at all; they do not sleep properly and they do not understand how these three components of good health interact with one another. Moreover, they do not consistently receive the sex education they need to function safely in our complicated society. Let us take up each one of these in turn and discuss what our children should know about health while they are in middle school and high school so that they can galvanize their understandings of proper health by the time they graduate.

Nutrition (diet)

For some years now, reports from corporate and independent news outlets have repeatedly announced the tragedy of obesity in the United States and child obesity in particular. Health professionals I have talked to or whose work I have read about the poor health of people in the United States and especially our children (from allopathic to homeopathic to naturopathic to chiropractic to acupuncture to ayurvedic to herbal) say the same thing: the so called 'American Diet' is responsible for the poor health of this nation. The fast-food industry, taking hold in the 1950s, has grown exponentially in the last 60 years and has brought with it an abundance of fat, carbohydrates, sugar and preservatives, in the interest of 'flavor' and a paucity of vitamins, fiber and other necessary nutrients, reducing costs to make this junk food affordable to the poorest among us.

Furthermore, there has been a systematic propaganda campaign (perpetrated by agribusiness, the American Dairy Association and others) to promote animal products as 'necessary' for proper nutrition. This is false. On the contrary, the major contributor to our poor health is the over consumption of animal products and other foods with low fiber and low vitamin and nutrient value.[38] That, combined with the poor quality of those animal products[39] and processed foods, routinely

---

38 See the monumental work of T. Colin Campbell and Thomas M. Campbell (2006) *The China Study: The Most Comprehensive Study of Nutrition Ever Conducted and the Startling Implications for Diet, Weight Loss, and Long-Term Health*, Dallas, TX: BenBella Books. This book should be 'required reading' in high school. The consumption of animal products is not necessary for health; in fact, it is deleterious to health. Colin Campbell has demonstrated that the consumption of beef causes cancer and that the elimination of beef and its replacement by a plant-based diet in cancer sufferers eliminates the cancer. Many people live very healthy lives without the consumption of any animal products, myself included.

39 The introduction of rBGH (recombinant bovine growth hormone) and rBST (recombinant Bovine Somatotropin), produced by Monsanto under the brand name Posilac, both used to accelerate the 'fattening' of cows (for milk) and of cattle (for beef), has proved to be problematic at the genetic level. 'Rendered' feed (the processed remains of other animals) is also used to speed up the maturation of beef cattle, giving rise in both cases to diseases, for which antibiotics are used on a regular basis to prevent epidemics in feed lots and other facilities for such animals. This is as a result of

What our children do not learn in high school **199**

made available to consumers, is what is making us unhealthy, inactive, sick and fat. In fact, they are killing us. In Einstein's words, "it is my view that a vegetarian manner of living by its purely physical effect on the human temperament would most beneficially influence the lot of mankind".[40]

The affordable junk food prepared by the fast-food industry targets the poor. Poorer people are less healthy than they could otherwise be, because they frequent these establishments more often than people of means. The disturbing fact is that eating at one of these places often costs less than buying groceries and preparing food at home. When working people come home after that long day, paid at minimum wage, they do not believe that they have a choice; they look to see what they have in their wallets and realize that some $8 can buy enough food at a fast-food eatery, whereas that same amount cannot procure from the market enough to feed the family. And there is the added work to prepare that food. Tired people do this more often than is safe for themselves and their families, no matter how many dollars are involved.

This condition continues until people are given an alternative that is not only more affordable, but also much more nutritious. If students were taught how to grow food on their own, the possibilities would be countless and most beneficial. If they were growing their own food either at home or in the community, as discussed above, they would not have that dilemma. All they would have to do is to stop by the community garden on their way home, after that hard day's work or school, and pick up some vegetables and tubers for dinner. The preparation factor is still a consideration, but the cost is massively reduced. This fact, along with the fact that this food is infinitely better for us, can boost enough energy in us to prepare this food ourselves. We need to cook more, from scratch. As we become familiar with many of the processes of cooking, they become 'second nature' and what, at first, seemed to be a mountain to climb becomes leveled.

In other words, with a little education, this scenario can change for the *much* better. This is where we can observe the real impact project-based education can have, not only in terms of the enlightenment of our children, but also in terms of how 'practicing good food production' can transform a situation of poverty into a situation of healthy consumption. Yes, I'm talking about the *children's* education. Mom and dad are pooped, exhausted from the hoops and hurdles they have to surmount all day; they don't have the time nor the funds to get educated. Children can teach their parents what is possible, even for the poorest of the poor. With education about nutrition and health that really matters and that can translate into the realities of their lives, children can help organize the practices in their families

---

decision-making, on the part of agribusiness, designed to make more money, not to produce safe food. All of these practices result in (along with the misery it causes the animals) poisoned food. Most of these animal products are purchased by the fast-food industry and end up in children who eat them.

40 Translation of Einstein letter to Hermann Huth (December 27, 1930) Einstein Archive 46-756 at https://ivu.org/history/northam20a/einstein.html.

200 Left Behind

in terms of food as nutrition, not only food to fill their stomachs. Here are a couple of principles to consider.

Fundamentally, the body works with a self-balancing system, called *homeostasis*, which tries to keep the body in equilibrium, part of which has to do with keeping the body at a roughly 80% alkaline to 20% acid balance.[41] If the diet constantly challenges this system, much energy is spent balancing the system and maintaining the immune system and less energy is available for many other things, including paying attention in class, having more energy to prepare that meal, having more energy to enjoy a better life. One easy way to monitor this balance in practical terms is to minimize the consumption of cooked foods (which, as a result of cooking, are acidic) and to maximize consuming raw foods (which are, by nature, alkaline). This simple fact about nutrition can place the student and his/her family in much better stead with regard to food choices. Our children need to be taught to become more adventurous about what they eat. They must become open to trying new foods; that is, foods that they are not used to and that are just as easily available. Sampling different foods helps to open up the palate. Broadening their options even at the level of that which they are already familiar can become the first step toward a more healthy diet. Chewing on a carrot or a celery stalk or biting into a tomato or apple or pear instead of potato chips, chicken nuggets or pizza will go a long way toward better health.

Meat and milk are concentrated proteins and, as such, produce a leftover acid ash in the stomach once they leave the stomach and move on to further digestion. This drives the body into imbalance, requiring *homeostasis* to compensate for this excess acid by 'stealing' calcium from the bones. Over time, this process of self-preservation has deleterious effects on the bones, often leading to osteoporosis. If we listen to the propaganda and routinely eat these foods, we are setting ourselves up to suffer diseases actually caused by that food we put into our mouths. Learning about these facts can help students and their families make informed choices that can obviate the consequences of a poor diet. Additionally, these foods – meats and dairy – are the most expensive foods in the market. While it is true that vegetables and fruits and nuts and seeds and herbs and grasses are becoming more expensive, especially the organic ones which are recommended more and more, so too are the meats and dairy products. Overall, I have found that buying organic produce costs less at the cash register than any combination of meats and dairy products.

Here's another fact: our bodies are not constructed to accommodate the portion of animal products recommended by the 'American Diet'. Human beings are not carnivores (meat [flesh] eaters). We are herbivores (eaters of many different kinds

---

41 Not to be confused with the body pH, the healthy range being 6.0 to 7.5. The symbol 'pH' is a measure along a continuum, favoring, for our bodies, the alkaline end of that spectrum. In order to maintain that pH, the alkaline percentage of the body should be approximately 80% of the acid/alkaline mix. Hence, our diet should also reflect those percentages. See http://draxe.com/balancing-act-why-ph-is-crucial-to-health/ and many other sites for details.

of plant foods).[42] This is not a matter of choice; it is a matter of biology and physiology. Our digestive system does not produce the kinds of enzymes in the quantity necessary to digest the volume of animal products that people consume in the United States. True (obligate) carnivores, like cats, do. This means that they *must* have meat, lots of it, in their diet, because they cannot synthesize from plant foods the following nutrients: retinol, taurine and arachinodic acid; these are natural to the flesh they consume from predation or scavenging. This means that they eat raw meat from either kills or carrion. Human beings do synthesize these nutrients from plant foods and thus have no need to eat meat. The fact that people cook (roast, fry, bake, *sauté, etc.*) their meat, for the most part before they eat it, demonstrates further that we do not conduct ourselves the way carnivores do; they eat the meat raw and bloody, we do not. Also, cooking, in most cases, is necessary because animal products often contain parasites and other contaminants, such as antibiotics and growth hormones, that are administered to the livestock to 'fatten' them quicker and protect them from disease, danger from which is maximized because the animals are in such close proximity in the 'factory farming' system. True carnivores have the immune systems to counter this assault on their bodies; we do not.

Another fact is that true carnivores have a much shorter digestive track than we do; people roughly measure two to three times that of the cat, proportionally. The digestive track, from stomach to rectum, for human beings is between 17 and 35 feet, some six to eight times the length (height) of the person. This is too much distance for meat to travel in the intestines and colon to be fully digested before it putrefies; as a result, this putrefaction in the lower track is what causes problems for us, most notably colon cancer.[43]

In order to realize the simple relationship between food and health, teachers and school administrations must discard the nonsense they are told from the American Dairy Association and agribusiness. Posters about nutrition continue to dominate the classroom walls about what people should eat and how often, *etc.* These are advertisements for these mega-organizations, not credible programs for health. According to these corporate endorsements, animal products and dairy products make up a disproportionate share of what they would like to see us eat; and, most of the time, they are ingratiated, because overwhelmingly people follow these recommendations without engaging in any critical thinking.

If you look at the latest USDA version of the so-called 'food pyramid',[44] you discover that all of one-third, if not more, of what they recommend we eat each day is animal products. The latest food pyramid by the USDA (April 2005), they call "my pyramid", proposes that this guide is flexible and can be adapted to each

---

42 Some argue that we are 'omnivores', that we can eat pretty much anything. While it is true that human beings do eat 'pretty much anything', that does not make us omnivores. Eating 'anything' is partly responsible for the ill-health that is rampant in the United States.

43 See *What's Wrong with Eating Meat?* (1981) by Vistara Parham, Denver, CO: PCAP Publications.

44 See www.cnpp.usda.gov/mypyramid.

one of us, changing this here and that there to meet our particular needs. They admit that all of us should eat something from all of the different groups 'every day'. The different food groups represented in the diagram are grains, vegetables, fruit, fats (oils), milk and meats and beans. While this pyramid is different from the one I grew up with (the one that advocated fully one-half of all food intake to be from animal products), it maintains the same piety towards animal products (to be fair, it does recommend more grains and vegetables). They promote milk by emphasizing our need for calcium, which is added to the milk; there is more calcium in a leaf of lettuce than there is in a glass of milk. Furthermore, casein is a known carcinogen, a component of milk. Animal protein, in meats, are also known to create the environment for the production of various cancers. See Campbell and Campbell cited in Note 36. The "Harvard Pyramid" makes some important changes, emphasizing grains and vegetables, but also recommends two portions of dairy and up to two portions of meat daily.[45] In June 2011, the USDA created yet another version of recommendations for "healthier eating". This new scheme, to its credit, does advocate the consumption of more fruits, vegetables and grains, but, true to its affiliations with agribusiness, still promotes the routine consumption of animal products in the forms of meat and dairy.[46]

These industry recommendations run contrary to the nutritional science available to all of us for study. The leading consensus worldwide (of professional nutritional and medical journals that are not owned or funded by agribusiness or the AMA, *etc.*) is that, if we eat meat at all, it should be no more than 20% of food intake. And, the more we decrease that percentage, the better health we can achieve. *Not everyone must become a vegetarian in order to have proper nutrition.* All people have to do is to reduce animal product intake from 21 times a week to seven times. In addition, fruits, nuts and seeds, vegetables, rice and beans (complete protein) and starchy foods like potatoes and pastas must be the majority of the intake. The results, after a short period of time practicing this kind of diet: more energy, less weight, fewer aches and pains, fewer onsets of disease, a happier and more productive life.

What is more, eating less meat and dairy would reduce the need for the mega-production of animals for food. This would reduce the amount of water consumed by them, leaving water for people to drink. Water availability is waning fast worldwide and, if we do not do something (and this super-sized animal production represents the largest misuse of water, period) to minimize our waste of water, we will be sealing our own demise as a result. In addition, the waste from this system would decrease substantially, thereby reducing the pollution of our rivers and lakes and, in some instances, our ground water. It would also free up

---

45 See the work of Michael Pollan at http://michaelpollan.com.
46 See Editorial (June 3, 2011) "USDA Replaces Food Pyramid with 'MyPlate' in Hopes to Promote Healthier Eating". *Washington Post* at https://www.washingtonpost.com/national/usda-replaces-food-pyramid-with-myplate-in-hopes-to-promote-healthier-eating/2011/06/02/AGRE16HH_story.html?utm_term=.2d3b742e0126.

the land from such farming and allow the forests to rejuvenate. Trees on the same area of land, now relegated to growing feed for animal production, are much more sustainable, becoming home to varieties of other plants and animals. In the end, ceasing this production process would free up land to plant crops that could not only feed people in the U.S. but all over the world, effectively eliminating famine, as long as those foods were properly cared for and distributed globally.

This is an approach that has been tried and tested, yielding noteworthy results, sometimes fantastic results. Thousands of people each year learn about how badly they have been treating themselves by the way they eat. With some help in understanding alternative concepts and ideas and a little coaching, people discover that their eating practices are the cause of what ails them. Most of these people are adults, having done damage to themselves over many years. Why place our children in this position? Teach them early how they can avoid a majority of ailments and diseases, suffered by their parents and members of their extended families, simply by eating according to a few simple principles.[47] While becoming vegetarian is advocated by Einstein, good nutrition does not *require* it. All students and their siblings and parents need to do is to reduce their animal product intake, which will go a long way to a healthier life all around, to an increase in animal welfare and a reduction in world famine.

Schools can adopt such instruction with little disruption or fanfare. This course should be introduced as early as possible and built upon in subsequent years of public education. By the time our children graduate from high school, they would have become experts in nutrition and a lifestyle that will afford them a quality of life they may not have seen in their parents and a longevity that will surpass that of their parents.

Physical education (exercise)

When I was in elementary, there was no physical education (PE), as such. We had recess and played games/sports after lunch and during the mid-day break. When the weather was inclement, we didn't. In high school, participation in sports was mandatory. Whether it was soccer or football or baseball or ice hockey or skiing or basketball or tennis, one each season counted toward the accreditation requirement for 'physical education'. In other schools, I remember hearing about actual classes being held in their schools about how the body works and how to strengthen it and develop it; to be fit. In 1962, President Kennedy had introduced the 'JFK Challenge' at La Sierra High School in Riverside, CA.[48] It showcased the program

---

47 These principles are well-known and advocated by several successful institutions at which programs are set up to help people change their eating habits, in many instances, to save their lives. Here are some: www.drmcdougall.com; www.gerson.org; www.livingfoodsinstitute.com; www.hippocratesinst.org; http://cancercompassalternateroute.com/doctors-and-clinics/oasis-of-healing-treatment-center/; www.garynull.com; www.youtube.com/watch?v=ULciZ8jSgHA.

48 See JFK Presidential Library and Museum for details.

204 Left Behind

that he wanted to be adopted throughout the country. Unfortunately, this 'great national effort' did not last very long due to budget cuts, leaving the vast majority of schools in the country without proper programs for PE. While there still are schools that have some kind of programs, there have been progressively more and more budget cuts throughout the last 60 years across the country that have resulted in less and less PE, either its curtailment or its elimination in the United States. Wealthy schools have it; poor ones do not. A case in point: Naperville, IL, a relatively wealthy school district, under the tutelage of long-time PE coordinator, Paul Zientarski, has developed an early-morning program to help students who are lagging behind in reading and math. The connection between physical activity and learning is well-established and his program has made a huge difference for these students. All schools should have all of these facilities for PE.

The National Association for Sports and Physical Education takes the position that "physical education is critical to educating the whole child, and that all students in grades K–12 should receive physical education on a daily basis." Their national standards call for "a minimum of 150 minutes [of PE] per week [elementary] and 225 minutes [of PE] per week [middle and secondary school]". These standards have been advocated by the NASPE since 2004.[49]

When one investigates a little, one finds that those standards are not followed, not even close. According to the Centers for Disease Control and Prevention (CDC), some "[54%] of high school students [67% of 9th grade students but only 41% of 12th grade students] attended physical education classes in 2007".[50] Also, "The percentage of high school students who attended physical education classes daily decreased from 42% in 1991 to 25% in 1995…"[51] The story gets more complex: "Among the 54% of students who attended physical education classes, [only] 84% [of those] actually exercised or played sports for 20 minutes or longer during an average class".[52] This is not at all impressive and falls way below what one might expect when we hear that "education in the United States is the best in the world", often vaunted by people who want us to believe in the mythology of 'American Exceptionalism'.[53] Real PE comes from hard work, from individual students, from PE faculty and from the institutions that are supposed to provide the facilities to engage in proper physical training.

The high school for which I coached girl's ice hockey has a PE program; it is a school which is located in a privileged community, where the tax base is significant,

---

49 National Association for Sport and Physical Education (2011) "Physical Education is Critical to Educating the Whole Child", [Position Statement]. Contributing Author: Brent Heidorn. See hhttps://www.wssd.org/cms/lib/PA01001072/Centricity/Domain/581/NASPE%20-%20PE%20 Critical%20to-Educating-the-Whole-Child-5-19-2011.pdf; www.ascd.org/wholechild.
50 Centers for Disease Control and Prevention (2008) "Youth Risk Behavior Surveillance – United States, 2007". *Morbidity and Mortality Weekly Report*, volume 57, issue No. SS-4, 1–131.
51 *Ibid.*
52 *Ibid.*
53 See Chapter 11 on exceptionalism.

because most of the houses are very expensive and yield significant taxes available for appropriation to the school budget. The athletic director there,[54] David Schulz, avowed that, except for the cut in budget here and there, "We have all the funding we need to conduct a comprehensive physical education program." This includes the impressive sports program at the school. The success of that program was not only due to the funding that it enjoyed, it was, in large measure, due to Schulz's commitment and devotion. I highlight this to remind the reader that, while funding is the single most important component to the viability of school PE and athletic programs, many ADs, whether well-funded or not, do amazing things with what they have, because they are dedicated to their athletes and the whole student body at their schools. We owe them deep respect and thanks for their work.

Other communities do not enjoy such wealth for the development of our children and, as a result, their schools do not possess the same kinds of PE facilities.[55] Consequently, children in those districts/communities do not receive the instruction they need. The promise that has been continually repeated over the years by officials is that our children will be provided with only the best education has been consistently broken when it comes to PE. The perennial lament is that the budget is not adequate to continue this or that program; the humanities are also among the first to be cut. That is why the most important component of education is the proper funding made available to all our schools for all our children.

The three components of being fit I was taught are still valid today: eat properly, exercise routinely and sleep in accordance with your needs. Eating properly means consuming good, clean (organically grown) food on a regular basis and knowing when to eat and how much; routine exercise means engaging (weekly, if not daily) in the three major activities to keep the body fit (stretching, aerobic/anaerobic and resistance); getting enough sleep means knowing what our body needs to restore and repair what the body has 'suffered' each day.

Physical education in our schools should be reinvented to include all of the fundamental instruction that transforms our youngsters into people who understand their body physics. Instruction should include knowing how to breathe properly, to stretch one's muscles and tendons, to engage in strength training and engage in aerobic exercise to optimize the heart and vascular system.

Often, we have thought of PE as 'playing sports'. This is a mistake and must be rethought. Engaging in sports does not mean that the players know what they are doing with regard to their physicality; often athletes hurt themselves unnecessarily simply because they are not aware of some fundamentals of movement they have not had the opportunity to learn about as a regular part of their education. More and more experts in this field are developing programs to do the real work

---

54 During my tenure at Fairfield Ludlowe High School, 1998–2016, Mr. Schulz was AD from 2006 to 2016.

55 See chapters on poverty and discrimination for further discussion about the uneven distribution of educational resources.

of teaching children how to become acquainted with their bodies and learn how to maximize their physical fitness. I am not referring to the kind of training that Olympic athletes must endure; that is advanced training. This is basic stuff; it is about teaching our children how their bodies are supposed to move and how to keep them healthy and strong.

One program, developed and implemented by Richard Sirois, MS, LAT, ATC, CSCS, has already shown promise.[56] He is a certified athletic trainer and strength coach with Southern Maine Health Care Sports Performance Center in Saco, ME. He and his colleagues have been piloting a program at two high schools in Saco and Biddeford, ME: Biddeford High School (for four years), a typical school in Maine and Thornton Academy (for five years), a private and the largest secondary school in Maine. The program emphasizes the most fundamental of body movements (plyometrics) that all children should be able to perform, regardless of their physical abilities. Interest in this program came from the sports programs at these high schools. Coaches and athletic directors there recognized the potential of this training for high school athletes in various sports and for students, in general. While the program was not developed and designed for the purposes of athletic 'conditioning', Richard was willing to test the program on them, thereby providing a context to pilot-test these training concepts for nonathlete students.

The pilot and subsequent test years were conducted during the summer months (2011 through 2016) while classes are not in session. Students were administered a 'pretest' at the beginning of a six-week program to establish a baseline of performance. At the end of the six weeks, students were tested again on their performance of the same movements to detect the improvements they had made. Richard has registered significant results: *all students improved in some or most or all of the individual movement tests.*

I was fortunate to accompany Richard and his staff to both schools to witness the training activities. Groups of students, boys and girls, were formed based upon the general level of performance they had established in the pretest and the level of activity (movement) brought to the different groups was commensurate with that level. Hence, the program is sensitive to the needs of the students and encourages the achievement of goals which are on par with their abilities and within their reach. Progressively, in each group, they improve their performance in each category as they advance in the program. This is very important because one of the observations/complaints that we hear from parents is that "my son/daughter is not very physical and he cannot do that". With this program, that kind of retort evaporates; all students do what they can as they improve.

In my view, this is an impressive attempt to establish real physical education for our children and schools should adopt this kind of program. I asked Richard about the attitudes school administrators had about adopting his methodology as

---

56 See Appendix for details about this innovative program to teach youngsters fundamental movement and self-awareness. Results of this program are posted there.

the means to render real physical education to their students. He was not optimistic about any immediate movement in that direction. While establishing such a program is something he/they might like to realize, he worries that it is unlikely to happen, mostly because of the cuts in funding that continue to plague PE education and the inertia that has set in over the decades.

As a coach myself for some 24 years, I have assessed the efficacy of this program and have concluded that this and others like it could revolutionize our educational practice where our children's physical fitness is concerned. I was able to experience the mechanics of the program and, without a doubt, existing faculty, not only coaches, could deliver this training to students once they received the training (CEUs) they would need in order to implement it correctly. Once trained and assigned to PE classes, existing faculty could earn additional salary just like faculty members who coach this or that sport do already. Presumably, that training could come from Richard and his staff; they would certify the PE faculty member(s), who would, in turn, train other interested faculty members to contribute to the instruction.[57]

I am not attempting to undermine physical education professionals' area of expertise; obviously, they would not be able to take on this increase of instruction all by themselves in the present economic climate. This may be an intermediate platform upon which to build a real PE program which could accommodate all our children, dramatically raising the percentage of participation in PE to an acceptable level. They could take the lead that Naperville, IL established, even with reduced facilities; there is much that is possible with much less. ADs, PE instructors and coaches do that already. Once such a program were established, the tasks could then become the sole domain of the PE faculty again, presuming that funding would be made available to schools to hire more faculty for this purpose. All students could then benefit from this program or one like it across the country. This kind of program could solve the abysmal reality of PE in the United States today. Imagine how wonderful it would/could be if our high school graduates, instead of being physically deficient, imbalanced and sitting on the couch, were physically fit, with full equilibrium, and active members of society.

Athletics

My daughters played school sports. In elementary school, it was soccer; in high school, it was ice hockey. I was always athletic and it was no stretch to involve myself in that part of their education. I coached them throughout the years and learned a lot about them, their mates and myself. It did not take long to discover that much of what we taught them on the field or on the ice was not taught in the classroom. Notions of cooperation, teamwork and leadership are not in evidence

---

57 This scheme is not something Richard has planned, *per se*; it is something he and I speculated about as a potential beginning. If not this kind of initial modus operandi, then what?

as much in the classroom context; there, academic performance is. It seemed that, at the beginning of a sport-season, we (coaches) would find that new players had to be introduced to these skills, even freshmen in high school. How is it that these concepts are not adequately introduced and engendered as part of the regular educational fare?

Of course, some kids did understand these concepts; but they probably learned them attending summer camp or by being involved in the Girls and Boys Clubs or the Girl and Boy Scouts. I endorse these avenues for continuing education, not only for their physical components, but also for their attention to cooperation and sharing. They should be part of the broader educational experience for children. They should be required at the elementary level, especially middle school (6th, 7th & 8th grades) and continued in high school.

Are *curricula* so stuffed with requirements that there is no time for these kinds of skills? The short answer is "yes". Take any subject matter, from mathematics to science to languages to literature to sociology, and teachers are inundated with required texts and blocks of subject matter they must cover within a specific time period. And it is too much. History, for example, is most egregious in this regard. Of course, every year that passes, there is that much more history to cover. And, if many significant events and issues dominated that year, the more important it is to cover it. As a result, something suffers. This is a closed loop which always gets bigger, never smaller, unless there is a change in perspective about what we must teach our students. Consequently, the concepts I propose for your consideration presently are not typically introduced wherever they should appropriately appear in the *curriculum*.[58]

Athletics offer students an opportunity to learn about themselves, their mates and how to interact with them in a setting which *requires* cooperation and sharing and teamwork and leadership. In other words, much classroom work may not *require* familiarity with these skills. However, in team sports,[59] these are *essential*, not only desirable. One cannot have a well-functioning team without them. The dominant methodology of teaching in the United States places students in competition with each other, *e.g.*, grades, economic status, talent, *individual* awards, *etc.*, rather than in cooperation with each other. Hence, notions of sharing required in playing a team sport are expectedly undeveloped for them. Playing sports opens

---

58 To be fair, there are occasions in which students can be exposed to and develop some of these skills, *e.g.*, group study and interaction, orchestra and band, debate, field trips, *etc.*; however, often, there is a need for transportation to and from these random activities, usually not part of the budget – transportation *must* be included in the athletics program, if the school has one. Consequently, those other activities are often not supported.

59 I emphasize 'team sports' because these skills are essential in those contexts; individual sports like tennis, track and field, wrestling and swimming tend to highlight the individual effort more than the team effort. I do not disparage participation in these sports; they also have 'teams', the 'ski team' and so on; however, the dynamics are different and I want to draw closer attention to team sports, in which many players engage in unison.

up a personal and collective investigation into these matters, from which students benefit immeasurably.

How many times have I been approached (and this has happened to all my coaching colleagues) by players who thank me for all they learned about themselves and how to work together. Only occasionally have players approached with gratitude about how we made them better players. That is important too, but we have commented among ourselves how interesting it was/is that players get it: they understand how important playing a sport was/is in terms of their own development as people and their place in their realities at school, at home, wherever they are; not only in terms of playing the sport. This is the kind of education that makes a real difference. I remind the reader here about my philosophy of education which requires the "dialogical encounter" as proposed by Paulo Freire and the 'project-based' methodology of education, in which wonderful learning arises from the collective project in which students participate. The sports arena is perfect to engage players/students in this way.

What do they learn? Team sports, in particular, teach students how to cooperate with their mates to work toward common ends – in hockey, to break out, pass the puck to one another, shooting on net and score goals. Even if the skills of the players are not the best (prowess in a sport is not what I am addressing here), these activities require a goodly amount of self-awareness (knowledge of one's abilities and limitations), realization of the play before them (whether or not to pass the puck and to whom; decision-making), their commitment to their mates while on the ice (how they must always do their best, whatever that is) and know when to get off the ice (a tired player cannot do her best for the team).

They learn respect for their mates, for their opponents and for themselves. They learn restraint when harassed by an opponent who has not learned restraint. They learn to be selfless and pass the puck to their mate when they know that their mate has a better chance to score. They learn how to be happy for their mates when they make a good play and how to encourage them when they make mistakes. They learn how to muster all their courage and tenacity, especially when they are two goals down in the third period and the pressure is on because they know that they should have overtaken this team in the first period. They learn how to share their knowledge of the game and of other matters in their lives. The bonding that develops during the weeks of a season, or several seasons, can galvanize into life-long friendships and companions.

For some, not all, leadership skills develop over time. Captains are players who demonstrate an overall understanding and appreciation for the meaning of a team. They are the players, not necessarily the best players, who gain insight into what is needed when and how to solve problems in the making. They are the ones to whom their mates turn for encouragement and compassion and praise. Opportunities for leadership do arise elsewhere in schools: music, club membership, student government; and the leadership developed there and in team sports is constantly tested and, as a result, becomes solidified in the respect that is granted those captains by their playmates.

These are life-long skills that they will need in order to pursue their dreams. These are not temporary for the purposes of winning games or receiving trophies at the end of the season. These skills will carry them a long way to further understanding of themselves, others and their circumstances in life. This is what all education should do for our children: prepare them for life in the multifarious paths they will encounter. No one subject matter does that alone. However, if the *curriculum* is properly fashioned, the breadth and depth of that experience will serve them well and they will see the folly of the individualistic mantra that continues to dominate in today's schools. Instead, the *curriculum* would have prepared them from a critical base, rather than from a selfish and acquiescent one.

Some readers might think that the previous description has been a 'pie in the sky' version of how sports can influence player/students. In one way, they are correct. These opportunities for learning are ones that should be offered to all students; they are not. More often than not, such opportunities go to the 'athletes', not the whole population of students. The contexts of sports education should be afforded all our children, no matter of the level: beginner, in-house, JV, varsity, *etc.* My own experience was like that – one based upon those principles and others which helped me develop self-discipline and self-esteem.

However, more often than not, that is not the message that is left with our youngsters. Depending upon the sport – some are more egregious than others – other values are engendered. For example, while this is not universally true, football is the classic for teaching players to 'knuckle under'; to 'do what the coach says'; to 'go all the way', no matter what. Successful players are those who acquiesce to the military style training that is this sport. I have spent a fair amount of time witnessing football practice over the years, while jogging/running on high school tracks which surround football fields. From August onward, there are football practices, from try-outs to general conditioning to special-play practices. Throughout the practice time, one can hear the barking of the coaches and the responses of the players in unison "huh". This reminds me of the marine reply to orders "sir, yes sir". Along with this outward sign are more serious implications. This is where/when much of the attitudes of students are caste: fit in; don't make waves; learn how to respect the way things are; obey authority. Worse are the exaggerations of these values: we are better than them; stay away from those school kids from this or that school; they don't belong to our group. I am not arguing that any sense of discipline that arises from this experience is undesirable. I am only pointing out that discipline comes from within, not as a result of pressure and, sometimes, demeaning pressure, from outside.

I am reminded of George Carlin's contrastive descriptions of baseball and football in one of his 'shticks'. His keen attention to the ways we describe, that is the language-use which surrounds, this truly 'American' sport, has been codified in his words. I reproduce only the comments about football here:

> Football is played on a grid-iron in a stadium, sometimes called soldiers-field or war-memorial stadium ... In football, you wear helmets ... In football,

you receive a penalty ... Football has hitting, clipping, spearing, blocking, piling-on, late-hitting, unnecessary roughness and personal fouls ... Football is rigidly timed and it [the game PLJ] will end even if we have to go to 'sudden death' ... In football, the object is for the quarterback, otherwise known as the field-general, to be on target with his aerial-assault, riddling the defense by hitting his receivers with deadly accuracy, in spite of the blitz, even if he has to use the shotgun; with short bullet-passes and long-bombs, he marches his troops into enemy territory, balancing this aerial assault with a sustained ground-attack, which punches holes in the forward wall of his enemy's defensive line.[60]

His comic genius has made us laugh, but has also made us think about many issues that are manifest in everyday life. A master of ordinary language-use, he highlighted for us just how language works and how particular uses predispose us to understand our world in prescribed ways.

For our purposes, his comments are astute indeed. They punctuate how the way we use language can influence the ways we understand our surroundings. Arguably, this is how extreme ethnocentrism can and does enter our children's thinking. Sometimes this leads to ideas of jingoism, racism, nativism and xenophobia. Also, the extreme version of these sentiments "we are better than anyone" or "we are the best" or "those people are no good" can also obtain.

Certainly, there are other institutions which contribute to this kind of discourse that lulls us into a mode of thinking that accommodates these dangerous outcomes. However, while these outcomes are not universal (that is, in my view, good coaching strives not only not to develop such attitudes but also creates countermeasures against them), they occur often enough to perpetuate these kinds of attitudes in our students in school sports, whether in high school or college. The cries at sporting events that spur on 'our team' do not only galvanize the affiliations spectators have with their team members, but they also punctuate the separations that may exist between the opponents in the game and their fans, especially if the teams are 'rivals'.

A healthy sense of competition is not the problem here. Contests to discover the best teams/players in any game are not the issue. However, if what accompanies the competition, in the form of rhetoric or the introduction of false values (like "we are better than anyone"), which serve to transform the match at hand into something else, a fetishized version of the sports events, then the fundamental purposes of such sports become distorted and bear no resemblance to the formidably positive learning experience they could have been.

My own experience has been that, at least in the actual coaching of our players, these extreme attitudes have not been allowed. And, if we observed them in others (parents, students, spectators), we would call them on their conduct and not allow it to happen, at least during our events. What happens outside our purview is

---

60 See George Carlin's (1984) HBO Special, *Carlin on Campus*.

another matter and that is the point here. Even if we are mindful of such matters in our daily interactions with students around sports, the larger context of the society continues to embrace these notions and attitudes in so many different domains of life that the most astute efforts do not always make a difference.

While this is a serious problem in our society, I do not believe that the situation is so bleak that there is nothing we can do about it. The solution begins at the schools themselves. At the level of a shared, sound philosophy of education, sports included, there must be, at the very beginning for our youngsters (pre-school, kindergarten, elementary and high school), a comprehensive effort to transform existing practices of 'individualistic' thinking into modes of thinking that are critical and liberating, rather than those that limit the periphery of thinking to oneself. We must change the 'I, mine, me' attitude into a 'we, ours, us' one and team sports can help us do that.

Sleep (rest)

Children are often told by their parents and other significant adults in their lives to get enough sleep so that they can function correctly and be rested for the multifarious demands placed upon them in our frenetic culture. However, they are not often told what the best conditions should be for the best rest/sleep. Sleep is the state of being that is called 'basal metabolism'; it is that state that is inactive and at rest, a necessary part of daily life. It is the daily opportunity, not only for the body to rest, but it is the time for the body to self-repair. During our waking hours of the day, we go about our activities, some of which are sedentary and others of which require exertion of one kind or another to perform this or that task. The body, over the course of any given day, fatigues more or less commensurate with the activities of that day. We get tired in ways that involve our muscles, our bones, our nerves and our state of mind. These represent all sorts of warring down of our faculties, our strength and our ability to function in an alert and effective way. The cycle of hours during which we are awake and those asleep is natural to our organism. To the extent that we are aware of our needs to maintain an effective level of engagement in what we all have to do each day, to that extent, we are living a balanced life.

Without proper sleep and renewal, we would not be able to function efficiently for very long at all. So, what should we know about sleep that can predispose us to have the energy we need to take on the next day? There are only a few principles to follow. We need to know that the number of hours of sleep we need varies from person to person, even with children; although children need, on average, more sleep than adults. That is something that can be arrived at through a simple trial and error test to discover at which point in time we can enjoy optimum readiness to engage our day. If we function well all day, then we are probably getting enough sleep; if not, then we need to increase it. *Too much* sleep can affect us as negatively as *not enough*. This will not take long to determine and the timing may change as we age. However, once we make those determinations, we must follow the protocol that we adopt. Until something changes, and, early in life, there could be several alterations in our sleep needs, we must respect our plan and not waiver from it, or we will pay either in the ability to concentrate, make routine decisions or stay awake.

What is hidden in this test are the physiological parameters which are addressed during the repair process. When repair is engaged, the process that the body deploys to fix, replenish and re-energize all the parts of the body to optimize their potential for the next day, a certain queuing up takes place. First of all, no repair can take place before the stomach is empty. The reason for this is that digestion takes up most of the energy of the body to perform this task.[61] Repair is impossible until all the energy of the body can be devoted to it. Hence, if someone eats something before going to bed (less than three to four hours for the digestion of proteins, less than two hours for complex carbohydrates, or less than one hour for fruits), repair will be delayed until these food items are out of the stomach. Depending upon the person, complete repair will last from six to ten hours. If we eat something and go directly to bed, planning eight hours of sleep, repair will be delayed and truncated; the body will not be able to complete the process before we have to rise for the next day. So, a rule of thumb is not to eat anything (we can drink water anytime) at least three hours before we go to bed.

So, what is the trajectory for repair? A simplified overview looks like this: the first to be repaired are the vital organs, then the muscles and bones, then the nerves. That is it. Not surprisingly, people who have eaten too late before going to bed will rise with a headache or increased stress (waking up 'wired') that will affect their ability to function correctly that day. Because the central nervous system (CNS) is repaired last (we have no choice with regard to this; the organism is an intelligent one and does what it must according to its ontological rules), if we do not move into 'delta' sleep, we are being deprived of this reparation and we will suffer the next day. So, sleep is not just 'crashing' to rest; it is a vital part of the daily cycle which, if paid attention to, will serve us very well for the activity level in which we partake.[62]

These three components of health, nutrition, exercise and sleep, are the fundamental ones we should know about and whose interaction we should understand. If we do not eat the right foods, we are putting ourselves in jeopardy: we invite diseases and ailments; our bodies will not function correctly, causing us distress such as nausea, diarrhoea, gas in the stomach or intestines, *etc.*, predisposing us to long term conditions such as obesity, osteoporosis, diabetes, *etc.* When we don't feel well, we don't sleep well and we don't feel like exercising, and don't. If we

---

61 That is why we hear said that one should not do any extensive swimming immediately after eating. The energy required to swim is not available because the stomach is using it to digest the food one just ate, especially if that food is protein, requiring much longer to digest than anything else.

62 All of these matters are readily available to read and study on the Internet. With some minor variations, these parameters are well known and advocated across a wide spectrum of health practices.

214 Left Behind

do not sleep well, we do not function well; our energy level cannot cope with the demands we place on ourselves, including making sure that we eat well. If we are not well rested, we will tend to seek out fast food and become more sedentary. If we do not exercise properly, our bodies tend to become lethargic, driving us deeper into a less active life and what goes with it: weight gain, less energy, prone to eat more fast food, affecting our sleep patterns, often resulting in more sleep that we do not need or less sleep because whatever physical movements we do engage in strain our muscles and keep us awake. These three health bastions must be taught effectively.

Sex education

That we must take pause in considering the many ways that our educational practices fall short in the present context, the state of sex education is of the highest concern. I assert this because, when we spend two minutes, and I do not exaggerate, looking into how sex education in public schools is delivered, we discover immediately that something is wrong. First of all, there is no federal/national mandate for sex education; the kind of sex education that is offered in each state is determined by the school boards and political, religious institutions of those states. As I have demonstrated previously in this book, *curricula* are largely not decided by teachers (only ~25%), but by politicians, business people, clergy and ideologically motivated actors. This fact has given rise to an array of sex education policies that challenges the most astute observer.

There are two major trajectories for public school sex education in the United States: the 'abstinence-only-until-marriage' policy and the 'comprehensive' policy. The first is a simple pronouncement that students will not have sex before they get married; straightforward but problematic and consequential (more below). The second includes a broader set of considerations, but is inconsistent across states.

With a significant 'consensus' by teachers of what comprehensive sex education can consist, here is a sample across the spectrum of topics that could be included in such a program: anatomy and physiology, STIs (sexually transmitted infections) including HIV and AIDS, unintended pregnancy, the proper use of condoms, birth control, sexuality, gender, masturbation, sexual orientation and expression, awareness of and respect for LGBTQIA persons, interactional skills, communication skills, overall sexual health, abortion, sexual violence and rape. According to the NCSL, as of March 1, 2016,

> – 24 states and the District of Columbia require public schools teach sex education (21 of which mandate sex education *and* HIV education).
> – 33 states and the District of Columbia require students receive instruction about HIV/AIDS.
> – 20 states require that if provided, sex and/or HIV education must be medically, factually or technically accurate. State definitions of "medically accurate" vary, from requiring that the department of health review curriculum

What our children do not learn in high school **215**

for accuracy, to mandating that curriculum be based on information from "published authorities upon which medical professionals rely."[63]

It is significant that only "24 states and the District of Columbia *require*" sex education and that only "33 states and the District of Columbia" *require* instruction about HIV/AIDS and that only "20 states require *if provided*, sex *and/or* HIV education must be.... 'medically accurate'" [italics added]. What about the other states? Does this mean that all other states have no sex education requirements? I take it that the NCSL would have included those 'other' states had they reported that they offer in sex education in their schools. So, to find out, one would have to do a state-by-state search to obtain a complete picture of what is going on with regard to sex education in the United States.

Or would we? After searching a sample of states, I discovered that the details are not as clear as I would expect about just what kind of sex education is offered to those children. In Maine, under the auspices of the DOE, sex education subscribes to an 'abstinence only' scheme and is addressed virtually only in terms of HIV prevention, not in terms that actually educate students about sex.[64] In Florida, under the auspices of the DOE and the sub-category of "Comprehensive Health Education", the topics of HIV/STD Prevention, Teen Pregnancy Prevention and Sexual Health Education are included.[65] In Washington, the DOE is legislated (WAC 392-410-140) to include sexual health education (HIV/STD's, harassment, intimidation and bullying are mentioned.), which is "optional" due to "excusal of students" by parents.[66] In California, a new act, the California Healthy Youth Act (January 1, 2016; Education Code sections 51930–51939), requires that all students, grades 7–12, will receive comprehensive sexual health and HIV/AIDS instruction. The high school sex education curriculum, called "Be Real. Be Ready" is replacing a non-mandated policy. It stipulates that "Abstinence-only education is not permitted in California public schools".[67] You get the idea of the quagmire of unstandardized attention that states give to sex education. This is partly why we have so many sex-related problems in our society. Part of the problems arise from an unclear national policy to educate our children about sex and all its accompanying ramifications and part of them arise from the 'puritan' attitudes that still plague our culture. Comprehensive sex education, along with sustained and responsible parent participation is the only way to inform our children about this important part of their lives.

One element about this discussion that complicates this kind of call for good sex education is the parental 'opt-out' clause. If parents do not want their children to

---

63 The National Conference of State Legislatures, "State Policies on Sex Education in Schools", December 21, 2016. See http://ncsl.org.
64 See www.maine.gov/doe.
65 See www.fldoe.org/schools/safe-healthy-schools/healthy-schools/comprehensive-health-edu.stm.
66 See http://apps.leg.wa.gov/WAC/default.aspx?cite=392-410-140.
67 See www.cde.ca.gov/ls/he/se/faq.asp.

216 Left Behind

receive sex education, many of these programs make specific exclusionary provisions. While I accept that parents have a say in their children's education, I wonder about the motivation for exercising their decision-making options here. The advantages of parental involvement in their children's education is well known: children get higher grades; they attend classes regularly; they move from one grade to the next more smoothly; they have better social skills; they are more likely to graduate and move on to post-secondary education.[68] However,

> – Nearly one-third of students say their parents have no idea how they are doing in school.
> – About one-sixth of all students report that their parents don't care whether they make good grades in school or not.
> – Only about one-fifth of parents consistently attend school programs.
> – More than 40 percent never do.[69]

With such a poor record of parent participation, is it not interesting that this part of their children's education, sex education, attracts their attention? Here, I sense we have a disproportionate involvement of parents. Is this because parents want to inform their children about sex themselves? Is it because they disagree with the approach that the school system uses? Or, is it because they do not want their children to receive sex education at all? We already know that religious beliefs can influence such decisions, claiming that, *inter alia*, masturbation is a sin and should not be discussed in school; sex is sinful except for connubial 'procreation' and such instruction can encourage children to have sex; same sex intercourse is 'unnatural' and should not be introduced to children. Therefore, abstinence is the only option for these children. According to the NCSL,

> – 38 states and the District of Columbia require school districts to allow parental involvement in sexual education programs.
> – Four states require parental consent before a child can receive instruction.
> – 35 states and the District of Columbia allow parents to opt-out on behalf of their children.[70]

The abstinence-only program has a long history in the United States. Again, to appreciate details about this movement, one must conduct a state-by-state search.[71]

---

68 See National Education Association study "Research Spotlight on Parental Involvement in Education", based upon the conclusions of a 2002 report from Southwest Educational Development Laboratory, "A New Wave of Evidence".

69 See Lawrence Steinberg (1997) *Beyond the Classroom: Why School Reform Has Failed and What Parents Need to Do*, New York: Simon & Schuster, pp. 19–20.

70 *Op. cit.*, www.ncsl.org/research/health/state-policies-on-sex-education-in-schools.aspx.

71 One valuable publication which includes historical retrospectives from the 1970s onward is Planned Parenthood's "Sex Education in the United States" (March, 2012). It presents the several interwoven

Sadly, there have been problems with them as well. According to the Waxman Report, abstinence-until-marriage programs were often inaccurate and sometimes dishonest; among the findings,

> the curricula contained false and misleading information about the effectiveness of contraception, HIV prevention, and condoms ... about the risks of abortion ... blurred religious belief with science ... treated stereotypes about girls and boys as scientific fact ... girls are weak and need protection ... reinforce sexual aggressiveness among men, *etc.*[72]

A sentiment that is expressed in the Heritage Keepers Student Manuel is disturbing:

> girls need to be careful with what they wear, because males are looking! The girl might be thinking fashion, while the boy is thinking sex. For this reason, the girls have a responsibility to wear modest clothing that doesn't invite lustful thoughts.[73]

One state that has laws that prevent any sex education other than abstinence-only, *e.g.*, Utah, 2010 (HB363); all states have an abstinence-only component to whatever sex education program they have. Everyone is in favor of our children abstaining from having sex at an early age. However, it is naïve to think that because *we* want our children to wait until *we* think they are ready, we are deluding ourselves. Children in middle and high school are sexually active. The following details the age of our children and the kind of sexual activity they are having.

> In 2013, 47% of high school students reported having sexual intercourse. Almost three-quarters (70%) of teen females and 56% of males reported having their first sexual experience with a steady partner. Almost half (49.3%) of all 12th grade students reported being sexually active compared to almost 20% (19.6) of 9th grade students.[74]

---

complexities of sex education in public schools with regard to parental involvement and the abstinence-only program. Whatever one's perspective on this issue, the information contained therein is a good *primer*.

72 See Rep. Henry Waxman (D-CA) Report "The Content of Federally Funded Abstinence-Only Education Programs" (December 2, 2004); based upon 13 abstinence-only programs; www.democrats.reform.house.gov/Documents/20041201102153-50247.pdf.

73 See Heritage Keepers Student Manual, p. 46; www.heritageservices.org/abstinence_education.

74 Kann, L. *et al.* (2014) "Youth Risk Behavior Surveillance – United States, 2013". *MMWR Surveill Summ*, volume *63*, issue *4*.

218 Left Behind

And,

> Many adolescents are engaging in sexual behaviors other than vaginal intercourse: nearly one-half have had oral sex, and just over one in 10 have had anal sex.[75]

The fears that all parents have about their children are real. A CDC survey analysis revealed many ongoing problems with regard to teen sexuality; here are some:

> 41% had never had sexual intercourse.
> 30% had had sexual intercourse during the previous 3 months, and, of these:
> 43% did not use a condom the last time they had sex.
> 14% did not use any method to prevent pregnancy.
> 21% had drunk alcohol or used drugs before last sexual intercourse.
> Only 10% of all students have ever been tested for human immunodeficiency virus (HIV).[76]

Results like these will persist until we adopt sex education *curricula* that eradicate these outcomes. However, we must be circumspect about how we understand what course of sex education study our children should be offered. It turns out that many of the negative outcomes that parents fear can actually obtain regardless of the sex education they receive. Some will have sex sooner than they are ready; some will still contract STDs; some will get pregnant; some will fall into the trap of confused messages and cause sexual violence; and, yes, some will suffer rape. However, studies have shown that a comprehensive sex education program, including abstinence, can mitigate the horrors I just listed. A series of studies (115) of 48 comprehensive sex education *curricula* was conducted over a six-year period. They found that the *curricula*

> helped teens delay first intercourse; helped sexually active teens reduce the frequency of sex; helped teens reduce the number of sex partners; helped teens increase their use of condoms; helped increase use of other contraceptives; helped sexually active teens reduce their sexual risk through changes in their behavior.[77]

---

75 Chandra, A. *et al.* (March 3, 2011). "Sexual Behavior, Sexual Attraction, and Sexual Identity in the United States: Data from the 2006–2008 National Survey of Family Growth". *National Health Statistics Report*, number 36.

76 Centers for Disease Control and Prevention (August 4, 2017) "Sexual Risk Behaviors: HIV, STD, & Teen Pregnancy", at www.cdc.gov/healthyyouth/sexualbehaviors/.

77 See Douglas Kirby's *Emerging Answers* in the National Campaign to Prevent Teen and Unplanned Pregnancy (November, 2007), p. 102. www.TheNationalCampaign.org. This study was brought to my attention by Planned Parenthood (2012), *op. cit.*

What our children do not learn in high school **219**

There is nothing wrong with pledging not to have sex until married. However, that does not mean that pledging abstinence should be done *in the dark*; that is, without proper sex education instruction. When parents prevent their children from receiving comprehensive sex education, those children will be launched into society with incomplete information about their sexuality. Sexual activity is part of life; it is part of health; it must be understood and embraced, not shunned. The responsibility of the educational system is to teach and guide, not to judge and prescribe. However, the responsibility of parents is to work with their schools to create the best educational experience possible for their children, free of prejudices and arcane practices. For public schools, a comprehensive national sex education plan, including the impact of drugs and alcohol, must be put in place, decided by health and education professionals and teachers, that will cover all of the topics that our children need to understand about their sexuality, including learning tolerance and respect for those different from themselves. That means, as in all other domains of teaching, to instruct and discuss, not to proselytize.

The considerations in the previous collection of health discussions are very brief and do not delve into the complexities of the whole relational matrix among these components of health. A comprehensive health education plan taught in school would flesh out the details and drive home to students the critical nature of these matters. This should be taught as soon as possible in elementary, but no later than in middle school and all four years of high school, beginning with the basics for the first years and building more depth and breadth the following years; such that, upon graduation from high school, students have become intimately acquainted with their bodies and how to manage their own health.

The topics of discussions in this chapter are only a sampling of the many ways we can improve the quality of education in K-12. One of the overarching concerns is to provide education that makes sense to children and allows them to carry what they learn in school to their real lives outside the confines of the classroom. So much of what we do in these grades is done *to* our children; we need to do much more *for* our children. We need healthy, critical-minded, smart, probing, inquiring, persistent, independent, compassionate and patient graduates of high school.

Bibliography

American Montessori Society. (n.d.) "Introduction to Montessori Method". Retrieved from https://amshq.org/Montessori-Education/Introduction-to-Montessori

Associated Press (July 16, 2013) "Mitch Daniels and Academic Freedom". *Politico*. Retrieved from www.politico.com/story/2013/07/mitch-daniels-academic-freedom-094318

California Department of Education. (n.d.) "Frequently Asked Questions". Retrieved from www.cde.ca.gov/ls/he/se/faq.asp

Campbell, T.C. & Campbell, T.M. (2006) *The China Study: The Most Comprehensive Study of Nutrition Ever Conducted and the Startling Implications for Diet, Weight Loss, And Long-Term Health*. Dallas, TX: BenBella Books.

220 Left Behind

Cancer Compass – Alternate Route. (n.d.) Retrieved from http://cancercompassalternateroute.com/doctors-and-clinics/oasis-of-healing-treatment-center/

Carlin, G. (Writer). (1984) *Carlin on Campus* [Motion Picture].

Carlin, G. (Writer). (2005) *Life Is Worth Losing* [Motion Picture].

Centers for Disease Control and Prevention (2008) "Youth Risk Behavior Surveillance – United States, 2007". *Morbidity and Mortality Weekly Report*, volume 57, issue SS-4, pp. 1–131.

Centers for Disease Control and Prevention (August 4, 2017) "Sexual Risk Behaviors: HIV, STD, & Teen Pregnancy". Retrieved from www.cdc.gov/healthyyouth/sexualbehaviors/

Chandra, A., Mosher, W. D., Copen, C., & Sionean, C. (March 3, 2011). "Sexual Behavior, Sexual Attraction, and Sexual Identity in the United States: Data from the 2006–2008 National Survey of Family Growth". *National Health Statistics Report*, volume 36.

Chemtrail Central. (n.d.) Retrieved from www.chemtrailcentral.com

Community Bicycle Center. (n.d.) Retrieved from www.communitybike.net

Dr. Axe. (n.d.) "Balancing Act: Why pH is Crucial to Health". Retrieved from http://draxe.com/balancing-act-why-ph-is-crucial-to-health/

Dr. McDougall's Health and Medical Center. (n.d.) Retrieved from www.drmcdougall.com

Editorial Board (June 3, 2011) "USDA Replaces Food Pyramid with 'MyPlate' in Hopes to Promote Healthier Eating". *Washington Post*. Retrieved from www.washingtonpost.com/national/usda-replaces-food-pyramid-with-myplate-in-hopes-to-promote-healthier-eating/2011/06/02/AGRE16HH_story.html?utm_term=.2d3b742e0126

Educate-Yourself. (n.d.) Retrieved from www.educate-yourself.org

Einstein, A. (December 27, 1930) "Translation of Einstein letter to Hermann Huth". Einstein Archive 46-756. Retrieved from https://ivu.org/history/northam20a/einstein.html

Florida Department of Education. (n.d.) "Comprehensive Health Education". Retrieved from www.fldoe.org/schools/safe-healthy-schools/healthy-schools/comprehensive-health-edu.stml

Fulghum, R. (1986) *All I Really Need to Know I Learned in Kindergarten: Uncommon Thoughts on Common Things*. New York: Ballantine Books.

Gary's Vitamin Closet. (n.d.) Retrieved from www.garynull.com

Gatto, J.T. (January 31, 1990) reception speech of New Your City's Teacher of the Year Award. Retrieved from http://2bcreative.org/?p=1592.

Gerson Institute. (n.d.) Retrieved from www.gerson.org

Griffin, G.E., Murphy, M.J., & Wittenberger, P. (2010) *What in the World Are They Spraying? The Chemtrail/Geo-Engineering Cover-Up* [Motion Picture]. Retrieved from www.youtube.com/watch?v=q7Nn0AKFtGY

Habitat for Humanity. (n.d.) Retrieved from www.habitat.org

Heritage Community Services. (n.d.) Retrieved from www.heritageservices.org/abstinence_education

Heritage Community Services (n.d.) *Heritage Keepers Student Manual*, p. 46.

Heidorn, B. (2011) "Physical Education is Critical to Educating the Whole Child". Position Statement. Retrieved from www.ascd.org/ASCD/pdf/journals/ed_lead/el_197711_curtis.pdf

Herman, T.F.D.D. & Richards, G.W.D.D. (1920) "The Novum Organum of Francis Bacon", in *The Reformed Church Review*. Philadelphia, PA: The Reformed Church Publication Board, pp. 20–21.

Hippocrates Health Institutes. (n.d.) Retrieved from www.hippocratesinst.org

HOMEGROWN. (n.d.) Retrieved from www.HOMEGROWN.org

Jaschik, S. (July 17, 2013) "The Governor's Bad List". Retrieved from www.insidehighered.com/news/2013/07/17/e-mails-reveal-mitch-daniels-governor-tried-ban-howard-zinn-book

Just Label It! (n.d.) Retrieved from www.justlabelit.org

Kann, L., Kinchen, S., Shanklin, S.L., Flint, K.H., Hawkins, J., Harris, W.A., & Zaza, S. (2014) "Youth Risk Behavior Surveillance – United States, 2013". *MMWR Surveill Summ*, volume *63*, issue *4*.

Kirby, D. (November, 2007) "Research Findings on Programs to Reduce Teen Pregnancy and Sexually Transmitted Diseases". *Emerging Answers in the National Campaign to Prevent Teen and Unplanned Pregnancy*, p. 102. www.TheNationalCampaign.org.

Living Foods Institute. (n.d.) Retrieved from www.livingfoodsinstitute.com

Maine Department of Education. (n.d.) "HIV Information". Retrieved from www.maine.gov/education/hiv/

Matringe, O. & Moretti, I.M. (April 20, 2006) "'Big 6' Pesticide and GMO Corporations". United Nations Conference on Trade and Development (UNCTAD). The Center for Media and Democracy, Source Watch. Retrieved from www.sourcewatch.org/index.php/%22Big_6%22_Pesticide_and_GMO_Corporations.

Naperville Community Unit School District. (n.d.) Retrieved from www.naperville203.org

National Association for Sport and Physical Education (2011) "Physical Education is Critical to Educating the Whole Child", [Position Statement]. Contributing Author: Brent Heidorn. Retrieved from www.wssd.org/cms/lib/PA01001072/Centricity/Domain/581/NASPE - PE Critical to-Educating-the-Whole-Child-5-19-2011.pdf

National Conference of State Legislatures (December 21, 2016) "State Policies on Sex Education in Schools". www.ncst.org

National Education Association (n.d.) "Research Spotlight on Parental Involvement in Education". Retrieved from www.nea.org

National Conference of State Legislatures (December 21, 2016) "State Policies on Sex Education in Schools". Retrieved from www.ncsl.org/research/health/state-policies-on-sex-education-in-schools.aspx

Parham, V. (1981) *What's Wrong with Eating Meat?* Denver, CO: PCAP Publications.

Paul, R. (1993) *Critical Thinking: What Every Person Needs to Survive in a Rapidly Changing World, 3rd ed.* Santa Rosa, CA: Foundation for Critical Thinking.

PBS. (February 16, 2011) "A Physical Education in Naperville". Need to Know series. Retrieved from www.youtube.com/watch?v=ULciZ8jSgHA

Pfeiffer Medical Center. (n.d.) Retrieved from www.hriptc.org

Planned Parenthood (March 2012) "Sex Education in the United States."

Pollan, M. (n.d.) "Michael Pollan". Retrieved from www.michaelpollan.com

Rense, J. (n.d.) Retrieved from www.rense.com

Resource Center for Adolescent Pregnancy Prevention. (n.d.) Retrieved from www. http://recapp.etr.org/recapp/

Russo, A.J. (2010) "Decreased Serum Cu/Zn SOD Associated with High Copper in Children with Attention Deficit Hyperactivity Disorder (ADHD)". *Journal of CentraL Nervous System Disease*, issue 2, pp. 1–6. Retrieved from www.hriptc.org/pdfs/ADHD Cu Zn SOD Copper Paper.pdf

SourceWatch. (n.d.) Retrieved from www.sourcewatch.org

Southwest Educational Development Laboratory (2002) "A New Wave of Evidence". www.sedl.org.

Steinberg, L. (1997) *Beyond the Classroom: Why School Reform Has Failed and What Parents Need to Do.* New York: Simon & Schuster, pp. 19–20.

Taylor, C. (2008) *Food Fight: A Story of Culinary Revolt/Revolution Never Tasted so Good*. [Motion Picture].

Twenge, J.M. (2017) *iGen: Why Today's Super-Connected Kids Are Growing Up Less Rebellious, More Tolerant, Less Happy – And Completely Unprepared for Adulthood – And What That Means for Us*. New York: Atria Books.

United States Department of Agriculture. (n.d.) "My Pyramid". Retrieved from www.cnpp.usda.gov/mypyramid

Washington Administrative Code ch. 392–410, §140. (August, 2008) "Student Health Education—Definition—Optional Course or Subject Matter—Excusal of Students." Retrieved from http://app.leg.wa.gov/wac/default.aspx?cite=392-410-140

Washington State Legislature (n.d.) "Sexual Health Education". Retrieved from http://apps.leg.wa.gov/WAC/default.aspx?cite=392-410-140

Washington State Legislature. (n.d.) "Washington Administrative Code (WAC)". Retrieved from http://app.leg.wa.gov/wac/

Waxman, H. (December 2, 2004) "The Content of Federally Funded Abstinence-Only Education Programs". [Report]

10

"WHAT? I NEED TO LEARN A SECOND LANGUAGE?"

A man who has no acquaintance with foreign languages knows nothing of his own.
– Johann Wolfgang von Goethe[1]

One of the informal 'surveys' I have conducted for almost 40 years in my classes addresses which *spoken* second languages were represented in the class; that is, second languages, not foreign languages classes they took throughout their school years. The results were consistent over the years: very few foreign languages represented, maybe a dozen. What was also consistent was that the students who were bilingual had English as their second language. This means that students with a second language are students whose first language is other than English, which also means that they were either immigrants or children of immigrants, who virtually exclusively spoke their native tongue at home before entering the school system. While this speaks to the diversity that makes education more interesting and effective, it is also an insight into the sad realization that children born to English-speaking parents in the United States are ill-prepared for the continually shrinking world we live in.

In addition, while there were very few U.S.-born second-language speakers, virtually all of those students had had from one to three years of foreign language classes during either their middle or high school years or both. Some had had more

---

1 See Johann Wolfgang von Goethe (1906) Translated by Thomas Bailey Saunders. *Maxims and Reflections of Goethe*. Norwood: Norwood Press, p. 154, No. 414. Original German: Johann Wolfgang von Goethe (1809) Maximen und Reflexionen. Loschberg 9, Deutschland: Jazzybee Verlag Jurgen Beck. Also, see Kathleen Stein-Smith (2016) *The U.S. Foreign Language Deficit: Strategies for Maintaining a Competitive Edge in a Globalized World*. New York: Palgrave MacMillan.

224 Left Behind

exposure to classes in the same foreign language, but they still did not speak it adequately. My daughter had nine years of Spanish, elementary, middle *and* high schools; while she is well introduced to the language, she still does not speak it other than in simple, structured interactional situations. Her understanding of the language largely relies upon the rate at which her native Spanish-speaking interlocutor speaks: the slower, the better. She certainly could not undertake anything that would rely on her spoken and comprehension skills like say taking a class in Spanish history. By contrast, this is something that students from foreign countries do all the time as they come to the U.S. for university; this because they have had early childhood *immersion* in English. It is not only that they have had instruction, it is that the instruction they have received is within a context that *bathes* them in the language. Some have had the same experience in two or three languages. We have not learned how to do this in the United States.

This is a serious problem. People from all over the world are more and more accessible; the probability that someone from one part of the world will encounter someone from another country thousands of miles away increases every year. The fact is that most of the people in the world outside of the United States are better prepared, to a significant degree, to interact internationally and better able to communicate with other people who do not share their native language. Observably, most of those countries require English as that second language. For example, most European countries require instruction in two foreign languages, some only one – English is required in all of these countries.[2]

I remember, when I was a kid, that the official language of diplomacy (used in the United Nations and the diplomatic corps) was French. Today, it is predominantly English.[3] Accordingly, it is sensible that countries opt to require English to be taught in their schools. We have come to live in an Anglophone world. However, this does not mean that students in the United States should rely on the linguistic competence of people from other countries and 'get a pass' on learning a second language.

To say that English is the official language of diplomacy does not mean that it is *exclusively* so. Take, for example, the efforts made by the seven nations[4] to engage with Iran over the alleged nuclear weapons program there. All of those diplomats speak English on some level; but, for the sake of precision with regard to the nuances available in all languages, representatives from each country had at their disposal translators to verify that all parties understood what the details of the discourse was in those proceedings. Indeed, as a matter of course, there are hundreds of translators at the United Nations to facilitate communication

---

2 See Kat Devlin (2015) "Learning a Foreign Language a 'Must' in Europe, Not so in America", *Research Center*, July 13.

3 Actually, the U.N. has *six* official languages: Arabic, Chinese, English, French, Russian and Spanish.

4 The nations, meeting in Lausanne, Switzerland and achieving full implementation of the Irean Nuclear Agreement on 16 January, 2016, were China, Russia, France, England, Germany, Iran and the United States.

"What? I need to learn a second language?" **225**

among all countries. People outside of this context do not have translators to help them.

Admittedly, European countries are relatively smaller in geography than the United States and with many more contiguous neighbors who speak different languages; hence, the incidence of encountering someone from one or several of those countries is increased and the immediacy of knowing different languages for them is essential. However, we in the United States are witnessing a significant increase in immigration from all over the world, giving rise to *our* need to communicate with those people, who are all around us, in all states, counties and towns. Therefore, the instruction in second and third languages should hold an elevated place in our educational *curricula*.

"Why learn another language"? students ask. "We can address any issue and potentially solve any problem in English!" they exclaim. This attitude has certainly contributed to an ambivalence, lack of interest or indolence on the part of people in the United States in general and on the part of the institutions (particularly educational) in particular, leading in part to the devaluation of foreign language instruction.

Foreign language instruction varies greatly in the U.S. According to Pufahl and Rhodes, elementary schools in the U.S. offered foreign language instruction as follows: 17%, 24% and 15% during the years 1987, 1997 and 2008 respectively. In middle school, instruction declined from ~70% to ~50% from 1987 to 2008 and in high school, during the same years, offerings hovered around 90%. However, only some 14% offered 'immersion' methodologies.[5] According to the Education Commission of the States, there are at least 17 states that have no requirement for foreign language instruction in high school; several others have minimal 'units',[6] one or two, of instruction.[7] There is no 'national/federal' requirement for foreign language instruction in the United States. The implication is that students in those states cannot receive language instruction other than in English, or they must seek such instruction from private sources.

There is a difference between the foreign language courses in high schools and those offered in colleges and which courses those schools require students to take. Enrollment in these courses, more and more, seem to be left to students. Two hypotheses are offered by Lewis to explain the deficit:

---

5 "Foreign Language Instruction in U.S. Schools: Results of a National Survey of Elementary and Secondary Schools" by Ingrid Pufahl and Nancy C. Rhodes of the Center for Applied Linguistics in *Foreign Language Annals: The American Council on the Teaching of Foreign Languages*, Summer 2011, page 258 ff.

6 'Carnegie Units' represent 120 hours of instruction in any course of study; hence, each unit equals one 'credit' toward graduation. This computes to one period of study every day, five times per week, one year of instruction.

7 See report "50-State Comparison: High School Graduation Requirements: Foreign Language" by the Education Commission of the States (2007), compiled by Jennifer Dounay, Project Manager; www.ecs.org.

226 Left Behind

First, Americans may be reverting to a belief in "English language exceptionalism." Yes, English is the accepted *lingua franca* of international business and U.S. students may therefore feel another language is unnecessary. Perhaps if their only competitors in the global job market were other monolingual Americans, there would be no cause for concern. But the global job market will include a very crowded field of well-educated graduates from Europe, China, Mexico and many other countries who have mastered English on top of their mother tongue ... A second explanation for anemic language enrollment may be that students are taking the easy way out. There are no quick rewards in the study of another language. Language skills must be built over time; real fluency comes easily for very few and must be constantly cultivated if it is to be maintained.[8]

Hence, the 'lack of interest' on the part of students in studying a foreign language is, in part, actually generated out of state departments of education. The call for foreign language instruction is muted by the lack of action at the legislative level of state government. No wonder our children are not inclined to desire second language instruction; their own leaders do not accord to foreign language instruction the proper attention and emphasis it deserves. We need a foreign language instruction mandate from the U.S. Department of Education, instituted across the country, not only to prepare students for job-related reasons, but also for the simple expansion of their minds and cultural awareness. This is not only desirable, but necessary, considering the growing diversity in all aspects of life.

A first step would be to institute a national standard requirement that would place all students on the same footing. Standards of this kind are well established for mathematics and English (reading and writing) and efforts are being made in science;[9] why not foreign languages? This is not an 'academic freedom' issue. No one is arguing here that criteria for instruction should be dictated to teachers from 'on high'. No, I am arguing that there should be a national level *curriculum guide* for foreign language instruction. What must be instituted is an *intermediate level baseline* for foreign languages. That means that students would have achieved a level of competence that would allow them to have a conversation in that language beyond the situated contexts highlighted in current foreign language instruction. Some languages would be mandatory options for students, say Spanish and French (considered the first and second two most useful languages to learn[10]); others could be regionally decided, based upon the demographics of the population. The requirement should be one yearly credit, in the same language, for each year in middle school, 6th, 7th and 8th grades. Then, two years of foreign language instruction, in

---

8 See Clayton Lewis (2015) "Monolingual Myopia", *U.S. News and World Report*, March 12.
9 In the global arena, in spite of the recent increases in funding for the STEM Program, the United States is not doing well in science and mathematics; see Chapter 7 on the teaching profession.
10 See Luca (2017) "Which Language to Learn? The 7 Most Useful Languages".

the same language, in high school, taken in the freshman and sophomore years and a third, during the year/semester abroad, taken in the junior year (more below). This program would bring all students at least to an intermediate level, by the time they graduate, and some to a more advanced level, depending upon their propensity for language learning and/or level of study in the foreign country.

Yet another area of dismay is the virtual elimination of the foreign language requirement at the college level. That 'requirement' is often satisfied when incoming high school graduates have taken six semesters of or achieved an intermediate level[11] of proficiency in a foreign language. Judging from the spirit of the previous discussion, this scenario is not acceptable. Even though students may have been busy at the high school level, they should press on in their quest to speak that foreign language while in college. However, many universities do not require any further training in foreign languages. Why? Because they have the power to do whatever they want to do. Even the different schools within a university each have different requirements for foreign language 'proficiency'. This does not bode well for our youngsters; they are being launched into the most diversified world we have ever known. This is not what I mean by equal, high-quality public education for all our children.

In recent years, colleges have been offering fewer foreign language courses, often due to cuts in funding for the humanities. As a result, colleges do not offer an adequate array of foreign language choices, because they rely on the work students have done in high school; it is a lazy way out of spending the money on this necessary part of a college education. This is partly how government agencies can argue for cuts to funding for the humanities. It is difficult to require foreign languages in the *curricula* when there are no faculty to teach them. Or is it the other way around? It has become a circular trap. It is difficult to fund foreign language instruction when there are no requirements for it.

Native, English-speaking, U.S. students are so limited in their foreign language abilities that they are stunted in their appreciation and understandings of other cultures and their people. Because our society has become so ethnocentric,[12] students do not understand how important learning other languages is in broadening their skills in order to reach out to members of other cultures in their midst; they rely on those from other countries to master English as their second or third language. This lack of preparation is most consequential for our children's opportunities in life in a shrinking world.

The chosen methods of instruction continue to impose on students the memorization of vocabulary and grammar, leaving little time actually to speak the language. Even when programs do require that students speak, say "only Spanish in

---

11 This 'intermediate' level does not coincide with the one I advance here; it refers only to the nomenclature of the course(s) the student took in high school. Hence, the student has not likely reached a level of competence to have a substantive conversation in that foreign language.

12 See Chapter 11 on ethnocentrism.

228 Left Behind

class" (a kind of pseudo-immersion, which I take as an earnest attempt on the part of teachers), the contexts in which this kind of exercise is undertaken are artificial and do not deliver the common sense experience that can result in a *genuine* understanding of what takes place in a naturally occurring setting. I laud teachers who attempt this methodology and sympathize with them about the *curricula* constraints imposed upon them by the school system in which they practice. In other words, I am aware of the frustrations expressed by teachers of foreign languages about their circumstances, many of whom would much rather see established the kind of program recommended here, a remedy that is offered by virtually everybody in education, globally: the real 'immersion' solution. I recommend, indeed argue, that the best scenario for such immersion is to travel to countries in which the language of choice is spoken.

Travel

> Travel is fatal to prejudice, bigotry, and narrow-mindedness, and many of other people need it sorely on these accounts. Broad, wholesome, charitable views of men and things cannot be acquired by vegetating on a little corner of the earth all one's lifetime.[13]
>
> *– Mark Twain (1835–1910)*

One of the best ways to learn about the world is to travel the world. Most often, that means the occasional visit here and there on vacation. While this kind of travel can be meaningful in many ways, it is limited by time, by money, by location and by the commercial connections that are made for this or that trip. For the wealthy, such trips abroad can be quite rewarding because these limitations do not apply. However, for overwhelmingly most people in the world, vacations of this kind are probably, if at all, a one-shot experience. Relying upon holidays and vacations to experience what the many countries and cultures have to offer in terms of *education* is unrealistic. There is too little time to absorb the breadth and depth of what such places can offer. For most people, family or individual budgets do not allow for extended visits. Where the vacation takes place is also a factor: most people arrange their vacations with travel agencies, whose parameters are often targeting the 'tourist traps' that most countries have to satisfy tourists' yen for a 'good time' and to fill the coffers of the tourism industry. Learning about the people and customs of a new culture is not a priority. Even though vacations can be very rewarding in general ways to learn about other cultures, they are not the occasions to learn a foreign language. Most people take vacations to relax and to appreciate the sights and sounds of a different kind for a short while.

Learning a foreign language requires *immersion* in the culture. Some ways to

---

13 Samuel Clemens (as Mark Twain) (1911, originally published in 1869) *The Innocents Abroad*, New York: Harper Bros.

mimic immersion is to engage in group meetings with native speakers in which only that language is spoken, with the inclusion of variable scenarios to broaden access to different contexts of interaction. This can help, but does not provide the immersion that is really necessary to be awash in the culture, where one can hear, in context, the use of the language, thereby developing an intuition in the language. Hence, travel to different countries is by far the best way to avail ourselves of the innumerable components of what it means to speak another language.

Learning a foreign language through travel requires a more systematic arrangement of parameters that can accommodate the expectations of such education. It must become part of the education that we provide all our children as part of the *curriculum* itself. If this component of education is to be comprehensive and global, which is what I propose here, it requires an intricate network of sharing and cooperation on the part of all participating countries in the world. More specifically, the educational institutions of these countries must establish infrastructure and programs to make such travel efficient, affordable and available to all students all over the world. These 'mechanisms' of cooperation among countries are not limited to language learning; they are also applicable to a myriad of other subjects: political science, sociology, history, anthropology, philosophy, *etc.*

This may seem impossible at first glance, but it could be done if the leaderships of participating countries were to get together and negotiate the elements of such a system. We already have the United Nations Educational, Scientific and Cultural Organization (UNESCO) which promotes collaboration among nations, conducts studies, facilitates knowledge sharing. Its main goal is "to bring education to all". Why couldn't we have this august organization systematize such a global cooperative effort and actualize the slogan? This question is no doubt somewhat loaded in the sense that the United Nations has a lot to do already and funding is limited, even when all nations pay their dues. However, I propose only that UNESCO apply the organizational skills they already have to this global project. Each country pays an additional small fee as part of their dues to fund this clearing house of exchanges among nations. All U.N. ambassadors coordinate with their respective counties to affect the connections necessary to establish points of entry for the students in the program. At first, such points will be few and perhaps targeted to areas with easier access and where better infrastructural accommodations exist. Eventually, these points could expand to include less accessible areas. All points would have a host school, either secondary or university or both, that each participant would attend while abroad.

Yes, this program would be for high school and college students, both. It would be mandatory in either the junior or senior year of both high school and college/post-secondary vocational school. Each semester, there would be an exchange of students so that the schools would accommodate foreign students in their junior or senior year. The level of exposure to the language/country of choice would be established in such a way as to place students correctly in their year of study (I am aware that some students are more advanced than others of the same age). This annual exchange would be doubly beneficial to all systems of education: each

230 Left Behind

school population will benefit from the influx of foreign students every year; and each student in the program for that semester will surely benefit from the experience in a foreign country.

Funding this global program would be relatively simple and inexpensive. All students would be subsidized by their countries of origin for travel to and from their target country. The educational institutions of each country would pay for the in-country part of the travel expenses of the students. The airlines, as part of their social service, would donate the cost of the tickets for each student. They could claim these tickets as a loss on their tax returns. In cases in which geographical distances were considerable, say for Australia, or when nations are halfway around the world, flights would be subsidized by tax-based funds from the country of origin.

While in their target countries, students could be cared for by families of the students who are also in the program that year/semester. This balances out the cost of everyday living expenses. The coordination for these exchanges would be administered by the officials of all countries, monitored by UNESCO. Obviously, not all countries would participate with all other countries: several countries are not always ready or willing to cooperate with some others, *e.g.*, the United States would not likely cooperate as well these days with North Korea, Saudi Arabia, Syria, *etc.*, as it might with England, France, Germany, *etc.*

Here's the thing: these kinds of exchanges, if enthusiastically embraced, could help dissipate international conflicts and engender different attitudes in people (maybe slowly at first). Certainly, the student participants in this kind of program would experience fundamental changes in their knowledge, their attitudes, their world view such that, over time, global attitudes might change enough to promote global peace instead of global mistrust, fear and war. In other words, the benefits of this kind of program would greatly surpass those to the individuals in the exchange programs and the initial reason for its creation: second language instruction. It would be a boon for global *rapprochement*.

In the United States, we badly need this kind of program. Our students/people are too often frighteningly ignorant of people from other countries. Yes, this, in a country that boasts of its variety of peoples. We are a country of people who live one town over or down the street from people who come from a variety of countries, who speak a myriad of languages, who practice a multiplicity of customs, who are just like us, fundamentally, and yet we don't know much about them. This is sad and unnecessary.

In my own travels, I have visited many countries and witnessed many cultural practices. I was fortunate to be able to do this, mostly because I was stationed in Europe while in the military. What I learned is unquantifiable and has become part of who I am. Students – it doesn't matter from where – would learn so much more in that foreign country, including its language, than from any textbook about that country read at home. They would actually learn a different language and, along with that, a different culture. They would learn about themselves and how they operate in the world, in their own native country as well as in their target country.

"What? I need to learn a second language?" **231**

And they would be able to do this twice, once in high school and once in college/ post-secondary vocational school, in different (or the same) countries, all as part of their educational experience. Think of how rewarding that could be for everybody: increasing trust, decreasing fear, deepening understanding and maximizing cooperation and sharing.

Critics, even those who may actually agree that such a program should be established, say that the cost is too much and that "we can't do it". If we continue to think of education in the ways we have been, then such 'throwaway' conclusions will continue to dominate decision-making in this regard. We must abandon this myopia and begin to see that the cost in human terms is much greater if we do not implement a comprehensive international program to address this chronic problem.

Thinking that language instruction can take place in a meaningful way constrained by the four walls of a classroom is absurd. By definition, language is the most important component of a culture. Cultures, while they do have 'boundaries,' do not operate within the confines of four walls. Members of any given culture largely participate in everyday activities and relationships in the open, enabling other cultures to observe and experience various social practices within that culture. This could never be replicated in the classroom.

I can vouch for this, based upon my own experience with German, a language which many believe to be particularly difficult to learn. Because I was exposed to everyday life *in Germany*, paying attention to the nuances of the language in context and being obliged actually to speak German every day, the gradual process of learning German became organic. That is not to say that the different syntax of German versus English was not a challenge, particularly at first, and the familiarization with the different sounds did take time and was, on occasion, frustrating. Absolutely, but that is part of learning any language and indeed anything of depth and significance, no matter where or according to whatever conditions might be imposed. The simple fact that I was living the language made my grasp of it relatively straightforward. Most people immersed in this process will experience similar frustrations and delights.

While students are learning the language, they are also immersed in the culture, gaining an intuition in the language, something that cannot be taught, only experienced. Students are able to connect with the people in whatever country in a way that is impossible without living among them. What students learn is not limited to the language, but reaches out to the broader context which includes experience with people at large, the institutions, the practices, the norms, values, *etc.*, of the natives of that country. These learning experiences may be even more important in the long run than learning the language, but at minimum, they are *part of* learning the language.

The latest attempts to create a facsimile of an immersive context are interactive CDs or online language programs which use images and videos to simulate the immersion. While these methods may bring the learner closer to the desired experience and have a measure of success, they remain a mere social construction of the preferred 'lived engagement'. Three or four months in a foreign country not only

232 Left Behind

accelerates the acquisition and learning of a language, it also affords the learner the opportunity to experience, *in situ*, the contexts of its use.

Students would return home having *genuinely* learned a foreign language, having been exposed to a different culture and thereby being better able to appreciate people from other countries and broadening their outlook on the world. This is not a new idea; many students have already experienced this form of second language learning, but they likely had their own funds, making this kind of education available only to the economically advantaged or those who have won a scholarship. Imagine what kind of *entente* among peoples of the world could be made possible if this program alone were implemented.

To take a practical approach to this kind of program, I recommend that students spend one semester abroad in high school and a full year in college, (junior or senior year). In the case of high school, students would have a choice to go abroad during either of the junior semesters or the fall semester of the senior year, at the latest. (Students would want to be with their graduating classmates their last semester.) For college students, that year abroad would more than satisfy any of the requirements I have seen for specific degrees or majors. The apparent confusion among colleges about a proper language requirement could be mitigated by such a program and could actually be seen as a global standardizing incentive, creating a dialogue with other universities to raise the level of overall academic achievement for either country's students. A very few students of mine have taken advantage of such programs, usually for one semester, but each has returned massively enlightened. The benefits may be immeasurable from the standpoint of standardized testing, but they are real and immediately observable.

Taken in the broader context, such a program would foster in students the importance of many principles such as cooperation and sharing, while engaging in their respective studies. This generation of students would become, very quickly, citizens of the world and ambassadors to and from countries, galvanizing their deeper understanding of one another. This would go far in establishing international cooperation instead of competition, trust instead of suspicion and compassion instead of indifference. One organization that supports this orientation is the Global Nomads Group. They assert:

> GNG operates at the intersection of international and peace education, serving as a vehicle for awareness, bridging the boundaries of cultural misconceptions, and instilling in our audience a heightened appreciation and comprehension of the world in which they live. GNG's programs prepare students with the 21st century competencies to be flat career ready: the abilities to collaborate, empathize, and interact effectively with individuals from around the world.[14]

---

14 Part of mission of the Global Nomads Group; see www.guidestar.org/profile/75-2750127.

Critics of these kinds of offerings will, no doubt, concentrate on how such a program could be frustrated due to the lack of collaboration 'on the part of other countries' or because funding will not be forthcoming from politicians who have different agendas or because mandating such a program for all students would 'just not work'. The nay-sayers of our country will always find excuses to thwart common sense progressive policy proposals. Witness the obstructionist response to the Obama Administration's attempts to change the health care parameters in 2009–2010: "NO! NO! NO!" was the response, no matter what was proposed. In spite of all this, the Affordable Care Act was passed, a significant step toward a universal plan, and has been in effect since. Now, with Trump in the White House, those same legislators are doing all they can to repeal the Affordable Care Act (Obamacare) and have no plan to replace it. It is doubtful that those who are steeped in partisan (party over common sense and the common good) visions of the world will ever be won over. They will be relegated to the same place others have been when progressive ideas win currency in our society, *e.g.*, the abolition of slavery, the Civil Rights Act of 1964, desegregation of schools, *etc.* We must take up this challenge and see it through.

The concept of this program is very simple and easy to understand. The problem, granted, is its implementation which, at first, will seem daunting. However, if we use the avenues of communication that already exist in the U.N. (UNESCO), this can be done in a relatively short time, say five years. Even down the road when the inevitable problems present themselves (we are aware that the U.N. does not always work as efficiently as many of us would like, but it is an established force in the world that can become the hub of this effort), we must encourage this institution to operate according to the most elementary principles of cooperation, communicatioin and respect.

As this program slowly takes on a life of its own, the benefits will become more and more evident across the world and could, actually, become a model for other global programs of cooperation. The attitude here is optimistic, but it is also realistic, if federal, state and local funding sources are properly aligned. As I have noted elsewhere, to start with, we must triple the federal funding for education, 6% to 20%, and follow through by monitoring what more we may need to establish proper funding for our children. I know that such a program cannot be established overnight there are powerful factions working against this kind of innovation. Nonetheless, we must press on to move ahead and create tools for our children to bring the world together in these meaningful ways (not only those ways that bring people together as a result of globalization or wars or natural disasters). Otherwise, we will never realize the human potential that is made possible by the extraordinary spirit of our species.

Sacking the Humanities

What is it that people want to do when they are awake and not working? We want to be entertained or participate in distractions that take us beyond our daily conditions to revitalize us or to calm us, *etc.* What is presupposed here is that most people are not *happy* in their work and, accordingly, seek out 'happiness' from other sources, those not related to their work, perhaps dropping by the bar for 'happy hour'. People who *are* happy in their work will also seek entertainment outside of work, but as a source to enhance their wellbeing, not as something to replace their humdrum work day. No matter which activity people choose to partake in, such activities or distractions are possible because of the humanities. Other than labor and the cooperation that has always been necessary to satisfy the basic needs of human beings in a community (water, food, shelter, safety, health, clothing, *etc.*), what is it that we can observe throughout the history of human evolution that we have consistently sought after and achieved? It has been to feed or to express our most essential of feelings, such as anger, sadness, joy, enthusiasm and a host of other emotions and sentiments of all kinds? It is music, dance, story-telling, games (including sport), theatre, drawing (and painting), architecture and cuisine; these are not only sought after, they are foundational to our very being. These are the activities and spectacles that human beings seek out to relax, to imagine, to test one's limits, to learn a foreign language, to create social commentary or poke fun at something, to interpret 'reality', to express, through movement, what life looks like, to create sounds that touch the profundity of our nature, to create cultural spaces for functionality and beauty and to please the palate. This is the stuff of the humanities. This is what people in every culture not only want to experience but crave on a regular basis. When we are not doing the things required of us, those things that are our responsibilities (work, caring for children, chores, *etc.*), what do people tend to look to and for? We want to watch television (witness the [2017] threat against PBS with cuts to the Corporation for Public Broadcasting from the Trump Administration), listen to music, go to the theatre or the cinema, attend a concert, a symphony presentation, go to the art gallery, cook a fabulous meal, visit places where extraordinary edifices, in beauty and design, have been erected or marvel at the movements of dancers of any kind, who celebrate the bodies we inhabit. And yet we dare slash or eliminate the programs designed to teach our youngsters how to do all of these things we rely on so much to make us whole?

Human communities throughout history have created these wonderful expressions and have guaranteed, in one way or another, their perpetuation, not only because they are forms of enjoyment, available to all, but because they are cultural forms which characterize who they are. These expressions are part of the legacy of the culture and components of the artifacts of the civilization they constitute as theirs. I do not have to remind the reader of the extraordinary pyramids of Egypt, the Great Wall of China, the Golden Gate Bridge, *etc.*

Education has always, in one form or another, included the humanities. Even before formal educational institutions, members of any culture were steeped in the expressions that were at the core of their society. Children sing, dance, busy themselves with coloring books, draw, paint, build structures with blocks, build castles in the sand. They learn how to entertain themselves, either alone or with their pals. They mimic their older siblings or their parents or their friends in the

"What? I need to learn a second language?" **235**

neighborhood. There is never a question about engaging in these kinds of play. We take it for granted that they are part of the course of activities that routinely engage the attention of children and adults alike. Not to participate in some of these would indicate that something was 'wrong' with that child, because all of these forms of 'recreation' are embedded in the culture. Later on, when children go to school, they realize that all of those activities they engaged in are actually taught as legitimate subjects; that there are methods and details to know about so that one can become conceptually informed about them, to become specialists in this or that art. Indeed, whether or not we become *adroit*, we learn to enjoy and appreciate those kinds of expressions along with all the other subjects that are part of the *curriculum*.

Is it reasonable to assume that these kinds of activities will always be there for us to participate in whenever we have the inclination? Are these artistic expressions *sui generis*? No, they do not. Or must we diligently preserve the cultivation of these expressions so that they may be, passed on to members of the culture in order to survive? Just like the very language we speak, we must perform these art forms in order to keep them alive and to pass them on to our children.

In early societies, before written records, shamans were charged with keeping the 'secrets' of the society in order to pass them on to new members. Among them were cultural forms. Those shamans were relied upon to do this correctly and without interpretation, by and large. This cultural knowledge was what character-ized the society and made it 'unique' or recognizable to its members; it comprised their cultural identity.

Today, the task of perpetuating cultural forms is relegated to the institutions of learning. Unfortunately, this relegation has not been very successful. The humani-ties have suffered huge funding cuts and their importance has been savaged. Terry Eagleton, foremost supporter of the humanities, revives that importance in this sentiment:

> The humanities should constitute the core of any university worth the name … In the end, the humanities can only be defended by stressing how indis-pensable they are; and this means insisting on their vital role in the whole business of academic learning, rather than protesting that, like some poor relation, they don't cost much to be housed.[15]

The enculturation and socialization of these cultural forms are just as important as other conventional forms: norms, beliefs, values, common sense and specialized knowledge. Cultural expressions are as much who we are as any other dimensions in society, the economic, the political, *etc.* In other words, the humanities, and I

---

15 See Terry Eagleton's (December 17, 2010) "The Death of Universities", *The Guardian* at https://www.theguardian.com/commentisfree/2010/dec/17/death-universities-malaise-tuition-fees.

236 Left Behind

emphasize 'language' and second languages here, are as much a part of, if not more than, what contemporary educational philosophies tend to take for granted.

Why is it, then, that the humanities are the first to be cut back or eliminated altogether when economic woes appear over the horizon? The answer to this question requires a discussion of some matters often overlooked. One issue often overlooked is that education has sadly become an institution to entrain children to 'fit into' society according to the needs of dominant special interests. This is a fundamental truth; we develop an ethnocentrism that allows us to understand which cultural group is ours and to appreciate who we are according to its terms. Unfortunately, with economic institutions dominating our every move, it is corporate interests and political exigencies which dictate the kinds of considerations we should have on our minds. For example, in contemporary U.S. culture, being a 'good consumer' is utmost in our consciousness, instead of say the engagement of others according to the fundamental principles of sharing and cooperation, values which were dominant in early societies, when egalitarian traditions and customs more often characterized the ongoing activities of their cultures. Education is proposed by the business model as a way to prepare our children for the work force, to fall into line, and to be absorbed into a commodity-driven economy, for which there is little to no need for cultural expression other than that of the corporate culture. This mode of thinking has been in evidence for more than 100 years, but its current expression has exceeded any prior experience.

It is not important, for the purposes of working for this or that corporation, to know about music, its history, its contribution to our cultural identity and its power to move people. While corporate executives may disagree, their sole interest in people has conventionally been to what extent workers can perform the duties of their occupational/professional positions for the benefit of the corporation. Such corporations would assert that they also want to hire 'well-rounded' individuals, who have been involved in sports, the arts, *etc.* and that their applications for employment request information about these activities and interests. In the last analysis, they are most interested in someone who can do the job the way they want them to do it, nothing more, nothing less. They are very rarely interested in 'creativity' on the part of their functionaries. To be 'marketable' in the work place really means how well you can fit in and follow instructions. Indeed, much of education today involves paying attention to directions: how to study for the test, oral or written, how to practice taking the test, how to improve your ability to answer the questions posed therein. There are lots of questions and answers but very little, if any, context or discussion surrounding those questions and their prescribed answers.

So, in the eyes of special interests, the articulation of ruling ideas, the society does not need creative expression, unless it is of the kind that advances innovation in the interest of the maximization of profit. A result is, as recently manifest in the STEM program, funds are made available for science and taken away from the humanities. Both should properly be funded.

To whatever extent a school fulfills a humanities *curriculum* is not solely based

"What? I need to learn a second language?" **237**

upon its commitment to a fulsome education. As expressed elsewhere in this book, it is also based upon the commitment of the state and the federal entities which fund schools. Surely, cutting mathematics or science from the *curriculum* would bring on a barrage of criticism from the mainstream society, citing how important these skills are to the overall education of the individual in society. Such an outcry is inaudible when the humanities are cut. Other than the few who are committed to the arts, all we observe are the shrugging of shoulders and the sighs of acqui-escence. We could hear said, "Oh well, if the budget is not there to support all the elements of education and we have to cut something, it's better to cut the music program rather than the science program." What we are persuaded to do is to accept that the budget is in trouble, and not to question how the budget was managed and what we, as citizens, can do to assure that all components of a well-rounded education be preserved. Asking those critical questions and following through to a viable conclusion at the local, state and federal levels is the only way we can hold our officials' feet to the fire.

Here is something that is always taken for granted: teachers will always be there to take care of those programs. False! The cuts proposed can be more subtle than simply cancelling courses in the arts. They can take the form of laying off the teach-ers who provide the arts instruction. If there are no teachers, the arts are not taught. Take, for example, the fact that teachers do retire; and, when they do, adminis-trations can choose not to replace them, because of 'fiscal difficulties' (and these kinds of decisions are sometimes made without the knowledge of parents in the community, until their children do not have an arts class anymore). These teachers have been touted as essential to a good education while they were on the job; but, as soon as they retire, their positions somehow lose their import and the school can get along without that part of the *curriculum*.

A case in point: I recall when I began teaching at a state university, there was a modest full-time humanities cohort on staff. There was a pianist who taught music; an artist who taught drawing and painting; a dancer who taught movement and a variety of dances; a French teacher, and a Spanish teacher. There was also a part-time German teacher, and a teacher who taught a course in architecture. In every case, when these faculty members retired or left for other reasons, none of them was replaced, citing "rough economic times".

This should never happen. Education should be at the top of the social spending priorities list,[16] along with health care and other social programs that carry the poor and needy through difficult times, not the machines of war, occupation of other countries and blatant control over other peoples in the world. It should be tax based and require nothing more. There should never be a 'shortage' of funds for education. It should be treated like the most fundamental institution that it is and granted the utmost priority for social funding.

16 See Chapter 3 on the business model.

Bibliography

Clemens, S. (as Mark Twain) (1911, originally published in 1869) *The Innocents Abroad*. New York: Harper Bros.

Devlin, K. (July 13, 2015) "Learning a Foreign Language a 'Must' in Europe, Not so in America". *Pew Research Center*. Retrieved from www.pewresearch.org/fact-tank/2015/07/13/learning-a-foreign-language-a-must-in-europe-not-so-in-america/

Dounay, J. (March 23, 2007) "50-State Comparison: High School Graduation Requirements: Foreign Language". Retrieved from www.ecs.org/high-school-graduation-requirements/

Eagleton, T. (December 17, 2010) "The Death of Universities". *The Guardian*. Retrieved from www.theguardian.com/commentisfree/2010/dec/17/death-universities-malaise-tuition-fees

Goethe, J.W.v. (1809) *Maximen und Reflexionen*. Loschberg 9, Germany: Jazzybee Verlag Jurgen Beck.

Goethe, J.W.v. (1906) *Maxims and Reflections of Goethe*. Translated by Thomas Bailey Saunders. Norwood: Norwood Press, p. 154, No. 414.

Global Nomads Group (n.d.) "Mission". Retrieved from www.guidestar.org/profile/75-2750127

Lewis, C. (March 12, 2015) "Monolingual Myopia". *U.S. News and World Report*. Retrieved from www.usnews.com/opinion/blogs/world-report/2015/03/12/american-students-opting-out-of-foreign-languages-are-making-a-mistake

Luca (June 25, 2017) "Which Languages Should You Learn? The 7 Most Useful Languages". Retrieved from www.mosalingua.com/en/7-most-useful-languages/

Plutte, C. Part (n.d.) "Mission statement of the Global Nomads Group". www.gng.org

Pufahl, I. & Rhodes, N.C. (2011) "Foreign Language Instruction in U.S. Schools: Results of a National Survey of Elementary and Secondary Schools". *Foreign Language Annals*, volume *44*, issue *2*, pp. 258–288.

Stein-Smith, K. (2016) *The U.S. Foreign Language Deficit: Strategies for Maintaining a Competitive Edge in a Globalized World*. New York: Palgrave MacMillan.

11

CULTURAL ARROGANCE

I believe only in French culture, and regard everything else in Europe which calls itself 'culture' as a misunderstanding. I do not even take the German kind into consideration.[1]

– Friedrich Wilhelm Nietzsche (1844–1900)

Ethnocentrism

One of the most important cultural structures in any society is ethnocentrism. It is developed, mostly during the early socialization process, from the time children become *linguistic* until they take steps to venture out on their own in life. These are the formative years during which we all develop a sense of self and of cultural identity.

Mostly manifest in the language we speak, our sense of identity follows us all our lives. While I was born in the United States, my cultural heritage is Francophone Canada. This was a result of having been raised in a French Canadian enclave and exposed overwhelmingly to French in the home. While I was exposed to some English in the larger context, I did not learn English until I was introduced to the 'outside' world of school, where I followed a bilingual *curriculum*, French and English, through elementary and high school. Hence, my ethnic center was French Canadian with Anglophone influence around the edges.

Because culture is primarily based upon language (culture cannot exist without it), the sense for one's center is also a linguistic phenomenon. When

1 See Nietzsche's (1911) "Why Am I so Clever?" in *Ecce Homo*, p. 37. New York: The Macmillan Company.

240 Left Behind

one is socialized simultaneously in two cultures, side by side (or actually *one* culture which is bilingual), one develops certain sensitivities to the differences between them, as well as their similarities. As the process progresses, one realizes that one can move in and out of this or that linguistic situation seamlessly because of the simultaneous socialization in both. This circumstance is not usually a problem in terms of cultural identity. I mention this only to illustrate that whatever our particular experiences may be, it is that early formation that stays with us all our lives and affects the ways we understand who we are and where we come from.

This sense of belonging is essential for anyone's self-identification. Without it, for whatever reason(s), one could suffer what Emile Durkheim called *anomie*[2], a social *unhingement* from one's family, friends and ultimately one's cultural connectedness. The enculturation and socialization process takes place almost unnoticeably and unproblematically for many years; one's sense of cultural identity is part of the conventional commonsense knowledge we come to have at our disposal. Overwhelmingly, people 'absorb' and acquire their cultural heritage without much difficulty and fanfare. Cultural identity is expressed in a multiplicity of ways: of course, the language we speak, the beliefs we hold, the values we espouse, the norms we follow, the clothes we wear, the activities we engage in, the music we make and listen to, and so on and so on.

Our ethnocentrism is so embedded in our daily activities that it largely goes unnoticed; we take it for granted. It only becomes a matter of note if it is ignored or treated in a way that is condescending. Any challenge to our ethnicity is a challenge to our very being because we embody the culture we belong to, that culture which lies at the center of our lives.[3] Without its members and speakers of its language, the culture cannot exist.

Consequently, ethnocentrism is inherently not a problem; it is a natural part of the very culture, any culture, reflected in the multitude of cultural institutions that are developed and maintained in all societies.

Extreme ethnocentrism

While ethnocentrism is necessary for providing members a sense of belonging to a particular culture, exaggerated forms of this fundamental cultural structure can become problematic. Extreme ethnocentrism is a form of discrimination. It is different from other forms of discrimination, *e.g.*, racism or sexism, in that the motive for such discrimination is based upon cultural traits, not physical characteristics. If, for example, one's sense of self generates a sense of superiority and exclusivity, we can say of it that it is an 'extreme' form of ethnocentrism. In fact, expressions of

---

2 See Emile Durkheim's (1997) *Suicide: A Study in Sociology*, New York: Free Press.
3 Someone who is 'culture centric' might take this to the extreme and interpret every cultural challenge one that rises to the level of an actual 'cultural assault'." I do not mean that here.

Cultural arrogance **241**

such an attitude, verbal or physical, toward people who are not members of one's culture range from being hurtful to being violent in different ways and to being deadly. Overall, they stand in the way of cooperation among the many peoples of the world.

There is a well-established propaganda system in the United States that repeatedly communicates to our youngsters (and the larger population as well) the sense that we must preserve that which is 'American' and exclude those from other countries from participating in what constitutes *being an American*. The problem is exacerbated when we witness the exclusion of predominantly 'black' and brown people, giving this practice a racial patina. Consequently, an instance of extreme ethnocentric discrimination can be (but not necessarily) accompanied by an instance of racial discrimination.

Everybody who lives in the United States has come from someplace else (except for the indigenous peoples, who either suffered genocide or were relegated to living on 'reservations'), from the colonial experience to the present. The ongoing morass about immigration policy by the dominant group, 'white' Americans, plays out this extreme ethnocentrism and teaches our children that the language people speak, the clothes they wear, the food they eat, *etc.*, all matter to the point of exclusion. This is the stuff of which extreme ethnocentrism is made. And, when it permeates the dominant culture, like it has from the beginning, it is ugly and becomes something even more insidious; it can become exclusionary, while asserting that those who are members of that dominant group are 'exceptional', thereby creating a mythical set of claims that present that culture as *above* all others, which deserves special treatment.

'American exceptionalism'

What is 'exceptionalism'? It is an enigma to most people, including lexicographers and Microsoft Word. However, we can construct a characterization of it. The qualifier 'exceptional' is used to describe someone or something that is beyond 'average' or 'adequate' and above 'very good' or 'excellent'; indeed, it is an ultimate superlative. It comprises the notion that some phenomenon, in our case the United States, possesses such qualities as to be set apart from others and that such a status be ensconced as part of the very essence of, in our case, 'being an American'. In other words, the countenance of the United States displays all that is 'exceptional' about it, which should be patently obvious to anyone who observes it. Another understanding that can be included is the idea that the United States is the 'exception' to this or that (abstractly speaking); like the exception to a rule of some kind – as a rule, we all must do this or that; but, because we are who we are or what we are, we are the exception and, as such, do not have to do this or that. We are exempted from having to comply because of our exceptional status. We are over and above the others to such an extent that we are excused from these rules and our very presence should be enough for anyone to see that we deserve such accolades; therefore, we are 'exceptional'.

242 Left Behind

Apart from being arrogant, such descriptions present an ideological[4] characterization of the United States. As introduced before, the concept of 'ideology' contains the logical properties of 'partly true' and 'partly false'; that is, ideologies are linguistic expressions which are significantly partly true and significantly partly false, simultaneously. So, to say that "there is equality in the United States" is an ideological expression because it is partly true – equality is part of the rubric of the Constitution and the Declaration of Independence – and partly false – the daily experience most anywhere in the United States belies this claim – at the same time. Raising this matter here is to highlight the fact that, while there may be some features of U.S. experience one could correctly identify as 'exceptional', we discover that others are actually reproductions of pre-existing experiences found in other countries, making them not exceptional at all or exceptional to all. Hence, to say that the United States is exceptional is an ideological statement and thereby partly true and partly false, at the same time.

If we review the formal histories of the United States, the ones used in our schools, we are told at every turn that the American experience is unique and unprecedented in history (some version of this kind of ethnocentrism is practiced by all countries; but, in the United States, this practice rises to the level of what has come to be referred to as 'exceptionalism'). Furthermore, the exceptional nature of these experiences is personified in the 'great men' version or the 'Founding Fathers' accounts of history.

The whole notion of 'American exceptionalism' begins with reference to the "Declaration of Independence,"[5] a unique expression of the principles espoused by *les philosophes* of the 18th-century 'enlightenment'. Thomas Jefferson, the Declaration's main author, crafted a most astute document, representing the radical idea that the people, not a monarch, should have the power to govern, that only self-government could veritably serve the needs of the people. "We hold these truths to be self-evident, that all men are created equal, that they are endowed by their Creator with certain unalienable rights; that among these are life, liberty and the pursuit of happiness."[6] Nowhere had such principles been expressed in document form before; "governments are instituted among men, deriving their just powers from the consent of the governed";[7] and "when a long train of abuses and usurpations, pursuing invariably the same object evinces a design to reduce them under absolute despotism, it is their right, it is their duty, to throw off such government, and to provide new guards for their future security."[8] 18th-century queens and kings were not enamored of this kind of sentiment, especially when it was expressed in writing, because it called for the demise of monarchies, either by

---

4 See Chapter 2 on the press.
5 "The Declaration of Independence", July 4, 1776.
6 *Ibid.*
7 *Ibid.*
8 *Ibid.*

being pushed into the background, as in the case of England, or by way of the *guillotine*, as in the case of France. This was radical stuff! This was indeed 'exceptional'! In addition, the idea that a place could accommodate people from a multiplicity of cultures is exceptional indeed. The promise of inexpensive, if not free, land available to begin a new life, unencumbered by remnants of feudal constraints was also unprecedented in the previous European experience.[9] This too, was exceptional.

However, many claims to being exceptional, unlike those for which we can find solidity, are unfounded; that is, ones which belie the facts, either historical or in substance. For example, the claim that the American Revolution secured 'liberty' is partly true and partly false, and hence ideological. It is true that Americans were free from the British king; but it is not true that liberty extended to all. Slavery was maintained for another hundred years after independence. The liberty to own land (something that had not been possible in the 'old country' because of the already crowded conditions), no longer controlled by the feudal relationship, was made available to people; but not until the indigenous populations had been systematically decimated by the extreme ethnocentric and racist killing machines brought to the 'new world'. This ethnic cleansing process was "essential"; no one wanted to live alongside these 'savages', who didn't even believe in God. These kinds of contradictions populated the foundations of our 'democracy'.

Commonly known are other features of 'Americanism', whose fundamental flaws stand out as 'exceptional' during most of the more than 240 years of this fledgling experiment: slavery from the beginning and the more than 100 years of Jim Crow Laws – slavery by another name – that exploited African peoples and their children, upon whose backs this country was constructed, free of charge. Yes, nowhere else, in the last 500 years, have modern infrastructures been developed so quickly as in the United States, thanks to the brutal treatment of slaves in the form of back-breaking work during long hours to the death in the absence of any remuneration. The United States and no other country could have afforded this massive undertaking under normal economic conditions. This exploitation did not end until very recently; it was the passing of the Civil Rights Act of 1964 that abolished Jim Crow. This is truly exceptional; exceptional in the sense that our country was built by people who actually do not have equal access to the benefits that they made available through their exceptional effort because, unfortunately, they continue to suffer the same discriminatory practices that the letter of the law guarantees against.

---

9 That original intent has deteriorated. Former Governor Jan Brewer signed into law the Support Our Law Enforcement and Safe Neighborhoods Act. "SB 1070 mandates the carrying of proper documentation for any alien in Arizona, and it levies a misdemeanor on any person who is found without such documentation. It also requires state law enforcement officials to determine an individual's immigration status during any routine stop, detention or arrest when the official has a reasonable suspicion that an individual might be in Arizona illegally. Additionally, SB 1070 strengthens penalties for hiring, sheltering, and transporting illegal immigrants." U.S. News and World Report (April 23, 2012) "Is Arizona's SB 1070 Immigration Law Constitutional?" at www.usnews.com/debate-club/is-arizonas-sb-1070-immigration-law-constitutional.

244 Left Behind

Moreover, immigrants from all over the world would populate this continent, responding to the invitation, expressed in the inscription at the base of the Statue of Liberty:

> Give me your tired, your poor,
> Your huddled masses yearning to breathe free;
> The wretched refuse of your teeming shore,
> Send these, the homeless,
> Tempest-tossed to me
> I lift my lamp beside the golden door![10]

I do not quarrel with such claims of exceptionalism as proposed in these early expressions during the developments of the 'new world'. I do, however, challenge these expressions such as they have become separated from the practices originally espoused, whereby they have been transformed into an ideology; one that, as Hodgson comments, countenances the extreme ethnocentric position that the United States "is not just the richest and most powerful of the world's more than two hundred states but is also politically and morally exceptional".[11] Anyone who investigates this claim is hard-pressed to demonstrate its truth; it may be partially true in its intent, but, in practice, it is false. Nonetheless, this kind of claim continues to be commonly expressed today and identifies a *superiority complex* that serves only to alienate 'Americans' from other peoples.

MSNBC's Chris Matthews did a 'promo' spot which ran in 2011 in which he is shown standing on a rooftop with the White House in the background. He tells the story about how, no matter how long someone not from China or Japan lives in China or Japan, one will never become Chinese or Japanese. However, anyone not from the United States who lives in the United States can become an American. He claims that this is 'American Exceptionalism'. Not necessarily true but not an unfair comment. However, he then points behind him at the White House with his thumb and makes reference to the then President Barack Obama, implying that even a black man can become president. This juxtaposition is curious because Obama was born in the United States. So, this flawed apposition confuses the message for the viewer. This is not unusual when it comes to these lofty constructs—another is the 'American Dream'.[12]

---

10 Written by Emma Lazarus in 1883, this is the last portion of the sonnet, poem, entitled "The New Colossus"; it was inscribed inside the base of the Statue of Liberty in 1903. The Statue of Liberty was a gift from the French people in 1886, offered with the sentiment: *La liberte eclairant le monde*, Liberty enlightening the world.

11 Godfrey Hodgson (2009) *The Myth of American Exceptionalism*, New Haven, CT: Yale University Press.

12 The following are the only references I could find to this promo. See William Fisher's Op Ed (August 29, 2011) "American Exceptionalism", *Truthout* at www.truth-out.org/opinion/item/3002:american-exceptionalism and Richard K. Barry (June 25, 2011) "Would Someone Please Tell Chris

Cultural arrogance 245

Overall, the corporate media continue to refer to 'American exceptionalism' as a 'tradition' or something that has always existed. Much of the rhetoric revolves around the notion that the United States *is* the 'leader' in the world. As soon as someone makes a comment in public discourse to the effect that the United States should work with other countries on a level playing field, pundits will interrupt and demand that the United States should always be seen as the 'leader' of the free world; to 'lead the world'; to be 'number one' in everything because that is the 'tradition', and that is the way it has 'always' been. This kind of continued drum beat reverberates in the echo chamber of the mass media and becomes what is expected to be the only way to see the United States by our citizens *and* by anyone else. This kind of attitude which has been established for a very long time becomes the basis for the United States to do whatever it wants anywhere in the world. An example of this global overreach, witness the 'no-fly zone' by George W. Bush above Libya, which became a pretext to bomb Tripoli among other cities and to target Muammar Gaddafi and his family directly. Think about how that kind of action would go down in the United States if any other country decided to target the White House because those leaders deem U.S. intervention in their country to be a terrorist act. This is what is really meant by 'American exceptionalism', the idea that the United States can do virtually anything it wants with impunity. That is truly exceptional, meaning that it is indeed exceptional *to think* that way. However, this is not what those who invoke the concept mean; they mean that it is exceptional *that we can do that*. This takes extreme ethnocentrism to another level; hence, the concept of 'exceptionalism', something that they take for granted and as a matter of fact, regardless of any consequences.

I do not quarrel with such claims of exceptionalism as proposed in these early expressions during the developments of the 'new world'. I do, however, challenge these expressions such as they have become separated from the practices originally espoused whereby they have been transformed into an ideology; one that, as in Hodgson's comment above, countenances the extreme ethnocentric position of the United States. Anyone who investigates this claim is hard pressed to demonstrate its truth; it may be partially true in its intent, but, in practice, it is false. Nonetheless, this kind of claim continues to be commonly expressed today and identifies a superiority complex that serves only to alienate 'Americans' from other peoples, not integrate them into the originally intended practice of such a political and moral high ground.

Alexis de Tocqueville[13] had observed that, in the latter part of the 19th century, those same Americans, who had originally given their lives for 'liberty' and

---

Matthews What American Exceptionalism Means?", *The Reaction* at http://the-reaction.blogspot.com/2011/06/would-someone-please-tell-chris.html.

13 Alexis de Tocqueville (2004, originally published in 1835) *Democracy in America*, vol. I, Part II, Chapter 1, translation, notes and chronology by Literary Classics of the United States, Inc. New York: The Library of America.

246 Left Behind

'equality', something really *exceptional*, had already lost their yen for those lofty constructs and had established a disparity, which was most noticeable in income distribution (hence inequality), something which is currently at an all-time high. Accordingly, the cries for liberty and equality fell by the wayside in favor of creating and maintaining wealth in the hands of the few, a true hallmark of any republic, commensurate with Plato's conception and something not at all *exceptional*.

Hodgson identifies several *negative* forms for which America is also exceptional. He cites the following examples: gun ownership, *i.e.*, the ability of ordinary people to purchase assault weapons and automatic bullet-spraying machines; the continued practice of capital punishment in the context of virtual global abolition, in the company of only a handful of countries – China, Saudi Arabia, Pakistan, Iraq and Iran; in the area of national productivity: once the world leader in manufacture, now lags behind most of the EU, Russia, and China (this largely as a result of foolish international economic policies such as NAFTA, CAFTA, and the consolidation of the WTO and the US corporate rush to China for yet cheaper labor).[14]

Acclaimed author Joyce Carol Oates, who teaches at Princeton University, has derided the notion that there is a distinctly American idea, one that is distinguishable from the core concepts that have animated Europeans, Scandinavians, and other cultures.

> [T]ravel to any foreign country, and the consensus is: The American idea has become a cruel joke, a blustery and bellicose bodybuilder luridly bulked up on steroids, consequently low on natural testosterone, deranged and myopic, dangerous.[15]

Andrew Roberts has endorsed American exceptionalism in his own writings. He regards Professor Oates's comments as being a sign of a "psychiatric disorder" displayed by 'liberal' academics. Roberts said,

> America is not like any other country. It wasn't born like other countries. It didn't come to prominence like other countries. It's not holding its imperium like other countries…. It probably won't lose its supremacy like other countries. And so in that sense it is completely exceptional….[16]

Eric Foner asserts that some expressions of American exceptionalism are "parochial" and "chauvinistic". He said,

---

14 *Op. cit.* Hodgson, Chapter 5.
15 Joyce Carol Oates (November, 2007) *The Human Idea*, under the broader title: *The Future of the American Idea*, the 150 anniversary of The Atlantic.
16 David Austin Walsh (August 21, 2010) "What is "American Exceptionalism"? http://m.hnn.us/blog/126940.

So it leads to this kind of imperial frame of mind that we know best for everybody, we know that our system is better – and of course sometimes other people aren't as convinced of that … To think about ourselves [sic] as exceptional really is a very narrow vision in a world which is becoming more and more globalized every day … Throughout our history, many of the processes which have shaped American history – industrialization, urbanization, things like that – are not purely national phenomena.[17]

This debate continues. The reader must decide for her/himself how claims of American exceptionalism square with the abundantly available facts regarding the many contexts in which these claims are made.

Exceptionalism in education

While the idea that the United States is 'exceptional' continues to dominate public and private discourse, at least in the United States, we note that such talk includes notions that education in the United States is still 'the best in the world'. We can trace the basis for this attitude in the writings of the revolutionary founders, Thomas Jefferson in particular. For example, while a classist (and elitist) in his recommendations, Jefferson was most adamant about education being at the heart of maintaining a viable democracy. He understood that a democracy was impossible without a literate citizenry. For members of the working class, it was sufficient "to give every citizen the information he needs for the transaction of his own business."[18] These citizens should be taught reading, writing and arithmetic, history, geography and surveying (surveying, because land ownership had become a most important factor for settlers from Europe, where land was at a premium). Also, everyone had to understand that the new experiment included voting as part of a longer list of rights. Without literacy, voting could not be viable. For the "statesmen, legislators and judges, on whom public prosperity and individual happiness" had to be based, Jefferson offered a different set of academic requirements, "starting with no fewer than eight ancient and modern languages, including Hebrew and Anglo-Saxon, theoretical and practical mathematics, an exhaustive array of the natural sciences, together with law, political economy, and 'ideology,' in which he included grammar, ethics, rhetoric, literature, and the fine arts."[19]

Some elements of this kind of curriculum survived into the 20th century, e.g., when I was a youngster, I remember reference to the different tracks that high schools offered, e.g., the secretarial track (for those who would become clerical functionaries), the industrial arts track (for those who would work the trades such as

---

17 Foner as quoted in Walsh, *Ibid*.

18 As quoted in *American Education: The National Experience, 1783–1876*, Lawrence A. Cremin (1980), New York: Harper, p. 103. Remember the comments by Gates, Chapter 3 epigraph.

19 Jefferson as quoted in *op. cit.* Hodgson (2009), p. 46.

248 Left Behind

plumbers, electricians, carpenters, *etc.*) and the college preparatory track (for those who would pursue college studies, usually those whose parents were well-to-do because college cost money; it was/is not tax-based (but should be) like elementary and high schools are). In those days, few-working class high school graduates were able to attend college. In my own family generation, of the two brothers and 22 cousins I have/had, only four of us had the opportunity. In my case, it was only possible because of the GI Bill. This kind of elitist higher educational system only belies the claim that the U.S. has the best education in the world. Many other countries offer college and university opportunities to students at virtually no cost, subsidized by the tax base. They must suffer and pass entrance examinations. In the United States, save perfunctory requirements, *e.g.*, having a high school diploma and scoring at a prescribed level on the Scholastic Aptitude Test, it continues to be the case that, if one has means, entrance into the college of choice is still widely practiced. I remember teaching in a school of a university that admits students who really did not qualify to attend, but who had the means to deliver 'cash on the barrelhead'. This hints at how higher education in the United States has become a business, rather than an institution separate from the 'capitalist profit motive' of the larger society.

When educational achievements in the United States are matched with those of other countries in the same epoch, we find that there isn't much that is 'exceptional' about the American experience, especially as of late. Let us look at the three major categories of education, roughly shared among the United States and Asia: elementary, secondary and university. Also, let us look at three major parameters among them for comparative/contrastive purposes: year of establishment, quality of curriculum and universality of offering.

Massachusetts became the leader in education as the colonies advanced toward establishing infrastructural institutions to serve the people. The first public elementary education was established in 1639 in Boston, MA, known as the birthplace of public education. This one-room schoolhouse was called The Mather School and was supported by tax dollars and was open to students at no cost.[20] Not long after, *The Massachusetts Law of 1647* was passed, stipulating that every town populated with at least 50 families had to provide a schoolmaster to teach reading and writing. If the town had 100 families, the town had to establish a Latin Grammar School to prepare students for Harvard College. This law is significant because it was the first law in the colonies to require public education for children; that is, education that was tax-based and education that children could actually access.

---

20 BPS is the home of many *firsts in the nation*: first public school (Boston Latin School, 1635), first public elementary school (Mather Elementary School, 1639), first public school system (1647), first public high school (English High School, 1821). See www.bostonpublicschools.org/site/Default. aspx?PageType=6&SiteID=4&SearchString=points%20of%20pride%201635,%201639,%20 1647,%201821, "Points of Pride".

Cultural arrogance **249**

Such a *curriculum* was vaunted as the kind commensurate with the aspirations of this fledgling democracy. However, according to Hodgson,

> Education, in short, is one of many fields in which American exceptionalism has been nourished by ignoring both the interdependence between America and Europe, and the fact that Europe, in the course of the nineteenth century, was changing as fast, if not in precisely the same ways, as the United States.[21]

Hence, the claim that the United States provides the 'best education' is simply not true today, if ever it was. Educational systems in the United States were fashioned after the Prussian model. The Prussian system instituted compulsory attendance, specific training for teachers, national testing for all students (used to classify children for potential job training), national *curriculum* set for each grade and mandatory kindergarten. During the 18th century, the Kingdom of Prussia was among the first countries in the world to introduce tax-funded and generally compulsory primary education, comprising an eight-year course of primary education, called *Volksschule*. It provided not only the skills needed in an early industrialized world (reading, writing and arithmetic), but also a strict education in ethics, duty, discipline and obedience. Affluent children often went on to attend preparatory private schools for an additional four years, but the general population had virtually no access to secondary education, only the *Volksschule*, which was established in Prussia (1717) and in the Habsburg Austrian Empire (1840).[22]

The universal system deployed in Scotland predates education in the United States (in Glasgow, 1124 and in Dundee, 1239)[23] and also served as a model for the system later established in the U.S. Certainly, education in the U.S. is not the worst in the world; but, what some early observers claimed about education in the United States that it was/is superior or exceptional has been successfully challenged. In fact, I argue here that the quality of education in the United States has waned over the years, especially in the last 50. Most of the subjects invoked by Jefferson as part of a comprehensive education for 'leaders'[24] were taught in the 1960s in the high school 'college prep' *curriculum*. In my own experience, four years of a second language were required (in my case, English was the second language); Latin was mandatory, including literature and poetry (four years), French and English literature and

---

21 *Op. cit.* Hodgson (2009), p. 50.
22 See Jackson J. Spielvogel (1997) *Western Civilization: Comprehensive Volume*, 3rd ed. Eagan, MN: West Publishing Company, and James Van Horn Melton, (1988) *Absolutism and the eighteenth-century origins of compulsory schooling in Prussia and Austria*, Cambridge: Cambridge University Press.
23 See T.C. Smout (1985) *A History of the Scottish People*, Waukegan, IL: Fontana Press for details about the development of education in Scotland.
24 Incidentally, Oliver Van De Mille's (2006) *A Thomas Jefferson Education: Teaching a Generation of Leaders for the Twenty-First Century*, Cedar City, UT: George Wythe College Press delineates three systems of education, based upon Jefferson's two tier system. This education philosophy has come to be known as 'Leadership Education' and comprises much of the homeschooling *curriculum*.

250 Left Behind

poetry (four years); mathematics and the sciences: algebra, geometry, chemistry and physics, all required (one year each); history, American and European (two years); civics (one year); art, music and sports (four years). Admittedly, my experience was not typical of most 'college preparatory' *curricula*. Nonetheless, this kind of 'college prep' track, as a whole, was replicated all over the country. By and large, this is no longer true in the United States; many of the requisite courses in that *curriculum* (*e.g.*, Latin, four-year second language, physics, chemistry) were mostly curtailed rather than eliminated, except for Latin, which has been largely dropped. This is not true in many other so-called 'advanced' countries in the world, *e.g.*, all of Europe, Russia, Japan, *etc.*

In fact, the idea of 'universal education' was widely entertained as a result of the 18th-century enlightenment and the American and French Revolutions. The new meaning of 'democracy' as espoused by these scholars and events was not that of Plato's 'democracy for the few', but one that was for everybody. The revolutionary ideas of the Enlightenment were ones that included all; and attempts to establish institutions that could 'cash the check' on their promise were in process throughout the Western world and established in many other countries before the independence of the United States.

Much of the practice of education has to do with the books students have access to in the course of their learning. Since 1986, the American Textbook Council has compiled information regarding textbook adoption trends. As expected, their information is dominated by the big states, that is, those states which regularly set the agenda for the country, most notably Texas and California (and to a lesser degree Indiana, North Carolina, Florida and New York). Textbook publishers tend to concentrate on the big orders; it is more economical for them to run textbooks that are being adopted by the high-population states and, by using pricing strategies, to influence lower population states to adopt accordingly. As a result, choices made in, say, Texas, will influence the 'choices' in other smaller states. Consequently, and in a context of the media monopoly documented by Ben Bagdikian, also manifest in textbook publishing. The American Textbook Council reports that the following textbooks as comprising 80% of the current U.S. history textbooks serving eighth and 11th grade needs. This first group of textbooks is aimed at the 8th grade-level, even though some are widely adopted for use in high school classrooms as easy readers.

McGraw-Hill/Glencoe	Appleby	American Journey
Pearson/Prentice Hall	Davidson	The American Nation
Houghton Mifflin/McDougal	Garcia	Creating America
BL Harcourt/Holt	Stuckey	Call to Freedom

This group of textbooks is aimed at the 11th grade:

Harcourt/Holt	Ayers	American Anthem (new)
Pearson/Prentice Hall	Boorstin	A History of the United States
Pearson/Prentice Hall	Cayton	America: Pathways to the Present

Houghton Mifflin/McDougal	Danzer	The Americans
McGraw-Hill/Glencoe	Nash	American Odyssey
BL Harcourt/Holt	Boyer	Boyer's The American Nation[25]

What has happened is that the political penchant of high population states can determine the *curriculum* agenda for the whole country. If a *bona fide* claim to American 'exceptionalism' ever applied to education, it certainly does not apply in any credible way any longer.

There are contrasting accounts of 'American history' which challenge those official versions. Take, for example, the case of *Labor's Untold Story*,[26] a history that emphasizes the workers and their struggles and how, through their political activities secured for us better economic conditions, *e.g.*, how the American working class won the eight-hour working day for the world. Or, take *A People's History of the United States: 1492–Present*,[27] how it was/is ordinary people who move history along and that what we experience today results from the collective movements that people created to achieve much of what we enjoy today. Or, the *U.S. History Uncensored: What Your High School Textbook Didn't Tell You*,[28] which addresses the current problem of how the flaws in history textbooks instruct our children to misunderstand our historical experience. Or, Oliver Stone's excellent 12-episode, documentary series "The Untold History of the United States",[29] in which he takes on different epochs in succession, from WWII to the present, and unpacks their historical significance. Or, many others that chronicle the struggles of the people to establish, in practice, the ideals that Lincoln expressed "of the people, by the people and for the people".[30]

Problems with the educational system in the United States have become a weekly, and sometimes daily, topic of discussion in the media, albeit not the kind of attention that it should merit. More often than not, the discussion is about 'test scores', not about the basic philosophy of what we are doing. Until we begin to unpack the fundamental mindset that we entertain in the United States, we will not get at the root problem plaguing our system of education and we will continue to fail our youngsters in the most important experience they will encounter in their lives.

What is truly exceptional in the United States, and for some decades now, is the lack of care we take with regard to informing our children about the important

---

25 See www.historytextbooks.net/adopted.htm.

26 Richard O. Boyer and Herbert M. Morais (1955) *Labor's Untold Story: The Adventure Story of the Battles, Betrayals and Victories of American Working Men and Women*, New York: United Electrical, Radio and Machine Workers of America (UE).

27 Howard Zinn (2003) *A People's History of the United States: 1492-Present*, New York: Harper & Row.

28 *U.S. History Uncensored: What Your High School Textbook Didn't Tell You*, Carolyn L. Baker, 2006, iUniverse, Inc., New York.

29 *The Untold History of the United States* (November 14, 2012) Showtime, Warner Brothers, Oliver Stone Director, Producer Narrator and Peter Kuznich author/producer.

30 Last phrase of Abraham Lincoln's "Gettysburg Address", November 20, 1863.

matters of life. Teachers are being trained to teach to the test and students are learning how to take tests. I have asked high school graduates, anecdotally, about what they thought was most memorable about their high school education. The responses I get are disappointing and hold a dark vision for the future. They don't say that they really came to understand algebra or geometry; nor do they say that their reading comprehension has improved markedly; nor do they say that their grasp of biology or physics has prepared them for college. No, they don't offer those responses; they do say that they learned something about themselves while playing this or that sport; they say that a particular teacher, not all, influenced them to pursue their studies (in that subject); they say that they had a lot of fun and made a lot of friends. What they say the most about how high school prepared them for life is that they learned how to take tests, some better than others. This, they avow because they remembered spending so much time on strategies for test-taking and not on the content of those tests. How sad is this, that this is what students remember most vividly because they did it so much!

This is not education. This kind of operation is designed only to construct students, or should we call them really what they are: "obedient clients". They are prepared to enter the world of work at mundane jobs that require only the kind of skills they have excelled in while in high school: stimulus/response kinds of work, work that does not require much in terms of critical assessments of what is before them. I remember, while I was in the military, that we used to complain how little our jobs required of us, except on the off occasion when we had a particularly pesky problem to solve. Military jobs are fashioned to bring all tasks down to their most common of denominators so that anyone can perform them. We used to say that what we did was 'gorilla work': one banana, take out the malfunctioning part; two bananas, put in the functioning replacement. Is this the kind of fulfillment our students can hope to achieve in their lives?

Sadly, if these children get into college, the same kind of test-taking awaits them; the large classes (100 to 500 students); the paucity of opportunity to engage a teacher about what they are learning; the boring contexts created by the all-importance of elevating test scores. This is "exceptional" education?

One of the things that they are most prepared for is the domain of consumerism. They have become most astute about what to buy, where to buy it and how much more important they will be once they buy it. This superficial mindset is most disturbing. Is this what we have come to offer our children? They are all experts in trivia, the kind they get from the magazines they 'read', if they even do that. Most of those media are displaying pictures of celebrities and how they look. They are so unaware of so many important matters and so aware of, even experts at, such insignificant drivel. Is this what has become of U.S. exceptionalism? Even though we have acquiesced to some of the claims that the U.S. has been exceptional in the past, *e.g.*, the potential for opportunity, for multi-culturalism, for government by the people, nonetheless. This kind of exceptionalism is impossible in the present context, one dominated by preoccupations about trivial matters instead of those critical in our times, *e.g.*, understanding that it is the invasions and occupations of

Iraq and Afghanistan, and now Syria looms large, that have caused the financial mess the U.S. finds itself in at the present; that the U.S. must end its military presence all over the world and the "empire mindset" along with it; and that, unless the U.S., India and China (most particularly) commit to a serious decrease in CO_2 emissions (not much hope with a White House and congress full of climate change deniers), many species of the world will die off, human beings among them. These are the matters that do not, but should, press on the minds of our young people today. That would surely be exceptional! If this reads 'bleak' to you, this is partly why we need a paradigm shift in our education policies, *pronto!*

The American educational system is not exceptional and cannot be touted as such in the world, nor even on the North American Continent. Evidence for this is becoming more and more available. According to the Organization for Economic Co-operation and Development (OECD) and its Programme for International Student Assessment (PISA), the 2009 (reported in 2010) performance assessment for the United States was slated as "average",[31] placing at 47th[32] overall in the world, 14th in reading, 17th in science and 25th in mathematics,[33] this among the seventy countries evaluated. The U.S. was accompanied in this "average" category by Portugal, Hungary, U.K., Denmark, Taipei, France, Ireland, Germany, Sweden, Lichtenstein and Poland. Earning a rating of "significantly above average" were Switzerland, Estonia, Norway, Belgium, Netherlands, Australia, Japan, New Zealand, Singapore, Hong Kong, Finland, Korea and Shanghai.[34]

I leave you with these dire thoughts to contemplate what we should do to stop these deplorable results neglecting one of the most foundational institutions in our lives. Our children are not responsible for these outcomes; they are those who suffer because of them. They deserve much better from us, in the wealthiest nation on the planet. They don't need slogans about how exceptional and *great* we are in the United States, especially of the kind that Trump spouts; they need real greatness that starts with the best education we can muster for them.

Bibliography

American Textbook Council. (n.d.) "Widely Adopted History Textbooks". Retrieved from www.historytextbooks.net/adopted.htm

Baker, C.L. (2006) *U.S. History Uncensored: What Your High School Textbook Didn't Tell You.* New York: iUniverse, Inc.

Barry, R.K. (June 25, 2011) "Would Someone Please Tell Chris Matthews What American

---

31 Actually the U.S. has fallen into the 'below average' category since 2010. See the PISA 2015 Report.
32 While unable to find the overall rating for the U.S., it has dropped since 2010. See the PISA 2015 Report.
33 These three rankings have dropped since 2010; they are now 24th in reading, 25th in science and 41st in mathematics. See the PISA 2015 Report.
34 OECD (2010) Strong Performers and Successful Reformers in Education: Lessons from PISA for the United States, http://dx.doi.org/10.1787/9789264096660-en

Exceptionalism Means?" *The Reaction*. Retrieved from http://the-reaction.blogspot. com/2011/06/would-someone-please-tell-chris.html

Basler, R.P., Ed. (1953) *The Collected Works of Abraham Lincoln, volume 7*. New Brunswick, NJ: Rutgers University Press, pp. 22–23.

Boston Public Schools. (n.d.) Retrieved from www.bostonpublicschools.org/site/Default. aspx?PageType=6&SiteID=4&SearchString=points%20of%20pride%201635,%20 1639,%201647,%201821.

Boyer, R.O. & Morais, H.M. (1955) *Labor's Untold Story: The Adventure Story of the Battles, Betrayals and Victories of American Working Men and Women*. New York: United Electrical, Radio and Machine Workers of America (UE).

Cremin, L.A. (1980) *American Education: The National Experience, 1783–1876*. New York: Harper.

De Mille, O.V. (2006) *A Thomas Jefferson Education: Teaching a Generation of Leaders for the Twenty-First Century*. Cedar City, IL: George Wythe College Press.

de Tocqueville, A. (2004, originally published in 1835) *Democracy in America, vol. I*. Translation, notes and chronology by Literary Classics of the United States, Inc. New York: The Library of America.

Durkheim, E. (1997; originally published in 1897) *Suicide: A Study in Sociology*. New York: Free Press.

Fisher, W. (August 29, 2011) "American Exceptionalism". *Truthout*. Retrieved from www. truth-out.org/opinion/item/3002:american-exceptionalism

Hodgson, G. (2009) *The Myth of American Exceptionalism*. New Haven: Yale University Press.

Lazarus, E. (1883) "The New Colossus". Retrieved from www.poetryfoundation.org/ poems/46550/the-new-colossus

Lincoln, A. (November 20, 1863) "Gettysburg Address". Retrieved from http://teachinga-mericanhistory.org/library/document/gettysburg-address/

Melton, J.V.H. (1988) *Absolutism and the Eighteenth-Century Origins of Compulsory Schooling in Prussia and Austria*. Cambridge: Cambridge University Press.

Nietzsche, F.W. (1911) *Ecce Homo*. New York: The Macmillan Company.

Oates, J.C. (November, 2007) "The Human Idea". *The Atlantic*. Retrieved from www. theatlantic.com/magazine/archive/2007/11/the-human-idea/306286/

Organization for Economic Co-operation and Development (2010) *Strong Performers and Successful Reformers in Education: Lessons from PISA for the United States*. http://dx.doi. org/10.1787/9789264096660-en.

Smout, T.C. (1985) *A History of the Scottish People*. Waukegan: Fontana Press.

Spielvogel, J.J. (1997) *Western Civilization: Comprehensive Volume, 3rd ed.* Eagan: West Publishing Company.

Stone, O. (Director/Producer/Narrator) & Kuznich, P. (Author/Producer). (November 14, 2012) *The Untold History of the United States* [TV series]. USA: Showtime.

Walsh, D.A. (August 21, 2010) "What is 'American Exceptionalism'?" Retrieved from http://m.hnn.us/blog/126940

U.S. News and World Report (April 23, 2012) "Is Arizona's SB 1070 Immigration Law Constitutional?" Retrieved from www.usnews.com/debate-club/is-arizonas-sb -1070-immigration-law-constitutional

Zinn, H. (2003) *A People's History of the United States: 1492–Present*. New York: Harper & Row, Harper Collins.

12

ORWELL'S NIGHTMARE ACHIEVED: THE 'COLONIZATION OF THE MIND' VS. CRITICAL THINKING

War is Peace; Freedom is Slavery; Ignorance is Strength; 2 + 2 = 5
— George Orwell[1]

So, we are talking about evils of the colonization of the mind as well as of land and body.
— Gil Noble[2]

Excellence in thought, however, must be systematically cultivated...Critical Thinking is the art of analyzing and evaluating thinking with a view to improving it.
— Richard Paul & Linda Elder[3]

The epigraphs above encapsulate the subject matter of this chapter. First, the iconic slogans of Oceania in George Orwell's dystopian novel, *1984*, "War is Peace", "Freedom is Slavery", "Ignorance is Strength" and "2 + 2 = 5" remind us of how close we are to such distorted constructs in today's society. Second, Gil Noble's reference to the "colonization of the mind" in his discussion with those other

---

1 These were the slogans in the novel *1984*, that Orwell's tragic hero, Winston Smith, came to accept once he was tortured by the Thought Police in Oceania, the dystopia controlled by Big Brother.

2 Gill Noble was the host of a TV series entitled "*Like It Is*" in the 1980s; this comment by him is taken from the program aired June 13, 1982, WABC, New York. The discussion was about the colonial experience in the 'Americas'. He was interviewing Ivan van Sertima, John Henrik Clarke and Yosef Ben Jochannan.

3 Leaders of The Foundation for Critical Thinking; taken from their 2011 announcement of their 31st Annual International Conference on Critical Thinking, p. 2; see www.criticalthinking.org.

256 Left Behind

enlightened scholars helps us understand that colonialism was not only a physical displacement of land and resources in the 'new world' but also the replacement of ideas of the indigenous peoples with foreign conqueror's ideas. Something of the same happens to all of us through the mass media today. Third, the practice of critical thinking becomes the necessary element in education to ward off the impact of Orwellian 'doublespeak' and the 'mind-control' effects of the mass media. These constructs set the tone for the discussions ahead.

The reader will recognize these three topics, which I have addressed in previous chapters. Hence, the following is not a reintroduction to them, but an emphasis upon them. I discuss them together, because I want to stress that these are very closely related and go to the crux of the problems we have with regard to the actual skills we fail to teach our children. Namely, we fail to alert them to the pitfalls of the corporate media. They are not media savvy. Yet, they think they are because they know how to manipulate all those 'little boxes'; but, in reality, they are unaware that they are being *colonized* by the messages of those media. Further, they are not aware of the critical thinking skills that could render their experience at school so much more effective and rewarding. They do not know what insights they could unveil simply by checking their thinking, in the making, according to known conceptual tools. And further, they are unaware of what these two deficiencies in their education together predispose them to in terms of the way language is distorted with 'doublespeak'. All of these manipulations organize their ways of thinking, not *critical thinking*, making them unable to sort through the junk to find the 'truth' about anything and the sense that they have no control over their lives. This, in the midst of all the other issues discussed in this book, puts our students at a severe disadvantage if we want them to be savvy and happy.

Doublespeak

The reader may realize, having read George Orwell's *1984*, that many of the horrors of that 'futuristic' society have now been realized, compliments of the same kind of powerful institutions and their managers as in Oceania, Orwell's fictional state. In many ways, the United States has become Orwellian. In so many ways, from the constant use of doublespeak, to the manipulation of history, to perpetual war, *etc.*, our daily lives have become dominated by the distorted spectacle and 'Big Brother'-like reality of the American empire. This has been a gradual and deliberate effort, and is especially due to the ideological dimension – the most powerful parts of which are the mass media – that controls information, thereby controlling the conduct of members of society. The constant fear Orwell described in his novel has been replicated in the United States, most notably demonstrated by the establishment of a 'culture of fear' especially since the attack on the World Trade Center towers on September 11, 2001, and the passing of the Patriot Act. As in all instances of mass fear, those in positions of power can, and often do, regulate populations to think and do what they want. This set of circumstances has given rise to the

Orwell's nightmare achieved **257**

constant state of war we have experienced especially for the last 15 years.[4] Children in school today have not seen anything else since they were born. Let us look at these matters as they relate to current public education in the U.S.

I remember observing in the *year* 1984 that Orwell's dystopian imagination, expressed in his novel *1984*, had escaped the boundaries of that masterpiece and entered into the mainstream of the American experience. Orwell was most interested in how language worked; and I am highlighting the organized misuse of language in this discussion. Orwell made this preoccupation a central theme in his story and its controlling and torturous impact on the lives of the people of Oceania, personified in the protagonist, Winston Smith. Working in the Ministry of Truth, "Minitrue" in *Newspeak*, the official language of Oceania, his job was to change the newspapers of the past to make them square with the present. The party slogan stated that "Who controls the past, controls the future; who controls the present, controls the past".[5] This required a mindset of internal contradiction and acquiescence. This was a place where "War is Peace", "Freedom is Slavery", "Ignorance is Strength"[6] and "2 + 2 = 5"[7] were the required mindset. Orwell called these contradictory expressions 'doublethink'. He explained:

> Doublethink means the power of holding two contradictory beliefs in one's mind simultaneously, and accepting both of them ... The process has to be conscious, or it would not be carried out with sufficient precision. But it also has to be unconscious, or it would bring with it a feeling of falsity and hence of guilt.[8]

Erich Fromm, in his Afterword to *1984*, commented:

> Another important point in Orwell's discussion is closely related to 'doublethink', namely that in a successful manipulation of the mind the person is no longer saying the opposite of what he thinks, but he thinks the opposite of what is true. Thus, for instance, if he has surrendered his independence and his integrity completely, if he experiences himself as a thing which belongs either to the state, the party or the corporation, then 'two plus two are five', or 'Slavery is Freedom', and he feels free because there is no longer any awareness of the discrepancy between truth and falsehood. Specifically this applies to ideologies. Just as the Inquisitors who tortured their prisoners believed that they acted in the name of Christian love, the Party 'rejects and

4 Some people may think that 'wars' are in the past, i.e., WWII, the Korean Conflict, Vietnam. However, the wars that are still ongoing began in 2001 in Afghanistan and in 2003 in Iraq. The effects of these conflicts/occupations have been ever-present in our minds, including our children.

5 George Orwell (1961.) *1984*, New York: Signet Classic, p. 204.

6 *Ibid.*, p. 7.

7 *Ibid.*, p. 239.

8 *Ibid*, p. 176.

258 Left Behind

vilifies every principle for which the socialist movement originally stood, and it chooses to do this in the name of socialism."[9]

Doublethink is manifest in language-use or 'doublespeak'. Doublespeak can take on different forms: a 'euphemism' to conceal the truth, 'doubletalk' to confuse what is being expressed, or a form of 'stylized talk' to obfuscate what is being said such that one can be heard to ask "What did he say? What was that?" Orwell was writing about public discourse and its bastardization of the language in order to reformulate "arguments which are too brutal for most people to face and which do not square with the professed aims of political parties [or corporate policy-PLJ]. Thus political language has to consist largely of euphemisms, question-begging and sheer cloudy vagueness."[10] Orwell provided some examples:

> Defenseless villages are bombarded from the air, the inhabitants driven out into the countryside, the cattle machine-gunned, the huts set on fire with incendiary bullets: this is called *pacification*. Millions of peasants are robbed of their farms and sent trudging along the roads with no more than they can carry: this is called *transfer of population* or *rectification of frontiers*. People are imprisoned for years without trial, or shot in the back of the neck or sent to die of scurvy in Arctic lumber camps: this is called *elimination of unreliable elements*.[11]

Some more contemporary examples are: in the nuclear industry, a 'peacekeeper' is a nuclear missile, 'energetic disassembly' is an explosion and 'rapid oxidation' is a fire. In the medical field, 'terminal living' is dying and a 'negative patient outcome' is when a patient dies in hospital. In the military industrial complex, 'surgical strikes' are bombings and a 'vertical insertion' is an attack from the air. This kind of talk/writing has become routine in our era of the American empire. Language that confuses or hides the true meaning of discourse is the regular diet of communication that the monopolized media mete out to us today in very much the way the Minitrue did in Oceania.

To prepare the reader for how this misuse of language operates, let us consider its use in the context of working people, something that most people can relate to. One recent example was visited upon us by the National Right to Work Legal

---

9 *Ibid*, pp. 265–266. Fromm ends on Orwell's critique of Stalinism, what many in the United States take to be the same as socialism, due to the conspiratorial efforts on the part of U.S. governments, and their complicit minions in the mass media, since WWII. If a distorted conception of socialism could be accepted by the American population, capitalism would have an easier time exploiting labor and keeping the social rewards in the hands of the few. Socialism, on the other hand, advocates economic democracy and a fair distribution of wealth to all members of society.

10 George Orwell (1954) *A Collection of Essays*, (This quote is from his "Politics and the English Language" [1946]), New York: Doubleday Anchor Books, p. 173.

11 *Ibid*.

Defense and Education Foundation. They have advanced this construct, the 'right to work' (RTW) principle, which "affirms the right of every American to work for a living without being compelled to belong to a union".[12] "Compelled"? What a strange misapplication of a concept! Union representation is voted in by the rank and file, not imposed upon them. As for new employees who are entering a unionized context, who among them would refuse an uptick in pay? This and other benefits are typically won by the collective bargaining that unions provide; certainly not offered up due to the magnanimity of corporate owners and managers. The phrase 'right to work' brings with it a sense that people have the right to a job, a good job, one with a living wage and benefits, something that has rarely been guaranteed, but that is not what this is about. Actually, *good jobs* have often been associated with *union jobs*; that is, good pay, good working conditions and good benefits have historically been associated with the oversight of collective bargaining. Unfortunately, for the last 50 years, the right to a job like that has eroded significantly along with unionization; so much so that only some 10% of workers in the United States are represented by unions, down dramatically from the 1930s and '40s, when some 40% of workers were protected by unions.

Twenty-five states, in the South and the Midwest, have adopted this union-busting, RTW idea in the form of laws. According to the AFL-CIO in Minnesota, one of those 'right to work' states, there are several negative consequences not to supporting union labor:

> workers in states with so-called Right-to-Work laws have a consistently lower quality of life than in other states…

- On average, workers … earn $5,538 a year less
- According to the Bureau of Labor Statistics, the rate of workplace deaths is 52.9% higher
- Only 51% of nonunion workers have access to health care insurance as opposed to 78% of union workers

And this next one is most relevant to our discussion:

- Those RTW states spend $2,671 *per capita* less on elementary and secondary students than free-bargaining states[13]

So, policies that are expressed in one domain of life, in this case the regressive laws affecting our work places and relationships, can also have an effect on the education

---

12 See www.nrtw.org/right-to-work-frequently-asked-questions for details and a list of states which have adopted such a law.

13 See the Minnesota AFL-CIO website for details about these matters: www.mnaflcio.org/updates/right-work-laws-get-facts.

of our children; in this case the reactionary decisions regarding the funding of our schools, translated as a decrease in the expenditure *per capita* of our student populations.

The ways language is used by those in positions of power are most consequential in many contexts. Co-opting the language to hide and confuse can be very effective. To the noncritical observer, reading or hearing the phrase 'right to work' can elicit an understanding that is generally favorable; that is, everyone has a right to work and people could say: "What is the big deal? I support that." However, to the critical observer, such a phrase can elicit a more questioning attitude, one which would require more information and context to warrant an evaluation based upon significant factors, simply *because* it has a nice sounding ring to it. Reference to 'education' is actually included in the title of the foundation! National Right to Work Legal Defense and Education Foundation. This also misleads people to believe that this organization is in support of education and the relationships it has to 'work'. In fact, it advocates just the opposite. That is 'doublespeak'.

Now that we are familiar with this concept, consider the following example of doublespeak in the context of education. The reader will remember the fanfare the media made of the No Child Left Behind (NCLB) law of 2002. Failing public schools were blamed for the lack of standardization of goals, teacher training and the evaluation of students and teachers. The answer proposed was to impose new standardized testing, placing an inordinate amount of import upon them. What resulted was that too much time was spent 'preparing for the test', which translated into too much time 'teaching to the test'. One child left behind is too many; however, implementing the law actually increased the number of children left behind, not in the sense that more children were forced to repeat a grade, but in the sense that, based upon the faulty logic of the law, real instruction for our children waned and became virtually impossible to achieve. Contrary to these faulty goals, children, who had not received proper instruction, were pushed ahead to the next grade, based upon standardized testing that had been engineered to allow more students to pass the test. The logic of the expression 'No Child Left Behind' implied that the law would provide our educational system some guarantees with regard to delivering high-quality education for all our children; that is not what it did.

The doublespeak lies in this euphemistic character of the expression, while really implementing a lazy process of evaluation, based upon spending more time making sure that students passed the tests, 'guaranteeing' 'good score numbers', instead of more time ensuring that our children received the proper instruction, empowering them to understand the world around them and themselves. Such cloudy expressions give rise to misunderstandings and false expectations about the true nature of the law. Criticism of the NCLB law came gradually but surely from teachers, students, unions, education professionals, employers, *etc.*, because they were not witnessing the level of education implied, if not explicit, in the law. This was the case because the methodology of mass testing has not demonstrated anything of value toward the expressed goals of the law: you cannot evaluate educational performance through testing; you have to do it the 'old-fashioned' way of one-on-one assessments with each child to determine what their weaknesses and strengths and special needs are. So, while the title of the law sounded good, it could not deliver. The language used, the doublespeak, gave one to believe that this law was needed to solve the ever more serious problems in our schools; but 'the proof is in the pudding' and this 'pudding' was empty of substance.

Another more recent example specifically within our educational context is the introduction of the Common Core construct. On its face, one can have the common sense understanding that education is actually a 'core' component of our very cultural identity. So, of course, that seems reasonable. Further, the concept of 'common' also seems reasonable; it places the phrase in the midst of what people would expect in the context of education: for example, a common set of principles regarding common goals. Let us not forget also that education is, as argued in Chapter 4, part of the 'commons'. So, on its face the phrase 'Common Core' can elicit a relatively positive impression from regular folks. However, the substance of the Common Core program proposes that there should be even more standardized testing for students, the results of which we already know: it fails. The program, *via* the same recycled nonsense of standardized tests – this time on steroids – will not only 'evaluate' students but teachers as well. One would think that those who propose remedies to our mediocre education system would try something else. Truth is: the remedies are much simpler if they would pay attention to the suggestions many have made before me in this book, along with other proposals in a comprehensive package. The *modus operandi* of standardized testing should by now be well known not to work. Let's do something else that will actually address our educational woes and help our children.

Unless our children are made aware of the dangers of the manipulation of language, doublespeak being one of those mechanisms, and the distorted messages that are carried through that manipulation, we will only perpetuate the kind of context that abides these confusions, rendering our children even more perplexed than they are already. Paying attention to how the language works has always been at the root of all education; we must redouble our efforts to retrain our children to pay attention to the nuances of their language.

The 'colonization of the mind'

There are countless other domains of life that the corporate media infiltrate to influence us: who we are, what we do, where we go, when we act, why we feel and how we think. Indeed, the mass media today are ever present and dominate not only our daily conduct but they have 'colonized our minds'; that is, the media have 'moved in', they have replaced the 'good sense' we were 'born with'. Consider the following discussion among John Henrik Clarke, Ivan van Sertima and Gil Noble, host of the 1980s series *Like It Is*. This excerpt is about the power of colonization beyond the physical, *i.e.*, economic and political, domination of peoples of Africa – the domination of the mind.

> Van Sertima: This is a kind of duplication of the European … I was a European duplicate; I was a British duplicate … The kind of loyalty, allegiance to the enslaver that became part of our inheritance.
> Noble: You sang "God save the queen".
> Van Sertima: Not only sang, "God save the queen", I felt proud that I was in an empire that was able to put everybody in their right place …
> Noble: So, we are talking about evils of the colonization of the mind as well as of land and body.
> Clarke: We're talking about the rise of the evil genius of Europe and western racism. There was not enough soldiers in all Europe to hold down that vast world. They had to conquer something else other than the physical body; they had to conquer the mind. And, maybe, their most tragic and dubious achievement was the convincing of so many people that they were supposed to be ruled over by these Europeans.[14]

In the present context, I borrow this construct of "colonization" or "duplication" of the mind to describe what happens to all of us, and especially to our children because of their particularly impressionable minds. That is, because of the media's constant barrage of, at best, dubious information, our minds become oriented to the messages and frames that they provide. A result is that *we are not only told what to think about, but also how to think about it.* This is particularly dangerous for our children, who are constantly bombarded by all manner of media productions. To uninformed and uncritical people (overwhelmingly school children), this means that what they see, hear and read every day is the 'truth'. To critical thinking people, much of what they see, hear and read can become, at a minimum, suspect, requiring further investigation. Because of the absence of 'critical thinking' instruction in our schools, children have no idea that they are constantly being 'colonized' by questionable ideas and, in many cases, outright false information.

I ask the reader to contemplate for a moment the kind of 'media day' our children experience. During a typical school day, they wake up to the radio or the television or their 'little boxes' (their phones, tablets, *etc.*); while they ready themselves for school, they listen to and/or watch programming on television, either random

---

14 *Op. cit.* Noble (1982). This analytical construct emerged out of the work of John Henrik Clarke, History at Hunter College and Ivan Van Sertima, African Studies at Rutgers University, to illustrate how colonization was not only a brutal political economic process, but one which interrupted the very 'mental' of all colonized people; that is, they were forced to think in terms of the colonial conquerors, and eventually, in their languages, never to return to their own indigenous linguistic and cultural realities. Also included in the discussion was Yosef Ben Jochannan, Africana Studies at Cornel University, not quoted. See, among other works, Van Sertima's (2003) *They Came Before Columbus: The African Presence in Ancient America*, Random House: New York, and Clarke's (2011) *Christopher Columbus and the African Holocaust: Slavery and the Rise of European Capitalism*, Hunlock Creek, PA: EWorld. Incidentally, this was at the very time that the Israelis were invading Lebanon. See several articles I wrote about the U.S. mass media reportage of that conflict.

or prescribed; over breakfast, if they have one, they are checking out their 'little boxes' again, on their way out the door; either on the bus or the walk or in the car, they continue to engage in 'social media'; while at school, they are subjected to Channel One and surreptitious forays on their cell phones; during lunch and other breaks, they are checking out the new video hit or the trailer to the new movie; while in class, routine screenings of information, largely 'approved' by the administration, which reinforces the 'mainstream' nonsense they already know about; upon leaving school, they revert to the visual media, either on their latest electronic apparatus or at home on television; into the evening, they watch programming that is full of prepackaged notions of what constitutes the world, seldom challenged to think critically about any of it; when they go to bed, they are still needing that external stimulation of either visual or audio fabrications; as they fall asleep, among other things, they think about all the experiences they have had throughout their media day and, chances are, they dream about them.

All that stuff coming at them all day is not random; it has been organized for them and targeted to them by powerful corporations, whose only motivation is to make a profit on whatever they were propagandizing that day, from consumer goods to ideas that support the agenda of those corporations. I am not arguing that any of this exposure 'causes' anything in particular. I am arguing that the virtually complete blanketing of all types of 'information' predisposes our children to do or not to do this or that. There is, of course, the possibility that some children will pay no attention to any of it. Even so, how many? The hard reality is that overwhelmingly most of our children will be influenced, in one way or another in their conduct, by these texts, audio and visual messages and far too little of it has encouraged them to think critically about anything. All of it, whether expressly or inferentially, has been wittingly designed to instill in them a certain prepackaged set of activities (shopping) or set of ideas (corporate), or attitudes (self-serving), or aspirations (climb the corporate ladder), or dreams (live in a mansion), *etc.*

If children's minds are 'colonized' by hundreds of corporate-sanctioned messages as proposed here, then how does that affect their ability to consider or accept anything other than what they already 'know', because they hear/read/view the way things are on a regular basis on their smart phones? They become virtual *automata*, to whom any introduction of critical ideas or ways of understanding are 'strange' or 'foreign' and hence, either too difficult to sort out or not worth their attention. One of the issues here is that sound bites received on these 'little boxes' are ahistorical and decontextualized. Kids cannot make connections between and among phenomena, because transmissions are treated as 'stand-alone', independent fragments, without any need to place them in some reasonable context. As a result, children do not even strive to connect any of this. Maybe there is no connection, but, they don't know because they do not have the conceptual tools to unpack such data. That is what school is supposed to do; without proper instruction, they are abandoned, left behind. Whoever disseminates these bits and pieces of anything is not interested in 'informing' children; they are only interested in being able to report to their superiors as how many individuals to whom they sent that tidbit of

264 Left Behind

information and whether any of them purchased a given product. That's it. There is no interest in getting real information to them. That would take too long. In fact, the less they know about anything, the easier it is to train them to follow directions about what to do, where to go, what to buy – the real goal of any form of propaganda. If they, the media corporations, fill up our day with frivolous bits of 'entertaining' nonsense, as I have argued they do, our attention is misdirected. Instead, with good, critical learning in our schools, we would pay attention to the malevolent lengths to which many businesses go to confuse or obfuscate what they are really up to – galvanizing their control over the minds of our kids so that they are compliant and unquestioning and acquiescent to the 'free market' and oblivious to the sometimes criminal machinations of these companies; so that all they think about is what to buy next. Under these circumstances, our students realize that what they are doing is not in their own interest.

This scenario must stop, and we have the conceptual tools to do it. Once students are apprised of the common sense ways to question what they are confronted with every day, they will be able to fair much better when it comes to making decisions about all sorts of things, academic and practical. I am not arguing that there is a 'conspiracy' at every turn to confuse and control the minds of our children. However, being aware that there are some conspiracies operating out there that manipulate their thinking will position them to be prepared to face some of those potential pitfalls. Progressively, they will learn to manage each next would-be trap and sort out its logic and move beyond it. Our children deserve to be warned about these matters and given the tools to manage them accordingly.

Critical thinking

I save this discussion for last to highlight its most foundational importance. As I discussed in the chapter on the mass media and recapitulated here, our children's minds are 'colonized' by the misinformation that is bombarding us constantly by the corporate media. At the same time, there is still a concerted effort on the part of organized education not to make 'critical thinking' (CT) part of the *curriculum*.[15] Instead, those educational institutions provided a plethora of sustained exposure to the advertising of Channel One or the ubiquitous and unending access to 'social media' in the form of phones, tablets and laptop computers. On balance, students are virtually always besieged by the likes of the corporate media to buy, buy, buy or to believe, accept and consume, at face value, the junk, whether advertising, programming or 'news'.

Efforts to bring CT to our children must be made relatively early on, say the 4th grade, once they have been introduced to the concepts necessary to engage in CT. The program I taught for 20 years was developed by Richard Paul and Linda Elder of the Foundation for Critical Thinking, one of whose slogans is: "Excellence in

---

15 See Chapter 9 for my discussion about critical thinking.

Orwell's nightmare achieved **265**

thought, however, must be systematically cultivated".[16] One of their definitions: "Critical thinking is the art of analyzing and evaluating thinking with a view to improving it."[17] That means that CT does not just happen to us or appear in our discourse like a rainstorm or the wind. No, critical thinking skills are conceptually based and, as such, must be studied and learned. In addition, they must be practiced, not only in school, but throughout the varied domains of life. Over time, with diligent effort, they become stronger and more adaptable to multiple contexts. Because our children are not introduced to CT in the early years, they continue to be at a disadvantage once they enter high school and college. Without some knowledge of the principles of critical thinking, students' minds are ripe for the picking by the nonsense perpetuated by the corporate media and by those educational systems that espouse myopic and reactionary platitudes. The propaganda machine in the U.S. is the best oiled in the world and takes its toll on our children every day. The critical faculties that our children have, which must be developed, are suppressed by the consumer mentality.

Of all the different topics which relate to a new paradigm for education, the most important component that must change is: *we must begin to teach critical thinking*. This would truly be a *subversive act*. Those who wield power do not want a population that thinks for itself. One of the most fundamental reasons that things do not change for the better for ordinary people is because ordinary people are not taught how to take charge of their own thinking. Instead, they are lulled into a false complacencies; they are told to let the 'leaders' take care of things, precisely what President G.W. Bush told people right after the attacks on the Twin Towers on September 11, 2001: "and I encourage you to go shopping more". To be fair, the president was trying to tell us that we should not allow the horrors of the attacks to interrupt our daily routines to the point that we would become paralyzed. Fair enough. However, it is telling that he chose to convey that kind of sentiment in reference to what people actually do respond to in the United States, consumerism. True to the essential 'soul' of a consumer society, shopping is what people know how to do best. This observation is not an accident; it is 'inbred' in the United States.

This is unacceptable at a time when we witness multiple violent conflicts due to the intransigence of global leaders, the highest disparity in income distribution in decades due to the greed among the wealthy and the collusion of the corporate and political institutions and the growing instability of working people due to job loss, health care erosion and despair about their future. We need children who mature into people who ponder the conditions around them, who question the people who are supposed to lead them, for whom they presumably voted. Collectively, they can change the world for the better: actually to force their leaders to deal with

---

16 2011 Foundation for Critical Thinking pamphlet for their 31st Annual International Conference on Critical Thinking, p. 2; also at www.criticalthinking.org.

17 *Ibid.*

climate change, to force their leaders to abandon fossil fuel and adopt sustainable wind and solar power, to force their leaders to cooperate with one another, to force their leaders to create the economic and political environment that provides the necessary conditions to support the poor, the sick, the elderly and the children, globally and a host of other very important goals. In addition they must act directly to affect these changes and not rely only on their leaders. That kind of work requires that they be taught critical mindedness and that they become critical minded. Once they take control of their thinking, which will liberate them from the constraints of outside influence, all the rest, in spite of the struggle that lies ahead, will be much easier to achieve in the long run.

Bibliography

Clarke, J.H. (2011) *Christopher Columbus and the African Holocaust: Slavery and the Rise of European Capitalism*. Hunlock Creek, PA: EWorld.

Foundation for Critical Thinking. (n.d.) Retrieved from www.criticalthinking.org

Foundation for Critical Thinking (2011) 31st Annual International Conference on Critical Thinking, p. 2.

Minnesota AFL-CIO (November 29, 2010). "'Right to Work' Laws: Get the Facts". Retrieved from www.mnaflcio.org/updates/right-work-laws-get-facts

National Right to Work Legal Defense Foundation. (n.d.) "Right to Work Frequently Asked Questions". Retrieved from www.nrtw.org/right-to-work-frequently-asked-questions

Noble, G. (June 13, 1982) *Like It Is*. New York: WABC.

Orwell, G. (1961) *1984*. New York: Signet Classic.

Van Sertima, I. (2003) *They Came Before Columbus: The African Presence in Ancient America*. New York: Random House.

POSTSCRIPT

What to do?

— Provide equal, high quality, public education for all our children by energizing local, state and federal grass-roots direct action to influence legislative decision-making.

The reader will recall that I began the discussions in this book by delineating, in the Introduction, the five major structural dimensions in all societies, namely: the cultural, the social, the economic, the political and the ideological dimensions. I shall take each one of these, in turn, and make some further comments on and offer some recommendations for how to address their role in the mismanagement of our educational system.

Before I do that, I would like to comment briefly upon a methodology for change which is demonstrating its viability in the face of significant odds. I am referring to the work of the Community Environmental Legal Defense Fund, an organization co-founded by Thomas Linzey,[1] an environmental attorney. Linzey enlightens us about how communities can challenge corporate fracking operations, factory farming and the like, as well as the governmental protectionist laws that legalize their moving into communities. Many communities have successfully challenged these kinds of big business encroachments by guiding townships in passing legislation against corporate and government laws. One strategy they have deployed is the simple declaration that the ecosystems that are in jeopardy have rights; they

---

1 Linzey is author of *Be the Change: How to Get What You Want in Your Community*. The CELDF mission: "We work to preserve the natural systems on which all life depends." See www.edf.org/our-mission-and-values.

268 Left Behind

are rights–possessing phenomena and, as such, are conferred protections that supersede those rights accorded business interests.

One example of this kind of challenge that Linzey talks about in his presentations has to do with the "corporate charter movement".

> It's an understanding [the corporate charter, PLJ] that our activism is limited in the United States. We're, in essence, placed into a box, which is limited by something called 'corporate rights'. Corporations today have the same constitutional rights as you or I, but because of their wealth, of course, they can exercise those rights to a greater extent. So, even though you and I have First Amendment rights and Fourth Amendment rights and the Bill of Rights protections under the U.S. system of law, corporations have those rights too … we can't build a[n] … environmentally, economically, sustainable system if our activism is defined for us within that box. And so, we need to break out of that box somehow; and, one of the most amazing things about this/these particular community built rights, which is being amended into the Spokane City home rule charter is that it actually deals with that, declaring, in that bill of rights, that corporations don't have rights that can actually exceed those rights of people within the city of Spokane.[2]

Some 13 or more municipal and township communities have amended their existing charters/constitutions/home rule structures with bills of rights to protect their people from corporate encroachment. One controversy has been about the water in Alfred, ME (and several other towns in Maine), where Nestlé has been taking thousands of gallons of water from those sources and selling it as Poland Spring water, at huge profits. Those aquifers are part of the commons, as discussed in this book, and, as such, belong to the people, not corporations. Some of these townships are actively challenging this condition to oust Nestlé and return the water to the people. The strategy, described by Linzey, can apply here to establish a bill of rights that can foreclose on corporate mischief or challenge existing control over local resources of water by Nestlé.

Another example is the Dakota Access Pipe Line (DAPL) at Standing Rock, ND, which has been challenged by 'water protectors' (a categorial phrase deliberately chosen to distinguish them from 'protestors') of the Standing Rock Sioux Tribe (and many others from around the country) beginning in September 2016 and continuing. The demonstrations were met with violence from the Morgan County Sheriff Department.[3] Along with the demonstrations at Standing Rock, petitions were filed to challenge and disavow the construction permits. What is at stake in this action is to 'deny the easement' permit that was based upon the 'rights'

---

2 Interview with Linzey (2009) on www.democracynow.org, April 21, 2009.
3 See comprehensive coverage of these events by www.democracynow.org from September 4, 2016, and following.

Postscript **269**

of the Energy Transfer Partners corporation and replace the permit with a decree that reasserts the rights of the people. Part of the 'rights' of DAPL is based upon the purchase of the land upon which the pipeline is being built. The land that Energy Transfer Partners bought from a rancher is disputed as 'indigenous' land belonging to the Standing Rock Sioux Tribe. Hence, the sale of the land is in question too and, because the permit to build is predicated on the ownership of that land, the sale itself must be nullified, again in the interest of the rights of people, thereby setting aside the 'rights' of the corporation to buy the land in the first place. As of July 2017, these matters, with stops and starts, have still not been resolved. These are examples of how direct action is necessary to protect people from the actions of corporations, often not in the interest of people but of profits and often to the detriment of *the first LAW*, the protection of Land, Air and Water.

While this idea of community bills of rights was developed in the context of protecting communities from direct corporate shenanigans that affect ecosystems, economic viability and the quality of land, air and water, pollutions of all kinds, I want to suggest that this construct could be an efficacious avenue of pursuit to address the different intrusions by those in economic power, who influence the policies that our education institutions are mandated to follow. Such influence should come from the people whose children have to attend those schools, through their *bona fide* boards of education, whose members should be or have been teachers, not ones whose interests lie with corporate greed and/or political ideologies.

I have been advocating that control over our educational policies be kept in the hands of local actors, people who live in those school districts and send their children to those schools. I do not mean by this that local actors can do whatever they want. In fact, taken without caveats and overall guidelines, this attitude could prove problematic, if not dangerous: witness the decisions made by the Texas school board (*e.g.*, eliminating instruction of evolution and replacing it with creationism). The reason those decisions were/are problematic is because they violate the 'Establishment Clause' of the First Amendment or the separation of church and state.[4] In other words, people 'on the ground' cannot be advancing ideas/changes/policies that reflect their personal beliefs; those are fine for those individuals, but have no place in decision making about public education or any other issue in the *secular state* we claim to have in the United States. A federal/national set of guidelines must be adopted, a template upon which to craft any education policies that are befitting any particular community. With the guidance of local school boards, whose members are teachers, or former teachers, well-trained and committed to

---

4 While the phrase: "separation of church and state" does not appear in the rubric of the Constitution, it is clear that the body whose main task is to interpret the Constitution, the Supreme Court, has used that phrase, most notably in the decision of *Everson v. Board of Education* (5–4, in favor of the BOE, 10 February, 1947), stating that "the clause against establishment of religion by law was intended to erect 'a wall of separation between Church and State'" and in every ruling since. This has been the decision of the highest court in the land: that the Constitution created a 'separation of Church and State'.

adherence to well-hewn national rules, parents and interested people can work together to fashion policies that will serve their specific needs. Parents need to participate in their children's education in a meaningful way, with knowledge, insight, criticality and foresight with regard to how their school facility, program, faculty and *curricula* will be organized and implemented. Those decisions cannot be made driven by ignorance, personal opinions, superficiality, acquiescence or myopia. Education structures are artful, but they are based upon science and cannot be built on a foundation of politicized agendas or speculative impressions and preferences. There can be a meaningful cooperation between national parameters and the specific needs of all school districts. This kind of cooperation is not easy to achieve; it is hard work. It is work that is worth doing and must be done. Providing for national 'standards', without the detailed effort necessary to achieve the highest outcomes for all districts, is an exercise in futility. All educational contexts are not the same. However, all of our children must have the equal opportunity to achieve the multiple educational components they will need to embark upon a life well informed, with a depth and breadth of understanding and with confidence.

Remedies for the complicated troubles our public education system suffers are just as complicated. There are no 'silver bullets' that can target problems in short order and no 'well-paved roads' ahead that facilitate or welcome us on this most difficult journey. The layers of cultural, social, economic, political and ideological traditions, prejudices and stubbornness are multifarious and stand most obviously in the path of change and enlightenment about the quality and sustainability of our children's education.

By now, the reader will have understood that correcting the educational system in the United States cannot be a matter of reforming this or that, here and there. It cannot be a matter of replacing the people in positions of power here and there. It cannot be a matter of filling in this noticeable *lacuna* here and removing that abuse there. It cannot be a matter of firing this teacher and hiring that one. It cannot be a matter of purging this item in the *curriculum* here and including that one there. It cannot be a matter of appealing to this or that expert committee to advise us about this or that problem evident in this or that community. These actions should and will take place, but it cannot be a matter of thinking that doing anything piecemeal will bring any real change. Change will be incremental, but work for change must proceed on all fronts.

What must take place are comprehensive, deep-rooted and radical changes that start with the notion that our children are not 'property' to manipulate in this or that manner and to commodify for the purposes of profit-making. We must reclaim the posture that they are persons with rights. Only by adopting that attitude can we begin to rebuild what we all agree, regardless of political persuasion, religious belief or sexual orientation, must be available to our children. I have written about this attitude as requiring a 'paradigm shift', change that must come from the depth of our being. As in all movements, we must know what we want to change and what we propose that change to be.

I have organized the following presentation in hierarchical terms, lending more weight to one over another dimension. Hence, the discussion runs from the economic (in which funding public education must be a priority), to the political (in which our elected officials must be reoriented to the needs of our children and ordinary people must take charge to make changes with or without those elected officials), to the ideological (in which the information systems must be transformed to address educational problems in the interest of our children), to the social (in which protection of the commons must be secured and discriminatory practices eradicated) and finally to the cultural (in which, as a major component thereof, education itself must hold the highest place). However, this does not mean that the issues in the economic dimension should be addressed first exclusively. No, all issues must be addressed simultaneously. The hierarchy only highlights the general order in which progress must be made along the way, *i.e.*, efforts in any other dimension will always be hampered as long as funding is not properly applied to education. Then again, progress in any direction may influence the fundamental funding problem. Therefore, efforts must be expended in all directions at the same time.

In no way are the following proposals to be understood as '*the* solutions' to the massive obstacles standing in our way toward the changes that have to be made if we really want to reestablish and reassert our charge to provide our children with the best education possible. Change can only obtain, cooperatively, in and through the local, regional, state and federal struggles conducted by the people in those contexts. The people make changes as they engage the problems in their communities and work to revitalize our commons, to build constructive policies to support public education and to work towards a sustainable practice for our children. The following sections discuss some of the issues in each dimension and offer recommendations to address them. You will notice how closely related they are as you read through them on the broad subject of education.

The economic dimension

Predictably, the economic dimension is the most critical in our discussion, not because it possesses some essential primacy over the others, but because, without the proper funding for our schools and education writ large, very little of what I have proposed in this book will come to pass. Educational funding is ludicrous, *i.e.*, ~6% for education versus ~60% for war machines; this, because politicians, well-funded by the military industrial complex, have allotted overwhelmingly disproportional funds to them at the expense of domestic social services.

Who controls the funding? Government officials, elected and not, from the federal to the local levels control funding for all services. Who controls them? Corporate entities of all kinds, witnessing the electoral rules in place (*Citizens United v. FEC* and *McCutcheon v. FEC*, both Supreme Court decisions) that allow for huge private contributions to candidates for public office. That translates into an inordinate amount of influence on the part of the private sector. The assumption here is not that corporations do not care about education, it is that corporations care much more about making profits from government-approved projects and securing subsidies for themselves from public coffers, while funding for public responsibilities are truncated.

The lack of funding is the root cause of the crumbling state of public education in the United States. When funding is based upon the real estate taxation rates of communities, inequality in education is guaranteed. Poorer communities will not be able to sustain the cost of even 'adequate' instruction. In overpopulated urban areas, while their tax base may be arguably larger, the individual contributions are smaller and they continue to have budget appropriation shortfalls because the sheer number of students is overwhelming. Wealthy communities will always have the best available everything: physical plants, books, instructional facilities, sports equipment, music, dance, art, *etc.*, even though the humanities are always slated to be cut first in all communities. This system is, at its root, unfair and undemocratic. As I express the need for fundamental change, if these matters are not addressed and changed to accommodate all children in all communities, the material conditions of learning will never meet the challenge of equal, high-quality public education for all.

Private education has different problems, which can be substantial, but, as we are addressing the problems with public education, I only comment here. Tuition is virtually always charged for attendance in these schools and instruction programs are often supported by corporations or foundations or religious organizations of various kinds. Also, these schools are only bound in the broadest ways by *curricula* policies handed down by departments of education in those communities (*e.g.*, while teachers in private schools must also obtain an ongoing number of CEU's [continuing education units] each year, they still escape the 'certification' requirements mandatory for teachers in public schools). Their *curricula* reflect the priorities of those organizations and follow belief systems that may be at odds with the public sector. Their only mandate is to meet accreditation minimums.

Challenging the socio-cultural responsibilities of 'public' education, the attempts afoot either to replace public schools with private ones, or to support private education with public dollars, or to implement 'voucher' systems, are not acceptable. These are the goals of the 'charter school' movement taking hold since President Obama was elected and advanced by his Secretary of Education, Arne Dunken, and now by Donald Trump's billionaire Secretary of Education, Betsy DeVos, whose efforts are already moving our educational policies even further toward the privatization of our public schools. These efforts should be vigorously rejected. Private schools can do whatever they want, within the guidelines of the Department of Education – an institution currently in jeopardy – as long as they are not funded by *public* dollars. Those funds belong to the public, not private enterprises.

Funding should continue to come from a coordination of resources, local, state and federal, with the proviso that all schools have whatever funding they need to deliver the same quality of education across the country. This means that, whatever the specific needs any community might have, whether they be physical plant, grounds, maintenance, transportation, teachers, *curriculum* development, administrators, library, program facilities (science, language, practical training, *etc.*), project-based learning, books and all other resources and implements, funds from the larger contexts should be disbursed to satisfy potential shortfalls so that all communities possess all the means necessary to deliver the same high-quality education for all our children. When such policies, indeed laws, are enacted, at least from the economic standpoint, education inequality could virtually disappear.

For example, take the school system that is in an urban setting, where most poor families reside. Most of those people are renting; they do not own a house. Landlords are likely to charge more than the apartments are worth because the taxes are relatively higher than the surrounding communities. However, the appropriation for education does not reflect that rate. In other words, those urban communities will require more funding than their more affluent neighbors. It should not matter in which community people live; it only matters that all that is needed be provided. In more wealthy neighborhoods, less will be needed to complement and so on. This will not eradicate the preferential treatment that privileged people will always have, but it will elevate the circumstances of disadvantaged people to the level that the wealthy already enjoy with regard to education.

This scheme extends to all post-secondary educational institutions, not only colleges and universities. All trades schools and training programs that are not 'for-profit' should also be funded by the tax base. Regardless of vocational or professional direction, our children should be provided with the same vigor of financial support as students in public colleges. All of these avenues of life's work should hold equal status with regard to funding what is necessary for preparing our youngsters for their chosen field of occupation. No students should be left outside this system of funding for their advancement and enlightenment.

While high-quality education must be thought of as a social expenditure, not an endeavor for profit-making, that education should stay 'public' and not merge with corporate interests, even while they remain public in name. For example, public universities should not enter into *partnerships* with businesses which commit them to doing their bidding. If corporations contribute to public educational institutions, because they want to be 'good citizens', that is fine. However, it should never become a *quid pro quo*. Unfortunately, that is precisely what has developed over the years. These kinds of relationships compromise the educational goals of any institution by influencing decision-making at all levels, which compromises the character of what we are charged with as professors: protected by academic freedom, delivering education that is independent of moneyed, special interests. It also undermines the honesty of research findings when those dollars fund specific studies undertaken by the faculties of those public universities. Public dollars should flow directly to education, not to corporations in the form of subsidies (corporate welfare) and then to education in the form of partnerships that further benefit corporations.

On another side, these economic realities affect students in a personal, direct and lasting manner. Because public higher education is not tuition-free any more (in-state, land-grant institutions, which were tuition-free in the beginning, are now all charging tuition), overwhelmingly most students are forced to take out loans to attend college. These loans must be paid off once they graduate, at the rate of between $400 and $800 per month; and, if the student moves on to graduate school, that monthly amount will rise. This is a major flaw in the rhetoric of the 'American Dream'. Students are told that, in order to get a 'good job' and 'succeed', they must have a college degree. To do that, most of them must take out loans (grants are difficult to obtain due to the tough criteria; only the top students have access to such funds), which they have to repay once they graduate. However, the 'good jobs' that were promised do not exist for the most part, leaving most graduates in low-paying jobs, which cannot sustain the level of monthly payback that the lenders require. Even if students can negotiate lower monthly payments, they do this to their detriment because they only extend the debt into their middle life, because the interest which is applied only exacerbates the obligation. This is more like a nightmare, not a 'dream'. All education should be free of tuition and, in the meantime, all student debt should be 'forgiven'; students should be 'bailed out' just like the banks were in 2007–2008. Any further loans students may need should be interest-free and paid back at a rate that is commensurate with their earning capacity (say, 1% *per annum* to start), not according to some actuarial chart.

If we understand that delivering public education is the responsibility of our society, then we must also understand that such a project is a social expenditure to which the people and their representatives must be committed. While not all of the problems facing us in our corrective attempts will 'go away' just because we take the appropriate measures to ensure funding for equal, high-quality public education for all our children, we will be taking a major step toward those goals, which will lay the foundation for the other accompanying institutional challenges which also lie ahead.

The political dimension

I argue in this book that our children have rights, not only the unalienable ones ("life, liberty and the pursuit of happiness"), but also *human* ones guaranteed by organizations such as the United Nations and by U.S. Supreme Court case law that have arisen as a result of challenges to those rights. There is no controversy about these claims, in principle. What has eroded these fundamental rights is the enactment of laws to protect special interests. 'Black' people were not accorded basic human rights, which led to their enslavement and oppression. Women were not accorded basic human rights, relegated to subordinate placement in society. It was not until the 'laws' that put them in those positions were challenged, and defeated, that fundamental change took place. Protests of all types shine light on bad laws, but do not change them. Changing laws requires a concerted effort to replace laws that do not respect the fundamental rights and dignity of people with laws that do.

A basic democratic principle is that the people are able to elect representatives to carry on the full-time work of government, in the name of the people and in the interest of the people. This is part of the rubric of our Constitution. However, these days, more than any time in our history, government is conducted *in our name* (or maybe not; more and more special interests become more transparent), but *not in our interest*. Instead, each branch of government, our three estates, has been acting in favor of the wealthy or corporations. Especially since 1991, war, invasions and occupations (most notably Afghanistan and Iraq) have preoccupied our elected representatives. Despite the extraordinary cost of such illegal adventures, according to international law, and costs both in terms of lives and public funds, the corporate beneficiaries line up for their 'no bid' contracts, whether they be bomb-producers and other weapons of mass destruction merchants or mercenary corporations, to which are paid exorbitant per capita wages, or the companies which are poised to do this or that project to provide water and food for our troops or the construction companies which salivate at the prospect of any 'reconstruction' projects after the devastation has been delivered. All of these are part of the "military industrial complex" that President Eisenhower warned us about during his Farewell Address on January 17, 1961.

In the Executive Branch, most notably the presidency, then occupied by George W. Bush, not elected by the people, operated with impunity when he invaded Afghanistan (October 7, 2001, and counting under Obama and Trump) and Iraq (March 19, 2003, and officially terminated by President Obama on December 18, 2011; but with continued 'presence' numbering some 16,000 *personnel*, some troops some not, in the largest 'embassy' on the planet, $750 million to build on approximately one-half square kilometer). Under Donald Trump, the Pentagon and Secretary of Defense James Mattis have been given *carte blanche* to make 'in theatre' decisions in Afghanistan and Syria. The proposed increase in the number of troops in Afghanistan, with some 8,400 there already, is 1,000 to 3,000. Approval by Trump is still pending due to the controversy over whether to protract the occupation/war or to 'get out' of the longest war in American history. The point here is that these issues still occupy the minds of our country's leaders more than the delivery of social services to our people, including education.

The invasion of Afghanistan was presumably to seek retribution for the attacks on the Twin Towers on September 11, 2001; this with the immediate knowledge that most of the official perpetrators of the attacks were Saudis, not Afghanis. The invasion of Iraq was prosecuted on the basis of lies from Bush about 'weapons of mass destruction' (absent since 1998) and claims that Saddam Hussein was connected with 'Al Qaida' (absurd *prima facie* as Hussein was Suna and Al Qaida is Shia). The cost of these invasions and the subsequent occupations have been estimated to be $1–3 trillion. These are the expensive criminal acts that the Executive Branch has perpetrated upon the people of Afghanistan and Iraq, the results of which are hundreds of thousands of deaths and the spread of depleted uranium, and the people of the United States, the results of which have been thousands of deaths and domestic funding cuts for social services and education. Hence, the political dimension has been responsible for the extraordinary increase in discretionary funds for the purposes of prosecuting two invasions and occupations (with other military operations elsewhere) at the expense of domestic programs and responsibilities.

276 Left Behind

More than one-half of all discretionary funds has gone, and continue to go, to the Pentagon to support the slavish maintenance of these military operations.

The Legislative Branch has been complicit in the support for these illegal and criminal 'wars'. Our elected members of Congress have funded, time after time, these misadventures, in our name but against the overwhelming dissent of the people. Most egregiously and within the fever of the Neo-Con Project for the New American Century, they passed the USA Patriot Act in 2001, sacking many of our hard-fought liberties, many of which are encapsulated in the Miranda decision:[5] the right to remain silent, the right to an attorney free of charge, *etc.*, the Sixth Amendment to the Constitution, protecting our right to privacy and guaranteeing us due process of law and against search and seizure without probable cause, the Fourth Amendment, securing our right to a fair trial including the writ of *habeas corpus, etc.* This Act was passed in a frenzy of fear after the attacks and a culture of fear was perpetuated by the Bush Administration throughout the 2000s and continues today, under the mantra of global 'terrorism' lurking behind every corner and with pronouncements about a 'war on terrorism' necessary to protect us. In the midst of this hype, domestic responsibilities fell by the wayside, among them education.

Our representatives sold us out to a decade-long, and counting, frenzy of spending that has devastated the country in terms of infra-structure (our roads and bridges, our public transportation, our parks and forests, our ports, sea and air, our water, our air and our land are either inadequate, broken or contaminated), health care (some 50 million people do not have adequate care and another 100 million do not have proper coverage in spite of having insurance), education (schools are closing down or stand in disrepair or the 'commons' are being violated through privatization or *curricula* are being assaulted by ignorant and politically motivated boards of education, whose allegiance is to corporate interests or religious sensitivities) and social services (dwindling aid to families and single parents, incarceration of children for minor offences because of low-priority legal services) all of which currently suffer dire needs.

Politicians ignore these shortfalls, indeed the gutting of educational funding, resulting in inferior educational practice and claim that schools are 'failing' because they are 'public'. This absurd, knee-jerk perspective has no basis. Actually, 'private' schools are not doing any better; *i.e.*, replacing public schools with charter schools (private schools), does not necessarily make them any better than existing public schools, this in spite of the private and public funding made available to them.

The politics of education has never been more evident in public discourse, often in the person of a particular representative or representative body. When books are banned, as in the most recent case in Tucson, AZ,[6] academic freedom, won through long and costly struggle, in terms of human suffering and the waste of

---

5 *Miranda v. Arizona*; U.S. Supreme Court 5–4 decision rendered June 13, 1966.
6 One of the books banned in Tucson is the very book that informs the philosophical position taken in this book: *Op. cit.* Paulo Freire's *Pedagogy of the Oppressed.*

Postscript **277**

money, is in jeopardy. Stewardship over the *curricula* we teach our children shifts from the hands of qualified educators to the whims of politicians whose interests do not rest with principles of critical thinking and a practice of teaching which liberates students, but with the special interests of business or narrow-minded agenda, whether classist or religious or corporate or racist or sexist or homophobic. Because the overwhelming majority of our representatives, both Senate and House, are 'bought' by 'big money', they pledge allegiance to their corporate lords, not the flag and the people of the states represented in that flag.[7] Worse, when political parties seek to obstruct discourse and negotiation in the wells of Congress, they violate the very premise that laws are the means to rule the nation, not 'bullying' and 'obstruction', whether it be the filibuster in the Senate, or the refusal of the Speaker in the House to bring a motion or bill to a vote, or the signing of a 'pledge' to Grover Norquist "never to raise taxes", or to do anything, which Republicans have done during the Obama presidency, to embarrass, to denigrate and to disagree only for the purpose of, in the words of Senate Majority Leader Mitch McConnell "making Obama a one-term President". Now, we have Trump!

The Supreme Court, in *Bush v. Gore*, one of the most egregious decision in our history,[8] violated the Tenth Amendment, which secures elections in the hands of the states (something which is very problematic and wrong, but a discussion for another time). That decision effectively gave the election to Bush, because of the Florida vote, in spite of the fact that Gore received almost 544,000 more votes than Bush, or 48.38% vs. 47.87% of the popular vote, respectively. Incidentally, this scenario was repeated in the 2016 election: Clinton received some 2.8 million more votes than Trump, or 48.2% vs. 46.1% of the popular vote, respectively. We do not need the 'Russians' to tamper with our elections; we have been doing that very well at least since 2000 all on our own. However, the popular votes does not count when you have an arcane structure, the Electoral College, in place to trump (pun intended) the results. While our elected officials are busy tampering with our elections, *e.g.*, voter suppression *et al.*, and doing the bidding of the elite, they are not taking care of the people who elected them.

Moreover, the Supreme Court has given organizations, corporations, unions and 'super pacs' the green light to 'donate' unlimited funds to candidates for public office without disclosure. This was partly argued because corporations were accorded 'personhood' by the high court. Guess which institution will take the most

---

7 About flags – Trump falsely attributed professional sports players (NFL, NBA, MLB) taking a knee during the national anthem as disrespecting the American flag, the weekend of September 22, 2017. Not so; they were protesting the injustice that has manifest over the last ten years, in particular, with the police killings of black men and women.

8 The U.S. Supreme Court 5–4 decision, *Bush v. Gore*, December 12, 2000, settled that election in favor of George W. Bush; this in the tradition of elections resting in the authority of the states and taking away the franchise for voters. This, at that time, may have been the most egregious decision of the Supreme Court; however, the 'Citizens United' case trumps it because it lays down a continuous set of rules for how elections will proceed. The *Bush v. Gore* case decided a single discrete matter.

278 Left Behind

advantage of this? The decision in this case, referred to as "Citizens United",[9] cuts to the core of voting rights in the United States. In addition, the Supreme Court's McCutcheon[10] decision has lifted the limits on aggregate contributions to campaigns, thereby augmenting the amount that can be donated to candidates.

Our *vote* has deteriorated over the years. We already only 'ratify' candidates for election according to whom the corporate media parade before us. Now, funding for candidates in the interest of corporations will be maximized, while other candidates, funded by ordinary people at much lower rates, may receive less than adequate support to run proper campaigns. However, Bernie Sanders proved that comment at least partially wrong with his strong run in 2016.

With this kind of Supreme Court decision-making, empowering private, corporate influence in public affairs, how can we rely on our 'elected' representatives to understand and support the kind of education advocated in this book? We cannot. These kinds of decisions constitute a U-turn away from the direction we must pursue if we want to transform the practice of education and secure a viable future for our children. The most dangerous efforts to influence education in the United States are from corporations which want to privatize schools, all schools, so that they can have a direct hand in decision-making at all levels and of all kinds. If we are in trouble today with regard to corporate meddling in education, and we are, if this is the kind of 'justice' meted out by our highest courts in the land (and we can await more from them with the installation of Neil Gorsuch, April 10, 2017, as the new Justice of the Supreme Court), we can only expect that the 'commons' will continue to be co-opted or abducted by the powerful and single-mindedness of those who would transform everything in terms of the profit motive.

From a broad political vantage point, then, we are in dire need of a system which is sensitive and responsive to the needs of our people and, in particular, of those we cherish most, our children. If their education is challenged, at every turn, by the self-serving performance of our government officials, then the people must rise to meet that challenge and struggle to change that institution so that we will not only meet the needs of the people, but also work to create the circumstances necessary to enhance the conditions of life in general and of education in particular. This

---

9 This U.S. Supreme Court 5–4 decision, *Citizens United v. Federal Election Commission*, January 21, 2010, has already affected the 2010 mid-term elections and continues to in the 2012 elections with an unprecedented flow of money from 'super pacs' and multibillionaires. This decision may not stand long; the Montana Supreme Court, on December 30, 2011, in a 5–2 decision, challenged the 'Citizens United' decision and restored a 100-year tradition that banned direct corporate contributions to candidates in state elections. We await further challenges.

10 This U.S. Supreme Court 5–4 decision, *McCutcheon v. Federal Election Commission*, April 2, 2014, has also affected the 2014 mid-term election and the 2016 presidential election. There is mounting opposition to Citizens United and McCutcheon in the form of an amendment to the Constitution, along with many other changes that are needed on the subject of elections in general, including campaign financing, *etc.*; however, as long as Trump is in the White House and the Republican Party controls the House and Senate, there is little chance that such an Amendment will come to the floors of Congress, let alone pass as the Twenty-Eighth Amendment to the Constitution.

means that people must engage in the *politics* of their lives. They must organize to work for the conditions that their representatives will not. They must, in the varied contexts from the local to the global, take action either to force their representatives to do their bidding, as in Wisconsin throughout 2011, or take direct action, as in the Occupy Movement, making people aware of the shortcomings and failures of our elected officials and taking steps toward the corrective measures necessary to change the status quo into sets of rules or laws or codes that will galvanize the way toward a true security of our public lives.

Something that would go a long way to correct much of what I have highlighted above is election campaign reform that would change the way elections are conducted. Because current election laws rest at the state level, we must change some of them to streamline national elections. We must abolish the Electoral College and the concept of the 'delegates'; officials must be elected via popular vote. This would eliminate the contradictory voting of delegates; delegates are not always required to vote with the people in their delegation, thereby negating the popular vote of that constituency. We must pass a Twenty-Eighth Constitutional Amendment that would change election campaign laws and level the playing field for political candidates for federal, state and local office. Here are a baker's dozen:

- Repeal Citizens United and McCutcheon Supreme Court decisions.
- Redistricting must be limited and meticulously monitored by an independent agency, disconnected from the government, any political party and candidate, thereby eliminating the practice of 'gerrymandering'.
- Voter suppression tactics must be eliminated, *e.g.*, voter-ID legislation and voter log tampering, *etc.*, and voter registration and participation must be augmented.
- The Electoral College must be abolished.
- The Tenth Amendment must be amended not to include States' control of *national* elections; those elections should be controlled by the federal government.
- We must move towards proportional representation in both houses and retire the 'winner take all' format.
- Term limits for all elected positions must be reevaluated; *e.g.*, representatives and senators should have only two six-year terms, and life-time appointments should be abolished, e.g., supreme court justices and federal judges. and should suffer elections.
- The actual legislative language for campaign reform is the job of our federal and state legislators, not the Supreme Court.
- Candidates at all levels cannot use their own money to run for office.
- A \$100.00 maximum contribution from anyone or any corporation or institution or organization; these contributions are still necessary to pay campaign staff.
- If more than \$100.00 is offered, it is shared among all candidates running.
- Broadcast and print media provide free equal time/space for all candidates as part of their public service ('public interest clause' of license), in the form of

interviews, debates (media outlets have no say in who debates whom or the content of the debate), speeches on the campaign trail and promotions.

- Airlines, trains, buses, limousines, taxis, hotels, restaurants, provide all services free to all candidates and their staffs in all states, including gratuities.
- Media, travel, food, hotel and other providers are subsidized by our tax dollars from an election campaign fund managed by Congress; those providers can write off these expenses as a loss on their tax returns.

If we eliminate the costs of campaigning and stem the flow of money from the private sector, we can minimize the power any one candidate or set of candidates can have, thereby opening up the field to all candidates. This will provide the opportunity for all of us to listen to what all candidates have to say, instead of only those 'approved' by the powerful.

One last reminder: we must restore the idea that education is part of the commons, just like water and the fire department and the public park. The institution, however flawed it may be, does belong to everyone and no one. As the ever-changing phenomenon that it is, it must be cherished and maintained so that it can serve all our children, each next generation. It is our responsibility to guarantee its good health and viability because a society without an excellent education system available to its youngsters is one which cannot engender excellent people.

The social dimension

The Civil Rights Movement of the 1960s was significant in punctuating the forms of sustained discrimination that have plagued our society – racism, sexism, ageism, speciesism – and drawing our attention to what we needed to do to minimize or eliminate such unnecessary conduct. While I limited my focused discussions to racism, incumbents of those other '-isms' will recognize how they also pertain to them. Here we are more than 50 years later and we still witness discrimination of these kinds on a daily basis. Witnessing the conduct of the so-called 'Tea Party', we observe that many of the activities allowed under the Jim Crow Laws are being replicated today, for example, targeting President Obama with convoluted epithets of being a 'Socialist' and at the same time a 'Nazi', categories which belong to opposite ends of the political spectrum. The placards held by the participants in Tea Party rallies depicted the President in vile and demonic ways. The fact that the President of the United States was a 'black' man was not only *unacceptable* to them, but worse, it was something that could not be endured. They could not stand the idea that a 'black' man lived in the White House. President Obama's election gave way for those who were predisposed to reignite racist sentiments, however latent they may be, that have always been a part of our history. Indeed, this country was built, literally, by 'black' slaves, owned by 'white' people. This form of slavery was unprecedented in history and was the beginning of racism in the world. It is disturbing that such ignorant sentiments continue to inform how we think and what we do. Even those of us who may abhor racism, and even fight against it, breathe

Postscript **281**

it every day like everyone else. Of course, 'black' and brown folk suffer its effects much more than 'white' folk do. Accordingly, this racist reality poisons everything about our society. As many of us have observed, there has been a significant denunciation of racism in interpersonal relations by our young people. Racist thinking does not seem to have taken hold with them like it has in previous generations. However, our institutions have not followed that lead and institutional racism continues to affect the proper delivery of education to our children.

Sexism also continues to plague our reality in the United States. We still have not learned how important it is to recognize that there is very little difference between the sexes. Women are still treated as inferior to men; they are still controlled in terms of their reproductive rights (mostly by men), in spite of *Roe v. Wade*; their pay in equal jobs is still 20–30% less than that of men; their military experiences are wrought with sexual harassment if not rape; their bodies are still reduced to parts (reified) and women are paraded before us in the form of advertisements about what they should be or not be, wear or not wear, and portrayed in violent ways which allow for the mind to accept that women are expendable and useable for the pleasure or domination of men. Sexism also affects our female students in schools. Even with the best of intentions and legal changes, *e.g.*, Title IX, our schools continue to report how girls and women are seen as fundamentally *inferior* to boys and men. For example, witness how girls are treated by boys, who operate on assumptions that are misogynistic and sexist; they continue to view girls and women as objects for sexual satisfaction and, absent consent, abuse in the form of sexual assault and rape.[11] The paucity of and inconsistent sex education in our schools is putting our children at a disadvantage when it comes to sexual savvy and maturity about intersex interactions. In addition, misunderstandings of the LGBTQIA community give rise to the kind of violence we have witnessed, especially in the last two years in the case of transgender people.

Our children are so preoccupied with social media that they can barely hold a conversation with anybody without checking their little boxes or worse without being riveted to their electronic devices while social interaction is taking place; or is it taking place? With all these distractions, most of which are sound bites, seemingly the current mode of communication these days, how can our children pay attention to the important things around them? Am I correct in that there are limits on how many characters of text are allowable to transmit at one time? What this does is two things: one, it trains students to communicate within artificial parameters that satisfy the technology they are operating and two, it truncates their ability to engage in the full expression of their ideas. This translates into difficulties with oral and written discourse in the course of their daily learning. One cannot make an argument or explain anything in sound bites or 'tweets'. Learning requires discussion, not such limitations on utterances or sentences. Imagine students having

---

11 The reader is aware also of the false allegations that girls/women can bring against boys/men; while not equivocal, these false claims serve to ruin their lives as well."

282 Left Behind

to provide some discourse, say, in class that required a fulsome report on something and the student's oration would amount to a series of five- or six-word disjointed utterances instead of a flowing address on the subject. Same story in writing: a series of staccato sentences, largely disconnected which bears no resemblance to a paragraph. I am not arguing a *causal* relationship here, only a curious preoccupation that has serious consequences. This is a worrisome component of the social dimension; one which, left unaddressed, may cost us the full attention of our children in the educational setting. One partial remedy is to eliminate social media while students are *engaged in education*. At least, they would be free from this cacophony of noise as long as they are trying to learn something. I am not blaming students here; I am only pointing out that social media are a distraction from learning. This, of course, unless instruction is about social media or when part of the instruction itself requires it to fulfill the goals of the particular course of study.

One of the areas of difficulty that has emerged in the past few years is the notion that education can take place *online*; and this is primarily at the post-secondary level, but I have recently learned that K-12 on line programs are being offered by private companies. Frightening! While there is growing affinity to the implementation of these new technologies, it is worth considering what is lost in such a methodology. The imperative that is ontological to us *homo sapiens* is that we are *social*; that is, one of the most essential components of being *who we are* is that we *must* talk to one another. That is what we do to accomplish whatever it is before us. Language is the most important component of our lives; everything we do, think, *etc.*, is linguistic. That is, everything around us that we observe, interact with, create, destroy, *etc.*, is possible because of language. We cannot understand anything outside of our ability to access those things through the concepts that we develop along with acquiring and learning the language of our culture. *And*, that communication is best accomplished in person, *face-to-face*. It is from this realization that the phrase in French, having a *tête-a-tête* with someone, arises. In other words, we understand one another best when we speak *eyeball-to-eyeball* or *man-to-man* and *woman-to-woman*. These expressions are not frivolous; they mean that people are meant to converse in person. Doing so, brings people together and reduces the incidents of misrepresentation, misinterpretation, misunderstanding and confusion. Hence, we are meant to communicate, preferably, *face-to-face*. We can communicate otherwise, but they are not the most efficacious ways to achieve the best outcomes. Accordingly, while students can learn something in online courses, many of the nuances and non-verbal cues that are omnipresent in face-to-face interaction can be absent, thereby rendering such interaction considerably less than optimal when we are talking about educational interaction, something that should display the maximum of interactional components. Therefore, I fear that online education does not rise to the level of effective education and contributes to the deterioration of the teaching profession by creating the context for either the waning of teacher participation in their own profession or the elimination of teaching as a foundational necessity in any society.

Another concern is the lack of project-based education, learning that relies on interpersonal communication, the kind of communication which has primacy over any other form. This means that conversation is the first environment of communication in which we all participate. We acquire language mostly in our first two years and become linguistic by the time we reach 2 years of age. Those intimate interpersonal moments are what prepare us for the other environments of communication: thinking (we must have become linguistic in order to think), nonverbal (some of which is acquired along with the words and the rules of application), small group (requires having achieved/learned a language), public speaking (same as small group), organizational (same as small group) and the mass media (for which there is very limited 'feedback' and, as such, puts us in a more passive juxtaposition to them).

The reason I lay this out is because everything we do requires interpersonal communication. It does not matter in whichever other environment we engage, we must fundamentally participate in interpersonal communication. We hear about how the 'economy' is doing this or that; what we must realize is that the economy does not do anything, people are the *doers*. Institutions, foundations, corporations, *etc.*, do not do anything; it is the people in those domains of life who communicate with one another, have discussions, make decisions, *etc.* There is seldom only one person, the same person, talking and others only listening. No. Everything requires collaboration of some kind. So, if this makes sense, and I think it does, why do we commit our children to classroom contexts only to listen to teachers? Instead, why aren't they introduced into a collaborative and interactional context that not only requires them to be social, which is their nature, but also participate intimately in their education? I am not suggesting that all classroom situations have to be what I have expressed, but, I know that overwhelming most of them are. There is nothing wrong with some of that kind of methodology; however, project based education is much more conducive to participation on the part of students and requires of them to 'perform' learning. Discussions in class can be helpful too; however, if students find themselves in a variety of contexts other than a classroom, their attention span may increase and their interest may very well be enhanced, thereby yielding deeper insights. As you already know, I am a strong advocate for project-based education and encourage everyone who will take on some of the heavy load that changing education for our children will entail to look into how projects in your communities can become learning opportunities, not only for the sake of witnessing education in the making, but also understanding how all of the other subjects in school are embedded in all kinds of real-life situations, which can become projects to contextualize learning in the real world. Education must be connected to students' lives or they come to see learning as taking place at school, instead of all over the community. We should be seeing groups of students all over town, every day, engaged in one project or another. This enhances their learning experience many fold; they realize that they can learn from many more people than teachers: each other, the trades people, the baker, the bicycle maker, the chef, the lawyer, the police officer, the potter, the eco-system scientist and many more. And this does not diminish the teacher who plans out these projects; it makes his/her job easier and more rewarding and heightens the excitement and energy of the students. This is a major component of the social dimension and should be pursued with vigor.

284 Left Behind

Typically, high school children must board a bus from approximately 6:45 a.m. to 7:15 a.m. to arrive at school by 7:30 a.m., the beginning of their school day. At the end of their day, they board busses from approximately 2:30 p.m. and arrive home between 2:45 p.m. and 3:15 p.m. Elementary and middle school children board buses a little later in the morning and get home a little earlier after school. Let's concentrate on the high school schedule and allow the reader to extrapolate to the elementary and middle school schedules. So, for those outer-lying high school students, their day is eight-and-a-half hours long, somewhat less for their mates who live closer to school or don't take the bus at all. This seems excessive.

For more than 30 years, I polled my incoming university students on the matter of their high school experience, a very open question: "What are some of your impressions of your high school experience?" The responses I received were not as varied as we might think. There were always those idiosyncratic impressions expressed; interesting, but not what I was looking for. I was trying to obtain a more organic understanding of their impressions. In the broader context, many of their comments were about "too much homework" or "not enough time to take tests" or "having trouble getting into this or that course, because there were not enough sections offered" and more of the like. Two particular comments, expressed in different ways, really caught my attention: one was that *they spent too much time in school* and the other was that *a lot of time was wasted every week they spent in school*. Not time that they, the students, wasted (and there was plenty of that too); no, the time that was wasted during their school day, at school. It is interesting that the two most expressed comments were about the temporal factor of their experiences. Over time (pardon the pun), I came to reason that these were closely related: if there is a lot of "time wasted" in school, then it followed that they were spending "too much time" in school. Makes sense. We often dismiss the insights our children have about their own lives. Instead, we tell them just to "go to school and stop complaining; school is good for you, just go". In my view, these are missed opportunities to understand what is going on in their lives and in the institutions to which we expose them.

Please allow me to propose a broad overview of what a typical high school day could look like, which would address the "waste of time" and the "too much time" issues raised by former high school students. To start with, I agree with those hundreds of students: they spend way too much time in school. One of the reasons that it takes up so much of their time is that the *curricula* are fundamentally flawed; if properly organized, time would be much more efficiently spent and learning would be much more interesting for our children.

Arguably, the school day should be shortened. If the curricula are properly written; that is, the goals are reasonably set, the methodologies of instruction are well thought out and the parameters of learning are understood (many of which I address in this book), then we can expect that the learning day will be, realistically predictably, much more efficient and rewarding for both teachers and students. So, I propose that the school day be shortened to five hours, say, 9:00 a.m. to 2:00 p.m. (busing adding some time to this), with rotating lunch from, say, 11:30

a.m. to 12:30 p.m. (keeping in mind that students can have their lunch in some 20 minutes; the remainder of this time they are in class). Leading off with PE (no need for showers after this; these movement classes are not practices for athletics, which take place after 2:00 p.m.), followed by a light breakfast to freshen up ones constitution, moving on to the traditionally most difficult academic subjects, while reasoning potential is maximal, *e.g.*, mathematics and the sciences (the ones we do not do as well in as our CNS tires), and ending with less daunting classes, *e.g.*, art, languages and the social sciences.

First, there is too much time spent in classrooms; project based education would take them out of the classroom and into the community, according them a much broader context for learning. And, as detailed in Chapter 9, these routine outings would satisfy all of their academic requirements, while they connect their learning to the bigger context of their lives. You do not need seven or eight hours to do that.

Second, something we all know about our children: they have short spans of attention. Why not organize instruction to target, not only their *span* of attention, but also their *maximal physical and mental acuity*, when they are most receptive to learning. Hundreds of studies have shown that people are most alert mentally in the morning because their CNS (central nervous system) is at its optimum after proper repair overnight (assuming the parameters laid out in Chapter 9). Nonetheless, we observe some physical 'grogginess' that must be eliminated before effective learning can take place.

Third, that is when physical education should be scheduled, first period of instruction for students. In Japan and China, for example, all students partake in physical movement upon arrival at school. This awakens the body to allow for the best opportunities for successful learning. Once the body is enlivened, the body-mind connections are bolstered and ready for apprehension and reasoning. Then, teachers have the best scenario to bring the day's instruction to them, thereby minimizing interruptions, distractions and other modes of disruption during the learning day.

My colleagues are already railing! Of course, in order to achieve such a schedule, we would need the commitment of our five dimensions to allocate the proper funding to provide for the facilities, the faculty and staff, *etc.* in order to do this. Clearly, we do not enjoy such funding today (hence this book) and may not for some time to come (thanks to Trump and DeVos). However, we must work toward these goals so that our children can achieve their best.

There is considerable work to be done to address issues that are particular to the social dimension. As in all other dimensions, the society at large bears a huge responsibility for the troubles we observe in education. In other words, education cannot be discussed in isolation of all the influences at large in the society. While there are loads of social pressures outside of schools which must be addressed, there are also many social influences inside schools that vary from school to school. I have listed a few here, but the actual landscape of difficulties in the social arena must be identified by people in the communities and addressed according to common sense and a clear vision toward the best education we can provide for our children.

The cultural dimension

When I think of culture, I think of language, the essential requirement for culture to emerge in the first instance; when I think of cultural forms, I think of the arts: music, dance, painting, sculpture, film, *etc.*; when I think of those cultural forms in educational terms, I think of the humanities. Of all the subjects that are taught in schools, these are probably the ones that are most manifest in the everyday lives of people. That is, wherever we go each day, we will encounter the arts. What would we do without them? Our lives would suffer a great loss. The arts are where we go to please ourselves and our families and friends. They are what make us happy, especially when our jobs do not. We seek out these expressions of melody, of visual impact, of movement, *etc.*, because they accentuate our sense of ethnic belonging. It is through those cultural forms that we are reminded of who we are, where we come from, where we live and where we may be going. They represent our center (ethnocentrism); without them, life would be boring and routine.

If this is so, and I do not think that there are many who would challenge this kind of characterization, then the only reason that we continue to enjoy all of the arts is because they are taught; that is, teaching the arts is what allows them to survive and thrive. Artful expression can sometimes be observed to flow forth seemingly effortlessly, even by children, about whom we could hear said, "She is a prodigy". "He is a natural", "They are so talented". However in order to deliver sustained beauty in their art, they must participate in training and apprenticeships in the presence of lots of mentoring, if they want to become *experts*. And, it is the work of the experts that manifest all around us: the architecture we see against the sunset, the environmental art we see on our way to work or school and all the other art forms we encounter, including the very language we speak, that dynamic wonder that allows us to communicate in so many ways.

We must reestablish the foundational locus for the instruction of languages, music, dance, architecture, and all of the forms of artistic expression: painting, pottery, sculpting, photography, film, theatre, the fashioning of wood and metal, printing, cooking, *etc.* When people leave their chores and their work behind, they want to be entertained. The humanities provide that for them/us. If our children are not instructed and given an opportunity to perform these cultural expressions, how will they discover the artist within? If this is not sustained, where will people go to listen to music, to attend a play or an opera or a dance, to enjoy a painting or piece of sculpture or a photograph, to savor a culinary delight, to marvel at the design of a new building or bridge or subterranean thoroughfare? Those wonders will not be there if we continue to abandon this most important part of our children's education.

Consider my favorite topic in the humanities: foreign language instruction. As I expressed above, instruction in foreign languages has become a major problem in the delivery of cultural education. We have become lazy in the United States about requiring this kind of training. Granted, we have largely not grasped the methodologies for proper instruction in foreign languages: immersion; however, if there are no language classes in the first place, the methodology becomes moot. The programs of the past are just that *in the past*. I remember that some universities prided themselves in such instruction; Syracuse University, in particular, used to offer a litany of foreign languages and serious training. They still offer instruction in 17 different languages: the expected Indo-European ones and less expected ones like Arabic, Hindi, Farsi, Turkish, Chinese, Japanese, *etc*. I am not arguing that all public institutions carry the same level of program they do, only that we seem to have difficulty in maintaining a modest selection of foreign languages offerings. One of the ongoing problems is that, when university faculty members retire or leave, they are often not replaced because of the faulty policy that, if the language requirement is satisfied in high school, there is no cause to support a robust foreign language department. These conditions must be revisited and corrected if we want to offer our children a modicum of choice in this regard. Of course, as I also argued above, we must create a global exchange system for language instruction so that students from around the world can participate in immersion language learning around the world.

Because of the violent history we have had – the genocidal treatment of indigenous peoples, the enslavement of 'black' people, Jim Crow, labor struggles, *etc*. – which pitted one racial group against another and one ethnic group against another, the dominant 'white' population has developed, in addition to racism, a superior sense of self *vis-à-vis* other ethnic groups I have categorized as 'extreme ethnocentrism'. This is an attitude that creates division among the multiple ethnic groups that co-exist in the United States, groups our democratic experiment invited from all over the world in its beginning. Conflict arises and discrimination ensues. Such conditions persist in the United States and are tolerated in our schools, the victims of which are 'black' and brown and Asian people/students (indigenous people/ students are always in the crosshairs for this kind of treatment). These practices are not as overt as they used to be decades ago, but they are still effective; they have been institutionalized and are not expressed in personal affronts.

One of the more subtle, but very significant, ways that they suffer this discrimination is how the *curricula* are written; it often does not include the contributions of minority ethnic groups and minimizes their participation in the overall development of our country. It often leads to the attitude that has been long-standing in the United States: 'American' Exceptionalism, the extreme idea that 'Americans' are so much better than any other ethnic group as to be "exceptional". This kind of chauvinistic exclusion does not bode well for a multicultural education, something that is falsely vaunted to thrive in the United States. We must reflect upon these fundamental flaws and recreate the kind of inclusive practices and celebrate the diversity that has become so ubiquitous in the Unites States. The 'melting pot' metaphor of the past may not apply because the different ethnicities do not meld as well as implied in the metaphor; indeed, people continue to separate from one another along ethnic lines.

However, we have noticed that, in the context of different struggles – protests against the murders of young black males over the last three years in particular, the rallies to support the LGBTQIA community, the uprisings against efforts by the Republican party to repeal Obamacare, *etc.* – 'black' and brown and Latino and Asian people and those across ethnic backgrounds have collaborated to affect common goals. This is what students should know about and participate in for their enlightenment: witnessing people of all backgrounds cooperating to achieve something. Going to a rally or demonstration is an excellent example of project based education. While the Occupy Wall Street encampment was in place, I took thirteen students in my class on the subject of 'protest' there to witness what such protests entail and look like. Only two of them had been to a rally/protest before; the others had never witnessed one, in person, let alone participated. They all had to write an essay about their experience there, which counted as work for the course. There are so many opportunities to do this kind of education, regardless of the age of the students.

One last punch at standardized testing: aside from not measuring anything, these tests have been shown to be culturally biased and puts students of non-'white', non-Anglo heritage at a severe disadvantage. What with all the research on this, demonstrating the ineffectiveness of these tests, one would think that someone who is responsible for them would understand how futile these exercises are. The fact is that these tests are a huge money-maker for those who write them and print them and score them because every school district has to use them, by law. The four biggest companies are: CTB McGraw-Hill (the biggest for state tests, 96%) Harcourt Educational Measurement, Riverside Publishing (a Houghton Mifflin company) and NCS Pearson (the largest scorer for standardized tests). The annual federal budget for these tests is now in the hundreds of millions; this does not include state budgets for testing, varying state by state. A huge waste of resources, this fundamentally flawed practice should be abolished immediately and those funds redirected to areas of need in education.

The ideological dimension

The main question I have investigated in my academic experience has been: "How do people come to have the ideas they have?" Aside from the influence our parents have on us and the schools and immediate community (neighbors, religious, friends and acquaintances) impressions that stay with us, the major influences on our thinking, the ideas we subscribe to and the understandings we come to adopt come from the mass media. The main component of this dimension. In their first incarnation, they were *the press* and, in the United States, they were the 'fourth estate', that structure which was designed to check on the other three estates, the executive, the legislative and the judicial branches of government. They were supposed to be the 'watch dogs' of the powerful. The written word, echoing the slogan 'the pen is mightier than the sword' in the form of news and bulletins about the powerful would protect ordinary people from the tendencies of political power to become tyrannical, one of the conditions the 'Founding Fathers' desperately wanted to foreclose on in their new democratic experiment. There are different views about how well that went for the first 200 years. However, there is abundant evidence that, for the past 30 years, we have seen a drastic deterioration of our fourth estate: the corporate monopolization of the mass media. The results are devastatingly clear: we have five corporations controlling more than 90% of what we see hear and read every day. The five corporations are Time Warner, Disney, News Corp, Viacom and Bertelsmann. This stronghold on the media by these corporations, which we call the 'corporate media' now, has reduced the variety of voices and images that we used to have available to us down to five major voices and images that are virtually the same. They have become the 'lap dogs' of the powerful.

Here is an example that demonstrates how the corporate media are selective about how they report on events and issues: there was a series of hurricanes (the strongest of which were Harvey, Irma and Maria) that ravaged Houston, TX, the Caribbean and Florida in September of 2017. The coverage was 24/7 for days by the corporate media, from before landfall to the aftermath of the storms. There was virtually no mention of *climate change* the whole time these were reported. Discussion about this in the independent press and broadcast media expressed that not only should have climate change been mentioned, but that its scientific elements should have been explicated so that people could understand why these storms were so big and strong – a teaching moment. When discussed on the mainstream media, we heard claims that mentioning climate change would have 'politicized' the hurricanes – a teaching moment missed. Opportunities to instruct our children about some effects of climate change were lost, *e.g.*, while there is no data on its influence on the frequency of hurricanes, there is a correlation between climate change and the intensity of hurricanes. Actually, *not* mentioning climate change is what politicized them. The protectionist media avoided political fallout, because they knew that the Trump Administration is full of climate change deniers. This is what is meant by Marx's assertion: "The ideas of the ruling class are in every epoch the ruling ideas".

A very dangerous outcome of the monopolization of the mass media is that a unified voice is established that ignores the *real* needs of the people and supports the entrenched ideas and policies of corporations, which creates *false* needs, virtually muting opposing voices, the independent media, that hope to offer some kind of balance to the seemingly never-ending appeal for consumerism. Such intense broadcasting creates conditions that people can barely escape, least of whom our children. They are so bedazzled by the likes of commercial advertising and influenced by the presentation of product marketing that their minds become occupied by these hallmarks of capitalism and the quest for the possession of objects. They believe that owning these objects or services that they will be happy or happier. The public relations industry, because they operate on the emotional level, have been very successful in convincing our children that what these media bring to them is of high import. What this does, over time, is 'colonize their minds' to coincide with a certain way of thinking that does not serve them well. In fact, the kind of mindset that occupies their thinking distracts them from what they must engage in at school. Moreover, the fact that critical thinking is not taught anywhere

290 Left Behind

in the United States, in any systematic effort, makes our children 'easy pickings' to receive these detrimental messages. While our students are thinking about the next craze in consumer items, they are not honing their critical skills. As I have argued before, that is exactly what is needed in a 'consumer' society: acquiescent individuals, who just can't wait for the next wave of trinkets. I am not disparaging our children; they are the victims first. I am only pointing out just how vulnerable they are in the face of such powerful mechanisms of information dissemination, propaganda. They do not realize what is happening to them. That is why we need serious education changes so that we can establish, among many other programs, mandatory instruction in critical thinking.

This consolidation of voices also infiltrates our schools in the form of Channel One and the constant barrage of sound bites from the 'social media'. These realities have yet another unfortunate result: a generation of students who find it difficult to have any interaction with anybody without these 'little boxes' of electronic wizardry. This translates into the detrimental condition students now suffer: communicating in sound bites instead of free-flowing discourse through which one might glean and argument or explanation, impossible in sound bites. Understanding that this condition is one which is adopted over time, I recommend that they be reined in from these electronic devices while in school, except when they are the subject of instruction or in a project-based experience. I do not know what the future will bring, but I am certain that a continuation or exacerbation of this condition will compromise our educational efforts to a significant degree. Communication patterns are already altered: verbal discourse is limited to a few words, when a flowing oration is required; written work is truncated to simple disconnected sentences, rendering the production of a paragraph problematic. Good effective communication relies on a fluent command of the language. I am not disparaging students here; I am only pointing out some of the consequences of such practices, ones which have already diminished performance in the language. We must tackle this problem with energy and steadfastness; students should not be allowed to have hand-held electronic devices in school. They only distract them from the program at hand. Parents should also be alerted to this problem and encouraged to limit their children's exposure to them.

One phenomenon which has taken hold in the United States, actually from the beginning of our republic, is this notion of 'American Exceptionalism'. I write about it in this book and want to remind the reader of its impact. Just as our children's minds become occupied by consumerism, they also absorb the expressed attitude that "anything American is the best". Hence, we, Americans, are the best. Any suggestion that America is not 'in charge' or 'number one' or 'leading the world' is unacceptable. Our children are probably not taught these notions outright, but they are always in the background and supported at the local level. For example, take the weekly high school football game, at which students are told that they will win this game because they are the best, *etc.* They have rallies before the game to whip up the frenzy that will be 'necessary' to support the players on the field. To be fair, this kind of event happens all over the world for different sports; and, also to be fair, some of this is not all that bad – a healthy dose of competition does not hurt anyone. However, the dark side of this scenario can take over, that side which transcends these otherwise reasonable sentiments of *support our team* and moves in a direction of extreme ethnocentrism and even xenophobia, sometimes importing jingoistic attitudes of cultural superiority. Now it is *support our country* no matter what. Such misguided 'patriotism' can lead to very dangerous outcomes, such as the invasions of Afghanistan and Iraq, which would not have happened had the population of the United States not been in a state of fear after September 11, 2001. Ideological influence is at the root of these kinds of issues and events. Ideas do matter; and, depending upon who controls them, they can have very harsh outcomes.

One last pitch for teaching: the teaching profession is also in crisis. It has been challenged before, sometimes for good reasons, sometimes not. The current trend, however, is very subtle and, as such, could be the most severe blow it has ever suffered, and without good reason. What makes it subtle is the fact that it is masked by the fervor we witness for the most recent electronic innovations. The craze is to transform education from face-to-face instruction to online instruction. This is a frontal attack on the profession and on education. I am not lamenting that there will be changes in instruction because of the development of new technologies. I am warning of the disintegration and eventual elimination of *the teacher*. For students, because of the nature of online instruction, there is no guarantee that the person at the other end of the Internet connection is an instructor/teacher/professor. I ask, "From whom will our students get their instruction?" As this technology becomes even more sophisticated, there is a danger that the teacher's end of the connection could become automated in such a manner as to delete the teacher and install the 'cyber teacher', the program that will facilitate the instruction with pre-recorded voice-overs, much like the automated phone greetings we are plagued with when trying to reach a human being to discuss a matter. This is not paranoia nor is it out-of-the-pail in terms of its potential implementation. I trust that this has not become the norm yet, but I wonder if such strategies have already been introduced, without our knowledge, into the educational landscape. Stay tuned on this one; I truly hope that I am wrong about this concern.

I would like to leave the reader with the following thoughts: the sustained level of warfare and violence in the world, the rise in leaders who disregard the rights of people and the continued corporate/military destruction of eco-systems all over the world, resulting in Anthropocene climate change, could all be mitigated by establishing critical education, globally. I assert that, if we were to develop an array of global educational systems whose faculties, from pre-school to university, possessed the knowledge and insight and enlightenment that it should, whose *curricula* were up to the complicated task of education, in which critical thinking was at its core, influencing all the different subjects our children need to understand, we would not have the mess we have now in education and in the world. We already have such teachers and structures operating here and there in the global context, but not enough. If we could achieve these kinds of benchmarks across the world, we would not have dictators, and some elected leaders along with their lackeys,

292 Left Behind

- imprisoning people for their ideas;
- torturing journalists for telling the truth;
- bragging about having killed people without due process;
- oppressing women in the name of 'cultural traditions';
- continuing to develop nuclear weapons;
- stealing people's land in the name of 'religious entitlement' and 'military bullying';
- continuing to use of fossil fuel that exacerbates the already dire effects of climate change;
- calling for the targeting of people of this or that religion for persecution;
- still holding on to the practice of 'capital punishment', something that is over-whelmingly denounced;
- preventing women from accessing proper health care, including reproductive care and abortion;
- fixing elections to guarantee outcomes that will empower the rich and reactionary agenda

... and so on. Critical education is the starting point to answer all of these woes. There is no direct cause-effect relationship here; however, with all of the problems of so many different kinds, the common denominator that can effectively challenge them is a comprehensive effort to understand those problems and eventually to solve them for the benefit of all, not the few. It all begins with not allowing any of our children to be *left behind* by guaranteeing them all equal, high-quality public education.

Bibliography

Bush v. Gore, U.S. Supreme Court, 531 U.S. 98 (December 12, 2000) https://supreme.justia.com/cases/federal/us/531/98/

Citizens United v. Federal Election Commission, U.S. Supreme Court, 558 U.S. 310 (January 21, 2010) www.law.cornell.edu/supct/html/08-205.ZS.html

Democracy Now! (September 2016 and ongoing) Comprehensive coverage of DAPL. Retrieved from www.democracynow.org

Freire, P. (1968) *Pedagogy of the Oppressed*. New York: The Seabury Press.

Environmental Defense Fund. (n.d.) Retrieved from www.edf.org/our-mission-and-values

Everson v. Board of Education, U.S. Supreme Court, 330 U.S. 1 (February 10, 1947) https://supreme.justia.com/cases/federal/us/330/1/case.html

Linzey, T. & Campbell, A. (2009) *Be the Change: How to Get What You Want in Your Community*. Layton: Gibbs Smith.

Linzey, T. (April 21, 2009). "Envision Spokane: Coalition Works to Get 'Community Bill of Rights' into City Charter". A. Goodman, Interviewer [Video file]. Retrieved from www.democracynow.org/2009/4/21/envision_spokane_coalition_works_to_get

McCutcheon v. Federal Election Commission, U.S. Supreme Court, 572 U.S. (April 2, 2014) www.supremecourt.gov/opinions/13pdf/12-536_e1pf.pdf

Miranda v. Arizona, U.S. Supreme Court, 384 U.S. 436 (June 13, 1966) https://supreme.justia.com/cases/federal/us/384/436/case.html

APPENDIX: PLYOMETRICS MOVEMENT PROGRAM

Testing descriptions

1. 40 Yard Dash: The designated distance is set up and the participant is told to sprint as fast as possible through the finish line. The time starts on the athlete's first motion and stops when he/she crosses the finish line.
2. Squat Assessment: The examiner assesses the athlete's squat pattern from the side and front. The athlete is asked to place his/her arms straight out in front of them, take a shoulder-width stance and squat to a comfortable depth. The examiner assesses for compensations and risk factors such as a valgus knee position, excessive trunk lean, increased lordotic spine, instability, anterior knee position relative to the toes, fluidity of the pattern, *etc*.
3. Lunge Pattern Assessment: The examiner assesses the athlete's lunge pattern from the side and front. The athlete is asked to place his/her arms straight out in front of them, take a split stance and lunge to a depth just before the backside knee touches the ground. The examiner assesses for compensations and risk factors such as a symmetry, valgus knee position, excessive trunk lean, increased lordotic spine, instability, anterior knee position relative to the toes, fluidity of the pattern, *etc*.
4. Altitude Landing Assessment: The athlete stands on top of a 12-inch box. He/she is then asked to jump off the box and land into the bottom position of a squat pattern. The athlete is encouraged to only jump enough to clear the box to reduce the potential for injury. The examiner assesses for compensations and risk factors such as a symmetry, valgus knee position, excessive trunk lean, increased lordotic spine, instability, anterior knee position relative to the toes, fluidity of the pattern, *etc*. This pattern is more dynamic and allows for compensation to be easily recognized and will sometimes show risk factors even when the squat and lunge pattern are adequate.

294 Left Behind

5 Uni Squat to Box: The athlete stands in front of an 18-inch box. The athlete is asked to place his/her arms straight out in front of them, stand on one leg and control his/her body down to the box. This should take about 3–5 seconds to reach the box. The examiner assesses for compensations and risk factors such as a symmetry, valgus knee position, excessive trunk lean, increased lordotic spine, instability, anterior knee position relative to the toes, fluidity of the pattern, *etc.* This test allows the examiner to assess single-leg stability and control.

6 Pro Agility Test: The examiner sets up three cones, one at the start line, at 5-yard mark and 10-yard mark. The athlete starts in front of the middle cone at 5 yards. The athlete is told to sprint and touch one end of the cone, sprint across and touch the far cone and then sprint through the start cone. The athlete must touch the cone with his/her right hand if sprinting to the right and touch with his/her left hand when sprinting to the left. The athlete gets one repetition for each direction, and the time is recorded.

7 Plank Series: The examiner assesses for core control in the front and side plank positions. This is a muscular endurance test so the athlete holds the proper position until form falters. The examiner assesses for proper low back position, upper/lower body position.

8 Broad Jump: The athlete stands with a shoulder-width stance and jumps forward as far as possible and must land in a squat stance. The examiner measures the distance traveled from the start position to the back of the athlete's foot. This is a test designed to assess lower extremity power.

9 Squat with MedBall Toss: The athlete stands in a squat stance with a medicine ball held at chest height. The athlete gets into a squat stance and throws the ball as far as possible while maintaining his/her feet in contact with the ground. The distance the ball travels is measured. For consistency, the males utilize an 8-pound medicine ball while the females utilize a 4-pound medicine ball.

10 Push-Up Failure: The athlete performs as many push-ups as possible with proper technique. When form falters the athlete is told to stop. The examiner is assessing for proper low back position, arm/elbow relationship to the body and head/neck position.

11 Three Cone Drill: The examiner sets up three cones, one cone at the start, one cone at the 5-yard mark and one placed immediately to the right or left at a 5-yard mark. The shape represents the letter L. The athlete starts by sprinting to the first cone and back to the start line. He/she is then asked to sprint back around the second cone, then out and around the third cone. The athlete then sprints around the second cone through the start position line. The athlete gets one repetition for each direction, and the time is recorded.

12 Vertical Jump: The examiner utilizes a Vertec vertical jump testing device. The athlete stands under the device and reaches one hand up. The device is set to the proper position. The athlete is then asked to stand shoulder-width and jump up as high as possible and swipe the gates aside. The vertical jump number is then measured.

Name: _____

Date: _____

Sport: _____

Class YR: _____

SMHC
SPORTS
Performance
Center

1. 40 Yard Dash: _____ sec.

2. Squat 2 Trials (please describe any movement deficiencies):

   Anterior View: Lateral View:

3. In-Line Lunge with Dowel 2 Trials Bilaterally (please describe any movement deficiencies):

   1. R   1. L

4. Altitude Landing Technique:

5. Uni Squat to Box:

6. Pro Agility Test: _____ seconds

7. Plank Series Failure (please stop each plank when technique falters):

   1. Left Side: _____ seconds

   2. Right Side: _____ seconds

   3. Front: _____ seconds

8. Broad Jump (LE Power) 2 Trials (please measure to back foot/inches):

   1.   2.

9. Squat with MB Toss 2 Trials (MB should be roughly 5% of BW)

   1.   2.

10. Push-Up Failure (please stop athlete when technique falters): _____

11. Three-Cone Drill

   1. R   2. L

12. Vertical Jump 2 Trials (inches):

   1.   2.

The first part of the data pertaining to fundamental movement patterns reflects the amount of dysfunction present. Such movements as knee anterior sheer, knee valgus, lumbar extension, *etc.*, were noted in the pretest procedures and then monitored for changes during the posttesting procedures. These dysfunctions informed the assessment of the squat, lunge, altitude landing and single-leg squat to box. The data pertaining to the 40-yard dash, pro agility and three-cone drill would generally show a lesser time as compared to the pretest numbers. The remaining tests would generally yield an increase in outcomes between the pretest and the post test. Given that this program is designed hopefully to improve movement competency, we, as a staff, were very pleased with the decrease in movement flaws. "BHS" refers to Biddeford High School, Biddeford, ME and "TA" refers to Thornton Academy, Saco, ME.

296 Left Behind

BHS Pre Test Data

Number	40 yd	Squat	Lunge	Land	Uni Squat	Pro	Fr Plank
1	6.3	a/s	a/s, val, ext	a/s	R val	5.3	0.56
2	5.7	a/s	ext	a/s	B val	5	1.16
3	5.9	a/s, ext	a/s	a/s	B val	5.2	1.04
4	5.1	R dom		pre val	B val	4.9	1.37
5	6.1	a/s	val, ext	a/s, val	B val	5.2	1.21
6	4.8	trunk		a/s	B val	5	3.41
7	5.2	ext	a/s, ext	a/s	B a/s, val	5.3	2.20
8	4.8	trunk	B val	B val	B val	5.1	0.52
9	5.6	L dom	B val	L dom	B val	5.1	1.00
10	6.3	a/s	ext	a/s, val	B val	5.3	1.13
11	5	ext		a/s	L val, R a/s	5	1.48
12	5.2	a/s, val	val	a/s, val	B val	5.5	0.47
13	6.1	a/s, val	trunk	a/s	val, a/s	5.5	0.36
14	5	a/s		val	R val	4.5	1.15
15	5.1	a/s, val	a/s	a/s	a/s, val	5.1	
16	5	trunk	ext	ext, wink	B val	4.5	2.18
17	5.5	ext		a/s, ext	B val	4.6	2.20
18	5	ext				5.3	1.28
19	4.8	ext			B val	5.2	2.17
20	5.6	a/s	ext	a/s	B val, a/s	5.1	1.35
21	4.6	trunk			B val	4.4	2.03
22	5.7	ext	R val		B val, a/s	5.5	1.32
23	5.2	ext		a/s	B val, a/s	5.2	1.58
24	6.6	ext	val	val	B val	5.2	1.18
25	5.6	ext			B val	5.4	1.09
26	6.3	ext	val	a/s, val	a/s, val	5.3	1.13
27	5.1	a/s, ext	ext	val	B val	4.7	1.18
28	5.3	a/s		val	B val, a/s	5.5	2.15
29	5.4	ext			val, trunk	5	1.43
30	4.9	val	ext, val	a/s	B val, a/s	4.7	2.21
31	5.6	a/s, val	val	a/s, val	B a/s, val	5.4	2.30
32	5.9	val, ext	val	val, a/s	B val	5.3	1.55
33	6.5	val	val	val	val	5.5	1.05
34	5.6	a/s	val	a/s, val	val	5.6	1.10
Average-Pre	**5.482**	**41 flaws**	**53 flaws**	**37 flaws**	**86 flaws**	**5.1**	**1.44**
Average-Post	**5.6**	**11 flaws**	**16 flaws**	**9 flaws**	**31 flaws**	**5.5**	**1.52**
		★	★	★	★		★

9/14 category improvement

TA Pre Test

Appendix: Plyometrics movement program **297**

L Plank	R Plank	Bjump	MB Toss	Push Up	3 Cone	Vjump
0.35	0.28	67	308.00	8	10.69	19.0
1.08	1.07	65	183.00	25	9.78	20.0
0.45	0.35	68	224.00	22	10.24	17.5
2.05	1.19	76	243.00	35	9.91	18.0
1.13	1.24	62	219.00	21	10.26	15.0
2.22	2.03	88	248.00	43	9.86	23.5
1.25	1.25	78	239.00	30	9.69	23.5
1.34	1.04	79	255.00	37	9.64	26.0
1.10	1.19	67	234.00	24	9.68	19.5
1.01	0.35	64	196.00	21	10.38	17.5
1.25	1.17	76	264.00	32	9.58	23.5
1.07	1.09	73	272.00	36	10.23	20.5
0.30	0.25	69	246.00	8	10.74	21.5
1.47	1.58	91	276.00	65	8.28	24.0
		88	262.00	30	8.58	25.5
1.24	1.25		322.00	34	8.56	24.5
1.19	0.30	79	286.00	41	8.53	24.5
1.22	0.57	93	294.00	37	9.91	27.0
1.02	1.50	95	321.00	42	9.48	13.0
1.37	1.32	63	305.00	25	10.58	18.0
0.52	1.08	103	270.00	34	8.48	30.5
1.00	1.01	84	297.00	25	10.53	26.5
1.38	2.09	68	285.00	21	9.79	23.5
0.53	0.39	66	207.00	10	10.93	15.0
1.02	1.01	71	254.00	21	9.58	23.5
1.05	1.19	67	302.00	4	10.73	18.0
1.19	1.30	79	239.00	27	9.24	22.5
1.11	1.14	80	299.00	31	9.79	22.5
1.16	1.59	87	310.00	40	9.89	26.0
1.42	1.40	84	311.00	29	9.68	28.5
1.35	1.56	64	180.00	26	10.41	16.5
1.51	1.17	79	225.00	24	10.41	16.5
0.58	0.55	53	188.00	6	10.83	15.0
1.21	1.06	72	210.00	16	10.49	19.0
1.13	**1.08**	**76**	**258.06**	**27**	**9.8641**	**21.3**
1.06	**0.93**	**74**	**260.44**	**36**	**9.17**	**21.6**
			★	★	★	★

298 Left Behind

Number	40 yd	Squat	Lunge	Land	Uni Squat	Pro	Fr Plank
1	5.7	a/s, inst.	B val, ext	pre val	a/s, val	5.28	1.18
2	7	L val, a/s	B val, a/s	a/s, val	B val, a/s	6.61	1.00
3	5.2				B val	5.02	1.23
4	6.8					5.7	
5	5.3	B val	B val, a/s	val, a/s	B val	5.66	3.11
6	5.4	trunk	a/s	a/s	B val	5.33	1.05
7	6.4	val, a/s	B val, a/s, ext	val, a/s	B val	5.59	1.07
8	5.7	val, a/s	B val, a/s	val, a/s	B val, a/s	5.57	2.10
9	4.99	val, trunk	a/s	a/s	B val	4.8	1.30
10	5.3	val, a/s	B val, a/s	a/s	B val, a/s	5.32	1.50
11	5.7	a/s	B a/s	a/s	B val, a/s	4.98	1.02
12	6.2	val, a/s, tr	a/s		B val, a/s p!	6.08	1.35
13	6.5	val, a/s	B val, a/s	a/s	B val, a/s	5.59	0.35
14	5.5	B val, a/s		a/s	B val		1.10
15	5.3	trunk, a/s	a/s, candle		B val	4.93	1.21
16	5.3	val, a/s	a/s, B val		B val	5.56	1.10
17	5	val, trunk			B val		2.10
18	4.8	val, a/s	B a/s, ext	a/s	R val	4.78	1.32
19	5.66	a/s, val	B a/s, L val	a/s	B val, a/s	5.47	2.02
20	5.5	trunk	ext		R val, instab	5.08	2.00
21	4.6	L val		val	R val	5.06	2.03
22	5.1	val		a/s	B a/s, R val	4.53	1.42
23	5.5				B val	5.28	1.00
24	5	val	B a/s	a/s	B val	4.29	1.15
25	5.5	val, a/s	B a/s	a/s	B val	5.36	1.00
26	5.5	val, a/s	B val	a/s	B val	4.99	2.20
27	5.4	val, a/s	a/s	a/s	B val	4.66	1.01
28	5.8	val, trunk	B val	val	B val, a/s	6.01	0.47
29	6.5	a/s, trunk	B a/s	a/s	B val	5.88	1.46
30	5.9	trunk	B a/s, ext	a/s	R a/s	5.83	0.51
31	5	trunk		a/s	B val	5.11	1.01
32	5.1	trunk	ext			4.89	0.30
33	6	trunk	ext	a/s	B val, ext		0.36
34	5.93	R val	R val	val, trunk	B val, a/s	5.17	0.30
35	5.6	val, a/s	B val, a/s		L val	5.74	1.03
36	4.8					4.33	1.57
37	4.9					4.79	2.02
38	5.7	a/s, val	B val	a/s	B val, a/s		1.06
39	7.0	a/s, val	B val, a/s	a/s	B val, a/s	6.13	0.47
40	5.6	val, a/s	trunk, B val	val, a/s	B val, a/s	6.04	0.50
41	5.7	val, a/s	B val, a/s	val, a/s	B val	5.59	3.00
42	5.6	trunk	ext		B val, a/s	6.01	
43	5.2			val	B val	4.83	3.38
44	6.8	val, a/s	B a/s		B val	5.89	1.01
45	6.3	val, a/s	B val	a/s	B val	6.03	0.52
46	6.1	val, a/s	B val, a/s		B val	5.29	1.34
47	5.9	val	B val		B val	5.51	1.26
48	6.4	val, a/s	B val	val, a/s	B val, a/s	6.13	0.43
49	6.4	a/s, trunk	trunk	a/s	B val, a/s	6.16	0.34
50	5.1	trunk	B a/s	a/s	B val	4.91	1.03
51	5.2	a/s, trunk	a/s	a/s	B val, trunk	4.81	1.25
52	5.2				B val	4.96	1.50
53	5.0	B val, trunk	B a/s	L a/s	B val	5.06	1.00
54	5.7	val, a/s, tr.			B val	5.28	0.44
55	5.8	a/s	B a/s, ext	a/s, val	B val, a/s	5.80	1.04
Average-Pre	**5.6**	**84**	**93**	**46**	**117**	**5.37**	**1.24**
Average-Post	**5.8**	**29**	**32**	**20**	**37**	**5.22**	**1.29**
		★	★	★	★	★	★

10/14 categories improved

Appendix: Plyometrics movement program 299

L Plank	R Plank	Bjump	MB Toss	Push Up	3 Cone	Vjump
2.00	0.31	71	214.00	9	8.59	19.5
0.36	0.40	54	183.00	5	11.31	15.5
1.31	1.12	78	255.00	19	8.53	22.0
		64	204.00	15	9.52	18.5
1.41	1.25	77	264.00	25	8.78	21.0
0.47	0.44	78	237.00	9	9.03	22.5
0.48	1.04	62	193.00	10	9.38	17.0
3.01	2.30	58	220.00	44	9.53	16.5
1.30	1.30	72	185.00	31	8.34	19.5
0.47	0.50	80	278.00	20	8.94	23.0
1.06	1.00	86	279.00	10	8.19	23.5
0.34	0.26	58	217.00	19	9.28	16.5
0.12	0.31	70	226.00	1	10.88	18.0
1.20	2.12	83	203.00	17	8.47	22.5
0.56	0.50	90	207.00	33	8.18	25.5
0.40	0.30	71	214.00	10	8.66	16.5
1.45	1.46		294.00	39	7.28	28.0
1.03	1.01	106	273.00	23	7.81	31.0
1.10	1.30	57	209.00	24	9.37	17.5
1.00	1.00	86	323.00	20	8.44	27.5
0.59	1.06	98	276.00	31		30.5
1.15	1.17	104	297.00	29	7.95	31.0
0.38	0.40	79	296.00		8.13	25.0
1.15	1.15	92	306.00	37	7.91	24.5
1.00	1.00	87	330.00	17	8.57	22.0
1.08	1.18	88	242.00	20	7.75	20.5
1.03	1.00	98	388.00	34	8.13	30.5
1.02		64	224.00	20	9.41	17.0
0.31	0.40	68	274.00	16	10.00	18.5
1.12	0.34	70	224.00	10	9.53	14.0
0.50	0.40	95	331.00	24	8.53	28.5
1.00	1.00	102	322.00	43	7.66	27.5
0.30	0.27	82	320.00	8	9.00	19.5
1.09	1.00	67	178.00	35	9.53	18.5
1.14	1.29	74	312.00	6	9.12	19.5
1.17	1.10	109	410.00	54	7.03	28.0
1.01	1.01	107	338	48	7.94	28.0
0.26	0.43	70	203	3	9.28	19.5
0.34	0.34	52	224	3	10.62	15.5
0.30	0.55	59	232	25	10.44	17.5
1.30	1.30	82	266	30	9.72	21.0
		85	302		8.6	20.5
1.25	1.08	92	363	40	8.13	31.0
0.56	1.09	59	183	2	9.32	14.5
0.56	1.07	62	227	6	9.31	19.5
0.56	1.12	75	253	3	9.22	19.5
1.32	1.09	66	186	4	9.5	16.0
0.30	0.44	64	150	12	10.28	15.5
0.30	0.32	61	223	5	10.56	16.0
0.35	0.38	90	324	32	8.25	29.0
1.30	1.10	91	262	23	8.22	22.5
0.35	1.02	98	274	31	7.97	25.0
0.34	0.43	93	341	30	8.06	26.5
0.41	0.47	73	258	23	8.29	19.5
1.05	1.11	62	210	12	9.9	17.0
0.85	**0.87**	**78**	**258.67**	**21**	**8.90**	**21.6**
1.08	**1.04**	**78**	**257.13**	**25**	**8.72**	**21.5**
★	★			★	★	

INDEX

Affordable Care Act (Obamacare) 84n22, 100; health care 75, 90, 97, 99, 101, 233, 259, 265, 276, 288, 292

Afghanistan 9, 28, 253, 257n4, 275, 291

Alexander, M. 131

America's Promise Alliance 150

American Association of University Professors (AAUP) 147, 156–8, 161

American Dairy Association 27, 198, 201

American Diet 198, 200

American Dream 9, 12, 93, 244, 274

'American Exceptionalism' 12, 12n27, 204, 241–2

American Federation of Labor and Congress of Industrial Organizations (AFL-CIO) 259, 266

American Federation of Teachers (AFT) 156

American Legislative Exchange Council (ALEC) 99, 141–2

American Montessori Society 219; *Montessori Method* 180, 183, 219

American Revolution 35, 75, 243, 247

American Textbook Council 250, 253

Americans for Prosperity 99

Architecture 58–62, 189, 197, 234, 237, 286

Aristotle 3, 16

Arkush, D. 43, 55

Army Alpha written test 167n7

Arnold, M. 134, 161

Aronowitz, N.W. 124n48, 131

Astell, M. 77n7

Athletics 207–8, 285

Attention Deficit Disorder (ADD) 182

Attention Deficit/Hyperactivity Disorder (ADHD) 182, 221

Bacon, F. 184, 220

Bagdikian, B. 37–8, 54, 250

Baker, C.L. 251, 253

Barry, R.K. 244, 253

Bartleby Project: "I would prefer not to." 175n24

Barzun, J. 136, 161

Basler, R.P. 254

"Be Real, Be Ready" California *curriculum* 215

Beard, C. 7

Benyus, J. 5

Berard, T. 9, 111–2, 114, 131

Berger, J. 50n28, 55

Bernays, E. 45, 55

Bilmes, L.J. & Stiglitz, J.E. 10n22, 16, 108

Binet, A. 167, 169, 178

"Blaming the victim" 106, 120, 120n35, 133

Block, N.J. & Dworkin, G. 93–4

Blumenbach, J.F. 111, 131

Blumer, H. 166–7, 178; the 'variable' 165–7, 178

Boas, F. 7

Boyer, R.O. & Morais, H.M. 251n26, 254

BP (British Petroleum) 146–7, 162; Deepwater Horizon oil rig 146, 162

Brewer, J. (former Governor of Arizona) 243n9

Bridgeport vs. Fairfield, CT 117–18, 132

Brigham, C. 167, 168n8, 178

Brown, E. 132
Bush v. Gore 277, 292

Campbell, T.C. & Campbell, T.M. 198, 219
Campfield, S. (Tennessee Senator) 101–2
Cancer Compass – Alternate Route 220
Capitalism xix, xxiv, 6–7, 9, 11, 35, 50, 73–4,
    75n6, 77–8, 83, 87, 93, 96–7, 99, 106,
    108, 113, 120, 129, 132, 156, 193, 258,
    262, 266, 289; capitalist 9, 72n1, 76–8, 93,
    120, 148
Carson, R. 6, 16
Carter, J. (former President of the U.S.)
    18n6, 28n28, 32, 171n14
Casey, D. 124n50, 125, 132
Castro, A. 26n25, 32
Ceballos, G. 75n6, 94
Center for Budget and Policy Priorities 94
Center for Public Education 80n16
Center for Science in the Public Interest 46, 56
Centers for Disease Control (CDC) 204,
    218n76, 220
*Central American Free Trade Agreement
    (CAFTA)* 87, 246
Central Nervous System (CNS) 213, 285
Chamber of Commerce 150
Chan, A. 133
Chandra, A., *et al.* 218n75, 220
Channel One 31, 41–2, 45, 263–4, 290
Chavez, C. 26
Chemtrail Central 220
Chetty, J. & Friedman, J. 80n13, 94
Cheyney, E.P. 70, 72
Chicago School System 104, 149
Church 3–4, 14, 26, 45n21, 59, 129, 184,
    220, 269
Cilloffo, A. 83n20, 95
Citizens for Tax Justice 86n29, 94
Citizens United v. Federal Election Commission
    37n8, 47, 56, 195, 271, 277–9, 292
Citizenship Clause/Naturalization Clause
    (Article 1, Section 8, Clause 4 of U.S.
    Constitution) 21
Civil Rights Act of 1875 21, 22n15, 33
Civil Rights Act of 1964 21–2, 33, 120, 133,
    243
Clark, K.B. 115, 132
Clarke, J.H. xix, xxiv, 113n12, 132, 255n2,
    261–2, 266
College (university) xiv, 2, 8, 24–5, 44, 58,
    60, 62, 65–6, 69–70, 78, 81–2, 83–4, 88,
    90, 135–6, 140–1, 146–7, 152n31, 154–8,
    160, 172, 186, 224, 227, 229, 235, 237,
    248, 284, 287, 291

*College Entrance Examination Board Test of
    1901* 167
Collins, G. 129n70, 132
"Colonization of the Mind" xix, 41n14,
    255, 261–2
Columbus, C. xixn11, xxiv, 27, 113n12, 132,
    262n14, 266
Committee on Public Information (CPI) 45
Common Core 9, 173, 261
Common Dreams 119, 133
Common Sense Media 46, 56, 189n20
*Communication and Literary Skills Test
    (CLST)* 137
Community Bicycle Center 190, 220
Community Environmental Legal Defense Fund
    267
Comte, A. 164–5, 178
Conscientization (*conscientizacao*) xxiii
Continuing Education Units (CEU's) 272
Cooper, A. 195
Copernicus, N. 4, 16
Corn, D. 90, 94
Cornman, S. 80n15, 95
Corporate 'partnerships' 58, 68–9, 148, 173
Corporate vs. individual tax in 1940's &
    50's, 86
Coulter, J. 27–9, 33
Creel Commission 45
Cremin, L.A. 247n18, 254
Critical Thinking (CT) xvii, iii, xxiv, 14n36,
    41n14, 43, 45, 49–50, 58, 136n6, 173,
    174n23, 177, 184–7, 201, 221, 255–6,
    262, 264–6, 277, 289–91; "universal
    intellectual standards" 177, 186; "elements
    of" 186–7; "traits of" 187; "operations:
    identification, analysis and evaluation"
    187
curriculum/a xii, xvi–xvii, xix–xx, 6–7,
    13–15, 24–7, 32, 50, 92, 107, 110,
    127–31, 135–7, 142, 144, 148, 150, 159,
    161–2, 167–8, 171, 173, 175–6, 178,
    180–1, 183–4, 188n18, 190, 192, 194,
    208, 210, 214–15, 217–18, 225–9, 236–7,
    239, 247–51, 264, 270, 272–3, 276–7,
    284, 287, 291
'customer' hyperbole 63

Dakota Access Keystone XL Pipe Line (DAPL)
    145, 268–9, 292
Dartmouth College & indigenous tuition 88
Darwin, C. 26
de Blasio, B. (NYC Mayor) 102
de Tocqueville, A. 245, 254
DeNavas-Walt, C. 132

302 Left Behind

Department of Defense 42n16, 56
Devlin, K. 224n2, 238
DeVos, B. (current Secretary of Education)
13, 15, 58, 66, 88n35, 104n14, 151–3,
161–2, 168, 174, 178, 272, 285
Dewey, J. 7
Dickens, C. 74, 94
Dignity in Schools Campaign 125
Discretionary federal budget spending 79,
81, 88, 106, 275–6
Discrimination 12n30, 13, 19–20, 109–11,
14, 15n20, 117, 130–2, 157–8, 205n55,
240–1, 280, 287
"Doublespeak" 143, 147, 156, 158, 260–1
"Doublethink" 257–8
Douglass, F. 1, 16, 130–1
Dounay, J. 225n7, 238
Dr. McDougall's Health and Medical
Center 203n47, 220
Dred Scott v. John F.A. Sandford 21, 115
DuBois, W.E.B. 7n14
Duncan, A. (former Secretary of Education)
104, 149–50
Durkheim, E. 240, 254
Dyslexia 182

Eagleton, T. 235, 238
Ecole Normale Superieure 82
Economic Policy Institute 98n4, 108
Education 81, 83, 85–7; crisis in xii, 1, 8,
10–11; parental participation in 101;
philosophy of xiv–xvi, 135n2, 136, 209,
212; 'schooling' vs. 'education' xiii, 6,
42, 57–8, 71, 137–9, 249n22, 254; face-
to-face education vs. 'distance learning'
8, 12, 138–40, 142, 159, 188, 282, 291;
'literature-based' vs. 'information-based'
171; project-based x, xii, 24, 135–6, 140,
177, 189–90, 195–7, 199, 209, 273,
282–3, 290; health 6, 11, 19, 27, 44,
46n24, 47, 51, 56, 100, 105, 194–5,
197–203, 206, 213–15, 280; sex
214–15, 218n75, 219–220, 222, 237;
'comprehensive' 214–15, 218–20;
'abstinence only' 214–15, 218–20;
nutrition xii, 27, 46–7, 105, 182, 190, 195,
198–203, 213, 219; physical (PE) xix, 183,
190, 203–7, 220–1, 285; foreign language
91, 119, 128, 183, 223–9, 232, 234, 238,
286–7; *immersion* 224–5, 228–9, 231,
286–7; intermediate level 226–7; through
travel 228–30; Prussian Model of 249
Education Commission of the States (ECS)
225n7, 238

Education funding 20n9, 81, 83, 85, 86n27,
88; credit vs. debit column 79; tuition 58,
65; tuition-free 66, 81–2, 86, 88n35, 89,
273; pre-school 102, 212, 291
Einenkel, W. 125n53, 132, 203, 220
Einstein, A. 199
Eisenhower, D.D. (former President of the
U.S.) 9, 54, 81, 275
*Elementary and Secondary Education
Amendment of 1966* 21
El-Shabazz, E.M. (Malcolm X) 114n16, 133
Emancipation Proclamation 20n10, 115
Emanuel, R. (Chicago Mayor) 103
Employment (unemployment) 10n23, 87,
90–5, 97, 99–100, 139, 236
Enclosure Movement 72n1, 74
Enlightened (to become) 76
Environmental Protection Agency (EPA) 145,
148
"Equal Protection Clause" (Fourteenth
Amendment to the U.S. Constitution)
20, 116
Ethnocentrism 227n12, 236, 239–40, 242,
286; extreme 12, 211, 239–41, 245, 287,
291
Ethnomethodology 65n12, 71, 178;
categorization 65; category-related 65;
Disjunctive category-pair 27–8
Eugenics 92n45, 267
Everson v. Board of Education 269n4, 292

Fain, P. 158n39, 161
Fanon, F. xixn11, xxiv
FCC v. Pacifica Foundation 40
Federal Communications Commission
(FCC) 38–40, 44, 77
Federal Trade Commission (FTC) 39
Federalist Papers 19n7
Feeding America 105n19, 108
Feiveson, J.A. 144n14, 161
First Amendment 35, 37, 47–8, 268–9
First LAW (Land, Air & Water) 6, 74–5, 269
"First Voices Indigenous Radio" 74, 95,
98n5, 108
Fisher, W. 244n12, 254
Foner, E. 246–7
Food insecurity 105, 108; food stamps
(SNAP) 105
Foreign Language instruction 119, 225–7,
238, 286
Fort Lewis College 89; indigenous tuition
88–9
Fourteenth Amendment 21–2, 115n19, 116
Fourth Estate 14, 35–6, 288–9

Francois-Marie Arouet (Voltaire) 77n7
Freedom xvin5, xviii, xxii–xiii, 14n33, 16, 19, 35–7, 48, 114, 136n4, 138, 176, 180, 197, 255, 257; Academic freedom xvi, 3, 147–8, 156–7, 161, 219, 226, 273, 276
Freedom Works 99
Freire, P. xv–xvi, xviii, xx–xxiv, 181, 209, 276n6, 292
French Revolution 77n7, 250
Fresco, J. 10n23, 61, 79n9
Freud, S. 45
Fromm, E. 7n14, 257, 258n9
Funding for schools xx, 7, 9–11, 13, 19–20, 21n9, 69, 70, 76, 78–83, 85, 87–8, 95, 102–7, 110, 118–19, 128, 142, 145–8, 153, 171, 174–5, 195, 205, 207, 226n9, 227, 229–30, 233, 235, 237, 260, 271–8, 285

Gagne, S. 57n2, 71
Galilei, G. 4, 16, 149
Gamble, K.C. 57n2, 71
Gardner, D.P. 15n38, 16
Garfinkel, H. 114n15, 131, 167n6, 178
Garrity, A. (Judge, Boston school bussing) 22–3, 33
GasLand (documentary film, Josh Fox, Director) 145n16, 161
Gates, F.T. 57, 71, 247
Gatto, J.T. xvn4, xxiv, 57–8, 71, 175n24, 178, 197, 220
Genetically Modified Organisms (GMO's) 192; GMO labeling laws 193n27
Gentry, L. 112, 132
Gerbner, G. 52–3
Gerson (Max) Institute 220
Gettysburg Address 36, 251n30, 254
Ghosthorse, T. 74n5, 95, 98n5, 108
GI Bill 248
Gibson, W.E. 124n49, 132
Giroux, H. xvi–xvii, xxiv
Global Nomads Group 232, 238
Goddard, H. 167n7
Goffman, E. 50n28, 56, 114n15, 131
Goodman, A. 29n30, 30n32, 33, 102n9, 108, 125n55, 131n73, 132, 161, 292
Gorsuch, N. 278
Gould, S.J. 111n7, 132, 164, 167n7, 178
Grade Point Average (GPA) 169, 171
Gramsci, A. 147n23, 161
Great Charter of the Forest 73–4
Green, E.L. 153n34, 161
Greenwald, G. 36, 56
Grow our own food 190, 192–7, 199

Habitat for Humanity 189, 220
Hacking, I. 3, 16
Hagopian, J. 176
Haitian Revolution of 1781 114
Hannah-Jones, N. xixn9, xxiv
Harder, A. 145n18, 161
Hardy, P. 130
Harris, J. 46n24, 56, 221
Harris, T. 189n20
Hayes, D.; *Earth Day speech* 148–9, 161
Heidorn, B. 204n49, 220–1
Heritage Keepers Student Manuel 217n73, 220
Herman, E. & Chomsky, N. 38, 56
Herman, J.L. & Golan, S. 16
Herman, T.F.D.D. & Richards, G.W.D.D. 284, 220
Hicks, L.D. 23
High school xv, xvii, 2, 8, 12n29, 31–2, 42, 47, 52n33, 60n4, 82, 88, 90–2, 110, 118, 124, 137–8, 150, 167, 171–2, 175, 179–84, 186–7, 189, 191–2, 195, 197–8, 203–4, 206–8, 210–12, 215, 217, 219, 223–7, 229, 231–2, 238–9, 247–9, 250–3, 265, 284, 287, 290, 295
Hippocrates Health Institute 220
Historically Black Colleges and Universities (HBCU) 152
HIV and AIDS 214–15, 217–8, 220–1
Hobbes, T. 77
Hodgson, G. 244–7, 249, 254
Holbrooke, R. 28–9, 33
Holmes, J. 127, 132
HOMEGROWN 192, 221
Homeostasis 200
How does a house work? 191
How to act 40, 52
How to eat 40, 46, 197
How to look 40, 48
Hugo, V. 74, 95
Humanities 11–12, 61, 37, 103, 205, 227, 233–7, 272, 286
Hutchinson, K.A.M. 22n18, 33
Hydraulic fracturing ('fracking') 145, 267
Hyperlexia 182

Ideological expressions 26, 28
Ideology 26, 28, 32, 34, 56, 112, 242, 244–5, 247; 'partly true'/'partly false' 26–7, 32, 36, 186, 242–3
Iggers, G.G. 164, 178
Independent Media 14, 29, 40, 42, 44, 289; outlets 44
Industrial Revolution 5

Intelligence Quotient (IQ) tests 91–2, 94, 167
International Tanker Owners Pollution Federation Limited (ITOPFL) 146N21
Iraq war 9–10, 16, 28, 33, 108, 246, 253, 257, 275, 291

Jamail, D. 75n6, 95
Jaschik, S. 181n6, 221
Jefferson, T. xixn9, xxiv, 26, 129, 179, 242, 247, 249, 254
Jensen, R. 92n45, 119, 133
Jhally, S. 53, 56
Jim Crow Laws 20, 22, 119, 130–1, 152, 243, 280
Just Label It! 221
Juzwiak, R. 133

K.I.N.D. (Kids in Need of Desks) 20
Kaiser Family Foundation 46, 56
Kann, L. 217n74, 221
Katz, J. 54n37
Kennedy, J.F. (JFK) 203
Kennedy, T. 23n22
Keynes, J.M. 7n14
Kilbourne, J. 50, 56
Kimmel, M. 54n36, 56
Kind, R. (U.S. Representative, Wisconsin) 196
King Henry III 73
King John 73
King, M.L. xviii, xxiv, 26, 45, 60, 109, 133
Kirby, D. 218n77, 221
Knowledge xiv–xv, xx–xxi, 2, 6n13, 18, 28, 68, 76–7, 82, 128n62, 133, 137, 142, 168, 184, 229, 237, 275, 291; comprehensive 77n7; limited 77n7; commonsense 2, 17–8, 184, 196, 209, 240; practical 17, 184, 190–2, 209, 230, 235; specialized xiv–xv, xx, 2, 65, 135, 173, 175–6, 183, 235, 265, 270, 291; tacit 63; transfer of xv, xx, 11
Koch brothers 85, 99, 141, 145
Kohn, A. 172–3, 179
Koshhar, R. 83n20, 95
Kroh, K. 148n25, 162
Kroll, A. 37n8, 56
Krugman, P. 90n42, 95, 99n7, 108
Ku Klux Klan 22, 120, 130
Kuhn, T. 2–4, 16, 127–8

Landrieu, M. (Mayor of New Orleans) 30
Langton, S. (Archbishop of Canterbury) 73
Lasky, H. 8n14

Lazarus, E. 244n10, 254
Lederman, D. 147n27, 162
Lee, R.E. (statue removal in Charlottesville, VA) 30
Lewis, C. 225–6, 238
Lewontin, R. 92n45, 95, 111n7, 133
LGBTQIA 87, 110, 214, 281, 288
Liebling, A.J. 37, 56
Lincoln, A. (former President of the U.S.) 82; A&M programs 82; *Land-Grant College Act of 1862* 82
Linebaugh, P. 72n1, 73
Linzey, T. & Campbell, A. 219, 292
Little boxes (social media) 7, 55, 187, 188–9, 256, 262–3, 281, 290
Living Bible 123n47, 131
Living Foods Institute 221
Living wage 87, 89, 98, 106, 131, 156, 259
Locke, J. 77n7
"Logical geography of concepts" 63
"Logical properties of concepts" 63
Louisiana Rebellion of 1811 114
Low Power Frequency Modulation (LPFM) 40n13
Luca 226n10, 238
Lyman School for Boys 122

Machay, A.L. 165n5, 179
Mackey, S. 18n5, 33
Magna Carta Libertatum 72–4, 95
Mangan, K. 157n38, 162
Marsh, W.H. 115n17, 133
Marx, K. & Engels, F. 9n20, 16, 34, 56
Mass media xix, xxiii, 2, 7–8, 11, 14, 16, 26–9, 31, 34n2, 35–56, 66, 71, 93, 122, 131, 137, 145, 174, 178, 185–6, 189n20, 190, 221, 245, 250–2, 256–8, 260–5, 278–83, 288–90
Massachusetts Law of 1647 248
Massachusetts School Attendance Act of 1852 115
Matringe, O. & Moretti, J.M. 221
Matthews, C. 244, 244n12, 253
McCormick, M. 72n1, 73n4, 95
McCutcheon v. Federal Election Commission 37n8, 48, 56, 271, 278–9, 292
McFadden, R. 29n29, 33
McLaren, P. xviii, xxiv
Mead, G.H. 167n6, 179
Mead, M. 8n14
Media Education Foundation 50, 53n34, 54n37
Media monopoly 27, 37–8, 42, 55, 250
Melton, J.V.H. 249n22, 254

Melville, H. 175n24, 179
Mian, Z. of Feiveson, J.A. *et al.* 144, 161
Minimum wage 9, 84, 89, 92, 95, 98, 106, 199
Miranda v. Arizona 276n5, 292
Montagu, A. 111n7, 133
Morgan v. Hennigan 22, 23n20, 33
Morgan, M. 53
Morrill, J. 81; *Morrill Act of 1862* 81
Morris, Jr., K. 131–2
Mundow, A. 176n26
Munro, D. 33
Musu-Gillette, L. 80n15, 95

National Association for Sports and Physical Education (NASPE) 204, 221
National Center for Fair and Open Testing (Fair Test) 175
National Conference of State Legislatures (NCSL) 214–16, 221
National Education Association (NEA) 57N2, 157, 221
National Endowment for Democracy (NED) 77
National Institutes of Health (NIH) 145
National Oceanic and Atmospheric Association (NOAA) 146
National Right to Work Legal Defense and Education Foundation 260; "Right-to-Work Laws" 259
NBC Education Nation Summit (2013) 160n41, 161
Nell, W.C. 109
New School 7, 16
Newspeak 257
Nietzsche, F.W. 239, 254
No Child Left Behind (NCLB) 8, 23, 33, 169, 260
Noble, G. 255, 261–2, 266
North Atlantic Treaty Organization (NATO) 144
Nuclear power plants 3, 143–4, 258; nuclear weapons 144, 161, 224, 292

Oates, J.C. 246, 254
Obama, B. (former President of the U.S.) 28n28, 88n35, 90n41, 94, 102, 121, 142–3, 144n13, 145–6, 149–50, 173, 179, 233, 244, 272, 275, 277, 280
Occupy Wall Street 100–1, 279, 288
Office of Management and Budget 10n21, 79n10, 95
Oliver Brown v. Board of Education of Topeka 20, 115n20, 133
One minute for peace 108

Organization for Economic Co-operation and Development (OECD) 142n12, 162, 253
Orwell, G. xixn11, 14, 41n14, 111, 133, 153, 255–8, 266

Pacifica Foundation 44, 95
Paine, T. 36n5, 56, 77n7
Palast, G. 120n36–7, 133
Papoutsi, G.S., Drichoutis, A.C. & Nayga, R.M. 56
Paradigm shift (paradigm) 2–4, 5–7, 127, 169, 185, 253, 265, 270
Parham, V. & *Parent-Child Assistance Program (PCAP)* 201n43, 221
Paul, R. & Elder, L. (*Critical Thinking Foundation*) xviii, xxiv, 99n7, 136, 177n28, 186, 187n16255, 264, 266
Pearson Company 137n8, 288
Pedagogy of the Oppressed xv, xxiv, 181, 276n6, 292
Pew Research Center 83n20, 95, 238
Philosophy of Education xiv–xvi, 135n2, 136, 209; theory xv, 2n2, 11, 59; "banking" xv, xx, 10, 107n23; dialogical encounter xv, xxi, 140n11, 209
Picchi, A. 9n19, 16
Pilger, J. 29n30, 33
Pivin, F.F. & Cloward, R. 96, 108
Planned Parenthood 216n71, 218n77, 221
Plato's *Republic* 18, 77n7
Plessy v. Ferguson 20, 22, 33, 115–16
Plutte, C. 238
Political economy of education 72, 93
Pollan, M. 202n45, 221
Popper, K.R. 127–9, 133
Positivism 164, 167n6, 170, 177; 'measurement' vs. 'evaluation' 25, 137, 152, 170, 176–7, 288
Poverty 7, 9, 13, 16, 18, 61n7, 78, 85, 96–9, 101, 102n10–11, 105n20, 106–8, 116–17, 119n34, 132, 199, 205n55
Professors xiv, xvii, 25, 67, 141-2, 146, 148, 153-4, 156, 158, 160, 185, 273, 291; 'Research 1' institutions 154–5; teaching vs. research 154–5
Programme for International Student Assessment (PISA) 142, 162, 253–4
Project Censored 43–5, 56
Project for the New American Century 276
Prometheus Radio Project 40
"propaganda model" 38
Psathas, G. 28, 33
Ptolemy, C. 4, 16
Public Citizen 43, 55

306 Left Behind

Public Relations 45, 289
Pufahl, I. & Rhodes, N.C. 225, 238

Quid pro quo 68, 273

R.O.A.R. (Return Our Alienated Rights) 23
'Race' 21–2, 110–12, 165
Racism ix, 12, 18, 49, 110–13, 120, 132, 211, 240, 262, 280–1, 287; 'individual' 113–4; institutional 26, 113–14, 117, 126, 131; in education 114, 131, 152; economic 116, 119
Ramey, D. 126–7, 133
Rasmussen, D. 115, 133
Ravitch, D. 15n39, 16
Reckdahl, K. 146n20, 162
Reification 24, 91n43, 170
Rense, J. 193n29, 221
Revolution 3–4, 207, 222, 250; scientific 2, 3n4, 16, 127; technology 169
Right to education 6n13, 13, 17, 19, 21, 24, 31–2, 115, 151
Roberts, A. 246
Robinson & wife v. Memphis & Charleston R.R. Co. 22, 34n1
Robinson, J.H. 7n14
Roddenberry, G. 170n12, 179
Roe v. Wade 281
Romney, M. 83, 90n41, 94–5
Roosevelt, F.D. (former President of the U.S.) 99
Ross, J.M. & Berg, W.M. 23n19, 33
Rousseau, J.J. 77n7
Runnymede 73
Russo, A.J. 221
Ryan, W. 120n35, 133
Ryle, G. 63, 71

Sacks, H. 65n12, 71, 114n15, 131, 167n6, 179
Sanders, B. 66n15, 81, 88n35, 98, 178
Savio, M. 3, 15–16
Scahill, J. 29n30, 33, 35, 56
Schenwar, M. 121n40, 132
Schings, S. 67n18, 71
school closings 103
'school to prison pipeline' 110, 122, 125n55, 126, 132; Dontadrian Bruce 123; Kiera Wilmot 124
Schutz, A. 114n15, 131, 63n9, 71
Second language 223–4, 226, 230, 232, 236, 249–50
"separate but equal" *(Plessy v. Ferguson)* 20

Shaw, G.B. 96, 108
Shepherd, J. 18n4, 33
Silver-Greenberg, J., Cowley, S. & Cohen, P. 153n32, 162
Simon, J. 140, 162
Sirois, R. 206
Slavery xix, xxiv, 1n1, 20n10, 22, 30, 113, 116, 120, 131–2, 233, 243, 255, 257; Atlantic slave trade 130, 132, 262n14, 266; *chattel slavery* 20, 113–14, 280; mode of production 113
Sleep (rest) 198, 205, 212–14
Smiley, T. 96n1, 108
Smith, D. 169n10, 179, 223n1, 238
Smout, T.C. 249n23, 254
Social Physics 164
Social Security Insurance (SSI) & Medicare 84n22, 99–100
Socialism (socialist) 258, 280
Sociology of Knowledge 2
Socratic conversation method xiv, xxiv
Source Watch 221
Southwest Educational Development Laboratory 216n68, 221
Spielvogel, J.J. 249n22, 254
Spina, N.J. 170n13, 179
Stafford Loans 84n22
Standardized testing x, xii, 7–8, 16, 24, 104, 107, 137, 164, 168, 172, 174–5, 177–9, 197, 232, 260–1, 288; Armed Services Vocational Aptitude Battery (ASVAB) 92; Graduate Management Admissions Teat (GMAT) 172; Graduate Record Examinations (GRE) 172; Law School Admission Test (LSAT) 172; Measures of Academy Progress (MAP) 175–6; Pre-Scholastic Aptitude Test (PSAT) 171; Scholastic Aptitude Test (SAT) 167, 171, 248;
Standing Rock Sioux Tribe 145, 168–9
State departments of education mini investigation 128
Steiner, R. 146–8
Stein-Smith, K. 223n1, 238
STEM curricula 142, 144
'stock of knowledge' xxi, 18
Stone, M. 80n14, 95
Stone, O. 251, 254
Strauss, V. 151n29, 154n34, 162, 175n25, 176n27, 179
Structural Dimensions 1, 94, 113; cultural 1, 6n13, 7, 11–12, 26, 54, 59, 61n6, 62–4, 68, 75–6, 78–9, 88, 94, 113, 125–6, 134, 167, 190, 230, 232, 234–6, 239–40, 252,

261, 262n14, 267, 270–2, 286–8, 291–2; social xxi, 1, 4, 6n13, 7, 9, 11–12, 28, 62, 64, 65n13, 68, 85–7, 94, 96, 100, 113, 123, 127, 129, 133–4, 136–7, 160, 164–7, 169n10, 188, 197–8, 216, 230–1, 234, 237, 240, 263–4, 267, 270–1, 273–6, 280, 282, 285; economic 1, 6–7, 9–11, 13–14, 31, 39, 47, 67–8, 72, 77, 79n9, 81, 84, 86–7, 90–4, 94, 96–102, 105–7, 110, 113, 116–17, 119, 131, 134, 139, 142–3, 145–8, 150, 156, 190, 207–8, 232, 235–7, 243, 246, 251, 258n9, 261, 262n14, 267–8, 269–71, 273; political 1, 3, 6n13, 7–8, 11, 13–14, 20n12, 23, 26–7, 31, 35–7, 48, 58, 68, 72, 76, 81, 83, 87, 91, 92n44, 93–4, 96, 99–100, 102n10, 103, 106–7, 113, 115–16, 128n66, 130, 134, 142–3, 145, 147–9, 157, 159, 165, 190, 194, 214, 235–6, 244, 246, 251, 258, 261, 265–7, 269–71, 274–80, 288–9; ideological 1, 3, 6n13, 7, 11, 14–15, 25–8, 31, 34n2, 67, 94, 113, 134, 145, 147–8, 151, 214, 242–3, 256, 266–7, 270–1, 288, 291

Student loan industry 13, 81, 84n22, 87, 89, 94, 153n32, 162

Suber, M. 30, 33

Support Our Law Enforcement and Safe Neighborhoods Act 243n9

Taxes 10, 13, 75, 78–80, 82n18, 84n22, 86–8, 94, 100–1, 118–19, 20n36, 143, 205, 273, 277

Taylor, C. (documentary *Food Fight*) 194n32, 222

Teachers xiv–viii, xix–xxii, 8–11, 13, 20, 22, 24–6, 31, 39–42, 45, 50, 57, 59, 60n4, 64–9, 80, 82, 92, 102, 104–5, 107, 110, 118–19, 124, 128–9, 134–8, 141–2, 150–61, 169–73, 175–7, 180, 184n11, 185–7; 197, 201, 208, 214, 219, 226, 228, 237, 249, 252, 260–1, 269, 272, 283–5, 291; training xvii, 39, 82, 107n23, 128, 135–7, 139, 142, 172, 186, 207, 249, 260

Teachers' unions 151, 156, 159–60; AAUP 156; AFT 156–7; NEA 157

Teachers vs. functionaries xx, 142, 160, 188

Teaching xv, 7, 10, 14–15, 24, 42, 77, 109, 128, 134–6, 138–40, 142, 154–60, 168, 170, 172, 174, 176n26, 208, 210, 237, 248, 260, 282, 291; transfer of knowledge xv, xx–ii, 11, 51, 134; organic xviii, 10, 11, 13, 104, 172, 174, 177, 186, 195, 206, 219, 277, 286, 289

Telecommunications Act of 1996 39–41

Tenure 11, 154, 157–8

Texas Essential Knowledge and Skills (TEKS) test 25

Texas State Board of Education (SBOE) 2010; *curriculum* changes 25, 129–30

The 'common(s)' 20, 40, 44, 55, 68, 72–7, 79n11, 90, 100, 102, 153, 194, 261, 268, 271, 276, 278, 280

The German Ideology 34n2, 56

Think Progress 86n29, 148n25, 162

Thirunarayanan, M.O. 66n16, 71

Title IX 281

Trans-Pacific Partnership (TPP) 85

Turner, R. 65n12, 71

Turtle Island 6, 74

Twain, M. (Samuel Clemens) 228, 238

Twenge, J. 188n19, 222

U.S. Department of Education Office for Civil Rights 161

UNICEF 20n9, 33

United Nations Educational, Scientific and Cultural Organization (UNESCO) 229–30, 233

United Nations Universal Declaration of Human Rights 17, 19n8, 21, 33, 81

United States Department of Agriculture (USDA) 105n19, 201–2, 220, 222

United States v. Nichols 22

United States v. Ryan 22

United States v. Singleton 22

United States v. Stanley 22

Universe theory 4; geocentric 4; heliocentric 4

USA Patriot Act 54, 157, 256, 276

Van De Mille, O. 249n24

Van Sertima, I. xixn11, xxiv, 255n2, 261–2, 266

Veblen, T. 7n14

Venus Project 10n23, 16, 61n7

Veterans 79, 106

von Goethe, J.W. 223, 238

Voting Rights Act of 1965 120, 152n31

Wald, E.R. 145, 162

Walker, A. (founder of *Chez Panisse Restaurant*) 194–5

Walker, S. (Governor of Wisconsin) 85

Walsh, D.A. 246n16, 254

Walters, J. 148n24, 162

Waxman, H. (CA Representative) 217, 222

308 Left Behind

Weingarten, R. (President of AFT) 173, 174n22, 179
Wells, I.B. 20n10, 34, 40, 44, 50
Wells-Barnett, I.B. 34n1, 56
Wellstone, P.D. (the late U.S. Senator of Minnesota) 170, 179
Welsch, J. & Yousman, B. xvi, xxiv
West, C. 96n1, 108
White, J.L. & Cones, III, J.H. 113, 133
'white' privilege 112
Whiteman, D. 89n40, 95
Wisconsin State Budget Act of 2011 85n24, 95
Wittgenstein, L. 63n10, 114n15, 131

Wolff, E. 163
Wolff, R. 86, 26, 87n31, 97, 99n6, 108
World Trade Organization (WTO) 87, 246
Wright, F.L. 7n14
Wyler, G. 121, 133

Yaccino, S. & Rich, M. 104n13, 108
Yerkes, R.M. 167
Yusuf, M. 125n55

Zinn, H. 1n1, 16, 20n10, 33, 181, 221, 251n27, 254
Zuak-Skees, C. & Wieder, B. 126n56, 133